C0-AVV-250

Russia at Play

Russia at Play

Leisure Activities at the End of the Tsarist Era

LOUISE MCREYNOLDS

CORNELL UNIVERSITY PRESS

Ithaca and London

First published 2003 by Cornell University Press

Printed in the United States of America

Library of Congress Cataloging-in-Publication Data

McReynolds, Louise, 1952–
    Russia at play : leisure activities at the end of the tsarist era / Louise McReynolds.
        p. cm.
Includes bibliographical references (p.) and index.
    ISBN 0-8014-4027-0 (cloth : alk. paper)
    1. Leisure—Russia—History.   2. Middle class—Recreation—Russia—History.
3. Russia—Social life and customs.   I. Title.
    GV93 .M38 2003
    790′.0947′09034—dc21

                                                                    2002008359

Cornell University Press strives to use environmentally responsible suppliers and materials to the fullest extent possible in the publishing of its books. Such materials include vegetable-based, low-VOC inks and acid-free papers that are recycled, to-tally chlorine-free, or partly composed of nonwood fibers. For further information, visit our website at www.cornellpress.cornell.edu.

Cloth printing   10 9 8 7 6 5 4 3 2 1

to my mother,
who taught me how to play

Contents

Acknowledgments

I round up the usual suspects, arranged alphabetically in the lineup: Bob Edelman, David Hanlon, Mimi Henriksen, Beth Holmgren, Lynn Mally, Joan Neuberger, Dan Orlovsky, Don Raleigh, Richard Stites, and Reggie Zelnik, friends who are also willing to play the role of colleague and take time from their own work to comment on mine. They are also the quickest to remind me that, regardless, it's only a game. This work profited perceptibly by attentive readings of the entire manuscript by Don, Joan, and Richard; their input made this a much better book.

Outside the Russian field, Karën Wigen and Mary Louise Roberts read chapters and helped to give my work its comparative perspective. At the National Humanities Center, many other Fellows played with ideas with me in a delightfully stimulating environment. I also benefited from the help and advice of Neia Zorkaia and Evgenii Dukhov in Moscow. In Russia, I thank Boris Anan'ich, Alexander Fursenko, Natasha Korsakova, Tania Pavlenko, and Tania Chernetskaia, who enrich my time in Petersburg more than they can imagine. My oldest friends—Pam Chew, Les McBee, and Julia Hinkle Penn—are still always there for me: for this book "there" was, physically and psychically, Italy. My three younger sisters—Alice, Betsy, and Rebecca—continue to provide a corrective to the academic life, most of all because they, too, appreciate the game. And I must thank Betsy especially for the holiday spirit that infuses much of my leisure.

Several institutions supplied grants that made possible the completion of this project. Research was generously supported by the International Research and Exchanges Board (IREX), the Fulbright-Hays Committee, the National Council on Eurasian and East European Research (NCEER), and the Kennan Institute. I am exceptionally grateful for the three semesters spent at the National Humanities Center, my work there funded by the National Endowment for the Humanities and the Andrew Mellon Fund. In St. Petersburg, I have long depended upon the professionalism of the staff at the Saltykov-Shchedrin Library to complete my research, just as Pat Polansky of Hamilton Library has always supported my work in Honolulu. I thank Michael Kurihara and Iurii Pekurovskii for his help with the illustrations. At Cornell University Press, I thank John Ackerman for his enthusiasm and support, Karen Hwa for guiding the manuscript through the process of publishing, and Carolyn Pouncy for polishing my prose. And I would be remiss if I did not mention the University of Hawai'i's commitment to research.

Above all, I thank my mother. Every chapter has its origin in what I gained from her joie de vivre, her remarkable capacity for living: the Diana's Club melodramas; the devastating loss in Super Bowl I (and the Chiefs' revenge in Super Bowl IV); bus trips to the old Met to watch the Athletics play; stocking-stuffer tickets to see Pearl Bailey; the time we drove to Oklahoma because we'd never been there before; Debbie Reynolds at the Flamingo and Shoji Tibuchi in Branson; Kansas City's Starlight Theater; and Nelson and Jeanette on channel 5's *Million Dollar Movie*. Whatever success I enjoy today in a vocation that finds me digging into the past originated in the ways that my mother taught me to live fully in the present.

Some of the information in chapter 3 has been published elsewhere, in modified form: "Olympic Politics in Tsarist Russia: The Development of a Nationalist Identity," in *Problemy vsemirnoi istorii,* ed. B. V. Anan'ich, R. Sh. Ganelin, and V. M. Panaiekh (St. Petersburg: Vilanin, 2000) and "Tracking Social Change through Sport Hunting," in *Transforming Peasants: Society, State, and the Peasantry, 1861–1930,* ed. Judith Pallot (London: Macmillan, 1998).

In transliterating Russian titles, quotations, and names, I have used a modified version of the Library of Congress system, and I have conformed the old orthography to modern usage.

Introduction

People tend to forget that play is serious.

—David Hockney

Children of the Age (*Deti veka*), one of the many popular silent movie melo-dramas released in 1915, begins when two old school chums run into each other at Moscow's Gostinnyi dvor, the central shopping area on Red Square. The heroine, Maria, played by the silver-screen icon Vera Kholod-naia, believes that she is happy with her bank-clerk husband and baby in their small apartment. But her friend is living on a far grander scale, and rekindling their relationship takes Kholodnaia into the world of a wealthy businessman, with his elegant home and sporty companions. Enamored by the clerk's beautiful young wife, the businessman drives her home from a party at his house; later, he rapes her. Kholodnaia's sensibilities have been violated more deeply than her body, however, and she abandons her husband for the life of luxury that wealth offers. The banker tries to buy off the clerk, but the latter refuses, after having been fired for his integrity. As the husband walks home to console himself with his child, Maria decides that she wants the baby. She and her corrupting friend take the business-man's chauffeured limousine to reclaim the child. But as they attempt their escape, the limousine stalls. The director, Evgenii Bauer, heightens suspense with a montage sequence, cutting back and forth between the stalled limo and the husband sauntering homeward. The women escape with the baby in the nick of time. The disconsolate husband puts a bullet in his brain. End of film.

Shot primarily on outdoor locations, the movie is remarkable for what it exhibits of contemporary Russian culture, beginning with the two young women moving freely in public and enjoying the new pastime of consum-ing conspicuously. Social mobility is evident in the jobs held by the nu-

Moscow department store Miur and Meriliz, the quintessential palace of modern consumption

Her school chum gazes into the distance, where she will lead Maria. Vera Kholodnaia in *Children of the Age*. B. B. Ziukov, comp. *Vera Kholodnaia* (Moscow: Iskusstvo, 1995).

merous characters. The visuals on the screen can be compared to the displays in department stores: feasts for the eyes that piqued the appetite and testified to the presence of a bourgeoisie. Never mind that many in the audience could not have afforded the better shops at Gostinnyi dvor; simply attending a movie turned them into consumers, a practice that brought peasants watching a film on a makeshift village screen into contact with the ways of the modern city. Moreover, privileging women on screen reflected their increased participation in economic and social life as well as their presence in the audience. Ending the movie as he did with conspicuous consumption triumphant, though at a terrible cost, Bauer ensnared his audience in many of the contradictions inherent in modern life. His tense montage sequence highlighted the extraordinary capacity of the new medium to allow viewers to experience those contradictions both cerebrally, as they suspended preconceptions of time and space, and viscerally, as they had to decide which parent they favored.

This book charts the emergence of that commercial culture in late imperial Russia, which culminated in the birth of its movie industry. The primary actors in the book, like those in *Children of the Age,* are the middle classes who, like Maria, were negotiating the social ladder and looking for happiness in some of the new opportunities for self-fashioning opening up to them. Heretofore, Russia's middle classes have been studied primarily for their politics rather than their cultural activities. Analyzing this multi-layered social group according to a paradigm that couples a specific type of economy (free-market) to a particular political system (electoral and representative), scholars posed questions that would permit them to explain the consequential differences between Russian and western political structures. However, because their principal objective was to explain the failure of Russia's middle classes to establish their own political institutions when the autocracy collapsed, the paradigm historians constructed was skewed from the outset because it was based on a premise that accepted the western model as normative.[1]

As a result, tsarist Russia's middle classes found themselves victims of a self-fulfilling political prophesy according to which their primary historical significance became predicated on institutions they never built. This

---

[1] See, for example: Thomas Owen, *Capitalism and Politics in Russia: A Social History of the Moscow Merchants, 1855–1905* (New York: Cambridge University Press, 1981); Alfred Rieber, *Merchants and Entrepreneurs in Imperial Russia* (Chapel Hill: University of North Carolina Press, 1982); Jo Ann Ruckman, *The Moscow Business Elite: A Social and Cultural Portrait of Two Generations, 1840–1905* (De Kalb: Northern Illinois University Press, 1984); Edith Clowes, Samuel Kassow, and James West, eds., *Between Tsar and People: Educated Society and the Quest for Public Identity in Late Imperial Russia* (Princeton: Princeton University Press, 1991); Harley Balzar, ed., *The Professions in Russia* (Armonk, N.Y.: Sharpe, 1995); and James West and Iurii Petrov, eds., *Merchant Moscow: Images of Russia's Vanished Bourgeoisie* (Princeton: Princeton University Press, 1998).

book, however, drew inspiration from Peter Stearns's observations that it might prove more useful to investigate "a shift in personality traits and not just a change in political and economic structure" in the effort to identify a middle class.[2] By examining various ways in which these people enjoyed themselves, I look to leisure for indications of what those traits were and how they developed, investigating the new opportunities for people to imagine themselves in both public and private life. After all, attitudes toward the self had to change before ideas about political participation could emerge. Thus the evolution of a middle class becomes important for what it reflects about changing notions of self and society, regardless of political institutions.

Several terms require explanation at the outset. First, the "Russian bourgeoisie," like middle classes everywhere, is understood here to be in a constant state of emergence, that is, coalescing from a variety of social estates around a set of basic principles that privileged modernity over tradition. In this sense, "bourgeoisie" and "middle classes" can be used synonymously. Because these terms have become overladen with interpretive baggage, though, I use them infrequently and cautiously, more to describe an attitude than a social or economic position.[3] Never monolithic, the bourgeoisie is composed of individual members whose interests often conflict because each person also has other identities, not just the one rooted in social class. "Identity" follows Manuel Castells's definition: an "organizing principle . . . the process by which a social actor recognizes itself and constructs meaning."[4] Agreeing with philosopher Josef Pieper that "leisure has been, and always will be, the first foundation of any culture,"[5] I have selected five clearly defined leisure-time activities as the basis for this book: theater, sports, tourism, nightlife, and motion pictures.

My focus on leisure does not come at the expense of politics; quite the contrary, the politics implicit in commercialization and mass distribution is central to my analysis. Mary Louise Roberts's description of politics as "a series of personal changes in subjectivity and self-presentation that have real effects on how people act in the world" underscores the point that the emerging middle classes became politicized by virtue of their habits of con-

---

[2] Peter Stearns, "The Middle Class: Toward a Precise Definition," *Comparative Studies in Society and History* 21 (July 1979): 395–96. Stuart Bliumin, citing Anthony Giddens, has echoed the call to explore cultural experience as a source of middle-class identity in *The Emergence of the Middle Class: Social Experience in the American City, 1760–1900* (New York: Cambridge University Press, 1989), 10.

[3] The Russian language offers several equivalents: *meshchane* refers specifically to an urban social category, but abstractly it connotes the same pejorative as the simple translation *burzhui*. Both evoke more than a hint of the philistine.

[4] Manuel Castells, *The Rise of the Network Society* (Cambridge: Blackwell, 1996), 22.

[5] Josef Pieper, *Leisure: The Basis of Culture,* trans. Alexander Dru, with an introduction by T. S. Eliot (New York: Pantheon, 1954), 4.

sumption.[6] Borrowing from the influential works of the Italian Marxist Antonio Gramsci, I am looking for the ways in which commerce affected culture, and what impact this had on subsequent constructions of both the personal sense of self and ideas about how to interact in social relations.[7] For example, *Children of the Age* was produced for commercial consumption by a rationalized, capitalized movie studio, but the images it distributed raised compelling questions about class, gender, and conspicuous consumption that did not necessarily reinforce the studio's capitalist structure. And although every Russian viewer entering the theater was unique, each also shared a common stock of cultural referents and issues raised in political debates. Therefore, when watching movies or partaking in the other activities discussed here, they were forging individual identities within a broader, nation-based framework.

As leisure became increasingly commercialized, it extended its reach, resulting in the growth of a mass-oriented culture. Theoretically, "mass" culture distinguishes between culture produced *for* the masses and culture produced *by* them.[8] As I understand it, "mass" culture differs specifically from "popular" culture in that it is not a spontaneous expression by a group but rather a constructed product that represents the interests of the producer before it does those of the consumer. Therefore it is "commercialized" in both the financial and the pejorative senses of the word: mass culture allows money to affect values. Commerce supposedly trivializes culture, at the highbrow end by vulgarizing its aesthetics, and at the lowbrow end by destroying the authenticity of the vox populi.[9]

Mass culture is also distinct in that it is founded on business principles that inherently make it modern. "Modernity" here is understood to be both structural and attitudinal: it includes the deployment of industrial technology; rapid urbanization; capitalism as the primary economic mode; and mass transportation and circulation to keep people and information flowing. Intellectually, modernity organizes the world on the basis of reason. Though discussions of modernity generally call to mind images of work, it was just as much about new kinds of play. "Leisure" in this book, simply put, refers to time spent away from fulfilling mandatory job-related

[6] Mary Louise Roberts, "Gender, Consumption, and Commodity Culture," *American Historical Review* 103, no. 2 (1998): 842.

[7] *An Antonio Gramsci Reader: Selected Writings, 1916–1935,* ed. David Forgacs (New York: Schocken, 1988), especially 189–221. Among the potentially hegemonic institutions of popular culture listed by Gramsci, this project includes popular writers, the theater and sound films, and, in terms of reception, "conversation" between the more educated and less educated of the population (356).

[8] Dominic Strinati discusses this theoretical debate in *An Introduction to Theories of Popular Culture* (New York: Routledge, 1995), chapter 1.

[9] See especially Dwight MacDonald, "Mass Culture in America," in *Mass Culture: The Popular Arts in America,* ed. Bernard Rosenberg and David White (New York: Macmillan, 1957).

or domestic duties.[10] Both a time and a place, leisure presents multiple opportunities for employing mass culture in the search for a sense of self.[11]

Late imperial Russia offers remarkably fertile terrain for analyzing how leisure-time activities both mirrored and helped to shape the worlds of work, society, and politics—those outer worlds from which leisure purportedly offered refuge. When the tsarist government committed itself to industrialization following the military disaster in the Crimea in the 1850s, it upended traditional economic relationships and forced new patterns of social interaction. On the eve of World War I the urban population accounted for but 15 percent of the empire's total, yet this does not include the millions of other beneficiaries of mass-oriented technology beyond the cities' limits.[12] Because this largely agrarian society began to industrialize very quickly and comparatively late in the financial day, Russia developed a peculiar form of state capitalism according to which industries relied heavily on state subsidies because the country lacked a sufficiently strong infrastructure of private capital. This created a paradoxical situation in which the economy put the populace at odds with the autocratic state on the basis of "mass" participation. Mass production depends on mass consumption to remain viable, so it breeds a new social actor, the consumer. When autocratic subjects become consumers, they entertain fantasies of autonomy, made evident by the new opportunities for self-fashioning. Moreover, consumers confront those who control production by extending or withholding their financial support, which gives them a sense of participation.

Leisure developed first in private domestic settings, but commercialization pushed it out into public ones. The integral relationship between production and consumption, which collapsed the public/private binary, governed the development of these new forms of leisure.[13] Although the activities carried out in leisure time are intentionally nonproductive, they are nonetheless determined in large measure by the dominant forms of production.[14] The technological revolution, epitomized in entertainment

[10] Jan Huizinga, *Homo Ludens: A Study of the Play Element of Culture* (London: Routledge, 1949).

[11] On the significance of changing conceptions of time and space to the sense of how "modern" differed from that which preceded it, see David Harvey, *The Condition of Postmodernity* (Cambridge: Blackwell, 1990), especially part 3.

[12] On urban growth, see Boris Mironov, *The Social History of Imperial Russia, 1700–1917*, vol. 1 (Boulder: Westview, 2000), especially 255, 432, and 465. On economic growth, see Paul Gregory, *Russian National Income, 1885–1913* (Cambridge: Cambridge University Press, 1982), especially 192–94.

[13] As the sociologist Dean MacCannell has argued, leisure also holds some of the keys to postmodernity in the way that it "displac[es] work from the center of social arrangements." MacCannell, *The Tourist: A New Theory of the Leisure Class* (New York: Schocken, 1976), 5.

[14] As Roger Caillois has pointed out, an integral characteristic of play is that "it creates no wealth or goods." Quoted in Richard Schechner, *Performance Theory* (New York: Routledge, 1988), 9.

Pedestrians reflect the social change evident in Russia's city streets.

by the phonograph and the motion picture, made possible the mass production of sound and sight that increased exponentially the possibilities for a shared commercial culture. The mass circulation of music, information, entertainments, and personalities precipitated a whole new set of cultural referents that helped Russians to understand themselves and their empire.[15]

The term "culture industry," which captured the irony in the notion that culture should be financially profitable,[16] might well have been coined by Russia's cultural elite because it reflected their contempt for commerce. From the end of the eighteenth century onward, through successive generations, this self-designated *intelligentsia* enjoyed status as a social category, and entrance to it was based on political attitudes rather than economic or family status.[17] Denying self-interest and operating outside the govern-

[15] Yuri Lotman and Boris Uspensky would characterize leisure as I am employing the term as a "semiosphere," a "working mechanism whose separate elements are in complex dynamic relationships." In *The Semiotics of Russian Culture* (Ann Arbor: Ardis, 1984), xii.

[16] Max Horkheimer and Theodor Adorno coined the term "culture industry" with palpable opprobrium: "The stronger the positions of the culture industry become, the more summarily it can deal with consumers' needs, producing them, controlling them, disciplining them, and even withdrawing amusement: no limits are set to cultural progress of this kind." In "The Culture Industry: Enlightenment as Mass Deception," in *Dialectic of Enlightenment*, trans. John Cumming (New York: Continuum, 1997), 144.

[17] Martin Malia, "What Is the Intelligentsia?" *Daedalus* (summer 1960): 441–58. Richard

ment, the *intelligentsia* established its authority by virtue of its claim to speak on behalf of the interests of a variety of groups, especially those that lacked the skills to articulate their aspirations for themselves. The prestige that the *intelligentsia* accumulated empowered it to exercise what Gramsci characterized as a cultural hegemony, which meant that it extended its influence into all spheres, not just its private circles. I use the term *intelligentsia* to refer to those who identified themselves as such, and not to all educated Russians or even to all cultural elites. The avant-garde of the early twentieth century, for example, was more likely to celebrate mass culture than to denigrate its values, as the *intelligentsia* did.

Substituting cultural for economic capital, the *intelligentsia* fulfilled Pierre Bourdieu's maxim that those who control this form of investment in society can exercise powerful political mechanisms because of their capacity to determine the tastes that authenticate a system of values.[18] Philosophically, the members of the *intelligentsia* appeared most inclined to accept Aristotle's notion of leisure as "satisfaction of the truly disinterested interest, the achievement of understanding, which is man's highest goal."[19] Using Russia's elite culture to set the terms of their political critique, they conferred on the arts a transcendental truth that validated their own hegemonic position. As a result, culture carried a more overt political force in the Russian than in the western context.

Fetishizing Russia's highbrow culture, the *intelligentsia* provided both a frame of political reference and a stock of common symbols that influenced subsequent generations. Weaving its way seamlessly into Russian historiography, the *intelligentsia* established legitimacy that, in Stuart Hall's words, "appears not only 'spontaneous' but natural and normal."[20] Its members came to dominate as the lead characters in a master narrative that has only recently begun to incorporate interpretations of culture that competed with theirs. Their authority allowed them to set the agenda on critical questions about private property, the distribution of economic power, and the relationship of the individual with respect to the commu-

---

Pipes continues to argue for the overriding authority of the *intelligentsia* in his influential two-volume history of the Bolshevik revolution, *A History of the Russian Revolution* (New York: Knopf, 1990) and *Russia under the Bolshevik Regime* (New York: Knopf, 1993). The theme has been picked up by those who chastise the *intelligentsia* for the sad state of affairs in post-Soviet Russia, including Masha Gessen in *Dead Again: The Russian Intelligentsia after Communism* (New York: Verso, 1997), and Andrei Siniavskii, *The Russian Intelligentsia*, trans. Lynn Visson (New York: Columbia University Press, 1997).

[18] Pierre Bourdieu, *Distinction: A Social Critique of Judgment*, trans. Richard Nice (Cambridge, Mass.: Harvard University Press, 1984), 64–69.

[19] Ida Craven, "'Leisure,' According to the Encyclopedia of the Social Sciences," reprinted in *Mass Leisure*, ed. Eric Larrabee and Rolf Meyersohn (Glencoe: Free Press, 1961), 5.

[20] John Clarke, Stuart Hall, Tony Jefferson, and Brian Roberts, "Subcultures, Cultures, and Class," in *Culture, Ideology, and Social Process: A Reader*, ed. Tony Bennett et al. (London: Open University Press, 1981), 59.

nity. Holding fast to a position that denied a rightful relationship between "culture" and "industry," they rejected those tenets of western capitalism that celebrated competition and the personal wealth that resulted from it. Their position on these issues undermined subsequent acceptance of commercial culture.

Being a member of the Russian middle classes therefore meant fashioning oneself in relation to the politics and values expressed by the *intelligentsia*. However, just because commercial culture employed many of the symbolic codes formulated by this group did not mean that all parties used or interpreted them in the same way. In the process of self-definition, those evolving into the middle classes could not always escape insecurity about their status and at times sought the safety net of the familiar. When these Russians fell victim to the cliché that imitation is the sincerest form of flattery, they emulated those whom they imagined—on the basis of cultural stereotypes—to be their superiors, including westerners, aristocrats, and the *intelligentsia*. Their imitations left them vulnerable to parody, which exacerbated their anxieties about status.[21]

The imitators, though, ended up reconstituting many of the old ways in the light of their own ambitions and with respect to new patterns of consuming. Opera, for example, found itself recast in diminutive form as operetta, performed in nightclubs. The aristocratic "traveler" became the commercial "tourist," who experienced imperialism differently. When the Great Reforms began to undermine the old estate structure, not only did the moribund aristocracy find itself under siege from the emerging middle classes, but so too did the core of its critics, and the nascent commercial culture found itself caught between the Scylla of conservatism and the Charybdis of elitism. A nationwide revolution in 1905 resulted in an easing of political oppression, and the combination of an expanding economy and a relaxed censorship encouraged growth in the commercial leisure industry.

By carving out venues where the emergent middle classes could experiment with possibilities for developing individual identities, leisure-time activities contributed indirectly to the pressure for revolutionary changes, especially for increased participation in public life. Leisure, for example, demanded a reconceptualization of traditional ideas of free time and public space. "Free" time, or hours not spent at work or doing domestic chores, was not intrinsically new; "leisure" time, however—time spent in activities intended for "self-actualization through the arts"—was. And leisure broadened the category of "arts" to include the growing number of public spaces that had become commercialized, such as nightclubs, racetracks, and

---

[21] Rosalind Williams discusses similar status anxieties among the emergent French bourgeoisie in *Dream Worlds: Mass Consumption in Late Nineteenth-Century France* (Berkeley: University of California Press, 1982), especially chapter 2.

tourist hotels. Looking at the most popular leisure-time activities, this book explores some of the options from which growing numbers of Russians could choose in integrating themselves into the changing circumstances. Structured topically rather than chronologically, it examines each activity on its own terms before connecting it with others. Although the main part of each story takes place after the middle of the nineteenth century, earlier histories of the various entertainments are discussed to provide the context for change. My analysis takes each activity through the Great War, offering new insight on the old question of the effects of the war on social change.[22] All activities were affected, but in different ways, rendering a single verdict inadequate. References to analogous western activities also frame this story because they highlight the broad effects of modernity while bringing attention to the individuality of the Russian experience.

Capitalist organization, with its rational structuring, dependence on professionalization, and new modes of financing supplies the foundation for each activity, its institutional structure. From there the chapters explore both the producers of leisure and its consumers to see how leisure was practiced, experienced. In the process, this book resurrects a lifestyle and characters that vanished, literally and figuratively, from the spotlight in their prime. Like members of the collective audiences, certain individual personalities cross chapters to enjoy the variety found in the venues of play: an athlete becomes a movie star; a waiter rises to manage a chain of nightclubs; a movie scenarist takes to writing restaurant reviews. The sources were obtained from the impersonal businesses that organized the activities and from the personal, the memoirs and archives of both players and fans. The periodical literature that circulated specialized information and gossip about these various people and enterprises also provided a wealth of information. History rarely allows for balance in source materials, which has resulted in some people and activities being more fully described than others. I risk analytical symmetry in places for the sake of providing details about unfamiliar issues.

The legitimate stage presents a natural starting point because it was the first such organized, spectacular, mass-oriented medium that sought financing from the ticket-buying public. Several of modernity's performative properties surfaced on stage, from the social issues acted out to the audiences' adulation of its stars. The sociologist Richard Sennett found the analogies between stage and street in the nineteenth century so compelling that he connected the theatrical world to the emerging bourgeois society as a means of charting the evolution of the modern sense of self, which he portentously entitled *The Fall of Public Man*.[23] Like other national

---

[22] Leopold Haimson, "The Problem of Urban Stability in Urban Russia, 1905–1917," *Slavic Review* 23, no. 4 (1964): 619–24; and 24, no. 1 (1965): 1–22.

[23] Richard Sennett, *The Fall of Public Man* (London: Faber, 1986).

theaters, Russia's was never fully commercialized, but it would be artificial to exclude the imperial stage, because the state theaters set the national theatrical standards, enjoying the right of first refusal for any published play and serving as magnets for the best talent because they offered the highest salaries and most generous retirement benefits. The state theaters also exemplify the uneven geographical sweep of this book, concentrated in the two capitals but spreading out from them, following the touring companies into the provinces.

The significance of the stage to the process of transformation warrants two chapters. The first covers the essential aspects of the theater's historical origins, setting up the patterns that will be followed by subsequent topics. It highlights the life and works of A. N. Ostrovskii to illustrate the commercialization of the theater, both behind the stage and on it. The pivotal figure on the nineteenth-century's legitimate stage, Ostrovskii merits special attention because his wildly popular plays put on stage issues about postreform Russia that he was trying to actualize in the theater itself. He influenced the state to lift its monopoly on the theater in 1882, which permitted the growth of a private stage, the subject of chapter 2. The second chapter illustrates the many effects of privatization, again both on stage and off.

Performance also dominates chapter 3, on sports. Organized athletics was more about participation than display, however, and this chapter examines the role that sports played in the development of modernity, including the creation of hierarchical and rationally structured teams, competitive games that mimicked the marketplace, and fans seeking role models with whom they could identify. Quintessentially physical, sports situated the human body at center stage. As athletics joined the larger movement to make the body healthy, it enticed increasing numbers of both men and women into taking part in competitions that affected their attitudes toward modernity.

The workforce of the new culture industry performed a paradox: by presenting work as play, the stars of stage and sports blurred an important distinction between those who produced and those who consumed, which had implications for why and how their fans emulated them. The tremendous popularity of exceptional personalities inspired chapter 4. Modernity had different requirements for men and women, which led to a gendering of social roles. This chapter analyzes how idols from the entertainment world, an actress and a wrestler, reflected the gendering of identity at the turn of the century, when traditional roles were no longer competent to manage the future.

Supplementing these ideas about changing notions of selfhood, chapter 5 uses the growth of the tourist industry to examine an important way that Russians learned to see themselves as both nationalists and imperialists. The burgeoning tourist industry used developments in transportation to broaden significantly opportunities for travel, taking advantage of the growing numbers of those with both the money and the desire to expand their worldview into a new vision of Russia. Tourism has been described by James Buzard as "fundamental to and characteristic of modern culture"[24] because of its effect on cross-cultural contact. The broad range of travelers included soldiers, serfs, and religious pilgrims, but this chapter examines how the tourist industry developed as a commercial appropriation of the aristocratic notion that travel was a prerequisite for refined sensibilities. It commodified Russia's imperial expansion and suggested new ways of understanding what it meant to be, and to behave as, a citizen of the empire.

Two chapters on evening entertainments step out into the commercial night. Like leisure itself, the night functioned simultaneously as both time and place. If the day was primarily about work, then nighttime turned into playtime. The natural act of eating became the social act of dining, eclipsing several important distinctions between public and private interaction. The music, comedy, and other entertaining routines performed for evening recreation permitted audiences to experiment with identity and to encounter social difference in a seductively conciliatory environment. Song and spoof defused potentially combustible relations by removing them from the context that gave them political meaning, domesticating them to please a crowd. The first of these two chapters examines the places, and the second, the contents of these entertainments.

The eighth and final chapter uses the nascent motion picture as the linchpin to secure tsarist Russia's culture industry. Movies combined the radical potential of technological innovation with an equally profound social democratization of leisure. The cinema, with its astonishing capacity to engage a socially mixed audience, was an international phenomenon that revolutionized the nature of experiencing culture itself.

The Bolsheviks bring this project to the logical conclusion set by political chronology and punctuated in 1917. Reading Marx literally, the Bolsheviks saw commercial culture as evidence of a bourgeoisie that must either be absorbed by socialism or be destroyed. Party leaders identified themselves as *intelligentsia,* and they found common cause with many members of the cultural elite in pushing a political agenda that severely undermined the possibilities for independence found in commercial leisure. It must be recognized, though, that leisure-time activities had already affected the values and expectations of the audiences awaiting the revolutionary political production about to take center stage. How the successors to both autocracy and *intelligentsia* dealt with these audiences tells a story

---

[24] James Buzard, *The Beaten Track: European Tourism, Literature and the Ways to Culture, 1800–1918* (New York: Oxford University Press, 1993), 3.

very different from the one told here, but that story must begin with the cultures in place at the end of the old regime. Therefore, in lieu of a conclusion, *Russia at Play* ends with an epilogue that explores how the embryonic Bolshevik government co-opted leisure. It suggests ways that the new regime used the bolshevized forms of the activities discussed here to affect the formation of state-based identities that helped them to consolidate and maintain and maintain their precarious and ultimately short-lived hold on power.

The Origins of Russia's Legitimate Stage

The concept of a "legitimate" stage originated in Europe with the rise of the absolutist state; governments "legitimized" theaters by granting them permission to perform plays with spoken dialogue. This marked a formal separation of organized performance from the more commonly understood notion of "public theater" as fairground performances meant to entertain rather than to edify. It also brought the state directly on stage, so although legitimacy had the advantage of government subsidies, this boon was counterbalanced by the onus of an increasingly interested censorship. Long after autocrats had been replaced with representative parliaments in Europe, governments continued both subsidies and censorship. The question had become essentially one of national culture, which was considered too important to be left to the public. "National culture," though, defied consensus and put bureaucrats at odds with artists in Russia as elsewhere. The theater earned its social legitimacy by staging many public debates that playwrights and performers also hoped to resolve.

Russia's national theater was, characteristically, a western import. Having heard much about the theater from foreigners living in Moscow's *Nemetskaia sloboda* (foreign quarters), Tsar Alexei (1645–1676) arranged with Lutheran pastor Johann Gregori for a full-scale production of the biblical story of Esther in 1672.[1] The enraptured Alexei sat agreeably through the ten-hour performance in a theater built especially for the occasion at his residence, but the recalcitrant boyars he had compelled to join him in the

---

[1] Simon Karlinsky, *Russian Drama from Its Beginnings to the Age of Pushkin* (Berkeley: University of California Press, 1985), 39.

14

audience showed less enthusiasm.[2] Dependent on western materials, Alexei used the multilingual clerks of his Foreign Office to translate plays into less-than-poetic Russian. Simeon Polotsky, a monk who had studied in both Poland and Italy, became Russia's first official playwright with his stagings of biblical parables, especially the one that made for captivating pyrotechnical theatrics, *The Fiery Furnace*.[3]

Alexei's third son and heir, Peter the Great (1682–1725), developed a taste for performance during his tours of the European continent.[4] Peter viewed the legitimate stage as an emblem of civilization and therefore something that his Russia *must* have. He opened Moscow's first public theater on Red Square with inexpert stagings of Shakespeare and Calderon, translated by government scribes and performed by clerks impressed into service as actors. But his most effective productions were the dazzling public spectacles staged to celebrate his military feats.[5]

Russia lacked a receptive audience early in the eighteenth century because of some of its other cultural deficiencies, the most important being the absence of a literary language. Because the intellectual currents that had enjoyed the greatest influence in Europe, the Renaissance and the Reformation, had had only minor impact on Russia, the tsarist empire did not have the ambience that had generated the humanistic moral dramas that kept Shakespeare relevant across time and that made Molière so humorous. Russia needed to develop both philosophically and linguistically to establish a theater.

The influential tsaritsas who followed Peter patronized the arts, and their combined efforts resulted in the initial flowerings of Russia's national opera, ballet, and legitimate stage. Under Anna I (1730–1740), Elizabeth I (1741–1762), and Catherine II (1762–1796), intellectual life began to flourish through the education of the cadet corps, the opening of the first university in Moscow in 1756, and a series of provincial educational reforms. Russian identity and cultural independence were contested throughout the eighteenth century because of the foreign cultural imports, and theater emerged as a major forum for intellectual debates.[6]

---

[2] Ibid., 37–43.

[3] On the early history of the Russian theater, see V. N. Vsevolodskii-Gerngross, *Russkii teatr ot istokov do serediny XVIII v.* (Moscow: Akademiia nauk, 1957) and *Russkii teatr vtoroi poloviny XVIII veka* (Moscow: Akademiia nauk, 1960); B. V. Varneke, *History of the Russian Theater, Seventeenth through Nineteenth Century,* trans. Boris Brasol, rev. and ed. Belle Martin (New York: Macmillan, 1951), chapters 1–2; Marc Slonim, *Russian Theater from the Empire to the Soviets* (New York: World Publishing, 1961), chapter 1; and. J. Patouillet, *Le Théâtre de moeurs russes (1672–1750)* (Paris: Bibliothèque de L'Institut Français de Saint-Petersbourg, 1912), 17–28.

[4] Varneke, *History of the Russian Theater,* 21.

[5] Patouillet, *Le Théâtre de moeurs russes,* 29–40. See also N. S. Tikhonravov, *Russkie dramaticheskie proizvedeniia 1672–1725 gg.,* vol. 1 (St. Petersburg: n.p., 1874).

[6] Vsevolodskii-Gerngross, *Russkii teatr ot istokov,* 250–52. On Russia's cultural identity, see

Elizabeth was infamous for her love of entertainment; she might take two years to respond to the king of France, but every Tuesday she could be found at a masked ball.[7] In 1756 she appointed writer A. P. Sumarokov as director of Russia's first national theater, although like her grandfather she had to command the gentry to attend.[8] Sumarokov struggled, despite lack of funds, to mount respectable productions, and finally in 1759 he successfully lobbied to have the theater included in the Department of State Domains, which ensured subsidies for purchasing sets and costumes and paying salaries, including pensions.[9] Elizabeth also founded the Imperial Theater School, open to both sexes and all social estates, the only restriction being that students must be members of the Orthodox Church.[10] In addition, she built the first permanent indoor stage designed to be open to the public (*obshchedostupnyi*); the locale was initially so infested with rats that the tsaritsa had to send three hundred cats as exterminators before the carpenters could begin work.[11] Establishing a permanent site made it easier to regulate production and to establish a schedule for the customers, who paid according to the location of their seats.

Developments begun under Elizabeth continued to flourish under the enterprising Catherine, who penned several plays herself, possibly with help, and translated others.[12] Catherine oversaw the compilation and editing of forty-three volumes of Russian plays, though this included translations. Russian fans still depended largely on touring companies from France, Italy, and even Germany until the end of the eighteenth century, but they began staging amateur productions in peoples' homes or private clubs, which continued even after the extensive commercialization of the stage. This included the Romanov family; Catherine had built an intimate theater at her Hermitage, which was still being used by the last tsar's sister Olga, a great aficionada who performed with amateur troupes there until the end of her family's dynasty.[13]

The popularity of the theater in Catherine's time reflected philosoph-

---

especially Hans Rogger, *National Consciousness in Eighteenth-Century Russia* (Cambridge, Mass.: Harvard University Press, 1960).

[7] Baron N. V. Drizen, "Staryi Peterburg," *Ves' mir*, no. 10 (1918): 7.

[8] Baron N. V. Drizin, *Stopiatidesiatiletie Imperatorskikh teatrov (po novym arkhivam svedeniiam)* (St. Petersburg: Izdanie direktsii imp. teatrov, 1906), 10.

[9] Vsevolodskii-Gerngross, *Russkii teatr ot istokov*, 231. The Senate made the theater official on August 30, 1756, but the real support came when it became a department of the Imperial Domain and therefore had access to the state budget.

[10] RGIA, f. 472, op. 50, d. 1662, contains information about the school throughout its history, until 1917. Prospective theater students took a course on "The Lies of the Catholic Church," ll. 28–44.

[11] Drizen, "Staryi Peterburg," 26.

[12] Grigorii Gukovskii, "The Empress as Writer," trans. Mary Mackler, in *Catherine the Great: A Profile*, ed. Marc Raeff (New York: Hill and Wang, 1972), 64–89.

[13] V. A. Teliakovskii, *Vospominaniia, 1898–1917* (Petrograd: Vremia, 1924), 99–106.

ical shifts associated with the Enlightenment being expressed on stage. Catherine provided valuable financial subsidies to numerous French philosophers, but she fell short of embracing the Enlightenment's ideal of personal emancipation through theater.[14] Despite the limitations she set on intellectual importations, during her reign both secularism and satire began to flourish on the Russian stage. Russia's first "classic"—that is, a play that transcended the historical frame in which it was written because the issues raised had relevance beyond the immediate setting—appeared during her reign: Denis Fonvizin's *The Minor* (1782).[15]

The next tsar to levy significant impact on theatrical developments, Alexander I (1800–1825), inserted the state's presence more firmly through his bureaucratic restructuring and reorganization of censorship. A new statute invoked in 1804 subjected plays to pre-performance censorship by newly organized committees under the auspices of the Ministry of Education. The statute differentiated between performing plays and publishing them, with attitudes more lenient toward the latter. In 1811 supervision of production was transferred to the local police, which found itself under the political umbrella of the Ministry of Internal Affairs. The guidelines for censors told them to look out for disrespect for the royal family, the Orthodox Church, and materials that could potentially foment conflict between social estates.[16] However, no central body judged plays; instead, every theater manager needed approval from the local authorities for each play staged. Approvals were not uniform, and censors in one region could force changes in local productions that would not be repeated elsewhere, an action that put police agents into the creative mix.[17] This license for confusion and arbitrary decision making subverted any attempt at interpretive coherence, a situation appreciated by some directors as an opportunity for ingenuity.

Despite being known as the "Iron Tsar" in politics, Alexander's successor, Nicholas I (1825–1855), was something of a bon vivant who enjoyed drama as passionately as he did the lovely leading ladies.[18] The ornamental state theater that still stands in St. Petersburg today was opened in 1832 and named for his wife, Alexandra Fedorovna, and affectionately called the "Alexandrinka." One actor recalled Nicholas's reign as the best for the

---

[14] S. Zhizlina, "Iz istorii narodnogo teatra," *Narodnoe tvorchestvo*, no. 12 (1938): 56.

[15] On the theater in Catherine's era, see especially V. N. Vsevoloskii-Gerngross, *Russkii teatr vtoroi poloviny XVII veka* (Moscow: Akademiia nauk, 1960).

[16] S. S. Danilov, "Materialy po istorii russkogo zakonodatel'stva o teatre," in *O teatre: Sbornik statei*, ed. S. S. Danilov and S. S. Mokul'skii (Moscow: Iskusstvo, 1940), 177–200.

[17] I. F. Petrovskaia, *Istochnikovedenie istorii russkogo dorevoliutsionnogo dramaticheskogo teatra* (Leningrad: Iskusstvo, 1971), especially 45–58; and Alek. Ures., "Teatrovedy v gorokhovykh pal'to," *ANTRAKT*, no. 1 (1991): 3.

[18] Theatrical histories and memoirs from the era always note the tsar's keen enjoyment of the theater. See, for example, the *Autobiography* of one of the leading actresses, P. I. Orlova-Savina (Moscow: Khudozhestvennaia literatura, 1994).

theater "because he loved the artists as a father loves his children."[19] So popular did theater become during this era that Nicholas could end the family practice of requiring nobles to attend.[20] The consummate fan, Nicholas raised the social status and economic security of professional performers by extending legislation, first passed in 1783, that provided pensions for actors at the state theaters, "for the stimulation of talent and the fitting remuneration of lengthy service and the zealous fulfillment of duty."[21] His most significant action, however, was to integrate actors and actresses into Russia's official social system by assigning them a formal position (*sostoianie*) that reflected their professional expertise.[22]

Nicholas laid the foundation for a government monopoly by putting public performances in the two capitals under the aegis of the imperial theaters in 1827.[23] Legislation also addressed the role of playwrights, who were not expected to support themselves on the money earned from the performance of their works. This legislation placed greater monetary value on plays written in rhyme than those in prose, betraying a cultural prejudice that undermined the stylistic innovations that accompanied the evolution of realism by mid-century. Nor were plays considered heritable property; that is, authors could not will proceeds from copyrighted works to posterity. The criminal code tried to back up an implicit authorial right by threatening punishment to anyone producing a play without the author's permission, but these laws proved unenforceable.[24]

In a point with more far-reaching implications, the 1827 provisions made all plays submitted for performance the property of the imperial theaters, which then would classify them according to length, style, and originality. Playwrights would now benefit from more appropriate remuneration; for example, the honorarium for a five-act drama would be larger than that for a translation or a vaudeville.[25] Whether or not a play sold tickets did not figure into the calculations for payment. As an added bonus, likely borrowed from the familiar French tradition, playwrights were supposed to receive numerous tickets gratis, which they were then free to sell; an especially popular play could earn the author substantial additional income. But this practice was left to the discretion of the theater managers, and in 1869 the embittered Ostrovskii noted that despite having written

[19] A. Sokolov, "Iz teatral'nykh vospominanii," *Istoricheskii vestnik*, May 24, 1889, no. 4.

[20] Karlinsky, *Russian Drama*, 43.

[21] RGIA, f. 472, op. 66, ed. khran. 448, l. 2.

[22] Slonim, *Russian Theater*, 48; and Drizen, "Staryi Peterburg," 5.

[23] Catriona Kelly, "Popular, Provincial and Amateur Theatres, 1820–1900," in *A History of Russian Theatre*, ed. Robert Leach and Victor Borovsky (Cambridge: Cambridge University Press, 1999), 124.

[24] The earlier legislation was discussed in A. Gol'dman, *A. N. Ostrovskii. Predsedatel' obshchestva dramaticheskikh pisatelei* (Moscow: Vserossiiskoe teatral'noe obshchestvo, 1948).

[25] Ibid., 6–7.

eighteen successful plays he had yet to receive complimentary tickets to either of the imperial theaters.[26]

Nicholas's eldest son, Alexander II (1855–1881), did not share his father's enthusiasm for the theater, though he was known to drop in for the after-pieces, or late-night vaudevilles that followed the plays. Dubbed the "Tsar-Reformer" because of his sponsorship of the Great Reforms, Alexander was never quite certain how to deal with the theater. Although his censorship reform of 1865 significantly ameliorated the process whereby plays were approved, they did not substantially alter the substance of the statute nor end the censorial distinction between publication and performance.[27] More infamously, Alexander instituted the state monopoly over the theater. In 1856 and 1862 the government had passed resolutions stating that "private theaters are not allowed in the two capitals" and "public staged performances are exclusively the right of the imperial theaters."[28] Limited in any case to the two capitals, the monopoly was enforced only during the reform era, between 1856 and 1882, and haphazardly at that.

The reformist government never clearly articulated what it intended by the monopoly, and its economic policies favored commerce and private competition. The short-lived monopoly arrived too late to have real influence over the already legitimate stage. Performances of musical numbers and in foreign languages were still permissible, and private clubs could and did charge admission for plays that met most criteria for quasi-professional performances. The flaws of the monopoly could be counted in the twelve individual theaters in Moscow and fourteen in Petersburg that were negotiating with playwrights to perform their works in 1874 eight years before the monopoly was repeated.[29] But the imperial stage could always attract the best talent because it offered fixed salaries and retirement benefits that the financially unstable private theaters could not.

The Play's the Thing

Legislation provided one essential framework, but it was the plays and the performers who interpreted them that gave the theater its cultural significance. Well into the eighteenth century Russian writers were imitating western styles rather than inventing their own. Native playwrights con-

---

[26] Ibid., 11.

[27] The censorship statute was issued April 6, 1865, no. 41988 in the Law Code. Once a play had received an official imprimatur, it could be performed anywhere—thus depriving the local police, at least in theory, of its ability to intervene at will. The official *Pravitel'stvennyi vestnik* regularly published lists of plays approved and disapproved for performance.

[28] Danilov, "Materialy po istorii russkogo zakonodatel'stva," 178–83.

[29] RGALI, f. 2097, Obshchestvo russkikh dramaticheskikh pisatelei i opernykh kompozitorov, op. 1, ed. khran. 76, ll. 11, 13.

An amateur production by noble thespians, circa 1900

tributed few original pieces, but when they translated western European works, they demonstrated their creativity by russifying dramatic situations and characters; Sumarokov, for example, reconfigured *Hamlet* so that it resembled intrigue at the Russian court.[30] This developed as something of a new genre, distinct but not completely separate from faithful translations. But by century's end, Russia began to assert a more pronounced cultural maturity in its relationship with western Europe. Not wholly complacent with the rationalism espoused through the Enlightenment, the first genuinely original playwright, Fonvizin, borrowed the European genre of satire but created thoroughly Russian personalities: dull-witted nobles who clung to the old ways in clear defiance of reason, and others who worshiped before the altar of French fashions. This theme was especially significant at the creation of Russian drama because it highlighted national self-perception at the moment of its intellectual formation.[31] Fonvizin's *The Minor*—which with its mnemonic characters of "Starodum" (Old Thought)

[30] Victor Borovsky, "The Organization of the Russian Theatre, 1645–1763," in *History of Russian Theatre*, ed. Leach and Borovsky, 51.
[31] Patouillet, *Le Théâtre de moeurs russes*, 53–68.

and "Prostakov" (Simpleton) ironized the nobility—survived him because his clever dialogue bespoke the perseverance of obtuse bureaucrats and provincial ineptitude.

Fonvizin's popularity aside, the theater in the early nineteenth century was far from "mass" culture. But it was taking shape as a site in which issues of public culture were being hammered out by a socially and politically diverse audience. The most prolific playwrights of the first half of the nineteenth century, Nicholas Polevoi and Nestor Kukolnik, wrote plays that responded to the rising tide of nationalism and that reflected the post-Enlightenment Romanticism sweeping Europe. Kukolnik's *Almighty's Hand the Fatherland Has Saved* (1834) and Polevoi's *Parasha the Siberian Girl* (1840) offered an identity steeped in nationalism, emphasizing a sense of land and peoples. Criticized for creating cardboard patriots who spoke in stilted dialogue, these two dramatists never entered the pantheon of writers, but their plays provide valuable mirrors of new audiences finding some of their needs to understand Russia's expanding imperialist mission and "great power" status answered on stage.

The first production of Alexander Griboedov's *Woe from Wit* in 1831 marked a conceptual turning point for the Russian theater, moving away from Fonvizin's satire toward a more realistic depiction of characters. The author, murdered in a riot while on a tour of duty at the Russian embassy in Persia in 1829, rested his genius on this single oeuvre.[32] The chief protagonist, a tortured intellectual driven away from official society by its shallowness and willful ignorance, evidenced great psychological depth. Following *The Minor, Woe from Wit* took Russia to the next level of the modern theatrical age, where author, audience, and contents merged to form "theater"—a place where cultural ideals could be expressed, contested, and ultimately legitimized by the enduring support of fans. Both plays introduced political themes that still present obstacles to Russian cultural life: *The Minor* dealt with Russia's ambiguous relationship with the West, and *Woe from Wit* questioned the social and political responsibilities of the intellectual.

The "Talented Ones and Their Admirers"

The next step was for the performers themselves to find a level of social respect commensurate with their growing popularity. The distance between performers and audiences was not simply social: physical, spatial relationships between performers and viewers affected both presentation and appreciation of a work. When in the mid-eighteenth century David

---

[32] On Griboedov's satire, see especially ibid., chapter 7.

Garrick banned playgoers from sitting on the stage at London's Drury Lane Theater, and then developed lighting techniques that focused attention on the actors, he liberated performers to show off the characters they had assumed.[33] Departing significantly from the old style where roles such as Hamlet or Lady Macbeth were presented as articulations of transhistorical values, new talents had to portray psychologically motivated individuals, which led to audience identification with individual actors.

At first, the tsarist government had little success with the clerks impressed into service as actors and found itself importing stage performers, just as it did scientists. Official training for the stage began in 1738 in the State Dancing Academy, which included courses in the dramatic and operatic arts. The students would have been members of the cadet corps, the scions of Russia's better aristocratic families.[34] Serfs provided the other primary source for actors, which made the stage the one place where the two estates mingled openly.[35] The noble Sheremetev family at Kuskovo, in the suburbs of Moscow, for example, boasted one of the country's best acting companies, and the impresario Count N. P. Sheremetev married his favorite actress, a serf, and moved her to his theater at his estate at Ostankino.[36] Unlike western Europe, Russia had no intrinsic cultural prohibition against women on the stage.[37] Catherine Semenova, one of Russia's premier tragedians, was born a serf but later taught acting to the cadet corps. As early as 1757 an advertisement appeared in *Moskovskie vedomosti* (Moscow gazette) soliciting actresses to join the male company forming at the university.[38] To increase the talent pool, both Moscow University and the State Foundling Home began to teach acting in the 1770s.[39]

Russia's first quasi-professional acting company sprang up in the provincial city of Yaroslavl in the middle of the eighteenth century, under the directorship of Fedor Volkov, a merchant's son. Sumarokov brought Volkov's troupe to Petersburg, where the silver-throated Volkov thrilled audiences who favored the classical lyricism in which he excelled. But as Sumarokov's classicism found competition from other genres, satire and realism in par-

---

[33] Voltaire has also been credited with having playgoers removed from the stage, but Garrick institutionalized it. Richard Sennett, *The Fall of Public Man* (London: Faber, 1986), 80.

[34] Borovsky, "Organization of the Russian Theatre," 47–49; and Drizin, *Stopiatidesiatiletie Imperatorskikh teatrov.*

[35] The social backgrounds of the first generation of actors and actresses varied widely, from priests' sons to cadets to serf girls. For a collection of biographies, see I. N. Bozheranov and N. N. Karlov, *Illiustrirovannaia istoriia russkogo teatra XVIII veka* (St. Petersburg: n.p., 1903).

[36] Vsevolodskii-Gerngross, *Russkii teatr vtoroi poloviny XVIII veka,* 31. See also Varneke, *History of the Russian Theater,* 101–2.

[37] Varneke, *History of the Russian Theater,* 82, suggested that the difficulty lay in finding "a woman with enough courage to dedicate herself to so hazardous a venture as a career in the theater."

[38] Reprinted in Iu. A. Dmitriev, ed., *F. G. Volkov i russkii teatr ego vremeni: Sbornik materialov* (Moscow: Izd. Akademii nauk, 1953), 144, 147.

[39] Varneke, *History of the Russian Theater,* 88.

Mikhail Shchepkin, center, in Griboedov's *Woe from Wit*

ticular, another actor appeared from the provinces to introduce a new style, emancipated serf Mikhail Shchepkin.[40]

Originally from Kursk, the bright and talented Shchepkin was able to receive an education and to perform in local productions before his big break came in 1805 in true theatrical fashion: when the profligate leading man could not go on at a benefit for an important provincial actress, Shchepkin, familiar with the part, shone in his stead. Still legally enserfed, Shchepkin nonetheless joined a touring company and played to such applause that an influential enthusiast, Prince N. G. Repin, persuaded his owner to set him free in 1818. When Shchepkin ended up shortly thereafter at the imperial theater in Moscow, he established himself as Russia's preeminent character actor.[41]

Shchepkin's moment of historical consequence came when he assumed

[40] Vsevolodskii-Gerngross, *Russkii teatr ot istokov*, 241–45. See also Dmitriev, ed., *F. G. Volkov*, for reprints of relevant documents.

[41] Laurence Senelick, *Serf Actor: The Life and Art of Mikhail Shchepkin* (Westport: Greenwood, 1984). Shchepkin's own memoirs are also available: *Zapiski aktera Shchepkina*, ed. A. B. Derman (Moscow: Akademiia nauk, 1933).

the role of Famusov, the dim-witted bureaucrat in *Woe from Wit*.[42] The actor's artistic appropriation of this role moved the Russian theater to the next level by employing methods of comedy, which depends on character development—rather than farce, which registers through stereotype—to create multidimensional personalities.[43] For example, an actor performing in the comic opera *The Miller as Sorcerer, Deceiver, and Matchmaker* in the 1790s was praised because "his ways and manners are those characteristic of the common people, but at the same time they were ennobled";[44] in other words, actors had to simulate type, not play a personality.

The first major actors who performed as expressions of their fans off-stage as well as on- were the two great tragedians of the era, Pavel Mochalov and Vasilii Karatygin. Both sons of actors, they established rival performing styles that carried over into competition between their fans in the cities on whose stages they appeared—Moscow and Petersburg, respectively. Their contrasting interpretations of Hamlet in Polevoi's rather too freely translated version of Shakespeare's dramatization epitomized the debate.[45] Karatygin concentrated on painstaking historical accuracy, whereas Mochalov decried any technique and relied completely on his intuition, which made him far more popular with audiences than with his beleaguered costars, who never knew what to expect next on stage. Mochalov's womanizing and abuse of alcohol further distanced him from Karatygin: passionate, temperamental Moscow versus cold, bureaucratic St. Petersburg.

These actors, especially the colorful Mochalov, led their private lives in public.[46] In an apocryphal rumor, Mochalov was said to have attended a performance by Karatygin incognito, and when the audience began shouting down the reserved actor, the magnanimous Mochalov stood up to quiet them down.[47] Police had to be called in to separate fans whose partisanship had led to fisticuffs.[48] Moscow's merchant fans reportedly collected more than three thousand rubles to give Mochalov a vacation abroad, and many closed their shops for his funeral.[49]

Their competitive styles brought the *intelligentsia* to the theater on the

---

[42] Initially Shchepkin had problems developing this new kind of character. Varneke, *History of the Russian Theater*, 285.

[43] For Shchepkin's own articulation of the art of acting, see Varneke, *History of the Russian Theater*, 287. Senelick, *Serf Actor*, xiv, credits Shchepkin with the primary influence behind the realistic style developed later by the Moscow Arts Theater and through it, "the entire Western theatre."

[44] Quoted in Varneke, *History of the Russian Theater*, 94.

[45] Ibid., 243–44.

[46] Both actors left published memoirs. P. A. Karatygin, *Zapiski*, ed. N. V. Koroleva (Leningrad: Iskusstvo, 1977), and P. S. Mochalov, *Zapiski o teatre, pis'ma, stikhi, p'esy*, ed. Iu. Dmitriev and A. Klinchin (Moscow: Iskusstvo, 1953).

[47] *Iskusstvo*, no. 8 (1883): 75–77.

[48] Arsen'ev, "Iz teatral'nykh vospomi nanii," *Golos minuvshego*, no. 2 (1917): 239.

[49] Joseph MacLeod, *Actors across the Volga* (London: Allen and Unwin, 1946), 14.

watch for politics. Literary critic Vissarion Belinskii, the most influential intellectual during their years of stardom and himself a failed playwright, wrote on the theater for a number of the so-called "thick" journals, monthly periodicals that specialized in cultural critique.[50] Arguing that Karatygin represented the repressive aspects of autocracy and Mochalov the pent-up frustrations of living under such a government, Belinskii identified the stage as a political forum. Appropriating the actors for *his* readers, Belinskii was making essentially the same point as the merchants collecting for the vacation: actors performed more than just their stage roles.[51]

Personal identification with, or adoration of, individual actors also figured directly into how much money the latter earned. Those who had contracts with the imperial theaters enjoyed job security, a pension plan, a credit union, and educational support for their children.[52] But they also had a fixed income, which could work against the interests of the most popular stars who brought in the biggest audiences. A major secondary source of income came from the "benefits," or special performances allowing the featured performer to collect part of the ticket sales. Advance publicity also made this a night for the fans to come out and pay tribute, often giving personal gifts to favorites. The right to have a specific number of benefits was written into contracts for both state and private stages. In fact, contracts differentiated between two types of benefits: those included as a part of the player's salary, and those listed as "rewards" for the most popular stars. This method of supplementing salaries, known in England as the "golden ticket," was as controversial in Russia as elsewhere. In preparation, the performer being honored had to make the social rounds, inviting the wealthy to attend and hoping to coax them to pay extra for their tickets. This particular ordeal could be an amusing social occasion or an excruciatingly humiliating one. An indication of creeping commercialization, the administration responded to the loss of income by restricting benefits first in 1883 and again in 1892, abolishing them finally in 1903.[53] Top stars, continued to demand that one "reward" per annum be written into their contracts, but all protested at the obligation to appear gratis in productions to raise money for official charities.[54]

---

[50] Patouillet, *Le Théâtre de moeurs russes,* 135–39.

[51] Belinskii's comments on the two actors are reprinted in V. Vsevolodskii-Gerngross, *Khrestomatiia po istorii russkogo teatra* (Moscow: Khudozhestvennaia literatura, 1936), 213–19 and 222–41.

[52] Figures on salaries, pensions, and the credit union are scattered throughout the archive for the theatrical administration, RGIA, f. 468. On the history of the pension plan, see op. 44, d. 158, l. 6. See also RGIA, f. 472, the Archive of the State Domains, op. 66, ed. khran. 448. The educational funding, though, was miserly: f. 468, op. 14, d. 111.

[53] Despite the official abolition, evidence of the continuation of this practice reappears throughout the archives. See, for example, RGIA, f. 468, op. 44, d. 158, ll. 1–3 about benefits for 1910.

[54] Teliakovskii, *Vospominaniia,* 90–92. Performers were more pliant during the Russo-Japanese and First World Wars. See also complaints in RGIA, f. 468, op. 14, d. 406, ll. 1–2.

Those who wrote the plays also had reasons for ambivalence toward these benefit performances. Actors were constantly in need of new material, and a benefit for a popular actor offered a splendid opportunity to showcase a new play. The crowd favorite Shchepkin, for example, could prompt his friend the great novelist Ivan Turgenev to write short pieces, which kept both their names before the public.[55] The 1827 legislation, however, guaranteed that the performers reaped more from these arrangements than the writers.

The expansion of the theater and the interest in the popular personalities it was creating sparked the publication of specialized theatrical journals, beginning in 1808 with the short-lived *Dramaticheskii kur'er* (Dramatic courier), founded by playwrights A. A. Shakhovskoi and I. A. Krylov in an unsuccessful bid to save classicism.[56] In 1840 *Panteon russkogo i vsekh evropeiskikh teatrov* (Pantheon of Russian and all European theaters) began a decade of intermittent publication, with more information about Russia's provincial stages than those in Europe. Periodicals from newspapers to "thick" journals regularly covered the theater.[57] *Iskusstvo* (Art), which began publication in 1860, dedicated to "theater, music, painting, sculpture, architecture, and literature," introduced a new style. Despite a pretentious editorial policy that professed faith that artists must work for "the general good," this was a prototype of future gossip-oriented magazines that prattled about Mikhail Glinka's and Richard Wagner's childhood deficiencies.[58] *Iskusstvo* fed the fan who identified with the stars personally, and it heralded a spate of commercially funded magazines devoted to the various aspects of a consumer culture, serving up as "history" the delicious scandals that had embroiled past stars, the editors' apparent concession to decorum being that they kept away from the private lives of current performers.[59] A. R. Kugel's *Teatr i iskusstvo* (Theater and art), 1897–1918, became the most influential of these publications, critiquing actions on stage while also keeping a gossip reporting from behind the curtain.[60]

Realistic Theater: The Politics of Genre and Social Change

The evolution of realistic situations and acting underlay the theater's ability to generate audience identification with the action and the people on stage. According to the dictates of realism, actors "tried to equate the

---

[55] Senelick, *Serf Actor,* 178–79.

[56] Varneke, *History of the Russian Theater,* 187.

[57] On theater publications, see I. F. Petrovskaia, *Istochnikovedenie,* 109–69.

[58] See the various articles in *Iskusstvo,* no. 1 (1860).

[59] See, for example, the series run in 1883 on "Padenie Kokoshkin!" nos. 4–6, about numerous scandals in the imperial theater's directory in the 1830s.

[60] Petrovskaia, *Istochnikovedenie,* 156.

truth of what was done on stage with the truth of the lives of the audience."[61] Even before the term was coined toward the middle of the nineteenth century, realism enjoyed political life as a literary aesthetic, the purpose of which was to shine light on society's ills so that they could be identified and treated.[62] Therefore, it involved not just a new way of watching the action, but a new way of understanding it as well. Belinskii spoke for the *intelligentsia* when he argued that the arts must not only hold a critical mirror up to social reality, but must also provide a transformative vision.[63] For him, Griboedov's *Woe from Wit* offered the social critique required of Russian culture: "What a lethal power of sarcasm, what an analysis of characters and society, and what language, what verse . . . so very Russian."[64]

Griboedov wrote in verse and used satire; his realism lay in his politics. Nikolai Gogol, who had begun his artistic career as an untalented actor cast "only for parts without speeches,"[65] wrote the next Russian stage classic. His *Inspector General* (1836) broke new ground, and after Belinskii had seen Shchepkin perform the role of Khlestakov, the hapless clerk mistaken by the corrupt officials in a provincial town for one of the tsar's investigators, somehow Griboedov's realism no longer seemed sufficiently real.[66] Shchepkin himself wrote excitedly to thank Gogol for creating this remarkably imaginative sort of character, saying that he could "live a new life" by performing him.

The political implications of realism gave the theater a new seriousness of purpose without denying the entertainment value that brought in so much of the audience. In the 1850s, a decade wracked first by war and then by the realization that government and society could no longer avoid enacting sweeping reforms, stage plays were recognized as media where some of these issues could be presented for public consumption. The playwrights A. F. Pisemskii and A. A. Potekhin, relatively unknown today, produced the common themes and character types that marked the new social realism. Using drama rather than comedy, they attempted verisimilitude,

[61] MacLeod, *Actors across the Volga,* 18.

[62] Victor Terras, *Belinskij and Russian Literary Criticism* (Madison: University of Wisconsin Press, 1974), 133. Noted *intelligent* Mikhail Saltykov-Shchedrin argued that realism "should always carry a notion of the ideal . . . and serve to 'remind man of his humanity.'" Cynthia Marsh, "Realism in the Russian Theatre, 1850–1882," in *History of Russian Theatre,* ed. Leach and Borovsky, 150.

[63] On Belinskii, see Patouillet, *Le Théâtre de moeurs russes* 135–39. On the *intelligentsia* and realism, see Irina Paperno, *Chernyshevsky and the Age of Realism: A Study in the Semiotics of Behavior* (Stanford: Stanford University Press, 1988), especially her introduction.

[64] Quoted in Slonim, *Russian Theater,* 44.

[65] Quoted in Varneke, *History of the Russian Theater,* 299.

[66] Belinskii wrote that people should see no one but Shchepkin in the role. Varneke, *History of the Russian Theater,* 289. Belinskii also found *The Inspector General* one of "those profoundly true creations, by which Gogol so potently contributed to Russia's self-consciousness, enabling her to look at herself as through a mirror." Ibid., 307.

but were heavy-handed in their moralizing. *Tinsel* (1858), one of Pote-khin's best-known plays, extolled the capacity of education to transform backward and corrupt Russia. This theme underscored the pressure felt by audiences to find ways to assimilate the serfs and accept the changes for themselves.[67] Made an honorary member of the Academy of Sciences in 1900, Potekhin's work survives him as nostalgic glimpses into the bygone world of serfs and the guilt of liberal Russia toward them.[68]

The production that perhaps best captured the imagination of a public anxious to display its repentance on the eve of the emancipation was Pisemskii's most famous play, *A Bitter Fate* (1859). A melodrama about a genuine love affair between a married serf and her noble owner, by whom she bore a child, this play made every individual character sympathetic, even the peasant husband who murdered the baby born to his wife. Pisem-skii demonized Russia's social structure, indicting a situation that de-stroyed possibilities for personal choice. *A Bitter Fate* shared the prestigious Uvarov Prize for best new play with newcomer Alexander Ostrovskii's *The Storm* in 1860.[69] Whereas Pisemskii described the end of one era, Ostrov-skii had the talent to anticipate so many aspects of the one unfolding.

Initially, it was hoped that the Great Reforms would fulfill the promises of modernization first made by Peter the Great. But legislative innovations were dependent on cultural acceptance of increased socializing among the various estates. For example, the impending transformation of Russia from an agrarian to an industrial economy could not succeed if the bourgeoisie were regarded as pariahs or the peasants as chattel. But centuries of custom would not evaporate with the steam from the new factories. Ostrovskii made brilliant use of the theater to illuminate the expectations and failures asso-ciated with the reform era and the commercialization of Russian culture.

Ostrovskii Stages the Middle Classes

Alexander Nikolaevich Ostrovskii, 1823–1886, was the first Russian playwright to generate a sizable corpus of original works: almost sixty, ap-proximately 10 percent of them coauthored in his last years. He covered every genre, from historical patriotism to fairy tales to short comic vaude-villes, creating more than seven hundred individual characters. His forte, though, lay in the carefully crafted multiact comedies and dramas that de-

---

[67] On Potekhin and Pisemskii, see Marsh, "Realism in the Russian Theatre, 1850–1882," 149–51.

[68] N. G. Zograf, *Malyi teatr vtoroi poloviny XIX veka* (Moscow: Akademiia nauk, 1960), 46–48, 102–6, 399–401.

[69] *Iskusstvo*, no. 1 (1883): 51–52, provides some behind-the-scenes drama from this com-petition.

picted contemporary Russian life. Reflections of his audience, his characters came from all backgrounds. The Malyi Theater in Moscow, built in 1824, was considered Ostrovskii's theater of residence because he premiered his plays there. However, he usually set the action in the provinces. Most famous for his memorable merchants, Ostrovskii in fact described the middle classes as they were: a congregation of social estates who were forced by the circumstances of industrialization to adjust their attitudes to accept social mobility and the commercial marketplace.

Ostrovskii belongs in the company of western playwrights who transformed the stage in the nineteenth century through what was considered not simply a bourgeois ethos but also a bourgeois aesthetic. The plays that characterized this theater were deemed bourgeois because of the social origins of their primary characters and because of the neat interweaving of situations in the structured plottings, building scenes toward an emotional climax with the implicit promise of resolution at the final curtain. The standard setting, the bourgeois sitting room, was as significant as the narrative design because it relocated dramatic tension away from the traditionally more public places and into the private home. These staging innovations were facilitated by technological advancements in lighting, first with gas and then electricity. Lighting the entire stage gave it a heretofore unreachable depth, and actors enjoyed increased mobility. Moreover, sets no longer served merely as backdrops: the sitting room enhanced the familiarity of the situation on stage.[70]

One of the most remarkable characteristics of this theater is the extent to which the era's most productive and popular playwrights have not withstood the test of time. French dramatist Eugene Scribe is most closely identified with the bourgeois drama through his concept of the "well-made play" (*pièce bien faite*). Extraordinarily prolific and elected to the Académie Française in 1834, Scribe nonetheless never enjoyed much critical respect. Yet his influence was striking: Emile Augier, Victorien Sardou, and Alexandre Dumas (*fils*) were Scribe's direct aesthetic descendants. They dominated the French stage throughout the century and had their most popular works translated into other languages, including Russian. Sardou, derided by one critic for bringing to all his plays "the same technical ability and the same poverty of thought,"[71] must also be remembered for creating some of Sarah Bernhardt's most memorable roles and for his successful suit against composer Puccini for plagiarizing *La Tosca*. When George Bernard Shaw mocked the contemporary theater as "Sardoodledom," he was offering a begrudging recognition to a tremendous influence.

[70] Freddie Rokem, *Theatrical Space in Ibsen, Checkhov, and Strindberg: Public Forms of Privacy* (Ann Arbor: UMI Research Press, 1986), 15.

[71] *The Oxford Companion to the Theatre*, ed. Phyllis Hartnell, 3d ed. (New York: Oxford University Press, 1967), 350.

The ignominious "Sardoodledom" proved instrumental in developing a large theatergoing public with expectations that Shaw's biting social critiques would have to satisfy. Shaw's immediate British predecessors, including Tom Taylor, Thomas Robertson, and Arthur Wing Pinero, suffered the same lack of critical respect as their French counterparts. All three specialized in dramas presenting the complex realities of the changing social structure, and Robertson came closest to earning the title of the English Scribe with his so-called "cup-and-saucer" comedies, which also re-created the middle-class parlor on stage. Taylor's *Our American Cousin* turned into the most famous production in the United States in the nineteenth century: at a production of it at Ford's Theater in Washington, D.C., on April 14, 1865, John Wilkes Booth, scion of a famous acting family, assassinated the avid theatergoer President Abraham Lincoln.

Ostrovskii's critical reputation outlived that of Sardou, Taylor, and the others in their respective homelands because the transformation that he was dramatizing was never completed in Russia. After 1917 Ostrovskii offered a nostalgic familiarity with a past under devastating attack; so long as his plays could be interpretively performed as indictments of the fallen bourgeoisie, he passed the test of political correctness Soviet-style.[72] But in his prime he was staging comedies and melodramas in the dramatic structure of the "well-made play," presenting contemporary situations through characters speaking the parlance of everyday life.

The son of a lawyer, Ostrovskii initially followed in his father's footsteps. Assigned to the commercial courts early in his career, he became intimately acquainted with the local merchants. He broadened his acquaintances among that social group, which would supply him with types for his best known characters, in 1856 on a fact-finding tour of the Volga commissioned by the Naval Ministry. Because of differences in their historical development, Russia's merchants contrasted sharply with their more dynamic and self-confident western counterparts.[73] As a result, merchant culture remained corseted by tradition and mistrustful of change, especially when it came from a government that had done them more disservices than favors. But Ostrovskii appreciated how important this social estate would be to the future of the economic reforms, and when he gave in to his passion for the theater he took them to the stage with him.

While still practicing law, the future playwright mixed in several Moscow artistic circles with writers and actors of the Malyi Theater.[74] The strict censorial difference between publication and performance of plays aided the

[72] Lynn Mally, *Revolutionary Acts: Amateur Theater and the Soviet State, 1917–1938* (Ithaca: Cornell University Press, 2000), 196–97.

[73] Alfred Rieber, *Merchants and Entrepreneurs in Imperial Russia* (Chapel Hill: University of North Carolina Press, 1982), especially part 1.

[74] Marjorie Hoover, *Alexander Ostrovsky* (Boston: Twayne Publishers, 1981), 15–16.

The young A. N. Ostrovskii

early intellectual acceptance of Ostrovskii because his plays were read in political circles before they were performed. Like all the youthful intellectuals of the 1840s, he became ensnared in the Slavophile versus Westernizer debates, nationalistic polemics that contested the interpretation of Russia's past as well as the direction of its future. Equally at ease in both camps, to the puzzlement of his critics, Ostrovskii published in each of their "thick" journals: *Vestnik Evropy* (The herald of Europe), whose self-

31

evident Western orientation appeared in its title, and *Moskvitianin* (The Muscovite), which celebrated Russia's Slavic distinctions.

Ostrovskii's first play, *The Bankrupt,* appeared in *Moskvitianin* in 1849. So unflattering were his caricatures of a merchant's family and his business associate that the censors forbade performance. Agreeing that he had been unfair, Ostrovskii revised and retitled the play *It's a Family Affair, We'll Settle It Ourselves.*" Subsequently it became a standard in repertoires.

It was, however, a serious drama about the merchantry, published in the Westernizing *Sovremennik* (The contemporary) a decade later, that ensured his reputation as a social critic. *The Storm* was his first major tragedy, the story of a young woman trapped in a marriage based on social estate rather than love. The young heroine, Katerina, finds herself married to an alcoholic merchant's son and tyrannized by her mother-in-law, who runs the family business because her alcoholic son is incompetent to do so. Katerina falls in love with an idealistic student, but commits suicide when she realizes that she cannot escape her circumstances with him. This powerful drama received immediate and impassioned support from one of the most influential members of the *intelligentsia,* Nikolai Dobroliubov, *Sovremennik*'s literary critic. In his review Dobroliubov coined the phrase "kingdom of darkness," a biting metaphor for the ignorance and obscurantism in which he considered that the merchant estate lived.[75] Not only did he cast Ostrovskii in the role of severe critic of the merchantry, but he pressed the playwright to use the forum of the stage to take a political stand, noting that Ostrovskii's "clear depictions showed us the kingdom of darkness. . . . Sadly, he did not show us the way out."[76]

To turn Ostrovskii into an unforgiving critic of the merchantry, though, was to beg the question of why these very people flocked to his plays. They went because they heard in him their voice. His themes, his narrative structures, and his theatrical activities beyond stage productions made plain his intuitive grasp of the implications that modernization held in store for them. As Ira Petrovskaia discovered in studying reviews of *The Storm* in the provincial press, local critics did not see the play as Dobroliubov had, but understood the play as a commentary on modernization and the "new" women.[77] Where the Dobroliubov crowd saw Ostrovskii making social commentary about merchants, others found him speaking on their behalf.[78] Because this strata of Russian society was being asked to play a piv-

---

[75] N. A. Dobroliubov, "Temnoe tsarstvo," *Sovremennik,* part 1, no. 8 (1859): 17–78 and part 2, no. 9: 53–128.

[76] Ibid., part 2, 123–27.

[77] I. F. Petrovskaia, *Teatr i zritel' provintsial'noi Rossii* (Leningrad: Iskusstvo, 1995), 45.

[78] Kate Rahman argues for a broader view of the playwright than Dobroliubov's commentary allows in "Alexander Ostrovsky, Dramatist and Director," in *History of Russian Theatre,* ed. Leach and Borozovsky, 166–81.

otal role in the economic transformation, many of them could not help but meet their obligation with ambivalence.

Ostrovskii tapped into their cultural anxieties and prejudices. The name of one of his first merchant characters, Tit Titych Bruskov in *Hungover from Someone Else's Party* (1856), became a synonym in literary circles for the *samodur*, or petty tyrant. One has to wonder, though, how many who used this term pejoratively stayed to the end of the play: the *samodur* reveals the generosity of spirit behind his exterior by pushing his son to marry the girl he loves, despite the fact that her father is a poor school teacher. In his best dramatic form Ostrovskii reconciled social differences by showing how each had something to teach the other.

Moreover, Ostrovskii showed no inclination to privilege intellectuals over merchants or any others. For example Boris, the student in *The Storm*, could have saved the sensitive Katerina from her mother-in-law, but he ultimately proved too weak-willed. Another student, Meluzov in *Talented People and Their Admirers* (1881), keep his beloved from the man who could give her fame and fortune. These male intellectuals were not victimized by the same social circumstances that entrapped the women they loved; they were paralyzed by their impotence to take action. The students in his comedies suffered the same inadequacies, but they invited smiles rather than scorn. The description that gymnasium dropout Bulanov gave of himself in *The Forest* (1870) farcically conformed to his audience's stereotypes of intellectuals: "As you know, I didn't finish my education, so I don't go around with my hair uncombed. I bathe every day and I believe in dreams."[79]

Recognizing that the official categories of *soslovie* (estate) and *sostoianie* (position) still constituted a central aspect of personal identity in these times of change, Ostrovskii offered insights into the paradoxes generated by various estates struggling to retain part of themselves based on the old order, while still welcoming challenges to it. Value systems were changing, and Ostrovskii dramatized the new attitudes toward both production and consumption sifting down through society. Against the background of constant tension between the innovative and the familiar, both production and consumption became imbued with social value because they were good for the country: economically, they stimulated the local markets and reduced reliance on imports; socially, they contributed to the mobility intended to accompany the emancipation; and culturally, they incorporated increasing numbers of Russians into national life. However, despite these positive attributes, production still bore the stigma of dirty hands, and because consumption's primary concern was to feed selfish desires, it necessarily crashed hard against the *intelligentsia*'s utopian social ideals.

[79] *Les'*, act III, scene i.

Ostrovskii used comedy effectively to question the implicit negative undertones. Whether one wants to call Ostrovskii's plays "bourgeois," "*bien faites*," or "tea-glass-and-saucer," they followed the basic formula and setting constructed by Sardou. For example, he wrote a trilogy of short plays featuring Mikhailo Balzaminov, a low-level bureaucrat in search of a wealthy wife: *A Holiday Dream before Dinner* (1857), *When Your Own Dogs Are Fighting, Don't Toss in Another One* (1861), and *You'll Find What You're Looking for Once You Go after It* (1863), prophetically subtitled *Balzaminov's Wedding*. With help from his mother and a professional matchmaker, the hapless clerk-hero chases a series of wealthy widows unsuccessfully until the matchmaker catches one with no better looks or sharper wits than he has.[80] Such is a happy ending: Ostrovskii's comedic characters end up with whom they deserve. Fiscal irresponsibility and self-indulgence were not to be rewarded, but nor were they an evil in the nineteenth-century Russia where such profligate behavior was still both familiar and socially forgivable.

Those of Ostrovskii's clerks who are poor but honest end up with their true loves, as do Zhadov in *A Profitable Job* (1856) and Mitia in *Poverty Is No Crime* (1853). Those who pursue romance for financial profit alone, in contrast, are bound to be disappointed, as Appolon in *Wolves and Sheep* (1875) and Glumov in *Every Wise Man Is Also a Little Foolish* (1868). The title of *Truth Is Good but Happiness Is Better* (1876), offers the best summary of a stock Ostrovskii story: the scrupulously honest poor boy wins the hand of the rich girl through several convoluted duplicities by minor characters. Unaware of the others' deceptions, the hero believes that truth has won out, whereas another character reminds the audience in an aside that the hero's bliss is due to his ignorance; hence, truth is nice but happiness better.

Like Sardou's, Ostrovskii's plays were "well made": structured in four or five acts that led toward a predictable outcome, set primarily in the parlors of the lead characters, and dealing with issues most relevant to the emergent bourgeoisie. In *Easy Money*[81] (1870), one of his most popular works,[82] Ostrovskii used the vain and manipulative heroine, Lydia Cheboksarova, to personify the female in the new order as both a commodity and one who commodifies. One of her admirers argues that only a fool would marry her and keep her to himself, because "like frozen capital, her looks should yield interest. . . . The man who wants into the civil service could use her as bait for his superiors and a means to a quick promotion." He considered

---

[80] The directors of the imperial theater found the trilogy too common, but Ostrovskii threatened to stop writing it if they did not stage it. Hoover, *Alexander Ostrovsky*, 27.

[81] The Russian title of the play, *Beshennye den'gi*, would translate as "mad" in the sense of "rabid" money, but "mad money" has a different English connotation.

[82] In the 1893/94 season at the Malyi, the revival of *Beshennye den'gi* had sixty-seven performances. Zograf, *Malyi teatr*, 541.

Prov Sadovskii, center, in Ostrovskii's *A Profitable Job*

A production of Ostrovskii's *Last Victim* at the Malyi

his approach modern "because we live in a practical age."[83] Lydia herself did not confuse income and expenditure: "Who cares about economic laws? . . . The only laws for you and me, Mother, are the laws of the world of fashion. We have no time to think of laws; all we have time for is to go to a shop and to buy."[84] As her mother defended Lydia, "Why should she . . . know about things that everyone else does too? She's had a higher education."[85] Lydia at least came by her attitudes honestly: her bureaucrat father was living in Siberian exile because he "never distinguished between his money and the public's."[86] Her merchant suitor carries the day, bending her to his economic will and turning her from a spendthrift into a *Hausfrau*. After all, he had argued that it was easier to deceive a poet or a young woman with romantic fancies than "to get the better of a hard-headed businessman."[87] Still, Ostrovskii gave the last word to the amusing aristocratic ne'er-do-wells, who assure the merchant that "even if we haven't a single kopeck, we shall always have honor and credit. An old overcoat and an old hat can be worn with such dignity that people will make way for you. Virtue is respected even in rags!"[88]

Ostrovskii wrote numerous leading roles for women, which reflected in part the composition of his audience and the extensive role that women played in economic as well as social life. Most of his plays counterposed at least one strong woman to other, less confident ones. In *Wolves and Sheep*, for example, a comic battle of the sexes with each side putting forth both predators and prey, the euphonious Evlampia Kupavina gets the best of the more colorful Meropia Murzavetskaia with the help of a businessman, whom she decides to marry. "I used to dream of freedom, but I've come to the conclusion that for a woman to be happy she must be dependent on a man," says the feckless Kupavina. Her comical nemesis Murzavetskaia responds, "Don't slander women, my dear! There are all kinds. There are those who can manage not only their own affairs but those of the whole county."[89] Naive in business affairs, Kupavina evidenced a mature appreciation of the facts of life when she asked her middle-aged fiancé whether he had already "shot all his arrows."[90]

Berkutov, the fiancé who assured Kupavina that he was a frugal huntsman and guarding his reserves for her, was Ostrovskii's exemplary hero. A landowner with a firm business head, he moved fluidly between two worlds, that of the old and irresponsible aristocracy represented by Murzavetskaia,

---

[83] *Beshennye den'gi*, act I, scene iii.
[84] Ibid., act II, scene v.
[85] Ibid., act II, scene iv.
[86] Ibid., act III, scene xii.
[87] Ibid., act I, scene iii.
[88] Ibid., act V, scene viii.
[89] Ibid., act V, scene vi.
[90] *Volki i ovtsy*, act IV, scene v.

and the new business world that permits him to set Kupavina's affairs in order. When Kupavina, stunned that he would sell his own family's estate, asks if he has no remorse, he responds matter-of-factly, "Remorse, yes. Income, no."[91]

The confusion surrounding Russia's new legal system, reformed in 1864, also provides opportunities for Berkutov to reconcile the old and the new. The irrepressible Murzavetskaia used an elderly clerk retired from the old system as her solicitor, and although she loved taking people to court, as the clerk pointed out, "no one ever dreams of complying with her demands. We haven't won a single case."[92] Because he understood the cultural lay of the land, Berkutov did not prosecute Murzavetskaia. He needed only to insinuate that she could end up in the docket, which threatened her prestige. Ultimately, he gains her favor, too. Ostrovskii recognized that although the future might belong to those who had had "copper-money training,"[93] they would not accomplish their goals if they could not also operate according to the old ways.

If his comedies end formulaically with characters joining company with those whom they deserved, Ostrovskii's tragedies end far more soberingly in violent death. Larisa, the pathetic heroine of *The Girl without a Dowry* (1878), thanks her jealous fiancé for shooting her: she is grateful to be relieved of her desires for a life of pleasure and fame that could never be hers.[94] In *Everyone Knows Sin and Sorrow* (1863), a melodrama of mixed marriage between the wealthy merchantry and the impoverished nobility, the merchant husband murders his noble wife and then their baby when she confesses that she has never loved him and wants out. Katerina's decision to drown herself rather than return to her unhappy family situation at the end of *The Storm* is traditionally read by critics as a sign of the country writ large on the eve of the emancipation, when the old ways threaten to kill the new possibilities. Katerina's death, though, like Larisa's and the husband's murders, can just as easily be understood as lessons of decisive personal choice. Such an interpretation does not resolve the ambiguity of these endings, but like the silent movie melodrama *Children of the Age* discussed in the introduction, it enables the audience to decide moral questions for themselves.

In addition to his re-creations of contemporary situations and settings, through his innovative use of language Ostrovskii made another advancement in realism on the stage. His dialogues have been characterized as "ethnographic" because of his keen ear for the patois of geographical re-

---

[91] Ibid., act IV, scene v.
[92] Ibid., act I, scene iii.
[93] *Les'*, act I, scene i.
[94] He reputedly created this role for the prima donna of the Alexandrinka, Maria Savina. Hoover, *Alexander Ostrovsky*, 25.

gions and social groups.[95] His use of authentic slang generated problems for some actors both because it was difficult to enunciate, and because they felt threatened that these roles would relegate them politically to the Slavophile camp. Shchepkin, for example, raised early objections to the language because he had problems with the sing-song intonation of Volga speech patterns.[96] Ostrovskii needed performers who understood how styles must adjust; new actors Prov Sadovskii and Liubov Nikulina-Kositskaia found stardom demonstrating what could be accomplished through the use of the vernacular in character development.[97] Justifiably renowned for his faithful reconstructions of argot and customs, Ostrovskii extended his penchant for wordplay to the titles of his plays, the preponderance of which were from current slang that often seems incomprehensible in translation.

The ethnographic playwright also "made an extremely significant break with tradition (when he) named characters in such a way as to suggest that they were to be regarded as particular individuals in the contemporary social environment."[98] The protagonist in *Easy Money*, Savva Vasilkov, was immediately recognizable as a merchant because "Savva" was a common name with this estate. In *The Forest* (1871), a former serf turned butler carries the unfortunate but perfectly plausible name "Carp" and must suffer sundry fish jokes. Again, personality triumphs and the servant, inured by a lifetime of near-devastating subjugation, finds self-respect by identifying himself to others by the Latin word for the fish whose name he bears.

The Business of Writing Plays

Ostrovskii's artistic explorations of the mediating role of economics reflected a dominant concern in his own life: remuneration for performance.[99] Keenly aware of the opulent lifestyles that his French counterparts Sardou and Dumas (*fils*) enjoyed because of their royalties, Ostrovskii deeply resented the Russian system that netted him less than two thousand rubles in 1868–69, one of his most successful seasons.[100] Despite his pos-

---

[95] Ostrovskii himself preferred to listen to his plays backstage than to watch them. Varneke, *History of the Russian Theater*, 342.

[96] Senelick, *Serf Actor*, 188.

[97] As one critic compared the two, "Shchepkin portrays passions independently of the individual; Sadovskii plays the individual himself." Quoted in Varneke, *History of the Russian Theater*, 357.

[98] Thus does Ian Watt mark one of the steps in the development of literary realism in *The Rise of the Novel* (Berkeley: University of California Press, 1964), 19.

[99] Despondent over finances in 1866, Ostrovskii threatened to give up the theater altogether. Rahman, "Alexander Ostrovsky," 174.

[100] Hoover, *Alexander Ostrovsky*, 44. His *There's a Wise Man in Every Scoundrel* opened on both imperial stages that season.

itive impact on the coffers of the imperial stage, he was denied a pension until 1884.[101] Self-consciously commercial, Ostrovskii couched his demands that the writers receive appropriate financial recompense in terms that emphasized their property rights. He wanted playwrights to profit financially from their endeavors because he respected the role of the market as a negotiator among interested parties. This was a particularly precarious position for an artist to take in Russia's nineteenth century, because it questioned the origins and functions of creativity, pitting the value of art against that of entertainment. Moreover, it forced recognition of the significant differences between reading plays and performing them.

In 1865 Ostrovskii founded the Artistic Circle with other would-be playwrights, musicians, and actors, including Sadovskii. This group provided the core for the much more ambitious Association (*sobranie*) of Russian Playwrights in Moscow, organized in 1870 with the objective of defending their material interests. Officially chartered by the Senate in 1874, the renamed Society of Russian Playwrights (opera composers joined three years later) carried the weight of a legal body and functioned as tsarist Russia's rough equivalent to a union when the latter were prohibited. Appointed the society's first chairman, Ostrovskii held the position until his death in 1886. His training in law had schooled him well in how the courts could redefine the notion of literary property and the rights of the author. Throughout its history, which extended through 1927, the society kept a lawyer on retainer to handle everything from copyright to slander.[102]

Ostrovskii also appreciated the advantages of collective action and successfully built an institutional network throughout the provinces, defying the authority of the imperial theaters. When the official monopoly ended in 1882 he helped to produce legislation that recognized dramaturgy as a commercial enterprise. In that year he posed a rhetorical question to workers, asking how many of them would be satisfied to earn wages at scales paid in 1827, as he and other playwrights were.[103] Having experienced firsthand the tribulations of his characters, trying to negotiate between entrenched habits and fresh possibilities, he was the consummate transitional intellectual figure, the writer who worked to transform the expanding sphere of leisure.

The activist playwrights who joined the society lobbied to replace the 1827 legislation with laws that incorporated them into the financial structure of the theater. Skillfully, they based their appeals on their own inadequacies, arguing that the Russian theater was facing a crisis in talent and

---

[101] Ibid., 27.

[102] Ironically, only after the end of capitalism in 1917 did the lawyers prefer to work for a percentage of a case's profits rather than on salary. RGALI, f. 675, op. 3, d. 6, ll. 19, 50, 87.

[103] Gol'dman, *A. N. Ostrovskii*, 4. In the 1920s the society apparently capitalized on this ability to present its members as workers. RGALI, f. 675, op. 3, ed. khran. 6, ll. 51–57.

Members of the Society of Russian Playwrights, circa 1880

originality because writers could not afford to become playwrights. They pitched their battle to establish the property value of plays on several contradictory terrains. Alexander II had set up a commission in 1870 to integrate the theater into the legal system, but members wanted simply to incorporate the 1827 statute into the law code.[104] Ostrovskii and the society defeated this measure, and in the first legal test case, brought by the society against the operator of a fair booth in Petersburg for the unauthorized staging of a play, the circuit court sentenced the operator to two months in prison.[105]

Although this decision favored writers, it proved an exception to the general rule. Three years later, Potekhin brought provincial entrepreneur Pavel Medvedev up on criminal charges for producing his *Tinsel* without permission. The resultant suit illustrated unresolved issues concerning property ownership and commercialism. According to the 1827 regulations, plays to be performed, as opposed to being read, became the prop-

---

[104] Hoover, *Alexander Ostrovsky,* 36.
[105] Ibid., 52–53.

erty of the imperial theaters. The enterprising Medvedev cleverly interpreted the law to mean that officially approved plays were public property. The Russian legal system itself was contradictory on this point because article 1684 of the Criminal Code forbade "public production of any dramatic work without the author's permission." However, when Potekhin took Medvedev to court on the basis of this law, he lost because the law did not distinguish sufficiently clearly between the imperial and provincial stages. More important, it did not define which was the author's personal property: the physical manuscript of the play or an interpretive performance of it.[106]

Potekhin's defeat clarified the issues and thus helped the society to articulate its grievances and to take meaningful action. The issue of performance, as Ostrovskii had long insisted, was paramount: that was the point at which the written words achieved the author's intention, and it was also where the real money lay. Given the logistical difficulties of keeping the provincial entrepreneurs in check, it was necessary to strike some sort of accord with them. The first head of the legal division, O. N. Plevako, demonstrated some of Medvedev's cunning: he took cases to the Moscow justices of the peace, prompting entrepreneurs to settle out of court in order to save the time and expense of the trip.[107] Nevertheless, playwrights appreciated that entrepreneurs served as the vital cultural connecting link between the two capitals and the hinterland. Lacking the government subsidies available to the imperial stage, they ran fully commercialized operations and it was imperative to work with, not against them.

The society authorized a network of agents throughout the provinces to negotiate with the local entrepreneurs. The entire bureaucracy worked on a percentage basis, beginning with the playwrights, who contributed 30 percent of their take on original plays to the general fund. Because one of the society's aims was to stimulate native writers, those who translated plays for the Russian stage contributed 45 percent. The local agents collected 10 percent of the deals they concluded with entrepreneurs, whose payments followed complex scales depending upon type of play and locale. Well-known Orel entrepreneur D. P. Lazukhin became the first to officially sign on with the society, and by 1876 seventy-two theaters had joined—which almost equaled the number of member-writers.[108] After its first decade of operation, the society had 330 members, from playwrights with hopes of being commercially produced to others with business interests in the theater, including publishers, agents, and entrepreneurs. Working cap-

---

[106] Ibid., 17.
[107] RGALI, f. 2097, op. 1, ed. khran. 76, l. 23.
[108] Ibid., 64.

ital had risen from 25,000 to 67,000 rubles.[109] The original Artistic Circle, from which the society had sprung and was devoted to culture rather than business, closed its doors at this time for lack of funds. The transition to commerce was complete.

Because it found itself caught between official and commercial imperatives, the imperial theater played a contradictory role in these developments. Although it insisted on first rights to every play, and proprietorship over it for two years thereafter, this insistence hardly reflected contemporary reality, given that the first theater to negotiate with the society was the private one run by Moscow's Union of Nobles.[110] Moreover, many actors and actresses under contract to the imperial stage earned money under the table performing in "amateur" productions at clubs around town, a problem that persisted long after the monopoly ended. The society settled by offering the imperial theaters the right of first refusal of a play, which freed unselected plays to be produced elsewhere.[111] The stars of the imperial stage publicly supported Ostrovskii's aims because they depended upon him to stress the reality that people prefer to watch a great performance rather than to simply read a good play.[112] As future theater icon Konstantin Stanislavsky observed, "spectators come to the theater to hear the subtext (because) they can read the text at home."[113]

Whether fans wanted to read plays or perform them, the society faced an elemental problem associated with publishing: how to print and distribute multiple copies of plays needed for performance at numerous locations simultaneously. Once again, members turned to the market for the most effective personnel and mechanism. Their first contract, concluded in 1875 with A. F. Mozer, the librarian for the Alexandrinka, and I. I. Smirnov, publisher of *Teatral'naia gazeta* (The theatrical gazette) was based on commissions: the publishers would lithograph one hundred copies of each play, assuming publication costs themselves, and would receive 50 percent of all sales. Prices depended on length. However, after the first year only two of the forty-three plays published had sold even half of their print runs. Most sold only a few copies, and costs surpassed sales by three hundred rubles.[114] Production and sales improved in 1877, but the publishers still operated in the red.[115]

Enter another entrepreneur. In 1879 S. F. Razsokhin, the librarian at Moscow's imperial theaters, developed a marketing strategy that positioned the theater as fundamentally a business enterprise. A self-promoter

[109] Gol'dman, *A. N. Ostrovskii*, 103.

[110] RGALI, f. 2097, op. 1, ed. khran. 76, l. 1.

[111] RGALI, f. 2097, op. 1, ed. khran. 76, l. 4.

[112] Ibid., 79.

[113] Sonia Moore, *The Stanislavskii System* (New York: Penguin, 1988), 28.

[114] RGALI, f. 2097, op. 1, ed. khran. l. 80; and ed. khran. 81, l. 5–14.

[115] Ibid., l. 68.

and minor playwright, Razsokhin kept his library open eleven hours a day, seven on holidays, promising readers that they could find a copy of every Russian play ever published, plus most of the European classics. He negotiated the same commission as the others, but he increased his business opportunities by renting sets and selling makeup. After all, his primary business was to sell lithographs of recent plays, so he helped himself when he helped his customers to mount performances. Razsokhin advertised to writers and entrepreneurs alike, promising to use his knowledge and connections to guide plays through the potentially messy censorship process. In addition to plays he peddled jokes, couplets—practically anything meant for performance. When the theater industry began to boom in the 1880s, he had a network of contacts with agents in place. After his death around 1900, his wife and co-publisher Elizabeth continued the business until 1917.

Making a business of art must be regarded as one of Ostrovskii's major contributions to the self-confidence of the middle class and the dissemination of its system of values. The 1882 regulations greatly improved the financial remuneration for playwrights, but payments still depended on the length of play. Ostrovskii had hoped to go even farther and have compensation become contingent on the size of the audience. This was a revolutionary idea in his particular cultural context because it opened the door for writers to consciously commercialize the contents of their works, to play to the crowds rather than try to enlighten or uplift them. Even a Soviet historian who marshaled the appropriate direct quotes to show how Ostrovskii was committed to "edifying the public" by depicting the good and evil in human behavior admitted that his letters were preoccupied with financial issues rather than moral philosophy.[116]

Ostrovskii overshadowed all other Russian playwrights of his generation in both his talent and productivity to such an extent that it would be difficult to call them his competitors. After his death in 1886, revivals of his plays dominated the imperial stage every season. Through the content of his plays and the context of his actions, he demonstrated some of the potential benefits of commerce to Russians on several levels. By offering multiple identities to the burgeoning middle classes, he contributed to the growth of civil society. Some social groups, especially the merchantry, who had previously felt excluded from the public sphere began to develop a strong sense of civic consciousness that was reflected in their attitude toward the arts as well as in business and politics. Several community leaders, together with Ostrovskii, toyed with the idea of building a Russian national theater independent of the state, until the end to the monopoly

---

[116] P. A. Markov, *Iz istorii russkogo i sovetskogo teatra* (Moscow: Iskusstvo, 1974), 132–54, on "Ostrovskii's moralism."

made such private-oriented endeavors less pressing.[117] The establishment of independently operated commercial theaters, the subject of the next chapter, proved a boon to the middle classes in the search for a sense of place in the industrializing empire.

[117] The most influential merchant who involved himself directly in the Russian theater was A. A. Bakhrushin, whose estate is now the primary theatrical museum in Moscow. His son, Iurii, left memoirs that depict his family's sense of public duty. Iu. A. Bakhrushin, *Vospominaniia* (Moscow: Khudozhestvennaia literatura, 1994). On Ostrovskii's plans for this theater, see Vsevolodskii-Gerngross, *Khrestomatiia,* 404–9.

CHAPTER TWO

Commercializing the Legitimate Stage

As rapid industrialization pushed Russia's middle classes into social, economic, and political prominence, the need to establish and enforce values that reflected their concerns and contributions became all the more pressing.[1] When the imperial monopoly ended in 1882 and they were allowed to build their own theaters, this social group responded enthusiastically by demonstrating that commerce and culture were not on a collision course but could complement each other. New playwrights emerged to engage audiences in contemporary issues, and the dominant theme on stage was the reconciliation of capitalism with Russian traditions. The imperial stage never lost its pride of place, but it had to adapt in response to competition.

Characterizations of social types had to adjust to the fact that heredity was losing its capacity to define role-playing. The expanding commercial element included former lords and peasants as well as merchants, and avaricious businessmen began to appear on stage as unsavory protagonists, lightning rods of social angst. These characters did not personify evil in and of itself, but rather they functioned as foils to raise questions about the sorts of issues their positions represented to the larger society, reminiscent of how Gogol and Griboedov had made light of improvident nobles and the pervasive bureaucracy that structured life without giving it a moral core. When the Great Reforms shifted the state into a more aggressive mode, the locations of power and influence moved as well. Themes and roles were updated according to the circumstances of industrialization. The peasants,

---

[1] Nikolai Leikin, a journalist who chronicled the exploits of merchants, noted their dominance among theater audiences in 1888. RGALI, f. 853, op. 2, ed. khran. 45, l. 92.

who had largely provided backdrop for motivations for other characters on stage, were now becoming a proletariat that served the same dramatic purpose. The intellectual remained a stock character, someone of radical political ideas about "the people" and no visible means of support.

The *intelligentsia* and, later, Soviet historians criticized this theater for offering escapism. The popularity of light comedy ignited the accusation that the stage provided the middle classes with "laughs, glitter, and maudlin sentimentality," but that it had "lost the more lofty functions it had served in some earlier epics."[2] This dismissal, however, insulted the complex system of values meaningful to a great many people. For every *It's a Family Affair, We'll Settle It Ourselves* a *Storm* brewed on the horizon. On the twenty-fifth anniversary of Ostrovskii's death in 1911, *Obozrenie teatrov* (Review of theaters) eulogized the playwright by consigning his most famous creation, the *samodur,* to the grave.[3] Many Russians had changed in part because of him.

Because the theater was undergoing the same transitional anxieties as its audience, it needed a new genre as a mode of mediation. Thus appeared the social melodrama, a term used here to describe the application of melodramatic properties to domestic situations that were also identifiable as public concerns.[4] The domestic setting of the "well-made play" provided an especially appropriate background for this genre, because it put on display the tensions mounting in the generation gap that divided attitudes toward reform. Melodrama's patented preference for highlighting the effects of a dramatic situation over its causes resulted in the privileging of emotionalism over rationalism, which made it especially popular with female audiences. The theater was an important site on many levels for registering the growing presence of females in public places, exemplified by women who became managers of theatrical companies: E. N. Goreva, M. M. Abramova, and the best-known, V. A. Linskaia-Nemetti.[5]

The artistic elite reacted against the mundaneness they saw on the bourgeois stage, as in the other arts, and launched what later became known as the Silver Age. Resplendent in its modernism, the Silver Age was characterized by symbolism and decadence, because many of the younger generation hesitated to accept their commission from their *intelligentsia* ancestors and commit themselves to social welfare. In theater, the new wave led to novel stagings as well as inventive scripts. The Russian residence for this new kind of theater was the Moscow Art Theater (MAT), established in 1898 by Konstantin Stanislavsky and Vladimir Nemirovich-Danchenko. Al-

---

[2] John Brown, *Oxford History of the Theater* (Oxford: Oxford University Press, 1995), 341.

[3] *Obozrenie teatrov,* no. 1416 (1911): 5–6.

[4] I. F. Petrovskaia discusses the preeminence of melodramas in *Teatr i zritel' rossiiskikh stolits, 1895–1917* (Leningrad: Iskusstvo, 1990), 63–67.

[5] As Boris Mironov has pointed out, by 1897, 18 percent of women in the countryside and 29 percent in the urban areas were economically independent of men, numbers that continued to rise. *The Social History of Imperial Russia, 1700–1917,* vol. 1 (Boulder: Westview, 2000), 455.

though the latter had begun his theatrical career as a fairly traditional playwright, once he saw Anton Chekhov's originality he moved into production.
The MAT differed from other theaters both structurally and conceptually.
Directors rather than playwrights or performers controlled productions,
and the star system gave way to ensemble casts.[6] Naturalism dominated. At
Stanislavsky's insistence, his stage re-created life in accurate detail, physical
as well as psychological, exemplified by the crickets chirping on stage. Naturalism differed from realism in that it privileged form over the politics of
humanity implicit in realism, and traditional actors balked at assignments
that threatened to deny them emotionalism. The playwright most closely
identified with the MAT, Chekhov, found kindred spirits in these directors
after his *Seagull* bombed at the Alexandrinka in 1896. Chekhov, however,
who had begun his career at the private, commercialized Korsh Theater,
was not prepared initially to sever relations with the imperial stage. But the
MAT's innovative stagings of his plays infused them with an implicit political essence that marked his persona. A private enterprise, Stanislavsky's
"commercial amnesia" kept the MAT dependent on benefactors rather
than revenues. History has immortalized the MAT in the same proportion
that it has ignored the bourgeois stage, but the story being told here looks
at the MAT only as it affected other theatrical developments.[7]

The legitimate stage heightened its role of public forum after political
pressures erupted in revolution in 1905. All social groups and cultural
cliques competed to divvy up the political and economic spoils surrendered by the faltering autocracy. One byproduct of the revolution was a
growing pluralism, which resulted in possibilities for interaction between
such unlikely pairs as the MAT and the Alexandrinka. The view from the
stage favored the middle classes in attendance, growing not only in number but in variety of background and ambition as well.

Performers in the New Theater

Karatygin and Mochalov, Shchepkin and Sadovskii—personalities had
long reigned on stage, mediators between the actions and the ideas they dramatized. Once again, the great character roles, from Hamlet to Famusov,
would have to be reinterpreted to respond to the changes in cultural contexts. New Princes of Denmark took to the boards.[8] Prince A. I. Sumbatov-

---

[6] Both founders left memoirs: Konstantin Stanislavsky, *My Life in Art,* trans. J. J. Robbins
(Boston: Little, Brown, 1924), and V. I. Nemirovich-Danchenko, *My Life in the Russian Theatre,* trans. John Cournos (New York: Theatre Arts, 1968).

[7] Jean Benedetti, "Stanislavsky and the Moscow Art Theatre, 1989–1938," in *A History of
Russian Theater,* ed. Robert Leach and Victor Borovsky (Cambridge: Cambridge University
Press, 1999), 254–76.

[8] On this new wave of "Hamletism," see G. A. Time, *U istokov novoi dramaturgii v Rossii
(1880–1890-e gody)* (Leningrad: Nauka, 1990), 27.

Prince A. I. Sumbatov-Iuzhin, the masculine Hamlet

A. P. Lenskii

Iuzhin, with his handsome face and aggressively masculine presence, introduced a Hamlet resolved on revenge rather than one beset by doubts. Also
a playwright of some repute and from Georgia, Sumbatov-Iuzhin was a vig-
orous character well suited to embody an economically and militarily ex-
pansionist Russia in the 1890s, substituting muscular passion for interior

49

pondering.[9] In contrast, A. P. Lenskii presented an introspective and sensitive Hamlet, one more in tune with the intellectual temper of self-doubt raised by Russia's poorly regulated growth and the continued failure of liberals to persuade the autocracy to share government with them. He strove for psychological verisimilitude in his characters, reflecting the growing influence of psychiatry on society.[10] Both began as matinee idols at the Malyi in the 1880s and rose to direct the theater later in their careers.

Their romantic counterpart at the Alexandrinka, Iu. M. Iur'ev, combined psychology with good looks. The Alexandrinka also showcased the greatest comedian of the era, Konstantin Varlamov. Affectionately known as "Uncle Kostia," Varlamov used his considerable girth in slapstick fashion, delighting and enjoying tremendous intimacy with crowds. Like his comic counterpart at the Malyi, V. N. Davydov, he could be found moonlighting in comedies at popular supper clubs. Varlamov, Davydov, and Iur'ev, watching the future relocate from the stage to the silver screen after 1908, began to develop film careers. Aided by a popular press that circulated news about and photographs of them, they raised the stage actor to new heights of national celebrity.

Scenes calling for generous displays of emotion in social melodramas resulted in the scripting of numerous starring roles for women. As a result, actresses dominated the turn-of-the-century stage, a status apparent in the salary scale that reversed convention and gave some of the most popular women nearly double the wages of their male co-stars.[11] Petersburg's Maria Gavrilovna Savina and Moscow's Maria Nikolaevna Ermolova rekindled the capital cities' competition between Karatygin and Mochalov. The Russian public read politics into their performances: in Savina they saw the shrewd reformer, superb at drawing-room comedies and in the kinds of melodramatic roles that showed women victims of an exploitative system. Ermolova, like Mochalov, was something of an insurrectionist who excelled in portrayals of strong women victimized by circumstances, such as Johann von Schiller's *Mary Stuart* or *The Maid of Orleans*. Both actresses also had parts written especially for their personae. A renegade from the imperial theater, Vera Komissarzhevskaia, began to challenge their emotional styles with innovative interpretations pioneered at the MAT, but time was not on her side.[12] Even had she not died prematurely of smallpox in 1910,

---

[9] N. G. Zograf, *Malyi teatr vtoroi poloviny XIX veka* (Moscow: Akademiia nauk, 1960), especially 532–33.

[10] Ibid., especially 503. I. F. Petrovskaia, *Teatr i zritel' provintsial'noi Rossii* (Leningrad: Iskusstvo, 1995), 186–87, discusses the impact of psychiatry.

[11] Salary information is from the archival fond for the imperial theater: RGIA, f. 468, op. 13, d. 686, ll. 5–9 and op. 44, d. 158, ll. 99, 104. In the 1890s, for example, at the Malyi Lenskii received 7,200 rubles, and Ermolova and Fedotova 12,000. In 1911 Savina was earning 18,000, but Varlamov only 8,200 and Davydov 12,000. The men complained that they had to learn more parts than the women did.

[12] One of the circle of students who revered her remembered that she was both intimi-

Варламовъ (Снѣгурочка)

"Uncle Kostia" Varlamov as Grandfather Frost in Ostrovskii's *Snow Princess*

Maria Ermolova, darling of the radical youth

Давыдовъ (Горѣловъ)

V. N. Davydov, comic headliner at the Malyi and the Korsh

she would have had to face, with Savina and Ermolova, rivalry from the new media star: the movie actress, who enjoyed the incomparable advantage of youthful beauty up close.

The National Audience

As theater historian Ira Petrovskaia pointed out, in 1897 "Russia was the provinces."[13] The census taken in that year showed that fewer than two and one-half million Russians lived in the two capitals, as opposed to almost seven times that many in provincial cities. A nationally circulated theater press reached provincial fans, and the stars themselves toured the provinces during the summer hiatus at the imperial theaters. If a glimpse of Savina was a rare occurrence, she was nonetheless a known commodity. Moreover, provincial Russia had its own star system.[14]

The theatrical press kept audiences au courant on premiers and favorite celebrities. *Zritel'* (The spectator), associated the street with the stage by addressing its reader as "a viewer of politics and the theater." Launched in the 1880s by a consortium of popular journalists, playwrights, and actors, the staff included Nikolai Chekhov and Vasilii Nemirovich-Danchenko, the brothers of the two future founders of the Moscow Art Theater. A nationally circulated publication, *Zritel'* united the empire with anecdotes about touring performers, reprints of skits that could be performed anywhere, and illustrations suitable for framing.

This press sold itself by actively encouraging amateur performances. *Domashnyi teatr* (The home theater) began in 1895 as a supplement to the popular family magazine *Rodina* (The motherland); as its title suggested, this monthly offered a variety of plays, from vaudevilles to serious dramas, that could be performed at home. *Teatral'naia biblioteka* (The theatrical library) also published plays in serial form, especially suitable for provincial amateur productions. Others followed, including the popular *Rampa i zhizn'* (The footlights and life), which peeked in the most keyholes, and ultimately *Obozrenie teatrov,* a weekly booklet that mixed fillips of gossip with information about local repertoires, giving the essential consumer information such as show times, theater addresses, and plot synopses. Performers took to advertising themselves in journals that enjoyed national circulations.

With its broadening reach and popularity, the theater generated new op-

---

dated by and envious of the long reigns of Ermolova and Savina. Aleksandr Serebrov (A. N. Tikhonov), *Vremia i liudi* (Moscow: Khudozhestvennaia literatura, 1955), 88.

[13] Petrovskaia, *Teatr i zritel' provintsial'noi Rossii,* 5.

[14] When Fanny Kozlovskaia died young in an unidentified provincial city, three thousand mourners came to her funeral. Ibid., 201.

portunities for social interaction. Etiquette manuals began devoting increasing space to comportment in theaters, until by century's end the advice on behavior in the theater repeated what had been written earlier on behavior in church. With the well-made play, dialogue rather than impassioned speeches igniting the congregation advanced plot development. The result was a change in the elements of theatricality, not a loss of the latter. More than ever, the theater had become a place to see and be seen. Etiquette demanded that "young women should refrain from looking around the hall as much as possible through their lorgnettes; their role is to stimulate delight and admiration. In fact, the majority of women envy them this role, and that is why they are watching others through their lorgnettes! Men and women alike should refrain from looking around at the audience during the performance; this is considered showing off because it attracts attention to the self."[15]

Under penalty of potential social rejection, though, one was not to be *heard* in the theater. Quiet was stressed above all. Even "when you see your friends in the theater, it is impolite to gesture to them, and even worse to call out to them; you should only nod slightly, without getting up."[16] By 1910, the theater had opened its doors even further, as found in the counsel that "one may wear what one would at home or at work to the theater, as long as it is neat and proper. Only those who are sitting in the boxes and the first rows must dress up." Further admonitions against excessive perfume, or beer or tobacco on the breath, suggested that those who had previously frequented the pleasure gardens were now also attending the theater.[17] Before the reader assumes that these admonitions were directed solely at the lower classes, it should be noted that Nicholas II's stagestruck sister Olga was known to scandalize audiences by forgetting to wear gloves, and her mother at times smoked in the royal loge.[18]

The Commercial Stage: Moscow's Korsh and Petersburg's Suvorin

Ostrovskii's observation that "the bourgeoisie everywhere has had a beneficial influence on art"[19] applied emphatically to the endeavors of F. A. Korsh and A. S. Suvorin, founders of the most important independent theaters in postreform Russia. Businessmen first, but with aspirations to cultural clout, they can be classified as members of a "bourgeois *intelligentsia*,"

---

[15] *Zhizn' v svete, doma i pri dvore* (St. Petersburg: n.p. 1890; repr. Interbuk, 1990), 103–4.
[16] Ibid.
[17] A. Komilfil'do, *Khoroshii ton. Sbornik pravil, nastavlenii i sovetov, kak sleduet vesti sebia v raznykh sluchiiakh domashnoi i obshchestvennoi zhizni, s risunkama* (Moscow: Konovalov, 1911).
[18] V. A. Teliakovskii, *Vospominaniia, 1898–1917* (Petrograd: Vremia, 1924), 76, 99–106.
[19] Quoted in T. N. Pavlova, "Teatr F. A. Korsha" (dissertation abstract, Institute of Art History, 1973), 17.

a crossover category in an era infused with the ideals of both. The professional biographies of these entrepreneurs demonstrate how commercial success could complement cultural innovation.

The son of a military doctor, Korsh had trained for a career in law but returned immediately to his first love, the stage, when the government ended the monopoly in 1882.[20] Korsh chartered his theater with four professed objectives: to provide Moscow with a theater that would respond to its maturing aesthetic demands; to give provincial actors an opportunity to perform under more favorable conditions than they could locally; to improve contemporary drama by presenting productions of new plays, which he accomplished by offering special Friday night performances of experimental works; and to make the greatest works of Russian and international dramaturgy available to the younger generation at reduced prices, which included free Sunday morning performances open to students. Later the Malyi adopted this policy.[21]

Realizing each goal, Korsh quietly revolutionized the Russian stage. For example, although Ostrovskii was by far the most performed playwright at both the Malyi and the Korsh, the two theater directors interpreted his works differently, and some critics preferred the Korsh's productions.[22] The authors whose works premiered in Russia at the Korsh, usually on Friday nights, included some of Europe's most inventive playwrights: Hermann Sudermann, Edmond Rostand, Henrik Ibsen, August Strindberg, George Bernard Shaw—not to mention such local talent as Petersburg journalist Anton Chekhov.[23]

Known for giving actors an uncharacteristically free hand, Korsh attracted an impressive list of performers early in their careers.[24] Most, however, left him when the imperial stage called, including Lenskii. In his single instance of reverse enticement, Korsh recruited popular character actor Davydov, briefly, from the Alexandrinka. Operetta and light comedy stars Lidiia Iavorskaia and Mariia Bliumental'-Tamarina added a dash of glamour in the 1890s.

His faithfulness to his four principles, even in times of economic adversity, indicates that Korsh believed in the theater as a cultural force as well as a business enterprise. The theater nearly went bankrupt in his second season because Korsh invested far more in sets and costumes than could

[20] The primary archival fond for the Korsh Theater is maintained in the manuscript division of the Bakhrushin Museum in Moscow, f. 123. Much of the historical background is derived from this fond.

[21] *Kratkii ocherk desiatiletnei deiatel'nosti russkogo dramaticheskogo teatra Korsha v Moskve* (Moscow: I. N. Kushnerev, 1892), 48.

[22] E. Beskin, "Teatr b. Korsha," *Sovremennoe iskusstvo*, no. 23 (August 27, 1932): n.p.

[23] On Chekhov's *Ivanov*, which owed much of its successful revisions to the initial staging at the Korsh, see Pavlova, "Teatr F. A. Korsha," 13–14 and *Kratkii ocherk*, 29.

[24] "Rol' aktera v teatre Korsha," Bakhrushin Museum, f. 123, d. 295.256, l. 4.

be recovered in ticket sales for *Tsar Vasilii Shuiskii,* a period piece from one of the most potentially stage-worthy episodes in Russian history, the appropriately named seventeenth-century Time of Troubles. Written by the curator of the Kremlin Armory, the play surrendered a good story for the sake of historical accuracy in staging detail, and the audience stayed away en masse.[25] Korsh recovered through extensive reorganization and with help from the Bakhrushin family, Moscow merchants with a lasting commitment to the theater. He opened the 1885 season in his new, enlarged theater, the first to use electric lighting, and designed by M. N. Chichagov, a pioneer in the nationalist revivalist movement in architecture. Moreover, Korsh restructured the acting company as a profit-sharing business, appointing himself managing director.[26] His daughter worked beside him as a manager who also translated plays. Celebrating the theater's twenty-fifth anniversary in 1907, the numbers of tickets sold indicated that potentially every Muscovite had attended the Korsh four times.[27]

The Korsh Theater exemplified what the *intelligentsia* feared as the "dictatorship of the box office."[28] In 1892 Korsh himself translated Sardou's wildly popular comedy about Napoleon's ex-washerwoman, *Madame Sans-Gêne,* and dispatched its star, Iavorskaia, to Paris to make certain that the Russian production would not be remiss in any of the fashionable details.[29] In contrast, Lev Tolstoy premiered his *Power of Darkness* at this theater because he admired Korsh's basic democratic impulses.[30] As a sympathetic contemporary reviewer pointed out, Korsh's gravest sin lay in trying to offer something to everyone.[31] Perhaps the most appropriate historical evaluation of Korsh's theater is that his original building became home to the MAT, after being redesigned by F. O. Shekhtel', whose art nouveau architectural style matched the changes within.

Several private theaters opened in Petersburg, but not until Suvorin founded his in 1895 did an independent stage affect the Alexandrinka. Best known as the publisher of the influential daily newspaper *Novoe vremia* (The new times), Suvorin was one of the most compelling members of the new commercial aristocracy. He appears in history texts as a bulwark of reaction during an era when nonviolent revolution was still considered a possibility, and he has always posed a special problem for historians because his politics have overshadowed initiatives that would have been deemed

---

[25] *Kratkii ocherk,* 10.
[26] *Kratkii ocherk,* 15–16. The contract creating the new company is in the Korsh archive, delo 174370.
[27] Time, *U istokov,* 16.
[28] Beskin, "Teatra b. Korsha," n.p.
[29] Bakhrushin Museum, f. 123, d. 295.256, l. 5.
[30] Ibid., d. 295.257, l. 6.
[31] V. P., "Teatr Korsha," *Artist: Zhurnal iziashchykh iskusstv i literatury,* no. 43 (1894): 183–85.

progressive by critics sympathetic to bourgeois initiatives. At one point he and Chekhov were close, but their relationship foundered on Suvorin's unrelenting antisemitism. A noble himself, but highly critical of unearned, estate-based privileges, Suvorin made an articulate spokesperson for those who embraced the economic potential of industrialization and hoped that financial changes would have positive social and political repercussions. He never lost his desire to have a say in shaping Russia's future.[32]

The empire he had built from publishing allowed Suvorin to indulge his passion for the stage. His theatrical activities included writing plays himself, and as an impresario he displayed both extremes of his personality, from the progressive committed to enlarging a civic sphere to the conservative who fought to keep that sphere from becoming fully democratized. Thus the same producer who staged Lev Tolstoy's *Fruits of Enlightenment* could also prompt riots with Viktor Krylov's racist *Sons of Israel*.[33]

The theater grew out of the official Literary-Artistic Circle to which he belonged, together with such secondary writers as P. P. Gnedich and E. P. Karpov. Although their theater was officially named for the circle, it was commonly referred to as either the "Suvorin" because as the major stockholder he had the greatest influence, or the "Petersburg Malyi," because it was smaller than the Alexandrinka. Like the Korsh, the Suvorin differed from its competitors more in staging than in essential repertoire. A number of popular actors and actresses played on both stages, including Iavorskaia and Dalmatov.

A primary reason for Suvorin to support a theater was to showcase his authorial vanity. But even the imperial theater staged his work, so his plays represented more than pure egoism on his part.[34] The title character of Suvorin's most popular melodrama, *Tat'iana Repina* (1889), enacted the cornerstone of his self-styled liberalism, his championship of women's rights.[35] The tragedy of an actress who administers herself a slow-acting poison because she has been seduced and abandoned, *Tat'iana Repina* protested the reality that men enjoyed inordinately more license than women in contemporary society. In an impassioned speech the title character argues for another of Suvorin's favorite social philosophies, the su-

---

[32] Biographical information on Suvorin is from Effie Ambler, *Russian Journalism and Politics* (Detroit: Wayne State University Press, 1972), 37–59; and E. A. Dinershtein, "Izdatel'skaia deiatel'nost' A. S. Suvorina," *Kniga issledovaniia i materialy* 48 (Moscow: Kniga, 1984), 82–118. Suvorin left a diary, *Dnevnik A. S. Suvorina*, translated, annotated, and with a foreword by M. Krichevskii (Moscow: L. D. Frenkel', 1923).

[33] *Dnevnik A. S. Suvorina*, ed. M. Krechinskii (Moscow: L. D. Frenkel', 1923). See also Catherine Schuler, *Women in the Russian Theatre: The Actress in the Silver Age* (New York: Routledge, 1996), 145–46.

[34] Chekhov remarked caustically, but not incorrectly, of his former patron's dramatic characters that "they do not speak, but rather philosophize and editorialize." Quoted in Zograf, *Malyi teatr*, 443.

[35] A. S. Suvorin, *Tat'iana Repina* (St. Petersburg: Suvorin, 1889).

periority of talent over hereditary nobility. But the popularity of this play had more to do with its stage worthiness than its politics: Repina takes the poison before she goes on stage so that she will be able to bring her life and her performance to a sad, simultaneous end. In a scene that allowed actresses in this role to elicit cheers and tears in the same breath, she expires in her dressing room, listening to the applause.[36] Savina and Ermolova both excelled in the part.

Suvorin's *Exit the Past,* first performed in 1905, recalled the complexities of the transition between modernity and tradition erupting at that very moment in revolution.[37] The hero, a count who has recently retired from state service, hopes to live peaceably in the provinces. He has always prided himself on running an honest bureaucracy, and now, bored and frustrated, he contemplates entering local politics. The painful truth he must face, though, is how little he actually accomplished for his country in government service. In the long climactic speech, his future son-in-law explains how bureaucrats look but see nothing. Reactionary in some matters, Suvorin was revolutionary in others.

Forgotten Playwrights, Neglected Themes

Struggling to make a financial go of his enterprise, Korsh turned to writers who could populate the cheap seats for plays that would allow him to fill his theater during the week in order to subsidize the Friday experimental plays and the inexpensive Sunday performances. The champion playwright in his stable became I. I. Miasnitskii. Although his name is rarely recognized today, Miasnitskii was one of the principal writers in turn-of-the century Russia, a prodigious producer of commercial comedy. The adopted (and probably illegitimate) son of merchant publisher K. T. Soldatenkov, he churned out feuilletons for the local tabloids and wrote at least eighteen novels and short story collections, plus two volumes of plays. Miasnitskii supplied Korsh with farces, comedies of topical issues. On the rare occasion that the highbrow critics bothered with him, they could find only lamentable escapism from what they considered Russia's pressing problems.[38]

Miasnitskii is most closely associated with the merchantry, yet his plays are also peopled with bureaucrats, retired soldiers, sly servants, *intelligentsia* wannabes, and provincials fantasizing about city life. Miasnitskii

---

[36] Chekhov could not resist the excessive emotions and wrote a parody of Suvorin's play. Time, *U istokov,* 91.

[37] A. S. Suvorin, *Staroe ukhodit* (St. Petersburg: Suvorin, 1905).

[38] Review of Miasnitskii's novel *Gostinodvortsy* in the "thick" journal *Russkoe bogatstvo,* no. 10 (1896): 56–57.

pieced together a mosaic of subplots rather than "well-made plays." His stock characters included a young woman of marriageable age counterposed to a bossy wife or mother-in-law, a bevy of suitors with varying intentions, and a cluster of older men trying to make sense of the confusion. He used colloquial language to convey the social origins of his characters, whose aspirations for social mobility came across in words they could not pronounce. The matchmaker in *Krutozobov's Wedding*, for example, worried about catching "agronomy, a 'ristocratic illness" and liked to drink "sheempain" at the weddings she brokered.[39]

Miasnitskii compares favorably with his French contemporary Georges Feydeau, a specialist in the comic situations into which the socially pretentious could not resist entangling themselves.[40] Both understood how comedy could teach lessons in public comportment to an audience dizzy from social flux. In *Two Hundred Thousand* Miasnitskii used the instant wealth provided by a winning lottery ticket to burlesque the awkwardness of social climbing. The lucky merchant-hero plans to move his family to a section of town where the nobility lives, but he and his friends cannot handle champagne or dance the latest steps, and because he is not au courant with the local conventions, he inadvertently proposes to three women. The moral to this farce was "better to be first in the village than last in the city."

In one of his first plays for Korsh, *The Old Woman Makes a Fool of Herself* (1882), Miasnitskii presented a cast that could plausibly be sitting in his audience: a building contractor, a sales clerk, a coachman, a doctor, members of a clerical family that had left church service, and their sundry relatives and servants. The hero sorely regretted that his parents had christened him Finogen, in response to a fad they had misunderstood. His wife dreamed of going to Paris to "take the cure," despite the fact that Europe was "an incomprehensible nation." Gallicisms such as *bonzhur* peppered conversations, usually used inappropriately. One woman turned the French *mon amour* into the Russian *mramornyi* (marble). Not surprisingly, instead of Paris they decided to settle the district in Moscow where most of the merchantry lived; after all, they assured themselves, nationalist historian Nikolai Karamzin had found literary inspiration there.

Miasnitskii blended the popular variety shows with the legitimate stage. He wrote for spectators not interested in universalisms, allegories, or language that sounded unnatural to their ears. Cultural critics reproached Korsh for his concessions to the Miasnitskii crowd, but they failed to appreciate the possibility of overlap in audiences between the Friday night preview and the Saturday night farce.

---

[39] I. I. Miasnitskii, *Zhenit'ba Krutozobova* (Moscow: D. P. Efimov, 1898).

[40] The financial records of the Korsh Theater show Miasnitskii consistently earning the highest royalties. Bakhrushin Museum, f. 126, dela 163772–163803. See also Pavlova, "Teatr F. A. Korsha," 12.

Another popular writer who rarely merits more than a mention in theater history is Viktor Krylov, not only a prolific playwright but also the director of the Alexandrinka in the 1890s.[41] He earned a reputation as "the Russian Sardou" by transferring a number of the popular French writer's plays to the Russian stage, though his translations of Goethe earned him no comparable epithet. Krylov emphatically rejected any notion that he was stealing European originals, pointing out that he had to change much in every play he transposed to make it fit Russian circumstances. In a flight of imaginative vanity, he insisted that other Europeans borrowed equally from his originals.[42]

Beginning his career in the revolutionary 1860s, he made the unlikely career move from teaching geometry to writing plays. Employing the usual stereotypes of the era, in his first play, *Against the Current* (1865), he offered the standard tale of a despotic landowner abusive toward his serfs. This plot enjoyed lessening appeal in the postreform era, and Krylov made his mark with topical works either borrowed from Sardou, or at least mindful of the latter's situational comedies and dramas. Using the daily newspaper as inspiration, he took an article about a distinguished gentleman arrested for pestering girls on the street and turned it into *To the Justice of the Peace!* (1877). This comedy captured the astonishment of men of good standing now coming into contact with women other than prostitutes asserting themselves in public places. Arrested for annoying a woman whom he believed should be at home, one character observed that "they used to lock women up in terems [a special part of the house], but now you have to look at them differently . . . and you know, it's better now!"[43]

The quickness of his pen and the lightness of his touch put Krylov in constant conflict with his fellow dramatists. A member of the Society of Playwrights, the prodigious Krylov became Ostrovskii's bane by sneaking off to the provinces to negotiate independently with entrepreneurs. Because the society had to approve the plays it sponsored, and the most self-important members disdained Krylov, the latter bristled at a situation whereby his plays provided financial support for them. In addition, he cultivated theatrics in general with his ten volumes of short plays, peopled with few characters and modest sets, written specifically for small provincial and amateur troupes.[44] Many intellectuals referred disparagingly to

---

[41] Although Krylov used the name "Alexandrov," even in his day he was almost always identified as "Krylov," so I will use that surname as well. Biographical information comes from Krylov's foreword to his collected works, published in at least two editions, 1884 and 1892.

[42] Viktor Krylov, "Ot avtora," *Dramaticheskie sochineniia*, vol. 1 (St. Petersburg: G. Shreder, 1892), v–x. Sardou managed to escape the epithet of "the French Krylov."

[43] Viktor Krylov, *K mirovomu!* (n.p., n.d.), act III, scene xi.

[44] These appeared in the 1880s and 1890s, published by the Shreder firm and costing about a ruble for each volume, which contained four to six plays and skits.

the 1890s as the *krylovshchina,* or the "Krylov Era," in the same vein that Shaw scorned "Sardoodledom."[45]

Such plays as Krylov's *The Madcap* (1888) and *Summer Daydreams* (1892) have long disappeared from any repertoire, just as it is nearly impossible to find revivals of Sardou or Robertson. But to view these plays as historical documents is to glimpse scenes from a past in many respects similar to those produced by a daguerreotype, complete with the cultural distortions that come from constructing the pose for the camera. Things are less than they appear, but also more.

Modernity as Social Melodrama

Between 1882 and 1905, Russia's emerging middle classes struggled to accommodate to the myriad of changes brought about by rapid industrialization. These years are characteristically minimized in textbooks as "reactionary" because of the policies of Tsar Alexander III (1881–1894) that sought to "put a period" to the Great Reforms. Although the conventional narrative of this reaction includes a perceived stagnation in the arts, such an attitude treats Miasnitskii and Krylov too dismissively. A closer contextual reading of the theater during those years depicts a Russia trying to adjust to reform, not to revert to the old ways.

The first controversy of the postmonopoly theater evidenced the emergence of new attitudes toward social relations. It flared between fledgling playwright Sumbatov-Iuzhin and Potekhin, who had become director of the imperial stage. Sumbatov-Iuzhin's *Sergei Satilov* (1883) brought to the stage the political discord brewing between the old left and the new.[46] An overblown rendering of life on the prereform estate, *Sergei Satilov* reversed the characters of Potekhin's *Tinsel* and dramatized a love affair between a good serf and the wife of his cruel master. The quarrel arose over the minor characters, when Potekhin objected to Sumbatov-Iuzhin's representation of other serfs supporting their master against their comrade. Potekhin's victim-serfs could never have common cause with their oppressors. The young playwright, though, had injected realism into the paternalism that had traditionally colored social relations, including that of tsar to subject. Tsar Alexander III seems to have preferred a paternalistic relationship, but theater audiences, shifting in their seats, were ready to become citizens.[47]

[45] Zograf, *Malyi teatr,* 143–52, 274–85. The appendices to Zograf's two-volume history of the Malyi, which list six decades of productions at the theater, trace Krylov's ascent from the 1880s, only to have him disappear from the repertoire after 1905.

[46] Ibid., 428–29.

[47] On Alexander III, see especially Richard Wortman, *Scenarios of Power: Myth and Ceremony in Russian Monarchy,* vol. 2 (Princeton: Princeton University Press, 2000), part 2.

Consumption offered one step to citizenship, but however welcome the additional money was in circulation, the culture of capitalism could not simply transform values without discussion. The individualism associated with competition and profit seemed somehow very un-Russian. For example, a contrast between Nemirovich-Danchenko's *Our Americans* and Robertson's *Our American Cousin* reveals stark contradictions in how different societies evaluated the Yankee ingenuity associated with industrialization. In the British version, the guileless Yankee outshines his foppish British peers. In the Russian, though, American pragmatism represents cynicism and duplicity. The Russian factory engineer who has fashioned himself according to American industrial ideals turns out to be a villain with falsified credentials, exploiting his workers.

The merchant estate had been vaulted by economic circumstances to positions of consequence, and with this came a not always welcome celebrity. Sumbatov-Iuzhin's most famous play, *The Gentleman* (1897), won him the first of his two Griboedov Prizes and the ire of several of Moscow's most prominent merchant families. This play is especially important because it was a thinly veiled dramatization of a slice of local life, hence an inventive form of theatrical realism. The pseudonyms the author used did a poor job of concealing the people behind his characterizations. The title character was recognizable as Mikhail Morozov, scion of one of the most politically and economically powerful of the industrialist clans. The factual Morozov represented the new generation of merchants, the well-educated and well-dressed opposites of their forebears. A self-conscious "gentleman," the real Mikhail had attempted a scholarly career under the pen name "M. Iur'ev," which fooled no one. The character of Rydlov in Sumbatov-Iuzhin's play was also a businessman with literary ambitions, but the similarities did not stop there.[48]

The Gentleman capitalized on gossip about the Morozovs, its stage worthiness deriving from what this family represented to and about Moscow at the turn of the century. The main story line was drawn directly from Mikhail Morozov's reality: his young and beautiful wife, from an impoverished merchant line who had therefore married above herself when she wed him in an arranged marriage, had left him around the time the play was written. Although the errant Mrs. Morozova had returned home before long, speculation about their separation was rife when the play opened.[49]

Sumbatov-Iuzhin cast his explanation for this marital contretemps around

[48] Mikhail's mother, Varvara Alekseevna, who had taken over the family business upon his father's death, had long cut a high profile in Moscow and had already appeared in fiction as Anna Serafimovna Stanitsyna, the heroine of P. D. Boborykin's 1882 novelization of the Moscow merchantry, *Kitai-gorod*.

[49] Natal'ia Dumova, *Moskovskie metsenaty* (Moscow: Molodaia gvardiia, 1992), 64–67.

issues of new money vs. old *intelligentsia* values. Rydlov is not a bad sort; indeed, the stock *intelligentsia* characters show themselves more morally dishonest than he. Rydlov's pretensions become problematic, however, because he is writing a book and wants to publish a gazette, *The Abyss*, for the "new man," who is left poorly defined but suggestively inclined toward money. The play is rich in codes intimating capitalism's intrinsic propensity for corruption. The pretty wife becomes profoundly disillusioned with her husband, whom she serves dutifully but does not love. Having then fallen instead for a seemingly more idealistic writer, she leaves home, as in the true-life scandal. When she learns that the writer wants her love but not marriage to her, she returns to Rydlov, who is happy to welcome her home. After all, as he reminds her, he is a gentleman and respects propriety.

As a *pièce-à-clef*, *The Gentleman* brought an immediacy to the theater that rivaled the popular press. The significance, however, and the justification for the Griboedov Prize derived from the production's biting commentary on the increasingly influential role of merchant money in cultural developments. In the most oft-quoted scene, Rydlov applauds how "all of Russia awaits rescue by the third estate." He extols the virtues of displacing the old with the new social element, observing that "first the nobility provided the writers, but now it's our turn."[50] When *The Gentleman* premiered at the Malyi, the influential families persuaded the Moscow city government to halt production, but the prohibition lasted only one season and Morozov reportedly did not stay long offended. After all, his wife was back and perhaps he delighted in the notoriety.

The young Mrs. Rydlov, like the factual Margarita Kirillovna Morozova, had faced an intensely relevant social quandary: what to do about an arranged marriage when women were enjoying unprecedented freedoms. The "woman question," a contentious issue that crossed many other aspects of social and cultural transformation, took center stage. The title of *Chains* (1888), the play by Sumbatov-Iuzhin that appeared most frequently in repertoires, referred to the legal code's attitude toward unhappy marriage. The code prevents the hero-husband from divorcing the wife who abandoned him and their daughter and marrying the "other woman," who has lived with him for years as his common-law wife. The wayward wife is able ultimately to make peace with those whom she abandoned and to accept the woman who took her place. However, the author kills the wife off suddenly at the final curtain, the only way out when divorce is not possible.

Despite the deterrents, women could forge personal lives independent

---

[50] *Dzhentlmen*, act II, scene iii.

of bad marriages. Vladimir Alexandrov, also known as the "Moscow Krylov," enjoyed a modest following for the melodramas he wrote for Ermolova at the Malyi.[51] Another lawyer who preferred a stage to a jury, Alexandrov introduced a strong heroine in *A Matter of Controversy* (1893), performed regularly in its day. Olga is married to a successful architect and businessman, Stepan; and they have a small daughter, Katia. Olga grew up as the ward of a wealthy merchant's widow, whose estate Stepan now manages. No one will let Olga forget that she, a charity case, made a favorable marriage, and she is deeply unhappy because her husband cares only about money. When Olga learns that her husband has taken advantage of another woman's financial straits, she demonstrates her moral fiber by leaving him, taking their daughter with her. Later, she also discovers that Stepan has stolen credit for another architect's designs. She moves into furnished rooms, but has trouble finding work because Stepan, who exercises legal control over her as his wife, will not give her the documents that would allow her to work independently. He offers to exchange the documents for Katia; and when she refuses, he manages to take his daughter back through legal channels. Olga's moral authority, however, holds sway over his corrupted soul. Stepan returns Katia in an attempt at reconciliation. The play is left open-ended: Olga tells Stepan that her return depends upon his behavior but asks him to continue to visit them. Olga struggled for the freedom to work and the opportunity to raise her daughter, and she held fast to principles that challenged the status quo. In an earlier time she would have ended like Ostrovskii's tragic heroines, suicidal.

The unhappy marriage became one of the dominant concerns of the nineteenth-century stage because the lack of possibility for divorce impeded the kind of social mobility on which modernization rested. Growing numbers of disgruntled wives in particular pressed their cases from the 1890s onward, usually charging adultery or desertion, and with increasing success.[52] By connecting the newly emerging social groups with traditional moral values, playwrights were calling attention to a very fundamental issue that was representative of how the tradition was obstructing modernity: the flexibility in the modern social hierarchy would be stiffened by the continuation of forced and bad marriages. The divorce drama performed a social drama writ large, about freedom of individual choice. It was particularly important to recognize that a fundamentally private act had serious public repercussions.

---

[51] Four of his plays published by the Kishnerev Publishing Firm in 1894, all melodramas, had been performed at the Korsh and the Malyi.

[52] William Wagner, *Marriage, Property, and Law in Late Imperial Russia* (Oxford: Clarendon Press, 1994), 70.

The Generation Gap

The conflict between Sumbatov-Iuzhin and Potekhin was fundamentally generational, and it showcased how attitudes toward the same situation differed across the divide in age and experience. Reminiscent of Ivan Turgenev's classic novel *Fathers and Sons* (1862), the generation gap provided an appropriate dramatic structure in which to frame stories of social transformation. The pace of industrialization was sufficiently swift and sweeping to provoke profound family ruptures, especially because opportunities for professional mobility challenged the economic structure that had kept children in the family business. Perceptions of capitalist culture generated the deepest conflicts, most apparent in the hypocrisies seemingly inherent in the market economy. The sons, more susceptible to the seduction of the new ways, did not always fare well against fathers. In A. P. Vershinin's *Antonov's Millions* (1898), the father turned on his greedy, pseudosophisticated children and set fire to his money rather than allow them to inherit.[53] P. M. Nevezhin's *The Old Homestead* (1892) demonstrated the political shallowness of the new generation. A collection of merchants' children, disgusted by their parents' old-fashioned values, decide to emulate the populists of the previous generation. They "go to the people" to help raise the cultural level of the peasantry, but the female protagonist becomes bored with high-mindedness and pursues village flirtations instead.

The most famous dramatization of the generation gap appeared in 1901, Sergei Naidenov's *Vaniushin's Children,* which premiered simultaneously at the Korsh in Moscow and the Suvorin in Petersburg.[54] Like Stanislavsky, Naidenov had been born into the merchant Alekseev clan.[55] What set this play apart was that Naidenov created in Vaniushin the *samodur* capable of recognizing that the old ways bore considerable responsibility for the attitudes of the new generation. He saw the harm he had inflicted on both himself and his family: his children cower before him, but behind his back they lead deceitful, debauched lives because he has provided no moral guidance or understanding. His wife has lived so long in fear of his temper that she has lost all sense of self, striving only to maintain an outward semblance of order and quiet in the home. The secrets, however, build to the point that they threaten the facade of family harmony. One daughter's husband blackmails his in-laws because he married their ugly girl to hide an unnamed disgrace that threatened to destroy

---

[53] I. N. Potapenko's 1905 *Kryl'ia sviazany* also dramatized the generational divide.

[54] S. Naidenov, *Deti Vaniushina* (published as a supplement to the journal *Teatr i iskusstvo,* no. 1, 1902).

[55] Naidenov's next play, *Bogatyi chelovek,* failed in large measure because it borrowed the moral from *Gentleman* but without the details that inquiring minds wanted to know. F. Bat-ov, *Bogatyi chelovek, Mir bozhii,* no. 11 (1904): 16–21.

the family business if made public. The youngest son, expelled from school, already has a drinking problem and has had an affair with an older woman, one of his father's employees. The oldest son desperately wants an education, but his father has forced him to drop out of school to learn the trade and is now pressuring the young man into a marriage that will unite two firms rather than two hearts.

In a confrontation with the youngest son, who is leaving home because he is certain that he can only find happiness by escaping the family, Vaniushin at last faces up to the mess he has created. The son sympathizes with the father, who was simply behaving in the only manner he knew. Vaniushin vows to make it up to his wife and children. Just when it appears that the play is moving toward a happy ending, though, the despondent Vaniushin takes his own life. Symbolically accepting responsibility for the tragic state of contemporary life, the old order thus does away with its crippling manners and prejudices.[56]

Naidenov was quickly joined under the spotlight by Maxim Gorky, the flamboyant and politically leftist writer who was soon to become the most celebrated spokesperson for the new generation. Gorky's *Philistines,* which likewise used the scenario of generational differences to presage social change, tied with *Vaniushin's Children* for the Griboedov Prize in 1902. Although at least one disgruntled critic accused Gorky of borrowing too liberally from Naidenov, the similarities between the two plays rest on the immediacy of the social issue they both address and the use of the family as the dramatic backdrop against which to develop the action.[57] The significance of yet another disputed awarding of the Griboedov Prize signaled that the Russian theater was again on the threshold of transformation, this one becoming apparent as society drifted toward revolution.

Staging the Aftermath of Revolution, 1905–17

On the evening of October 14, 1905, when the Russian empire was grinding to a halt in the wake of a general strike, a performance of Ostrovskii's *The Heart Is Not a Stone* was slated at the Alexandrinka. Comedian Davydov went to the director with the veiled admonition that "my heart is not a stone either," and the theater remained dark.[58] For the performers, the politics of revolution offered the sort of intangible gains associated with a reduced censorship that would allow for more artistic freedom. For

---

[56] See, for example, "Kriticheskie zametki," *Teatral'naia Rossiia,* [number unknown] (1905): 12.

[57] Iurii Beliaev, *Aktery i p'esy. Vpechatleniia* (St. Petersburg: Ia. Berman, 1902), 254–67, contrasts the two plays.

[58] Quoted in M. G. Svetaeva, *Mariia Gavrilovna Savina* (Moscow: Iskusstvo, 1988), 244.

those who worked for the private theaters, it increased the possibilities for some form of unionization that could balance the power of the entrepreneur. The real significance of the revolution for the stage, though, lay in the theatrical questions of how to stage the political changes when it appeared that the autocracy would finally surrender some of its authority to elected representatives.

Naidenov tried to capture the postrevolutionary climate by rewriting the ending of *Vaniushin's Children* in 1907. In this version, the elderly patriarch does not take his own life, but rather becomes victimized by his corrupt and tyrannical oldest son, who has assumed control of the family business. Naidenov's indictment of the new generation did not fare as well with audiences as the original, but by shifting the locus of moral degeneracy he reminded viewers that those assuming power under the reformed government had to be just as mindful of accountability as their parents.[59] Society could not send the corrupted son, a player in the economic takeoff, to the State Duma, Russia's parliament.

The divorce drama returned in another Alexandrov vehicle for Ermolova, *The Story of One Marriage* (1913), posing a different set of questions. The characters of the play come from the common stockpile of prototypes: a dowager widow who runs a factory and wants her son and daughter to be more cultured than she; the daughter's voice teacher, played by Ermolova, a former concert star who married a dissolute baron who drank through both their resources; and the voice teacher's son, a writer, who marries his mother's wealthy pupil. Thus Alexandrov joined in matrimony the perfect social contradiction: the noble *intelligentsia* on its way down, and merchant money on its way up the power hierarchy. What Alexandrov added, though, was an indictment of the *intelligentsia* for its ineffectiveness, a sentiment being felt throughout post-1905 society.[60] The bourgeoisie had begun to assume the role of moral anchor on stage.

The climax of *One Marriage* comes when the wife/daughter, unhappy with her husband's inability to take charge of his life, has an adulterous affair with the local doctor. When her mother-in-law suggests that divorce is not necessary because adultery is "bourgeois" and that divorce would represent only "philistine moralism," the daughter/wife walks out. She wants neither to join the doctor nor to return to her family's fortune, but only to escape the tyranny of the self-delusional *intelligentsia*. In the final scene, the voice teacher promises her son that she will care for him always because although he has inherited his father's weaknesses, he also has her artistic nature. What future can this Mama's boy hope for? Or effect?

The impending contestation over membership in the *intelligentsia* had

---

[59] Review of a collected volume of Naidenov's plays in *Sovremmenik*, no. 6 (1911): 389–93.
[60] Vladimir Alexandrov, *Istoriia odnogo braka* (Moscow: Lomonosov, 1913).

surfaced earlier in A. I. Stoikin's *The Intelligentsia* (1911), a play that, like the title characters themselves in the eyes of the bourgeois audience, was longer on dialogue than on action. Stoikin set the first acts just after the 1905 Revolution, when Russian society was consumed with the relationship between intellectuals and the *narod,* the workers and peasants who had proven their revolutionary mettle on the barricades and in the country-side.[61] This relationship was as tense as it was tenuous; now that the riotous potential of the *narod* had become manifest, some public opinion held the radical intellectuals responsible for exhorting them to violence.

The heroine of *The Intelligentsia,* a one-time provincial actress, was mistress to a wealthy factory owner but had fallen in love with the factory's resident physician, the prototypical liberal professional. The good doctor is the focal point for discourse generated about the most appropriate relationship between intellectuals and the *narod,* and he functions as foil to a radical law student agitating among the workers. The student is a particularly reprehensible stereotype who dislikes the *narod* because they will not put themselves on the firing line for *his* ideals. Capital is represented by the factory's lawyer, who personifies the moral ambiguity of business. For example, at one point this lawyer proclaims that he would be a socialist if that were where the power lay, but because it lies in capital, he will remain in that camp.

The relationship between the doctor and the heroine provides the moral dynamic. The doctor, in fact, returns the heroine's love and assures her that he does not subscribe to "philistine moralism," that he would not reproach her in any way for her affair with the boss. She, however, mistrusts his sincerity. In the last act, five years later, the audience learns that she became the doctor's mistress for a while but left him because of her own fears, not because he reproached her. She returns to him in the end, though, to work with him at a village clinic where they can both devote themselves to helping the people. The radical law student, in contrast, has diminished into becoming a petty bureaucrat in local government. Fearful of being murdered by the *narod,* he has turned to alcohol to quiet his anxieties. Discredited and in a frightened, drunken stupor, he makes a new stereotype of the *intelligent:* the feckless failure, whose extremist views are now held up to ridicule.

The identity of the philistine was also up for renegotiation because those born into the estates associated with this boorish and selfish behavior were asserting their moral sway after being held in contempt for generations. Lev Ivanov's comedy *A Philistine among the Nobility* (1912) updated the interchange of these two groups passing each other on the social ladder.[62]

---

[61] A. I. Stoikin, *Intelligenty* (*Teatr i iskusstvo,* 1911).
[62] Lev Ivanov, *Meshchanka vo dvorianstve* (Moscow: S. F. Razsokhin, 1912).

The philistine in question is a chorus girl who married well above her station years ago. Her noble husband turned out to be a libertine, and she was returning to his uncle and aunt to ask for their help in divorcing him. Professing to have married their profligate nephew only because he had threatened suicide, she was now pleading for her freedom, rejecting their money, because he had taken up with a singer at the Aquarium, Petersburg's most popular nightclub. Other characters round out the milieu of social interchange: a doctor with his wife and daughter, a lawyer, and the merchant who lives next door. Two romantic inversions of the social scale blossom in the course of this comedy: the chorus girl and the doctor, and the doctor's daughter and the merchant.

Throughout the action, the various characters have plenty of opportunity to prove that "nobility" and "philistinism" are categories of behavior, not estate-based classifications. The doctor's wife, who objects initially to her daughter's suitor, reveals her own cultural level through constant allusion to her favorite literature: *The Mother's Grief and Her Lost Daughter, The Heroine of the Demimonde,* and *Secrets of the Court of Madrid.* More intertextual references abound when the merchant, whose surname was Churkin, was affectionately called "The Bandit" in reference to one of the best known hero-scalawags from pulp fiction, "The Bandit Churkin" (1881). In his attempts to impress his social betters, the merchant Churkin referred to a "Remington" (the word Russians used for typewriter) as a "Renaissance." He was, however, the first to show kindness to the chorus girl and won the heart of the doctor's daughter with his strong moral fiber. The chorus girl, too, demonstrated her upstanding character by refusing the lawyer because she feared that he would become tired of her uneducated mind. But happiness prevailed. Impressed by her integrity, her former in-laws bestowed a sizable dowry on her, provided that she overcame her unwarranted insecurities and married the lawyer. Thus was social change reinforced through a resolution that highlighted the advantages each side brought to the mix.

The Political World Becomes a Stage

By 1905, "everyone went to the theater just as everyone read a newspaper."[63] An exaggeration, but the millions empirewide who did one were most likely to do the other because they were interested in politics. The easing of censorship after 1905 inspired I. I. Kolyshko, a state servitor with experience at the upper echelons of several ministries, to put the new government on public display. So long as he kept the Romanovs out, Kolyshko

---

[63] Petrovskaia, *Teatr i zritel' rossiiskikh stolits,* 4.

found himself at relative liberty to dramatize the gossip about some of the most influential people in the empire. Despite writing a major play, Kolyshko does not appear in histories of the theater. However, the nature of his hit, the manner in which he brought the immediate political present to Russian audiences, earns him mention in this discussion of the post-1905 Russian stage.

Just as Moscow audiences had had no trouble identifying *The Gentleman* as Mikhail Morozov, so the empire at large recognized Kolyshko's *The Great Man* as none other than Count Sergei Witte—the architect of rapid industrialization, the diplomat who had negotiated a surprisingly favorable conclusion to the lost war with Japan in 1905, and the statesman who had then persuaded the recalcitrant Tsar Nicholas II to end the nationwide general strike in October later that year by conceding the quasi-representative Duma. Within a year of his striking successes, though, Witte had been banished into political exile, damned by conservatives for going as far as he did, and by liberal public opinion for not going far enough. Kolyshko, who had served Witte in the Ministry of Finance, aired the dirty linen on stage.[64]

The author insisted on his purity of political motives, protesting that he was presenting an issue reflective of the Russian system rather than the life of a specific individual. Arguing that his play was an exposé of the numerous "organic obstacles—envy, laziness, stagnation, intrigue, and mediocrity," which prevented those Russians with political talent from achieving their objectives, Kolyshko drew heavily from Witte's private life to tell this story.[65] In a world where numerous alliances were still forged and decisions made at social functions at the Winter Palace, the illustrious count's formidable negotiating skills had long been compromised by the scandal surrounding his second marriage.[66] V. A. Ishimov, the hero of *The Great Man*, found himself trapped in the intrigues of his wife Ira, whose affections for a penniless nobleman inspired suspicions, and the ambitions of other members of her scheming family. Ira's mother, for example, ran a salon not unlike the sort the real Mrs. Witte was rumored to operate, where officials played cards with some of society's more unsavory elements, facilitating bribery. Ira's cousin had questionable strategies for investment in the Russian Far East, not unlike the schemers who cost Witte his posi-

[64] See, for example, Kolyshko's bilious *Lozh' Vitte. Iashchik Pandory* (Berlin: E. A. Gutnov, 1923), a diatribe written under the pen name "Baiain'" in exile after 1917 that blames Witte for not seeing through to the consequences his reforms inaugurated. In keeping with his penchant for gossip, Kolyshko also reports on the homosexuals in the government, conspicuously in the Ministry of Foreign Affairs under Lamsdorf.

[65] From the introduction to *Bol'shoi chelovek*, reprinted in a pamphlet of reviews of the play entitled *Bol'shoi chelovek* (Moscow: A. A. Devinson, 1909), 6.

[66] Theodore Von Laue, *Sergei Witte and the Industrialization of Russia* (New York: Antheum, 1973), 69–70.

tion as minister of finance just prior to the Russo-Japanese War. Another character recognizable from Witte's entourage was the corrupt French journalist on whom both the factual and fictional ministers relied, for a fee, to fill the French press with deceptively positive pictures of Russian political and economic stability.[67]

The play's theme, according to its author, was that those who initially seek power as a means to a righteous end ultimately fall victim to the seductive appeal of power for its own sake. Ishimov sees his reform bills overturned by a conservative Senate, and his own integrity compromised by an attempt to manipulate the stock market. In a piteous final scene, he compares himself to the failed reformers who preceded him in Russia's history. The curtain descended without much hope for Russia's reformist future, just as Witte's ouster provided a prelude to a conservative restoration that dashed the expectations of many after the revolution of 1905.

The Great Man premiered at the Malyi and was a smash hit. Before taking it on tour, the V. A. Linskaia-Nemetti Company published a promotional booklet with reprints from the major newspapers in both capitals describing at least five standing-room-only performances in Moscow, the names of government officials in attendance, and the debate about whether the play offered a "photograph" of Witte or, as the author maintained, simply a picture of the basic political structure.[68] Although cost forced the touring company to drop one very popular scene, the ball that showed the social animals in their native habitat, the play was just as big a hit in the provinces. The great man in question, Witte, remained quiet on the subject of this betrayal by one who had held his confidences.[69]

As many reviewers pointed out, Kolyshko made a better journalist than playwright. Trying to repeat his success by dramatizing the Duma in *On the Battlefield* (1910), he could not quite pull it off because he did not have the kind of sexual scandal to work with that had brought the Witte character to life. Any play that made "the golden mean" its central character was bound to lack a certain dramatic tension.[70] Billing *Battlefield* as "Russia's first political play," Kolyshko fancied himself a Russian Ibsen, but unlike the Norwegian playwright, he had locked his characters in the specifics of Russia in 1910.[71]

[67] Louise McReynolds, *The News under Russia's Old Regime: The Development of a Mass-Circulation Press* (Princeton: Princeton University Press, 1991), 126–30, discusses Witte's essentially modern understanding of publicity.

[68] *Bol'shoi chelovek*, 6.

[69] B. V. Anan'ich and R. Sh. Ganelin, "Opyt kritiki memuarov S. Iu. Vitte," *Voprosy istoriografii i istochnikovedeniia istorii SSSR* (Moscow: Akademiia nauk, 1963), 310–18; 298–374.

[70] RGALI, f. 853, op. 2, d. 58, l. 106. Savina scored the only rave reviews.

[71] I. I. Kolyshko, *Pole brani* (St. Petersburg: Imperatorskoe russkoe teatral'noe obshchestvo, 1910).

Revolution behind the Curtains

For all the implicit criticism of the political ideals of the nineteenth-century *intelligentsia* on the contemporary stage, few in the theater crowd did not feel pressure to respond to artistic innovations at the MAT and the other experimental theaters that had followed in its wake. Even though audiences avoided such symbolist weirdness as Leonid Andreev's *The Life of a Man* (1906) and *Black Masks* (1908), the prematurely deceased Chekhov became something of a demigod among certain theatrical circles, who worshiped him in his Stanislavsky incarnation. The imperial theater felt heat from both its commercial and experimental competitors, and required a massive transfusion of rubles to update sets, costumes, and the buildings themselves after 1905. V. A. Teliakovskii, who had assumed the directorship of the theater in 1901, wanted repertoires refurbished as well.[72] More sympathetic to creative young directors than to his aging talent pool, in 1908 Teliakovskii hired the wildly inventive Vsevolod Meierkhol'd away from the MAT. Notorious for his direction of *The Picture of Dorian Grey*, Oscar Wilde's novella in which the portrait ages as its subject grows young, Meierkhol'd had brought one of modernism's defining texts to the Russian stage. Teliakovskii's hire sparked a backlash because not only did the established stars not care to experiment with modernism, they objected to inverting the artistic hierarchy and placing the director atop, as Meierkhol'd demanded.[73]

The reaction against modernism, symbolism, and the naturalism that reigned at the MAT resulted in a deep nostalgia for Ostrovskii. In 1909 *Rampa i zhizn'* celebrated the fiftieth anniversary of *The Storm* with a call to return to Ostrovskii because the current theater had gone bankrupt. What the editors missed most about Ostrovskii's style was his reconstructions on stage of *byt,* the Russian term derived from "to be" that refers to the practices of everyday life. They understood Ostrovskii because they identified with his characters, and were put off by symbolism's substitution of form for content and Stanislavsky's obsession with detail, because that took the life out of the people on stage. Recalling another contemporary debate, that of "art for art's sake," the editors feared "*byt* for *byt*'s sake." Just as art must be employed for the greater social good, so must *byt* be returned to the theater in the form of the realism that people could see as a reflection of their quotidian experiences.[74] A play should not be performed for its own sake; it had to mean something to the audience.

[72] Many of Teliakovskii's complaints and demands to the government about problems at the theater are maintained in RGIA, f. 497, op. 11, d. 24 and f. 69., op. 18. See also f. 468, op. 44, d. 158.
[73] Teliakovskii's gossipy memoirs expose the obvious strains in his relationship with Savina, whom he describes as an intriguer and a liar. *Vospominaniia*, 299–305.
[74] *Rampa i zhizn'*, no. 33, November 16, 1909.

In what can best be characterized as a serious comedy, A. A. Pleshcheev put the plight of the contemporary theater on stage in *The Star* (1910). The heroine, a provincial actress who heads a touring company, maintains her faith in the culturally uplifting capacity of the stage and will not allow economic hardship to divert her off course. Yet she finds herself in a vise, caught between a Stanislavsky-influenced highbrow culture and the low-brow world of trained circus animals. In a particularly poignant scene, the Star bemoans naturalism: "in my day people took actors at their word: if you said it was raining, they believed you. Now you need rain on stage!" And as to the source of this unwelcome change, she protested, "we had talent, and all we have now is directors!"[75]

The most portentous threat of all, however, came not from the MAT but from the most physical symbol of modern entertainment: the cinema. Not only does this new attraction lure away the Star's potential ticket-paying audience, but to heap personal insult upon financial injury, her manager embezzles their earnings to spend on the cinema's cashier. Unlike the frustrated feminists of the earlier generation, this heroine decides to quit the stage, marry the man who loves her, and tells him that she wants to "keep house, put up vegetables, walk around in a housecoat, and not worry about hideous hairstyles."[76] A comic rendition of theater life, the Star's surrender to the status quo says more about role-playing than antifeminism. Moreover, as a new member of the sedentary middle classes, the Star would have undoubtedly turned to the silver screen to re-imagine her possibilities as she reconstructed her sense of self in retirement from the legitimate stage.

Conclusion

On the bourgeois stage the world dwindled into a drawing room. In their self-enclosed stories, dramatic tension seemed to lose some of its capacity to raise themes of grand significance. Or so some of the critics thought. Accusations that the interests and problems of a single class had narrowed the cultural scope of the theater did not seem to take into consideration the extent to which this class was comprised of a mixture of estates, created by the same forces that had transformed the very nature of theater. Their social melodramas did not simply put new costumes on old problems by relocating the settings from aristocratic salons to middle-class drawing rooms. Power relations between those privileged and those excluded from power remained at the heart of dramatic conflict, and the moral of each

---

[75] A. A. Pleshcheev, *Liubimets publiki* (Moscow: Razsokhin, 1910), 43.
[76] Ibid., 71.

story had to come to terms with the new forms of exploitation. The enclosed buildings, boxed sets, proscenium arch, and great sums involved in making a hit play differed strikingly from the Biblical pyrotechnics, lyrical sentimentalism, and even social satires of the previous eras. If the idea that the world was a stage belonged to Renaissance sensibilities, then the flip side, that the stage was a world unto itself, was grounded in the commercialization that made the theater self-sufficient.

As the Western world marched indefatigably toward war, the theater thrived in its position as a bastion of middle-class cultural values. In 1914 Moscow boasted nineteen private theaters, numbers approached if not equaled in other major cities.[77] Teliakovskii even fought with limited success to keep his personnel free from the military draft, arguing that they provided an essential service to the home front.[78] But the war also exacerbated the social problems that had appeared on stage, left unresolved in real life. When the February revolution forced the tsar's abdication in 1917, the marauders who seized the Malyi punctuated the end of the bourgeois legitimate stage by stealing what they could carry and defecating on what they could not.[79]

---

[77] A. I. Mogilevskii, V. Filippov, and A. M. Rodionov, *Teatry Moskvy, 1917–1928* (Moscow: Gos. ak. khud. nauk, 1928), 5.

[78] RGIA, f. 472, op. 56, ed. khran. 56, contains communications about draft exemptions. Opera star Fedor Shaliapin was apparently eligible, for example, but was kept away from the front.

[79] Iuzhin-Sumbatov stood a sad witness to the destruction. RGIA, f. 497, op. 1, d. 1359 contains documents on the Malyi in 1917.

CHAPTER THREE

Sporting Life as Modern Life

In 1912 Petersburg playboy Boris Suvorin organized a boys' soccer competition and named the championship cup for himself, inviting ridicule for his pretensions.[1] The son of publishing and theatrical magnate Alexei Suvorin, Boris was using organized sports to purchase his entrée into the world of the new elite, athletes. Serving on the editorial board of *Illiustrirovannyi zhurnal atletika i sport* (Illustrated journal of athletics and sports) alongside some of Russia's most notable sports figures, Suvorin (*fils*) played upon the reciprocal relationship between commerce and mass communications that accounted for his family's fortune and political influence. That he used competitive and egalitarian-oriented athletics as his métier bespeaks the multiple levels of significance that sports held in postreform Russia.

Organized athletics have long provided a conventional marker of the transformation of an agrarian society into an industrialized urban one. Melvin Adelman listed six characteristics that distinguish modern from traditional sports, each of which designates a move from an informal approach to the rational structure that parallels the development of capitalist industry: organization, rules, role differentiation, public information, competition, and statistics and records.[2] Adelman could have added the transformation of social relations and the construction of new kinds of public spheres, which aided the growth of civil society. In addition, commercialization organized sports in many ways, from gambling to prize money, from salaries to advertising.

[1] *Budil'nik*, no. 23 (1915): 12–13.
[2] Melvin Adelman, *A Sporting Time: New York City and the Rise of Modern Athletics, 1820–70* (Urbana: University of Illinois Press, 1986), 6.

76

The rise of the athlete as a person of respect registered the social up-heaval that connected sports to modernity. Horse racing lost stature as the "sport of kings" once the "totalizator," or electronic pari-mutuel betting machine, enabled gambling on a mass scale and following the horses be-came a favorite pastime of the crowd. Hunting, too, lost its noble blush when the government modified regulations over land use to facilitate eco-nomic development. In addition, the increasingly inexpensive manufac-ture of rifles changed the provincial ecology by putting guns in tens of thousands of new hands. Circus strongmen drifting through villages to tan-gle with bears or village toughs found respectable celebrity among rich and poor alike when they moved to upscale urban arenas and wrestled each other according to refined rules for international honors. The wealthy formed yacht and automobile clubs, while the middle classes organized bi-cycling societies. British plant managers organized Russia's first football team ("soccer" in the United States), the ultimate athletic mirror of the ra-tional structure of the industrial workplace. Regulations, membership dues, and organized competitions indirectly taught the rules of industri-alization. When educators recognized the natural affinity between sports and health, athletics entered many public school curricula. Sports pulled Russia into international politics when the Olympics were resurrected in 1896, and its subsequent humiliation at the 1912 games taught Russians to appreciate the substance behind the symbolism of the strong body politic. Widespread interest fueled an array of sports journals, subsidized by the growing industry for leisure. From the pedestrian to the sublime, sports became a part of Russian experience.[3]

For all the undeniable significance of rational organization, though, ath-letic competition is intensely individualistic and emotional. At the personal level, sports helped to transform attitudes by forcing Russians to internal-ize the outer expression of controlled behavior implicit in the rules of the game. The quintessential site of athletics is deeply personal, the body it-self. Competition, evolving with the ethos of capitalism, provided the prin-ciple that merged body with soul: it demanded the combination of physical stamina and the psychological determination to be better than others. The Russian word to denote amateur status, *liubitel'*, translates as "lover," cap-turing the spirit of the Latin original that underscores personal passion. Spectators, consuming fans, through their personal devotion supplied the necessary funding that transformed athletics into big business. Fans also gave meaning to the games through their identification with athletes or teams they accepted as representatives of some of their larger, amorphous ambitions.

---

[3] Timothy Harte, "Game, Set, Stanza: Modern Sport in the Poetry of Osip Mandel'shtam," *Russian Review* 59, no. 3 (2000): 353–70.

Organized sports also cultivated the growth of civic consciousness among fans and athletes alike. Urban landscapes were transformed when areas were built for the paying crowds, which affected notions of public space. Time and again sporting clubs took the initiative in pushing for legislation that held larger implications for the commonweal, as when hunters pressed for improved land management and bicyclists for better roads. Simultaneously, though, sports offered up a civic anathema: gambling, which threatened to corrupt the lower classes into wasting wages better spent on educational leisure. However, unlike cards or dice, which depend on Dame Fortune for a fortuitous turn, sporting events supposedly calculate physical or athletic superiority and therefore do not simply leave the outcome to chance. Wagering on an event gave sports as much of a raison d'être as competing oneself. The entrepreneurial spirit necessary to take a calculated risk, when economic success or failure lay in the balance, surfaced in the betting endemic to competition.[4]

Democratizing the Imperial Turf

One of the most poignant passages of *Anna Karenina,* Lev Tolstoy's serial melodrama of adultery, describes how Count Vronskii, the heroine's lover, must shoot his beloved thoroughbred Frou-Frou when the horse is injured during a race. Although Tolstoy intended the scene to explore Vronskii's sense of honor, the setting in which the incident occurs captures the fading flavor of an era when noble officers depended upon their polished equestrian skills in battle. Vronskii will ultimately go off to fight in the last pre-mechanized war, against Turkey in 1876. Before trenches, machine guns, and tanks turned horses into pack animals, proficiency in the saddle gave officers the habit of braggadocio that was further reflected in the wager that Vronskii felt obliged to place on himself. His side bet revealed the heady mixture of self-confidence and recklessness required of those who rode into battle. Horses more fortunate than Frou-Frou performed in hippodromes for the gambling public.

Russia's first totalizator, the pari-mutuel betting machine that made wagering possible on a mass scale, went into operation in 1876 at the hippodrome in Tsarskoe Selo, the site of several imperial stables. Showing an immediate profit, totalizators were opened in Moscow in 1877 and spread to provincial cities until more than fifty were operational by 1910.[5] Pari-mutuel betting made good financial sense: it organized gambling by combining all sums wagered in one vast pool, calculated handicaps to encour-

---

[4] On the relationship of sports and gambling to social behavior, see Martin Shubik, *Game Theory and Related Approaches to Social Behavior* (New York: Wiley, 1964).

[5] *Vopros o totalizatore v Gos. Sovete* (St. Petersburg: Iu. Ia. Riman, 1910), 12, 14.

age betting on horses less likely than others to win, and paid the winners from the collective pool. The money that remained in the pool constituted the profits, which could be reinvested in breeding. Thus could the totalizator relieve the financially strapped tsarist government of the need to underwrite the extraordinary costs of breeding thoroughbreds, deemed necessary for the military.[6] From the fifteenth-century rule of Ivan the Great, Russia's rulers had personally committed extensive funds from state coffers to support breeding. Peter the Great had brought stallions as well as draftsmen from Holland. His extravagant niece Anna Ioannovna had increased the number of stud farms from four to ten, raising purebloods from eastern as well as European stocks. Recognizing the strain that the millions of rubles spent on breeding put on the state budget, Catherine the Great closed several state farms and encouraged private initiatives. The Napoleonic wars devastated the Russian stock in 1812, forcing Alexander I to restructure the stables. A few wealthy private breeders, such as Count F. V. Rostopchin, had established exemplary stables competitive with the government's. Numerous small societies of breeders sprang up in the first half of the nineteenth century, but the costs of breeding were such that these owners depended on state subsidies. It would take the tsar who freed the serfs, Alexander II, to liberate the state from the stables. Pressed to pay for the emancipation during an economic depression, he quite frankly needed the money.[7]

The first modern spectator sport, horse racing required a reorganization of social space in the construction of hippodromes capable of seating thousands, built by the government that would profit from the gambling. Pricing policies determined where spectators could sit, but racing was fundamentally democratic because it brought people of various backgrounds together to participate in the same activity, to share the common objective of identifying the superior horse. An urban sport, racing changed the cityscape with its grandstands and the building of transportation lines to move the crowds back and forth. Racing also helped to capitalize mass-circulation journalism: in addition to the separate racing sheets published on race days, the daily papers carried information about the track during the season. The sport itself changed, from having the same horses run long, multiple heats to fielding as many groups a day on the track as possible.[8]

The lifeblood of the new sport quickly proved its bane as well. Liberal activists concerned with public welfare raised their hackles immediately with images of the already impoverished working class frittering away

---

[6] Ann Kleimola, "Good Breeding, Muscovite Style: 'Horse Culture' in Early Modern Rus'," *Forschungen zur osteuropäischen Geschichte* (1995): 199–238.

[7] *Sportsmen* (*Izdanie, posviashchennoe voprosam konnozabodstva i konskogo sporta*) (Moscow: n.p., 1913), 7–15.

[8] Adelman, *Sporting Time,* 39.

money they could ill afford chasing illusory wealth. The state tried to compensate for this by mandating that one percent of profits from the totalizator go to organized charities. The Moscow city government proved the betting machine's most trenchant foe, positioning itself in a fight against the national government over control of local affairs. This dispute between state and city governments originated as one of land management: in 1831 the Ministry of State Domains had turned over a section outside the city proper to the local horse-breeding societies as part of its broader objective of stimulating private initiative. Three years later, the societies were empowered to sponsor races that would identify the superior animals for breeding stock. In 1872, however, Alexander II's municipal reforms created the electoral, representative duma, whose members wanted control over this land. As the population exploded, land use became increasingly critical. This hippodrome was located in Petrovskii Park, a prime location for urban entertainments and therefore quite valuable property.

Initially, in 1873 the city duma levied a tax on the breeding societies, who refused to pay. The duma then tried to force the state's Department of Horse Breeding to cover these taxes, arguing that the societies were serving state interests. The department also refused. The tax, fifty rubles per annum per society, was sufficiently modest to indicate that the fight was not over money. In 1877, when national law required that the totalizator give a proportion of profits to local governments, the duma denounced this money as morally tainted. Their snubbing of badly needed funds continued as a cause célèbre until 1917. Reformist mayor Nikolai Alekseev even went undercover in the 1880s to expose the Moscow race track as a festering pool of corruption. The muckraking mayor reportedly sat alongside "workers, masters, servants, and petty tradesmen," all spending their single day off gambling rather than engaging in wholesome activities. Racing's true colors showed in the riot that erupted at the track in 1889 when the totalizator malfunctioned. In a quote that surfaced repeatedly in subsequent tirades against the machine Tsar Alexander III called it a "great evil," but no Russian ruler could afford to outlaw it.[9]

State Councilor I. O. Korvin-Milevskii, and Count I. I. Vorontsov-Dashkov, former head of the imperial stud farms and noted breeder himself, rushed to assure the tsar that thoroughbred breeding could not continue without pari-mutuel betting.[10] In fact, the minimum allowable bet was raised from one to ten rubles, which translated into an anticipated rise of eight to ten million rubles per annum that gambling would contribute to state breeding.[11] Given that the government's cut was only 10 percent, this sum at-

---

[9] *Vopros*, 12–13, 28.

[10] M. K. Breitman, *Zametki o totalizatore* (St. Petersburg: Sport i favority, 1912), 14.

[11] *Vopros*, 9. Breitman, *Zametki*, 14, gave the official percentage as 10.5, which probably represents the 0.5 percent designated for charity.

tested to the degree to which legalized gambling had become a major business enterprise. In a concession to the critics, students were now forbidden to wager at the tracks.[12]

Comparable to the debate about the government's monopoly on alcohol, which also put money ill-gotten from the poor into state coffers, the controversy surrounding the totalizator allowed public opinion to voice opposition to the autocracy. Lawyer A. F. Koni, a dominant figure in the liberal movement, joined with the reformers, who kept pressure on the government and forced increased regulatory controls in 1889 and 1900.[13] In 1909 the State Council considered a bill to shut down the totalizator but decided against such a dramatic step in order to avoid the riots that had exploded in France and Germany following similar attempts at prohibition.[14]

Those who championed the "great evil" skillfully inverted its negative propaganda. The Petersburg governor-general countered Alekseev's fearful images of degenerate workers stealing to feed their gambling frenzy with statistics compiled in 1895–1901 that showed only twenty-two instances of crime associated with the totalizator. The totalizator became a "nerve of economic life for the local population"; jobs associated with the track numbered ten thousand even in defiant Moscow. A justice of the peace alleged that four of ten crimes he judged derived from gambling, but his claims could not be proved.[15] The totalizator's supporters invoked the name of venerated poet Alexander Pushkin on the basis of his attraction to risk taking, though without mentioning the sad fate of the protagonist of Pushkin's *Queen of Spades,* or of the brilliant novelist Fedor Dostoevsky and his addiction to cards.[16] But playing the horses meant rationally studying the animals, not courting Lady Luck.

Statistics gathered to illustrate the benefits of gambling to breeding demonstrated an indisputably positive influence. Between 1854 and 1907 the number of registered breeding societies jumped from 96 to 3,700; the number of race horses increased by 3,000, up from 260; and the number of hippodromes nearly tripled, from 20 to 54.[17] As long as the state found a direct connection between the totalizator and breeding stock, it would seem ill-advised to forgo substantial returns on the basis of amorphous platitudes. If the military need for good horses were not reason enough, some argued that breeding would also improve the stock of peasant workhorses.[18]

[12] Breitman, *Zametki,* 7.
[13] *Sportsmen* (Kiev), no. 9 (1909): 3. Moscow had filed official complaints in 1886, 1889, 1897, 1901, 1908, and 1909. *Vopros,* 11.
[14] *Vopros,* 91.
[15] Ibid., 44–47.
[16] Breitman, *Zametki,* 27.
[17] *Vopros,* 41.
[18] Breitman, *Zametki,* 12.

The most articulate defense of the totalizator came in 1912 from sports journalist M. K. Breitman, who considered gambling a basic civil liberty. Playing on several fashionable theories, insisting that risk taking was essential to human nature, he stressed the "civilized" and European connections of the sport. Politically, he argued that public officials should dictate the rights of individuals to take risks with their own money.[19] Where others had compared the totalizator to the stock market and the state lottery,[20] Breitman placed it where it belonged, with "other institutions for public entertainment and recreation." Pointing out that even the "most modest coffee houses and public gardens" would have to be closed because people spent money in them simply to enjoy themselves, he lamented the unwelcome intrusion of Puritan ethics into entertainment.[21] At this time the track in Moscow alone, built at a cost of approximately two million rubles, seated crowds of fifteen to twenty thousand during the season, from April to August, and awarded nearly one million rubles in prizes annually.[22] It would be difficult for an enterprise of this economic magnitude to disappear on the wings of virtue alone.

Breitman's happy pictures of racing as egalitarian because it caught the interests of people from all social strata exaggerated its democratizing potential, but this was the appropriate tack to take in a society that envisioned itself as progressive. The names that appear in the racing column included some of Russia's most distinguished families, such as the Gagarins, nouveaux riches such as Boris Suvorin, and merchants such as the Eliseevs. Members of the royal family and others prominent in society sponsored races, lending their names to the prize. The Trekhgornii Textile Factory recognized the publicity benefits of financing a big race and put up corporate sponsorship; suggestively, the manufactory offered more prize money than the royals.[23] Newspapers in provincial cities reported on racing with the same enthusiasm as those in the two capitals, and during the First World War Yaroslavl, far from the battle front, became Russia's horse-racing capital. Horse racing had become tsarist Russia's first true national pastime.

Hunting for Sport

I. S. Turgenev's *Annals of a Sportsman,* which appeared in 1852, inserted politics into sports on the eve of the Great Reforms. Turgenev's protago-

---

[19] Ibid., 6.

[20] *Vopros,* 55–57.

[21] Breitman, *Zametki,* 3, 26–29.

[22] Ruth Kedzie Wood, *The Tourist's Russia* (New York: Dodd and Mead, 1912), 38–41.

[23] *Sportsmen* (Kiev), no. 3 (1909): 1. The Trekhgornii Prize was six thousand rubles, as opposed to others at two thousand.

nist, who finds that "one of the great advantages of shooting, my dear reader, is the perpetual going from place to place by those persons who indulge in it,"[24] wanders through the last days of prereform Russia. The serf boys who accompany him, and whose humanity he describes in such eloquent terms, lacked not only basic civil liberties but also the rights to land use. After the emancipation, hunting actively helped to restructure social relations. Moreover, it became central to several debates that emerged from the capitalization of the countryside.

Hunting for sport, rather than for food or protection, is an organized social activity. All over Europe the hunt lost its traditional ritualistic element when feudal lands became subject to the private law of the lord. By the nineteenth century, as E. P. Thompson has described for England, the forest had become political terrain and hunting a medium of class warfare.[25] Surprisingly, Peter the Great supposedly objected to this facet of modernity because he found hunting cruel to animals.[26] On the very eve of the reforms Tsar Alexander II used the hunt to celebrate aristocratic hierarchy, an ironic last hurrah for a system he himself would begin to dismantle.[27]

In the first half of the nineteenth century official prohibition on formal organizations had pushed Russians into informal, interest-based networks best exemplified by the "circles" (*kruzhki*) into which the *intelligentsia* gathered and found common identity. In the spirit of the reforms, the government showed much higher tolerance for organized assemblies, so long as members agreed to leave politics at the door. In 1862 a "circle" of hunters received an independent charter as the Moscow Hunting Society. With sixty-seven founding members, it also received the right to establish provincial branches. The charter underscored civic concerns: the society would advise on gaming laws, with an eye toward protecting the environment, and promote the breeding of hounds. A government subsidy underwrote the journal, *Priroda i okhota* (Nature and the hunt), in return for which favor the society organized hunts for members of the royal family. As a community service, the society went out after predators in villages and suburbs, "with dogged determination, always committed to using the hunt to satisfy the needs of our fatherland."[28]

---

[24] I. S. Turgenieff, *Annals of a Sportsman*, trans. F. P. Abbott (New York: Holt, 1885), 109. Holt saw the leisure rather than the politics, including this translation in its Leisure Hour Series.

[25] E. P. Thompson, *Whigs and Hunters: The Origins of the Black Act* (New York: Pantheon, 1975).

[26] Lindsey Hughes, *Russia in the Age of Peter the Great* (New Haven: Yale University Press, 1998), 374.

[27] Richard Wortman, *Scenarios of Power: Myth and Ceremony in Russian Monarchy*, vol. 2 (Princeton: Princeton University Press, 2000), 54–57.

[28] *Russkaia okhota*, no. 1 (1910): 9–11. Between 1862–1910 the society took care of 155 bears and 700 foxes that threatened local populations.

Revision of the gaming laws in the 1870s facilitated the acquisition of hunting licenses, increasing the number of active hunters. By the end of the 1870s Moscow boasted three hunting societies, whose primary purpose was to share resources and to organize excursions.[29] A hobby rather than a livelihood, hunting took members out of the city and back to nature, however briefly. The most prestigious of these clubs, measured by membership dues and royal sponsorship, was the Moscow Society of Lovers of the Hunt. The drive toward exclusivity had driven membership dues to a phenomenal 50 rubles by 1911, which did not discourage the two hundred who enjoyed the club's posh surroundings.[30] The hundreds of nationwide imitators had forced the elite to retreat.

Many private societies published journals, joining readers in a national network, especially from the 1890s onward. These journals invited readers to submit personal adventure stories. The hunters' correspondence drew vivid images of the massive and kaleidoscopic empire: they chased bears in Siberia, tigers in Turkestan, as well as deer and other less exotic game through the European provinces. Descriptions of wolf hunts could thrill readers anxious to escape the monotony of the city, although enough stories detailing confrontations with wolves in city streets and at railroad stations suggest that industrialization was proceeding too rapidly for nature to keep pace. Active hunters presumably comprised the largest segment of readers, but those who stalked prey only in their imaginations could also find vicarious enjoyment. As one measure of the tempo of industrialization, by 1910 wolf hunts had become spectator sports, moved indoors to the hippodrome.[31]

Impressive technological developments allowed the hunt to keep in step with industry, and affordable firearms proved pivotal to democratizing the hunt. Determined to learn from the disastrous Crimean War, Minister of War Dmitrii Miliutin went shopping abroad and found faster, lighter, and ultimately cheaper rifles, especially in the United States where the recently fought Civil War had proved a boon to weaponry.[32] The economical guns spread briskly from the military into civilian life. Journal advertisements for sporting arms communicated the advancements: in 1879 *Nasha okhota* (Our hunt) sold rifles made in Paris; three years later they could be ordered from St. Petersburg, at the cost of seventy-five rubles each. That price had dropped to just under nine rubles by 1905. The professional journals greatly facilitated the commercialization of the new sport by

---

[29] "Okhota: K iubileiu Mosk. obshchestva liubitelei okhoty," *K sportu!* no. 1 (1914): 4.
[30] Ibid.
[31] "Sadki na volkov," *Russkaia okhota*, no. 1 (1910): 8.
[32] Joseph Bradley, *Guns for the Tsar: American Technology and the Small Arms Industry in Nineteenth-Century Russia* (De Kalb: Northern Illinois University Press, 1990).

84

negotiating special prices with equipment manufacturers for their sub-scribers.[33]

Like Turgenev's protagonist, the new hunters still depended on help from the local peasant population to negotiate their way through unfa-miliar terrain. In many of the true adventure stories, the author-hunters demonstrate the social boundaries that continued to separate them from their guides by using the familiar form of *ty* to address peasants, whereas the latter spoke back to them in the polite *vy* form. One hunter bragged that he had never lost either a dog or a guide to bears, recalling that cer-tain images from the prereform days continued to linger.[34] Others appre-ciated the increased professionalization of their guides, who returned the respect for genuinely skilled hunters.[35] Moreover, the shrewd peas-antry quickly adapted the new rules to their local economy. As one jour-nalist wrote, peasants had created a new cottage industry by blackmailing hunters with threats of false accusations to authorities in order to cover up their own poaching.[36] A British hunter out for Russian bear in the 1880s described peasants trapping quarry and then selling the right to shoot it, priced at a rate of rubles per pood (36 lbs.).[37]

Modern hunting did not so much inspire an egalitarian camaraderie be-tween hunter and guide as it introduced a new medium for negotiating their relationship: money. More than fifty years after *Annals of a Sportsman,* when merchant millionaire Pavel Riabushinskii retained several peasant villages to help him in (successful) pursuit of bear, he embodied the role of the moneyed economy in the sport.[38] One of Moscow's leading citizens, Riabushinskii spent the considerable sum he could afford in order to bag his impressive trophies.[39] His peasant guides were wage earners, several earning better than twenty rubles each.[40]

Industrialization pushed ecological concerns to the top of the hunters' agenda. S. A. Ozerov, who wrote under the pseudonym "Old Bachelor," epitomized the post-Turgenev literature of the hunt by focusing on poach-

[33] *Privolzhskii vestnik okhoty,* no. 19 (1890–91): 292.

[34] A. N. Lialin, "Okhota na medvedia po nasty," *Nasha okhota,* no. 4 (1907): 16.

[35] See, for example, A. Aleksandrov, "Na komel'skikh ozerakh," *Priroda i okhota* 2 (1898): 71; and "Na glukharinom toku," *Nasha okhota,* no. 1 (1907): 20.

[36] Editorial in *Privolzhskii vestnik okhoty,* no. 11 (1892): 3.

[37] John F. Baddeley, *Russia in the "Eighties": Sport and Politics* (London: Longmans, Green, 1921), 102.

[38] The archive for P. P. Riabushinskii is maintained in the Manuscript Division of the Rus-sian State Library (RGB), f. 260, karton 1, delo 35, contains bills for his hunt from 1915; he and his brother Sergei split the 252-ruble cost.

[39] RGB, f. 260, karton 7, ed. khran. 1, contains photos of the hunters with their kills. In one picture Riabushinskii is standing with others from his hunt party over the remains of five large brown bears.

[40] RGB, f. 260, karton 1, delo 35, l. 2.

ing and the spoliation of the Russian land. Rapid industrialization put nature under attack, just as the steadily increasing number of hunters had begun to deplete the quarry. "Old Bachelor" dated the decline from the 1870s, when he remembered fields still teeming with game. For him, peasant poaching did not pose as serious a danger, but the careless, unseasoned hunters out of ignorance killed mothers and babies in early spring.[41] In 1909 an interministerial committee produced new hunting regulations that spelled out everything from minimum age of hunters to type of dogs permissible during the various seasons.[42] Standard licenses cost five rubles, but those who wanted to pursue something more exotic, such as swans, could do so for forty rubles.[43] In addition, foreigners had to pay double what the Russians paid.[44] The Russian bear, a prized trophy, warranted the considerable expense.[45] Guidebooks for Europeans traveling to Russia indicate that hunting was becoming a significant tourist attraction.[46]

Hunters asserted their political consciousness during the 1905 Revolution. A special edition of the journal *Psovaia i ruzheinaia okhota* (The chase and the shoot) published that December encouraged hunters to learn from the "tactics, energy, and camaraderie" the revolutionaries had shown. The official organ of the Moscow Hunt Society, this journal also represented thirty smaller such clubs scattered throughout the empire. The editors implored their audience to protest hunting laws that discriminated in favor of the wealthy. They also wanted to boycott stores that charged "ungodly prices." Like the self-styled *intelligentsia,* hunters now fashioned their own estate (*soslovie*). Based on avocation rather than birth, the journal's editors included peasants by asking, "Who is closer to the peasant than his brother-hunter"? However, editors fell short of supporting unified action because they feared the loss of new freedoms, especially those relative to the hunt.[47]

The violence of the revolution combined with improved technology raised questions about gun ownership. The increasing affordability of firearms generated a new debate: the cheap guns not only depleted game because they allowed so many nonprofessionals in the field, but they also

[41] A. N. Savel'ev's obituary of S. A. Ozerov, in *Psovaia i ruzheinaia okhota,* no. 3 (1904): 51–53.

[42] The "Proekt pravil ob okhote" ("Draft rules for hunting") were published in *Nasha okhota* (May 1909): 31–58.

[43] "Proekt pravil ob okhote," statute 9.

[44] Ibid.

[45] Baddeley, *Russia in the "Eighties",* 153–58, describes some bear-hunting adventures with excited but unskilled comrades.

[46] See the *Handbook for Travelers in Russia, Poland, and Finland, including the Crimea, Caucasus, Siberia, and Central Asia,* 4th ed. (London: John Murray, 1888); and Karl Baedeker, *Russia with Teheran, Port Arthur, and Peking: Handbook for Travelers* (Leipzig: Karl Baedeker, 1914; New York: Charles Scribner's, 1914), xlii.

[47] *Psovaia i ruzheinaia okhota,* special issue (December 1905): 534–35.

made handguns more readily available in the city streets. Fearful of those who used "self-defense" as a justification to loosen restrictions on gun ownership, in 1911 the editors of *Nasha okhota* demanded gun control legislation that would check handguns, but not sporting rifles.[48] On the eve of World War I, though, this journal was advertising guns at "prices affordable for everyone!" and "pistols for defense from attacks," which could be obtained without a license.[49] Russians themselves had become fair game on the city streets. Acclaimed hunter S. A. Buturlin modulated this imminent threat with his *Hunting with a Camera* in 1912, suggesting that "hunt" no longer be equated with "kill."

Thus did technological change combine with attitudinal change to create a leisure-time activity in which having fun had perceptible political effects. If lord and peasant were not yet brothers at the hunt, the sport drew its participants from all rungs of the social ladder. As members of a self-styled *soslovie*, hunters found identity in retreat from the industrial city. Significantly, though, this retreat was intended to be only fleeting, because these sportsmen had no inclination to escape from the future.

The Athletic Professorate and Physical Education

Hard work, whether on the factory floor or sitting in a stuffy office, debilitated the body. The connection between physical and mental health resulted in the "physical culture" movement of the late nineteenth century, which moved east into Russia especially from Germany. Because the ideas that underlay this movement were reputedly scientific, its champions were tenured as "professors" of athletics, in Russia as elsewhere. Three such professors dominate the history of Russian sports: Count G. I. Ribop'er, Dr. V. F. Kraevskii, and I. V. Lebedev. Their backgrounds could have scarcely been more dissimilar, but their paths crossed at the formative point of organized athletics. Most important, collectively they represented athletics as an individual effort, something worth doing for the self rather than the glory of the competition. Their efforts resulted in the emergence of a widespread cult of the body, which by 1914 had reached into the public school system.

Ribop'er made his mark first. Born into extreme wealth in 1854, from a family with ties to Prince Grigorii Potemkin, the boy grew up in Italy. At age twelve he began studying gymnastics, from which he moved into all kinds of sports: "wherever there was a competition, that's where the count

---

[48] *Nasha okhota*, no. 17 (1911): 1–2.
[49] This is based on reading ads in *Nasha okhota* at various times during the journal's run. The pistol "Trevoga" (Alarm) was advertised as available for purchase "*without a license*" (emphasis in original).

would be." At fifteen, he answered a wrestler's challenge in a circus—and lost. When adulthood forced him into a profession, he chose a guards regiment and was seriously wounded in the Russo-Turkish War. The loss of agility caused by his infirmity inspired him to develop equestrian skills, and he founded a stable on the family estate in Kharkov. He also organized the Society for the Lovers of Purebred Hounds. After meeting Kraevskii around 1890, however, the elitist sportsman became one of the most influential in democratizing the physical culture movement in Russia.[50]

Vladislav Frantsevich Kraevskii, a Petersburg doctor, had met Berlin weightlifter Charles Ernst in the 1880s and begun working out with him. Intrigued by Europe's fad for physical health,[51] the Warsaw-born Kraevskii toured Austria and Germany for ideas about opening his own gym, which he did in his apartment in 1885. Lebedev considered this the "birth of Russian athletics," because Kraevskii took sports that had previously been considered no more than circus acts and turned them into cultured activities. Opening the doors of his gym to men of all social estates, he papered the walls of his gym with the photos of all who trained with him.

To emphasize the educational aspects, Kraevskii gave diplomas to those who finished his courses. He and his followers formed the Petersburg Circle of Amateur Athletes and sponsored the first national bodybuilding competition in 1895. Much more than sweaty bodies were on display: the program included an intriguing tableau vivant: "The German Girl Defending Herself from an Attack by Roman Soldiers." The entertainment aspect was part of the charter, which by authorizing amateur theatricals kept these societies open to various forms of leisure.[52]

In 1896 Kraevskii's circle expanded to become the Petersburg Athletic Society, which elected Ribop'er its chair. When the organized bicyclists joined with them two years later, the society could boast three hundred members and was forced to move its annual competition to a larger space offered by the manège. The list of Kraevskii's alumni included, among others, several of Russia's internationally competitive wrestlers: Ivan Shemiakin, Georg Gakkenshmidt, and V. A. Pytlianskii.[53] In sad irony, in 1900 Kraevskii slipped on the ice on the Anichkov Bridge, breaking his leg so badly that not even his lifelong commitment to health allowed him to survive the accident.[54]

[50] I. V. Lebedev wrote this short but adulatory biography of the count-athlete. *Illiustrirovannyi zhurnal atletika i sport,* no. 3 (1905): 48–50.

[51] By 1914 an estimated 4 percent of all Germans belonged to athletic clubs, a figure that acquires comparative significance when one considers that it refers to a much larger contingent of urban males. Peter Fritzsche, *Reading Berlin 1900* (Cambridge, Mass.: Harvard University Press, 1996), 80.

[52] *Ustav S-Peterburgskogo kruzhka liubitelei sporta* (St. Petersburg: S. L. Kind, 1896), 6.

[53] I. V. Lebedev, *Russkie silachi* (Moscow: P. P. Riabushinskii, 1910).

[54] I. V. Lebedev, "Vospominaniia o doktore V. F. Kraevskom," *Illiustrirovannyi zhurnal atletika i sport,* nos. 1–2 (1905): 10–15.

Count G. I. Ribop′er, amateur sportsman extraordinaire

Of the three, Lebedev survived longest in historical memory, largely because he guided wrestling into the Soviet era. He was the strongman, the wrestler who in the pre-Kraevskii generation would have continued much as he had begun, touring with a circus and wrestling for kopecks with volunteers from the audience. Instead, he helped to turn wrestling into the most popular and profitable sport after horse racing. Born in Petersburg in 1879, he graduated from Gymnasium No. 3 in 1898, where he excelled in sports. In his fuzzy autobiography, Lebedev recorded that he joined the law faculty at St. Petersburg University, but dropped out to become a professional wrestler. Though often referred to as the "Professor of Athletics," it is not clear whether he gave himself that nickname to show off his schooling, or whether, as he claimed, the crowds called him that because of his skill. He achieved his greatest fame as "Uncle Vania," wrestling's foremost impresario.[55]

Where Ribop'er was the rich boy who conferred social prestige, and Kraevskii the scholar who gave the scientific imprimatur of his medical degree, Lebedev was the entrepreneur who popularized the notion that athletic activity was beneficial for every individual, regardless of background or even gender. He taught bodybuilding through correspondence courses, contributed news and fiction to a variety of sports-oriented journals, and wrote a history of wrestling. From 1905 onward, he sat on the editorial board of *Illiustrirovannyi zhurnal atletika i sport,* the official organ of Tsarskoe Selo's Amateur Athletic Society. Among the first to promote Russian participation in the modern Olympics, later in his career he organized physical education at the St. Petersburg Military Academy and at the Forestry and Polytechnic Institutes.[56]

As "Uncle Vania," Lebedev combined the primitive appeal of the village strongman with the new interest in individualized bodybuilding. Tapping into what was initially a class-based phenomenon, he turned it into a highly successful commercial spectator sport. Significantly, he stressed athleticism rather than the brutality that had previously characterized this competition. The tsarist government held onto its class-based prejudices and prohibited professional wrestling until 1894 because it feared the explosive effects the matches might have on its presumed lower-class audience.[57] Under Lebedev's experienced hand, wrestling in Russia paralleled the path of athletic respectability and mass popularity it was taking in the West. Because wrestling, more than any other leisure-time activity, influenced changing notions of masculinity, it is discussed further in chapter 4. But it

[55] I. V. Lebedev, *Bortsy* (Petrograd: Gerkules, 1917), 2–3.

[56] Lebedev, *Russkie silachi,* 10. See also his article in *Tsiklist,* no. 160 (1897): 1; and no. 20 (1898): 11.

[57] I. V. Lebedev, *Istoriia professional'noi frantsuskoi bor'by* (Moscow: Tea-Kino-Pechat', n.d.), 31.

I. V. Lebedev, better known to legions of wrestling fans as "Uncle Vania"

was Lebedev's clear vision of new perspectives on the athletic body that made wrestling a spectator sport of such cultural impact.

"Wrestling as theater" became reversed into theater about wrestling in the 1907 play *The Professor of Athletics,* a dramatization of the extent to which organized physical exercise had become normalized. The title character runs workout classes for men and women of varying ages and is trying to sell the government on legislation to make exercise mandatory in public schools. Like Lebedev, he has written an inexpensive booklet *On Physical Development* for people to train at home. Selling hard the medical-scientific discourse about healthy bodies, the play also consistently contrasts the weakness of Russian bodies to the athletic prowess of the Germans and the British.[58] Though not performed on the serious stage, the play had many venues to reach an audience interested in these issues.

In the play the tsarist government approves the desired legislation, an exaggeration of official Russia's commitment to sports as a national issue. The empire's poor showing in the Russo-Japanese War in 1904 joined the Ministries of War and Education in common cause in support of gymnastics/athletics as a part of the national school curriculum. Subsequently, Nicholas II appointed Major General Voevikov as national director of the Committee on Physical Development, an oversight group that monitored the expansion of the professorate's activities. In Petersburg, for example, Professor Lesgaft stressed physical health in an "educational society (that) attracts more and more children every year."[59] Two physicians were instrumental in organizing football clubs in Moscow after 1896.[60] Others sought to move sports into the schoolyard where they could connect the healthy body to the healthy mind, condemning the ill effects of hard benches, stuffy classrooms, and "the harsh gaze of the overseer."[61] Educators argued that extracurricular competitions could be used to teach individual issues of personal safety, such as swimming and lifesaving.[62]

Enthusiasm for sports of all kinds fueled the growth of amateur athletic societies, fully chartered by the Ministry of Internal Affairs. The societies arose in the major urban areas in the 1890s, spread across the empire, and virtually exploded after the 1905 Revolution, when many Russians felt newly empowered. These societies served two significant purposes: first, in addition to disseminating information about athletics of all sorts, they offered opportunities for participation across a broad social spectrum; and second, they pulled Russians into structured organizations, with regulations, dues, possibilities for management, and competitions within the group

[58] A. Bakhmetev, "Professor atletiki: stseny iz zhizni shkoly fizicheskogo razvitiia v trekh deistviiakh" (St. Petersburg: Gorodskaia tipografiia, 1907).

[59] *Gerkules,* no. 6 (1913): 12.

[60] B. A. Pirogov, *Futbol: Khronika, sobytiia, fakty* (Moscow: Sovetskii sport, 1995), 7.

[61] *Sport,* no. 3 (1913): 1–2.

[62] "Prazdnik plavtsov v Shuvalovskoi shkole," *Ves' mir,* no. 25 (1914): 27.

and against similar societies. These amateur societies pulled thousands of Russians into the public sphere taking shape around them.

It seems more than simple coincidence that the 1890s marked the rapid escalation of both industrialization and club membership. If some of the nobility felt displaced by the new money, those who had it needed a forum to display their status. Potential club members enjoyed more free time and disposable income, and what better way to gain a sense of self than through association with like-minded individuals? The potential benefits of networking suggested a profitable return on investment in athletic clubs.

Although virtually all club charters declared themselves open to members of all social estates, in the absence of membership lists it is impossible to gauge just how well they succeeded. Those hopeful of joining clubs usually depended on recommendations from members, which one critic pointed out was inherently limiting. He also worried that only people already friendly with one another would join in the outings.[63] The smaller clubs could not afford a permanent residence and therefore had to rent halls for dances and other events, but these extra-athletic activities increased the numbers of participants in club activities. Though most clubs had predominantly male membership, women enjoyed the social occasions.

One of the first clubs, the Petersburg Athletic Circle, organized in 1895 and officially chartered two years later, articulated its goal as "the promotion of physical exercises beneficial for the development of the body and for the improvement of health among youth." The elected board organized both outings and seasonal competitions in a range of both individual and group sports, from shot put to bicycling. Unlike most clubs that succeeded this one, women were not allowed to join. The exclusivity came from most charters' rule that applicants required nomination by another member and approval by the majority.[64]

The Petersburg Athletic Circle initially focused on sponsoring contests, but according to its own records its members showed a greater inclination to sign up for excursions than to compete with one another.[65] Although it cost only three rubles per annum, its membership list read like the social register, including two sets of notable brothers: the ubiquitous Boris Suvorin and his older sibling Aleksei, and P. F. and N. F. Sumarokov-El'ston, titled nobility and tennis aces of international quality. Two of the era's major middlebrow writers also joined, the prolific A. V. Amfiteatrov and A. A. Pleshcheev. Whatever the discrepancy between ambitions and reach, the circle provided an organizational model that took athletics out of the privacy of Kraevskii's gym and into the public sphere.

[63] "O pomeshcheniiakh dlia obshchestv," *Velosipednyi sport*, no. 1 (1895): 2–4.
[64] *Pamiatnyi listok S-Peterburgskogo kruzhka sportsmenov* (St. Petersburg: Suvorin, 1900).
[65] Ibid., 7.

The Moscow Society for the Promotion of Physical Development, chartered in 1896, was less socially selective. Not only did it admit both sexes, it made education its central objective. In addition to its goal of "helping parents and educators gain practice in the proper physical training appropriate for young people," the society sponsored lectures, published brochures, and conducted courses in physical education that conferred certification upon completion. It also arranged competitions among students and excursions for members to enjoy the fresh country air.[66]

Founded in Petersburg in 1904, the Bogatyr Society for Physical Education became one of the most influential because it spread its reach well beyond the dues-paying membership. The inspiration behind this society, K. G. Alekseev, had abandoned a military career in the 1890s to devote himself to the physical education of schoolchildren. In 1900 he opened a school specifically devoted to physical education, collecting funding from others who shared his ideas.[67] By 1906 Bogatyr had seven locales around the city where children of assorted ages could train in various sports. Moreover, its directors organized biannual holidays for kindergartens to publicize the significance of organized exercise from the earliest possible age.[68] Almost more a charity than a club, the society funded its activities at best minimally through its three rubles per annum membership fees; the directors raised considerable donations through solicitations and sponsoring events, such as educational lectures, to which it charged admissions.[69] Moving against the tides of exclusivity, for twenty kopecks nonmembers could participate. The membership roll was a Who's Who: painter Ilya Repin, writer Aleksei Tolstoy, Count P. S. Sheremetev, a handful of princes and princesses (although none of the Romanovs), A. F. Koni's widow, and theatrical entrepreneur P. B. Pal'm.[70] Targeting the physically rather than financially weak, Bogatyr infused the healthy body movement into the school system with the money, prestige, and organization that could command attention from the top. With filial branches in other cities, Bogatyr organized playgrounds for children at least through 1914.[71]

The majority of amateur athletic societies were pale but competent imitators of the Petersburg Circle. As a general rule, their charters permitted

[66] *Ustav Moskovskogo obshchestva sodeistviia fizicheskomu razvitiiu* (Moscow: E. Lissner and Iu. Roman, 1896).

[67] Alekseev's obituary was published in *"Bogatyr," Obshchestvo telesnogo vospitaniia: Otchet za 1906* (St. Petersburg: Suvorin, 1907), 7–18.

[68] Ibid., 42.

[69] The lectures included such civic-minded topics as "A Women's University" and physical education in Japan, and its possible association with the Russian loss in the recent war. *"Bogatyr," Obshchestvo telesnogo vospitaniia: Otchet za 1907* (St. Petersburg: Vladimirskaia, 1910), 6. The financial report is in ibid., 50–53.

[70] Ibid., 79–91.

[71] See, for example, *Ustav Ekaterinodarskogo otdeleniia obshchestva telesnogo vospitaniia "Bogatyr"* (Ekaterinodar: Pechatnik, 1910). *Ves' mir,* no. 25 (1914): 29.

them to arrange dances, educational lectures, and excursions in addition to the athletic training. Consistently, the primary goal was "to facilitate the development of the various sports."[72] The Sparta Club organized in Petersburg in 1908 went beyond sports alone and organized its male-only members for "moral, intellectual, and physical development."[73] The cultivation of a specific kind of identity became problematic for revolutionaries when factories began establishing their own athletic societies. Designed to instill loyalty to the institution, factory clubs were criticized for undermining others' attempts to unionize along the broader axes of class and skill.[74] But the healthy body/healthy mind movement was national in scope, aiming for individual achievements among all Russians.

Yachts and Bicycles: Transportation and Sports

Just as horse racing grew out of military imperatives, and then turned into a socially prestigious enterprise because it offered access to royal circles, so too did yacht clubs originate in exclusion before being appropriated by the middle classes. The Imperial Yacht Club provided the prototype for this. Founded by Nicholas I in 1846, the club initially combined military with social objectives. The tsar sponsored sailing competitions that attracted foreign yachts. After the Crimean War depleted its coffers, though, the government had to turn it over to private initiative. Established in 1858, what became the Nevskii Yacht Club in 1892 underwent several name changes and reorganizations. Open to people "of various means and various social stations," the club's objective was "the encouragement of all sorts of water sports." This ultimately led to a fracturing into other clubs devoted to sailing and rowing. The entry of new clubs into the social scene sent the directors of the Nevskii Club to curry sponsorship from the royal family to ensure exclusivity. Alexander III's daughter Ksenia lent it her name, and the fifty-ruble membership fee eliminated many hopefuls. Prince Felix Iusupov, one of the clique who assassinated Rasputin in 1917, was a charter member.[75]

The significance of the Nevskii Club was not so much its membership, or even the upscale international races in which its flags flew, but rather that it represented the pinnacle of a fundamentally new type of organization, one that encouraged identification through a specific form of group

[72] This quote is taken verbatim from half a dozen charters, from various cities.

[73] *Ustav korporatsiia "Sparta"* (St. Petersburg: Iu. A. Mansfel'd, 1908).

[74] Steven Riess, *City Games: The Evolution of American Urban Society and the Rise of Sports* (Urbana: University of Illinois Press, 1991), 83, discusses teams and unions. B. Chesnokov, "Sport v staroi Moskve," *Fizkul'tura i sport*, no. 9 (1947): 12, suggests that football diverted workers from developing a political consciousness.

[75] *Nevskii iakht klub* (St. Petersburg: Isidor Gol'dberg, 1897), 1–5, 45.

membership. Like the hunt club that had sought a royal protector, the yacht club had to find ways of keeping people *out* in order to maximize the prestige of those it allowed *in*. The flattery inherent in imitation surfaced in the numerous nonimperial yacht clubs that sprang up around the empire. Moscow and other major cities that had no ocean ports nonetheless opened yacht clubs for river sailors, which then encouraged the growth of other water sports. By 1892 the empire had an estimated twenty-two registered rowing clubs in riparian cities, especially along the Volga.[76]

Democratization had its downside, however, and it was small wonder that the upper crust wanted some distance from its emulators. The Petrovskii Yacht Club, for example, brought its members together to gamble at cards rather than to set sail. News of its activities appeared on the police blotter rather than in the social columns. Although the yacht club named for Grand Duchess Ksenia undoubtedly witnessed its share of late night games where fortunes moved around the table, its restrictive membership limited the numbers of acid-throwing women and gigolos who joined the crosstown rival.[77] Yet the Petrovskii Yacht Club reflected just as sharply as its noble predecessor the opening of an uncommonly *public* space.

The yacht clubs that remained devoted primarily to water sports crossed membership roles with those devoted to the new land-based activity of riding bicycles. Like boats, bicycles were media of transportation with multiple uses, including competitive racing. A journal published for these combined sports estimated forty yachting and cycling clubs in Russia in 1892.[78] Bicycles had been known in Russia since their invention in 1866, but not until the appearance of the safety bike in the 1880s, with its equal-sized wheels, gears, and braking system could they function as a comparatively inexpensive form of transportation.[79] The Moscow Bicycle Club, founded in 1888, soon had branches or imitators in all the major cities—in all, seventeen clubs by 1892, plus two more in Moscow.[80] By 1897 its Petersburg counterpart boasted five hundred members.[81] The bicycle craze reflected the aspirations for mobility that urbanization was encouraging; for example, two of Petersburg's suburbs, Tsarskoe Selo and Strel'na, had bicycle clubs.

Bicycles served two goals of leisure: exercise and competition. They car-

---

[76] *Velosipedist i rechnoi iakht-klub*, no. 1 (1892): 2.

[77] *Azart*, no. 4 (April 2, 1906): 43. Police raids at the Petrovskii Yacht Club appear frequently in this journal, devoted to gambling.

[78] *Velosipednist i rechnoi iakht-klub*, no. 1 (1892): 1.

[79] Robert A. Smith, *A Social History of the Bicycle: Its Early Life and Times in America* (New York: American Heritage Press, 1972), chapter 1.

[80] The first bicyclist appeared on the streets of Moscow in 1882. Moscow's three tracks were located in Khodynka Field, Sokol'niki, and at the manège. *Fizkul'tura i sport*, no. 9 (1947): 13.

[81] *Tsiklist*, no. 1 (1897): 2.

The demimonde's Petrovskii Yacht Club

ried their owners outside the city on fresh-air excursions, or to the local cy-clodromes where the high-spirited could compete with each other while spectators looked on. During the summer, bicycles conveyed people back and forth between workplace and dacha. In the 1890s Russians joined in the fad for contests that today would be characterized as "extreme" sports in pursuit of speed or distance records.[82] Sergei Utochkin, a preeminent Russian sportsman well known for his careers in wrestling and aviation, be-

[82] Michael Kimmel discusses the analogous "bicycle boom of the 1890s" in the United States. "The Contemporary 'Crisis' of Masculinity in Historical Perspective," in *The Making of Masculinities: The New Men's Studies,* ed. Harry Brod (Boston: Allen and Unwin, 1987), 139. See also Smith, *Social History of the Bicycle,* chapter 6.

Contestants in the Moscow-to-Petersburg Race

gan his sporting life with competitive cycling, winning seventy-seven first prizes in 1895, his first year.[83] The misadventures of the English daredevil Robert Jefferson, determined to slog through the mud from Irkutsk to Moscow in 1896, for example, were faithfully reported in *Tsiklist* (The cyclist), the Moscow Club's official organ. The reportage on Jefferson along his arduous route showed the extent to which cycling had spread across the empire, as from one border to the next many fans rode beside him partway.[84]

Priced as low as one hundred rubles, cheaper for used ones, bicycles were affordable to the middle classes, including skilled and clerical workers. Requiring no special training or arena other than the city streets, bicycling had more commercial potential than many other sports, and by 1892 more than six thousand bicycles had been sold in Russia.[85] Because it was so fundamentally liberating, bicycling entered directly into numerous discourses of modernity. For example, it was popular among women and required the purchase of special clothing, such as bloomers, that would have implications for politics as well as fashion. Its detractors included the Orthodox Church, which disapproved of the undignified sight of clergy on bicycles.[86] Others feared that its speed and maneuverability

[83] *Velosipednyi sport,* no. 14 (1895): 252.

[84] The series of articles on Jefferson's journey, written by V. Raspolin, appeared throughout the spring issues of *Tsiklist* in 1896.

[85] *Velosipedist i rechnoi iakht-klub,* no. 1 (1892): 2.

[86] *Sport,* no. 2 (1897): 30 reprints an article from *Tserkovnyi vestnik.*

Moscow's Cyclodrome

would enkindle a crime wave, thieves peddling faster than their pursuers on foot.[87] Many were simply taken aback by the novelty, and the potential for movement it offered.[88]

Commercialism, however, would carry the bicycle forward. Manufacturers marketed their products by showing them off in races, just as the automobile companies would do later. The British Humber and Starley companies had bicycle factories in Russia, which competed with the na-

[87] *Sudebnaia drama,* no. 1 (1899).
[88] "Chto takoe velosiped?" *Velosiped,* nos. 31–32 (1892): 1.

99

tional Pobeda ("Victory") Company. Starley advertised a bicycle "produced especially for Russian roads," appropriately named the "Psycho."[89] Russia's first major race, sponsored by the Petersburg Society of Bicycle Riding, pitted cyclists against each other on the largely unpaved road from Petersburg to Moscow in 1895. Despite competitors from France, where bicycling was becoming the national pastime,[90] Russian Mikhail Dzevochko arrived first—in less than forty hours. The race was deemed so successful that a second race planned for 1896 would follow the return route, from Moscow to Petersburg.[91]

Tragedy struck one of the Russian entrants, I. N. Sheliaev, in the second race. He apparently rubbed his perineum raw on the bicycle's saddle. The race's organizers had anticipated the possibility of accident and provided for medical oversight. The doctor at the Novgorod base who attended him wanted to treat the wound, but Sheliaev insisted on continuing. Dzevochko won again, and the ill-starred Sheliaev's infected thigh turned gangrenous. After lingering for several days he died, and his death figured into various debates about the place of sports in general and cycling in particular in Russia.[92]

Sheliaev's death gave a new urgency to the issue of training. As several doctors pointed out, sports demanded psychological as well as physical energy, a strain that most people did not take into consideration when preparing to participate in an event.[93] Differences between amateurism and professionalism rose to the fore, especially over the issue of costs.[94] Lebedev, a member of the society that had sponsored the race, suggested that competitions no longer offer prize money, that cyclists should ride solely for the pure love of the sport and the moral and physical strength exercise provided. The business element won out, though, over the ideal of athletics for its own sake because "the most powerful Petersburg clubs, in terms of membership and quality of their competitors, came down on the side of monetary prizes."[95]

Bicycling represented commercialism in other ways that outstripped the profits from bike sales and contest money. The successful clubs published their own journals, subsidized by advertisements from bicycle manufacturers, and from local nightclub or theater owners targeting this audience, which was distinguished by its dynamism and willingness to dispose of its

---

[89] *Russkii turist*, no. 1 (1899): 2.

[90] In 1897 France already had more than a half million bicycles, which dwarfed Russian numbers. *Sport*, no. 1 (1897): 80.

[91] A report of the 1895 race appeared in *Tsiklist*, no. 22 (1896): 6.

[92] *Tsiklist*, no. 22 (1896): 7–13.

[93] *Tsiklist*, no. 21 (1889): 3 and no. 27 (1896): 2–3.

[94] Staryi Chempion, "Porazhenie amaterism," *Tsiklist*, no. 1 (1897): 2–3, and no. 137 (1897): 1–2.

[95] *Tsiklist*, no. 1 (1897): 2–3.

income.[96] The Cyclist Café opened in Moscow's Petrovskii Park in 1898, without alcoholic drinks on its menu. The Moscow Society charged membership dues of ten rubles per annum, and the money bought a considerable array of entertainments in addition to social exclusivity. Members' silver badges gained them entrance to ice-skating competitions, fencing lessons, and numerous social events, including cards, billiards, family picnics, amateur theater performances, and organized weekend excursions.[97]

One purpose of these clubs was to draw social lines, to separate members out from the crowd. When "hooligans" in the Strel'na district outside Petersburg threw rocks and clods of dirt in the direction of bike lanterns at night, they were not simply protecting their turf but defending it against a certain type of intruder. Female cyclists seemed to suffer singular abuse.[98] An illustration in *Tsiklist* of peasants tossing broken bottles onto the streets bespoke one element of class conflict.[99] A. G. Alekseev and P. A. Smirnov, scions of two of Moscow's most prominent merchant dynasties and both avid cyclists, showed off their bodybuilding skills as well when arrested for scuffling with some toughs who were harassing them and their friends.[100]

The Cyclist Café was near the race track at Khodynka Field, and newspapers reported the not infrequent skirmishes between the two groups of fans.[101] The first image to arise from these confrontations is one of class-based antagonisms: the more privileged cyclists zipping past gamblers stumbling home after a day's losses. But so reductive an evaluation glosses over the reality that "class" was in the formative stage. One of the key attributes of sports was its ability to "level the playing field," that is, smooth over past social differences to even the competition. This purported social egalitarianism introduced a new basis for competing, physical and mental agility. The hooligans throwing rocks at the Smirnovs were venting frustrations at new kinds of social upheaval, unconscious of the ways in which they themselves often benefited from the changes.

The cycling craze faded after 1900, despite the fact that bicycle ownership was increasing steadily; by 1903 Petersburg had more than twenty-five thousand licensed cyclists riding the streets.[102] One observer blamed the decline of the sport on the stress on competition that was taking the fun

[96] The journal *Velosipednyi sport*, however, refused to accept ads from bicycle firms as a sign of its editorial independence.

[97] *Tsiklist*, no. 48 (1896): 19.

[98] *Tsiklist*, no. 26 (1896): 26.

[99] *Tsiklist*, no. 23 (1898): 1.

[100] *Tsiklist*, no. 191 (1897): 3. Alekseev was related to the mayor who had so vigorously opposed the totalizator. His lawyer secured all the young men's release.

[101] When a bicycling club opened in Riga in 1899, it had to share quarters with the local society for trotters, an indication of a shared track.

[102] *Tsiklist*, no. 10 (1903): 7. In Moscow at this time, the provincial government fought the city duma to force bicyclists to take licensing exams. *Russkii turist*, no. 4 (1904): 93–96.

out of cycling.[103] But bicycles were losing their sporting panache, becoming identified more mundanely as modes of transportation. Although no direct connection has been found between the constant editorials in the cycling press for improved roads and the subsequent paving of city streets, it is logical to assume that the growth in numbers of bicycles reflected better roadways. Some bicycling clubs became absorbed by touring societies, which used their advantage of moderately priced transportation for brief excursions.[104]

Football: The Team and the Factory

Team sports parallel factory production by bringing the group together and sorting members out along a hierarchy, and the efficacy of the whole depends upon the proper fulfillment of each particular task.[105] Russians enjoyed group activities before the 1880s, such as the ball-and-stick game purported to be the antecedent of baseball, but they lacked the kinds of highly regulated team sports that characterize the modern era. The first such team came to Russia by way of England. In order to industrialize rapidly, many Russian manufacturers had to hire skilled engineers and managers from western countries.[106] The British men on temporary assignment in Petersburg brought a favorite leisure-time activity with them, football. Initially they played among themselves, with no larger ambition of re-creating the shop floor on the playing field in evidence. Their actions sparked sufficient interest for many Russians to want to join in the fun. The first reported match took place in Petersburg in 1879 between the British teams at the Sampsonievskii and the Nevskii manufactories. It took almost another twenty years for Russians to participate in championship competitions; the game between the Vasileostrovskii Circle of Football Players and the Petersburg Amateur Circle in 1897 is recorded in history as the inaugural Russian match. Both teams included British players alongside Russians, and the Vasileostrovskii team won handily, 6 : 0.[107]

In the next year's rematch, the Amateur Circle pulled an upset, 4 : 3. Despite growing Russian interest, the British still dominated the sport. The

[103] "Smert' ili spiachka?" *Sportivnaia zhizn'*, no. 11 (1911): 5–8. The author queried, had the sport died, or was it merely sleeping?

[104] For example, Petersburg's principal cycling club, founded in 1895, was named the Peterburg Society of Bicyclists-Tourists and published a journal, *Velosiped* (The bicyclist). In 1899 it changed the journal's title to *Russkii turist* (The Russian tourist) and in 1903 rebaptized itself the Russian Society of Tourists.

[105] Steven Riess, *Touching Base: Professional Baseball and American Culture in the Progressive Era* (Westport, Conn.: Greenwood, 1980), 226–28.

[106] See, for example, John McKay, *Pioneers for Profit: Foreign Entrepreneurship and Russian Industrialization, 1885–1913* (Chicago: University of Chicago Press, 1970), especially chapter 5.

[107] Pirogov, *Futbol*, 3–4.

"Playing the game"

three teams that formed Petersburg's first football league, Victoria, Nevskii, and Nevka had all been organized by foreign employees, and the Englishman Thomas Aspden sponsored the trophy from 1901 onward.[108] When the all-Russian teams ventured out against the league, they were trounced.[109] If these losses are to be read as metaphors for Russia's relative industrial backwardness, then improvements could be anticipated around 1907. Sure enough, a Russian team took home the Aspden Cup in 1908.[110]

Football in Moscow had the same origins. The first reported match took place in 1895, played by the English employees of the Hopper factory. Within a year Drs. Dement'ev and Pokrovskii of the hygiene society organized a football club in hopes of marketing the game as a form of healthy outdoor exercise, but for at least a decade this sport remained based at British-managed factories.[111] The four Charnock brothers, two of whom worked at the Morozov Textile Factory in Orekhovo-Zuev and the other two at the Konshin Factory in Serpukhov, collectively captained Moscow's

[108] Victor Peppard, "The Beginnings of Russian Soccer," *Stadion* 8–9 (1982–83): 156. I thank Bob Edelman for this citation.

[109] Ibid., 5. The first Russian team to compete for the Aspden Cup in 1902 lost all games by a combined score of 3 : 23.

[110] Ibid., 6.

[111] Pirogov, *Futbol*, 6–7.

first teams and dominated in league play thereafter.[112] Working for two of Moscow's most progressive merchant families, through their British Sports Club they persuaded their Russian bosses to provide money and a playing field, thus beginning the boom that led to the formation of a league with regularly scheduled matches in 1909.[113]

Most soccer clubs differed from other amateur clubs in that they associated themselves with place, adopting the name of the factory or district they represented, often that of the nearest railroad station. Other clubs, such as the Mercury, used their name to relay an impression, just as the new movie houses going up all around were doing. The factory club at Orekhovo was referred to simply as the "Morozovtsy," and owner Savva Morozov, the eccentric industrialist best known for his contributions to revolutionary parties and subsidies of the Moscow Arts Theater, reputedly advertised in the British press for engineers and other workers who could also play football.[114] This became the team to beat.[115] By 1915 there were so many teams that they were divided into three leagues, ranked according to competitive skills.

Distinguished sports reporter and former football player Boris Chesnokov, writing from the Soviet perspective in 1947, recast the formative years of football in Moscow in the narrative of class conflict, the elitist Morozovtsy against the working-class team. This former editor of the popular journal *K sportu!* (Let the games begin!) took readers on a stroll down memory lane through a classic rendering of the underdog allegory. His team, named for the nearby Rogozhskii Station, was an "outlaw" (*dikii*) group, so called because it was not permitted into the league. Members, primarily clerks like himself, forsook breakfast and walked endless miles, saving their kopecks for equipment. The evil Charnock brothers, in contrast, eager to win at all costs, entertained referees at Moscow's fancy Metropole restaurant.[116] The Vasil'ev brothers, members of the Rogozhskii team, earned extra cash by delivering pails of water because their district did not yet have a sewage system. Their team practiced in muddy fields and cemeteries, using logs for goals. Members shared responsibility for the single precious ball, rubbing it nightly with fish oil. Their adroit play attracted many spectators, whom the cops chased away because of their suspicious social origins. Needless to say, when their talent finally se-

[112] Alfred Rieber, *Merchants and Entrepreneurs in Imperial Russia* (Chapel Hill: University of North Carolina Press, 1982), 210–11. Konshin was the brother-in-law of a dominant figure in the Moscow merchantry, P. M. Tretiakov.

[113] Al'bert Starodubtsev, "Pervye shagi," *Sport Ekspress* (October 1999): 38–40.

[114] Pirogov, *Futbol*, 7.

[115] P. A. Kanunnikov, "Pobeda 'dikikh,'" *Fizkul'tura i sport*, no. 12 (1936): 6; and Chesnokov, "Sport v staroi Moskve," 12–13. See also Pirigov, *Futbol*, chapter 1.

[116] B. M. Chesnokov, "Ot bor'by 'dikareu' s 'aristokratami' . . . K olimpiiskim pobedam," *Sportivnaia zhizn' Rossii*, no. 12 (1960): 11.

cured their admission to the league in 1914, they conquered the stunned Morozovtsy.[117]

Whatever the blatant Soviet spin to this version of Chesnokov's story, before 1917 he had used his editorial page as a pulpit for the democratization of soccer.[118] Moreover, the story would have been told essentially the same way in the United States, or in any industrializing country where grit must defeat privilege. The primary parable here is that of the group, because although the team depends on individual talents, it can achieve victory only when functioning as a unit. This facet has allowed team sports to provide so many common metaphors for modernity, and for war. Success of team sports also depends on fan support in a way that individual athletes do not. Fans develop affiliations with teams, investing the group with a part of their identity. Teams stand in for the collective; they have the capacity to bring strangers together on the basis of a hope that the group of athletes could do what fans could not do as individuals: win, prove their superiority. Fans show their identification by sporting team jerseys, team colors.[119]

Football became organized according to a basic desire for representation. The neighborhood teams eventually formed the leagues which then competed for the championship of the city; by 1911 thirteen teams competed for the Moscow title.[120] The wealthy jeweler R. F. Ful'd sponsored the trophy. The first championship of Odessa was played in 1911, although because of the strong international presence in this port city, football had been played there since the 1870s.[121] Kharkov and Kiev, two large Ukrainian cities, began a title competition in 1912.[122] Then universities and other institutes of higher education began forming teams and competing with one another.[123] Next came the dream of a national championship. In 1913 the All-Russian Football Union was formed, joining together almost four thousand athletes from 155 clubs in thirty-three cities.[124] When cities faced off against each other, the teams they fielded were composed of local all-stars, selected from among the best players. In 1913, a match-up between the two capitals attracted ten thousand fans.[125] This was twice the number of fans who watched the Chicago Cubs defeat the Detroit Tigers in the last game of the 1908 World Series.[126]

---

[117] Chesnokov, "Sport v staroi Moskve," 12–13.

[118] Peter Frykholm, "Soccer and Social Identity in Pre-Revolutionary Moscow," *Journal of Sport History* 24, no. 2 (1997): 147.

[119] Ibid., 148–49, discusses the fan identification with the prerevolutionary Russian teams.

[120] Pirogov, *Futbol*, 7.

[121] Ibid., 8–9.

[122] Ibid., 9.

[123] *Ves' mir*, no. 44 (1913): 26.

[124] *Fizkul'tura i sport*, no. 11 (1955): 1955.

[125] Pirogov, *Futbol*, 21.

[126] In 1908 only six thousand were in attendance to see the Cubs beat the Tigers in the World Series (http://www.sportingnews.com/archives/worldseries/1908.html).

The Petersburg team gets set to play Moscow for the national championship.

Next came international competitions, where again teams were formed from the cream of the players. Prerevolutionary Russia did not fare especially well against other European countries in football, not even against its semicolonized brothers in Finland. Czech employees had played for Odessa teams, and the matches between the Czech national team and the Petersburg All-Stars in 1910 prompted the first instance of advance ticket sales. The more than four thousand Russians who attended were disappointed by the 3 : 1 loss.[127] The German national champions from Kiel proved just as powerful against Moscow two years later in a game that attracted five thousand spectators.[128] Russian teams continued the quest to compete internationally, including an embarrassing performance at the 1912 Olympics, until war erupted in 1914. Their record against foreign teams that ranged from Oxford University (to whom they lost) and Turkey (whom they defeated) was seven victories, seven ties, and twenty-one losses. Despite the poor record of success, crowd interest continued to grow.[129]

The British factory managers in Russia did not simply enjoy a favorite pastime, they incorporated their Russian friends and workers into an activity with political implications. Through their national pastimes of football and cricket, the British attempted to re-create their colonies in the

[127] Pirogov, *Futbol,* 11; and *Obozrenie teatrov,* no. 1194 (1910): 16.
[128] *K sportu!* no. 1 (1912): 9.
[129] Pirogov, *Futbol,* 10–14, discusses Russia's bleak position in the world football market.

image of their ideals of fair play and competition, just as the United States exported baseball to the Central American neighbors it dominated through the Monroe Doctrine and to defeated Japan after World War II. The Russians, like the Indians and Japanese, made the imported sport their own, as when they defined football competitions according to issues of class and nationalism. Still, Russians should be eternally grateful that their British factory managers were not cricket enthusiasts.

Russia's Female Athletes

Although sports were overwhelmingly male, a few daring women also joined the competitive fray. Some sports, such as swimming (on separate beaches), tennis, and bicycling,[130] did not threaten principles of masculinity because they were oriented toward physical health. Hunting, on the other hand, was gendered aggressively male, and the penetration of women into this sport was a prime indicator of social change. At first, females appeared in the hunting literature as antagonists, shrews bent on keeping their men from realizing their true masculinity in the woods.[131] Sporadically, though, women began corresponding in the journals. A 1905 article by "Princess S. G." in *Psovaia i ruzheinaia okhota* offered a uniquely feminine angle: observing a skirmish between a wolf and an inexperienced hunter and his hounds, she felt thrilled by the bloody battle but ended with a mild reproof for giving into her "sadistic" instincts. It might have seemed unmanly for a male hunter to express the desire to conquer the beast within.[132]

A few professional female hunters began to lead expeditions and to bag such highly esteemed prey as bears. However, as the editors of *K sportu!* pointed out in 1912, male hunters were generally loathe to accord women the same respect as they did each other. The journal named several outstanding huntresses: Maria Grigor'evna Dmitrieva-Sulima, who led expeditions from the North Pole to Sakhalin Island and wrote several technical books; Lydia Mikhailovna Mazzurina, a noble Annie Oakley, who had proved herself one of the best shots in the Imperial Hunting Society; and Anna Adol'fovna Gil'bakh, who had killed six wolves on a two-week hunt and had proved equally impressive when out for bear.[133]

---

[130] By 1897 at least, women were permitted to ride bicycles anywhere in Petersburg. *Tsiklist*, no. 140 (1897): 3.

[131] See, for example, V. Pavlovskii, "O, zhenshchiny!" *Priroda i okhota*, no. 2 (1894): 78–90.

[132] S. G. Kniaginia, "Moe pervoe znakomstvo s volkami," *Psoviaia i ruzheinaia okhota* 9 (1905): 94–100.

[133] "Zhenshchina i okhota," *K sportu!* no. 56 (1912): 21–23.

Fears of excessive independence, or that women would sacrifice their femininity, raised deliberations about gender and identity.[134] But intrepid women drove in automobile races and flew, first in balloons and then airplanes, competing for the "Feminina Cup" in 1910.[135] Russia even boasted a record-setting female weightlifter, Marina Loore, and a female basketball team in 1914.[136] Leaders of the physical health movement actively supported female participation, some suggesting that women needed exercise even more than men.[137] The kind of modern "barefoot" dancing made popular by Isadora Duncan also encouraged women to develop grace and strength. The United States, a leader in industry as well as collecting Olympic medals, nonetheless long opposed female competition at the Olympics. The Russians had no fundamental philosophical problems with sportswomen, but gender equity was elusive.[138]

Russian Olympians: Sports Nationalism Goes International

The revival of the Olympic Games in Athens in 1896 pulled industrialized nations into competitions that effectively mirrored their respective levels of modernity. Initially, organizer Pierre de Coubertin faced international indifference. After Athens, the games moved to Paris four years later, where they were a featured attraction at the Exposition Universelle. In 1904, when the unfamiliar American city of St. Louis added the Olympics to its World's Fair, only 122 of the 554 athletes participating were not from the United States.[139]

Yet even as it appeared that the Olympics were being transformed into fairground entertainment, prescient observers were taking stock of the possibilities for athletes to symbolize the strength of the nation. Not surprisingly, the most industrialized countries—England, Germany, and the United States—recognized the potential first. The London hosts for the 1908 games built the first independent stadium devoted to the games, capable of seating seventy thousand spectators. The American tourist who described Russians in 1912 as "not a very athletic people" was speaking comparatively, and she conceded that in wrestling and football "they have

---

[134] "Zhenskii vopros," *Sportivnaia zhizn'*, no. 17 (1911): 1–8.

[135] *Sportivnaia zhizn'*, nos. 1–2 (1910): 78; and *Vozdukhoplavatel'*, no. 1 (1911): 39–47.

[136] *Ves' mir*, no. 25 (1919): 28.

[137] *Velosipednyi sport*, no. 1 (1895): 9–15. This includes several articles on the significance of cycling for women, even naming Russia's top female cyclists. See also *Sport*, no. 6 (1897): 80.

[138] A special issue of *K sportu!* (no. 56, 1912) celebrated, for example, the numerous accomplishments of Russia's female athletes, from gymnasts to bear hunters. Many, not surprisingly, came from the nobility, but by 1911 girls' schools were organizing football teams, too.

[139] Allen Guttmann, *The Olympics: A History of the Modern Games* (Urbana: University of Illinois Press, 1992), 25.

Tennis champion A. K. Tomilina

given a good account of themselves."[140] By the time of the 1912 Games in neighboring Stockholm, however, an increasing number of Russians recognized international athletic competition as a source of "great power" status. The disastrous showings in Sweden, a "sporting Tsushima" (in ref-

[140] Wood, *Tourist's Russia*, 41.

erence to the naval disaster in the war against Japan), sent home a powerful message of national inferiority.

Nationalism, despite Coubertin's original intentions to compete on the purity of athleticism alone, turned the key that made the Olympics so successful. Instead of being united by a shared physical consciousness, athletes found themselves divided by nationalist sentiments. Another of de Coubertin's misjudgments was that by insisting that only amateurs compete he would be able to separate gentlemen and scholar-athletes from their rough brothers who used their brawn to earn a livelihood.[141] A Greek patrician had blithely offered her hand to the winner of the marathon, but she tearfully reneged when a shepherd boy brought home the gold.[142] Native American Jim Thorpe stunned the crowds in Stockholm, only to have the official committee strip him of his medals when it learned that he had played baseball for money. The debate that pits the amateur against the professional, which still hovers over the games, keeps the Olympics at the heart of multiple discourses of modernity and its dependence on professionalization.

In 1896, however, the tsarist government could sense no return on an investment in athletes and sent none to the Games, despite a Russian member of the first International Olympic Committee (IOC).[143] Private initiative held sway in 1908 when several Russian amateur societies, who had been organizing and sponsoring competitions among themselves for years, put together a team and sent them to London. The Petersburg Athletic Circle sent four wrestlers, including a doctor and a student. Living conditions were abysmal and training facilities no better. Sleeping two to a bed in a dusty flat and working out in a dirty basement "on a carpet of dubious cleanliness," the wrestlers nonetheless acquitted themselves well; from a group of one hundred competitors, Russians Alexander Petrov and Nikolai Orlov picked up two second-place medals in wrestling.[144] Figure skater N. A. Panin took home tsarist Russia's single gold medal.[145]

Buoyed by this modest success, representatives of various amateur athletic societies met in Petersburg in 1910 and organized a National Olympic Committee (NOC), naming V. I. Sreznevskii, former president of the Petersburg Society of Amateur Cyclists, as chair. General Voevikov, national director of the Committee on Physical Development, also participated, as did Chesnokov, then editor of *K sportu!* Voevikov's business interests in

[141] In 1866, for example, the British refused amateur status in racing to "all those who made their living through manual labor." John J. MacAloon, *This Great Symbol: Pierre de Coubertin and the Origins of the Modern Olympic Games* (Chicago: University of Chicago Press, 1981), 166.

[142] Ibid., 234–35.

[143] General Butovskii reported indifference at home. Ibid., 199.

[144] D. V., "Londonskii olimpiad i russkie bortsy," *Gerkules*, no. 6 (1913): 2–6.

[145] F. Borisov, "Vospominaniia byloe," *Sportivnaia zhizn' Rossii*, no. 8 (1960): 18.

mineral water showed that he had a commercial stake in the health of the empire. Among the committee's more demanding tasks was to solicit partial funding from the government, although they had to underwrite most of the plans themselves.[146] Deciding on uniforms—straw hats decorated with nationalist ribbons—was easier than selecting representatives, because more athletes wanted to participate than could go. The Ministry of Internal Affairs helped by granting the NOC the authority to put together a team.[147] Moscow clubs, fearful of over-representation by their Petersburg rivals, threatened to boycott the selection unless their athletes were guaranteed adequate placement.[148] The two capitals hoped to resolve their differences through a football match, which ended presciently in a 2 : 2 tie.[149]

Most of the athletes sailed together on the *Burma,* a cargo vessel, with the idea that they could train on deck and stay in shape by helping the crew. They would also bunk on board during the games, as did the American team on their ship, the *Finland.* Tsar Nicholas II brought his children to the dock to see them off with royal good luck. Moreover, because the *Burma* had contractual obligations and had to lift anchor before all the athletes arrived—-tennis ace Count P. F. Sumarokov was one who missed the original sailing—Voevikov commandeered the imperial yacht *Strela* to get the latecomers out to the ship. The *Burma* sailed into Stockholm with high hopes, especially for tennis, fencing, and weightlifting.[150]

Wrestler Georg Bauman epitomized the turn of bad luck that plagued the team from the outset. Having bulked up before leaving Petersburg because he did not intend to eat on shipboard for fear of getting seasick, he found himself assigned to a higher weight class, where he could not compete effectively.[151] Russia's two tennis stars had to face each other first, thereby eliminating one immediately from competition. Sumarokov, the victor and early favorite, though, failed to win a medal. The imperial officer corps, which included Grand Duke Dmitrii Pavlovich, made a poor showing, winning only the bronzes in shooting and sailing. The football team was humiliated its loss to Germany, 16 : 0.

Scandinavian solidarity also proved problematic. The scorekeeping in the 1908 London Games had been sufficiently suspicious to cause the IOC to mandate that officials, too, be multinational, and now the Russians lodged complaints against "Swedish arithmetic."[152] And although Finland

---

[146] Ibid.

[147] "Olimpiiskie igry v Stokgol'me," *K sportu!* no. 23 (1912): 5.

[148] *K sportu!* no. 27 (1912): 3. The provincial clubs, despite the umbrella committee, found themselves virtually excluded from the Olympic team.

[149] Pirogov, *Futbol,* 15.

[150] *Gerkules,* no. 1 (1912): 2–6.

[151] *Gerkules,* no. 2 (1913): 6. In 1913, back at his normal fighting weight, Bauman won the world championship. Ian Dymov, *I druzhboi sil'ny bogatyri* (Kiev: Molod, 1983), 184.

[152] *K sportu!* no. 34 (1912): 1; and Borisov, "Vospominaniia byloe," 18.

was technically a part of the Russian empire, the Swedes allowed the Finns to march under their own flag and to compete independently, as the Irish had done at the London Games. The Russian football team considered it an affront to be matched up first against the Finns; especially galling was the Finnish victory, 2 : 1. Finnish wrestlers split the gold with the Swedes in this sport, and many Russians credited Finland's success to its greater national attention to physical development.[153] Had the Finns competed under the imperial flag, the Russians would not had to limp home with a miserable three medals and ranked thirteenth out of sixteen competing nations. Hardly a position for a "great power," as one sports editorial writer noted.[154]

Russians responded enthusiastically to the challenge. Boris Suvorin answered the call by sponsoring competitions in ice skating as well as football.[155] Two all-Russian Olympics were staged, the first in Kiev in 1913 and the second in Riga in 1914, to prepare for the Berlin Games projected for 1916. The outbreak of the Great War postponed the Olympiad and put the young men who should have been competing with each other for medals in deadly combat instead. But the war also stimulated interest in athletics, for the obvious reason that hard and aggressive bodies were needed at the front. Russians held another Olympiad in the provincial city of Yaroslavl in 1915. The organizers were cheered that fans came from all walks of national life and all social estates.[156]

The war effort intensified every aspect of sports. The number of clubs and amateur societies multiplied, and schoolchildren received more courses in physical education.[157] Schoolboys took the places of team mates called to the draft.[158] The athlete became a soldier, and vice versa, taking the civic consciousness that had been fundamental to organized athletics from the playing field to the battlefield. By 1917 it was clear that sports was changing the nation, while simultaneously the nation was changing sports.

[153] *K sportu!* no. 34 (1912): 7, and no. 44 (1912): 15.
[154] *K sportu!* no. 32 (1912): 2.
[155] *K sportu!* no 48 (1912): 11 and *Sport*, no. 2 (1913): 2.
[156] *Pervaia Iaroslavskaia olimpiada* (Yaroslavl: K. F. Nekrasov, 1915).
[157] See articles in *Ves' mir*, no. 25 (1914): 27, and no. 37 (1916): 27.
[158] *Ves' mir*, no. 43 (1916): 26.

The Actress and the Wrestler: Gendering Identities

Maria Savina and Ivan Poddubnyi: the actress who ruled the Alexandrinka for forty years and the only Russian twice crowned wrestling's world champion. If the two ever met, it would have been by chance, possibly selling government bonds during the First World War. Each was, though, an influential prototype for changing notions of appropriate sex-based social roles during the turbulent decades of industrialization.[1] Through their culturally constructed images, they offered instruction to Russians who needed to learn the new rules for behavior, the changing ways of presenting themselves in the public world under construction by the emergent consumer economy. Female and male, Savina and Poddubnyi offered imagined ideals of femininity and masculinity. Commercialism transformed them into representations that were "rendered invisible and subordinate within cultural and political frameworks . . . where what it means to be a man [or woman was] in fact highly regulated, conventionalized, and left by and large unsaid."[2]

Whatever else he might have miscalculated, Karl Marx had correctly perceived that industrialization would rearrange social relations. Industrial capitalism's need to ensure an efficient economy called for new forms of social control, including, as Michel Foucault has pointed out, a new set of sexual categories that would classify difference according to the de-

---

[1] In the words of Michel Foucault, the two celebrities represented "the set of effects produced in bodies, behaviors, and social relations." Foucault, *The History of Sexuality,* vol. 1, *An Introduction,* trans. Robert Hurley (New York: Vintage, 1980), 127.

[2] Paul Smith, *Boys: Masculinities in Contemporary Culture* (Boulder: Westview, 1996), 3.

mands of the new economy.[3] Moreover, because industrialization apportioned power unequally between the sexes as it did among classes, it depended on the ideology of capitalism to find a way to manage the conflict destined to erupt from the systemic inequalities. When the "woman question" arose to interrogate the rationale for women's subordinate status, biological science was called in to lend the weight of positivism to "naturalize" the hierarchy.[4] Capitalism compensated women who accepted their assigned roles, however, by increasing the benefits of femininity, tying it to consumption through a vast array of cosmetic rewards and enhancements. Men produced what women consumed.

Enter the actress and the wrestler. The biographies of Savina and Poddubnyi provide background perspectives on the social change that allowed them to emerge as what Philip Rieff termed "modal types of personality," or "bearers of the new culture."[5] Both used talent and ambition to clamber up from the lower rungs of the social hierarchy into which they had been born. Never mind that their chosen professions would still have distanced them from certain elitist circles: they embodied the creation of a new kind of aristocracy, not an imitation of the old. And certainly many from the old guard wanted to be publicly associated with them and were not content to stand in the shadow cast by their limelight.

Significantly, Savina and Poddubnyi hid their hard work behind a luminary status and were celebrated for results rather than for the energy expended achieving them. A fundamental aspect of this capitalist culture was the ascendance of consumption over production as a social value, which, as Warren Susman and others have argued, had implications for what would be considered desirable personality traits.[6] The actress and the wrestler represented celebrity converted into an article of mass consumption. As performers, they put their personalities on display, and some of their traits were manufactured for purposes of mass marketing. Icons of the secular age, whether in the concrete form of photographs or postcards or in the identities they inspired through public performances, images of Savina and Poddubnyi circulated as commodities. Like other celebrities, they must be understood as fetishes as well as individuals, and their personal experiences as stand-ins for social issues popularized by what they represented to their mass audiences.

[3] Discussed in Jeffrey Weeks, "Discourse, Desire, and Sexual Deviance: Some Problems in a History of Sexuality," in *The Making of the Modern Homosexual*, ed. K. Plummer (London: Hutchinson, 1981).

[4] Viola Klein, *The Feminine Character: History of an Ideology* (London: Routledge, 1971).

[5] Philip Rieff, *The Triumph of the Therapeutic: Uses of Faith after Freud* (New York: Harper and Row, 1966), 2.

[6] Warren Susman, "'Personality' and the Making of Twentieth-Century Culture," in his *Culture as History: The Transformation of American Society in the Twentieth Century* (New York: Pantheon, 1984), 271–85.

Although this chapter spotlights the lives of the stars, it uses them to explore their larger meanings for fans. The issue of fandom is crucial here because it explains popularity in terms of identification.[7] Specifically, Savina and Poddubnyi have been enlisted to illuminate how gender roles were evolving—that is, how social behaviors assigned to the sexes were changing to meet the demands posed by modernity. Because gender is about representation rather than pre-existing reality,[8] subjects such as performers who attract a mass audience through the persona that they present function as agents of cultural change, not simply mirrors of it. Imitation does not simply flatter: the imitator wants to be able to locate parts of him/herself in the idol by adopting aspects of his/her dress or style. The relationship is not one-to-one, but rather polyvalent, with fans picking and choosing individually and often haphazardly. As modal types, Savina and Poddubnyi became popular for the multiple opportunities that they offered for the construction of selfhood.

The Actress

The Great Reforms of the 1860s laid the foundation for citizenship, but the social structure that resulted from them remained tightly gendered. A high-minded minister of war opened the doors of the military's surgical academy to women in the 1870s, but his successor closed them. Performing on the stage offered women one of the few acceptable accesses to public space, although the line between two types of public women, actresses and prostitutes, was sometimes vague in the social imagination. But as Rita Felski has argued, commercialization turned the professional actress into "the paradigmatic symbol of a culture increasingly structured around the erotics and aesthetics of the commodity."[9] Once consumption acquired the same degree of importance as production, actresses found a new role to play.[10]

[7] As Janice Radway has argued, an audience is an "interpretive community" that makes specific selections "because essential features of their social life create needs and demands that are somehow addressed and fulfilled." Quoted in Jay Blumler, "Recasting the Audience in the New Television Marketplace?" in *The Audience and Its Landscape,* ed. James Hay, Lawrence Grossberg, and Ellen Wartella (Boulder: Westview, 1996), 101.

[8] Gayle Rubin first articulated the "sex/gender system" in "The Traffic in Women: Notes toward a Political Economy of Sex," in *Toward an Anthropology of Women,* ed. Rayna Reiter (New York: Monthly Review, 1975), 157–210.

[9] Rita Felski, *The Gender of Modernity* (Cambridge, Mass.: Harvard University Press, 1995), 20, 4.

[10] Susan Glenn has argued persuasively that America's female performers at the turn of the century were insistently political by their individualism, before feminism had articulated its platform. Much of Savina's life has parallels in this work. *Female Spectacle: The Theatrical Roots of Modern Feminism* (Cambridge, Mass.: Harvard University Press, 2000).

Of the many actresses who graced the Russian stage at the end of the Old Regime, Savina overwhelms all others for a variety of reasons, evidenced best by her unparalleled four decades as a star. She could say with accurate pride that "*I* am the Alexandrinka!" Ostrovskii commented glowingly on her ability "to drive audiences out of their minds."[11] After her Petersburg debut in 1877, the newspaper *Grazhdanin* (The citizen) referred to "the sad history of the Russian theater before Savina (*bezsavinshchina*)."[12] Humorist Nikolai Leikin noted her ability to compete for local fans with such foreign imports as Sarah Bernhardt in 1888.[13] Anticipating that she would become Russia's contribution to the international stage, her fans considered her "the Russian Duse." Although her 1899 tour of Prague and Berlin enjoyed a warm reception, it was not so successful as to warrant further stints abroad.[14] The Russian mass-circulation newspapers followed her tour with great fanfare, keeping readers at home informed throughout with reviews and interviews.[15] These fans became incensed over a perceived slight of Savina by Bernhardt on the first of "La Grande Sarah's" three tours of Russia in 1881, but Savina magnanimously spoke to the press to assure them that she and Bernhardt enjoyed deep professional respect for each other.[16] Comfortably a nationalist, Savina lamented the insecurity of those Russians who looked westward for art and culture.[17]

Remarkably, theater historians have not preserved Savina's memory well. Given the antipathy toward bourgeois values registered by the Soviet culture vultures, their curt dismissal should be read as a sign of her genuine popularity with the wrong crowd, the conspicuous consumers. Adored especially by the female audience, Savina played best in roles that dealt with contemporary issues, from drawing-room comedies to social melodramas. She took her position as role model quite seriously, from costuming herself in the fashions her fans expected her to wear to her personal involvements in charities. Her biography tells a classic version of the paradox between feminism and femininity in the evolution of modernity—that is, between the woman who establishes herself as an equal in the

[11] *Gordost' russkogo teatra: Mariia Gavrilovna Savina* (St. Petersburg: T-va khudozhestvennogo pechati, 1900), 2, 9.

[12] M. G. Svetaeva, *Mariia Gavrilovna Savina* (Moscow: Iskusstvo, 1988), 131..

[13] RGALI, f. 853, op. 2, ed. khran. 45, l. 92.

[14] *Gordost'*, 21–22. Savina knew some French but refused to perform in it. Svetaeva, *Mariia Gavrilovna Savina*, 232–36.

[15] In 1909 Savina's third husband, A. Molchanov, sponsored an official publication of a massive tribute to this tour, which included reprints of her diary and press clippings. *Russkoe stsenicheskoe iskusstvo za granitsei: Artisticheskaia poezdka M. G. Savinoi s truppoi v Berlin i Pragu* (St. Petersburg: Tip. Glav. Up. Udelov, 1909).

[16] The newspaper articles and correspondence about the "Bernhardt scandal" are in RGALI, f. 853, op. 2, ed. khran. 35.

[17] Interview in *Peterburgskaia gazeta*, December 29, 1909, no. 357.

г. САВИНА, фотогр. Импер. ТЕАТ.

Maria Savina, tsarevna of the Alexandrinka

man's world and the one who uses her personal appeal to hide that she has positioned herself thus.

Born in 1854 to an eccentric village schoolteacher and his beleaguered wife, the young Maria Gavrilovna led a particularly precarious existence both physically and emotionally. She wrote of her life before she conquered the Alexandrinka, aptly entitled *Hardships and Wanderings,* but left biographers to work without the aid of her memories after 1877.[18] Her father taught penmanship and drawing, but his true passion lay in acting. Ostrovskii once described the provincial stage as "the refuge for failures of all sorts," which perhaps unfairly characterized Savina's father and many others who influenced a career that began in her childhood.[19] Her identity fell into crisis early, when her father left the security of a state job, took the family to Odessa, and changed their name from "Podramentsev" to the more stage-worthy "Stremlianov." This was Maria's first name change; the "Savina" came from the first of her three husbands. Her mother, who harbored no artistic aspirations, joined Maria and her older sister on stage to earn extra money to pay for their squalid quarters.

The details of her early life are unclear, probably repressed in the unhappy memory of being abandoned by her mother, who left Maria alone with her feckless, womanizing father. Savina's life during these years, bounding from one provincial town to the next in the constantly shifting company of theater folk, gave her a stock of personal experiences from which to draw for the emotionally taxing roles in which she would later excel. Once, driven out of their lodgings by one of her father's revolving mistresses, the young Savina fell violently ill and was nursed back to health by one of the many actresses who functioned as her surrogate mother.[20] Not yet fifteen, Savina became a professional actress out of self-defense, to earn the money to free herself from her irresponsible father. Despite a lifetime of neglect by both parents, however, she refused to abandon her family as they had her, even to the point of adopting her sister's child and keeping her father employed as an extra at the Alexandrinka.[21]

Despite her inadequate and interrupted schooling, Savina never lacked in stage smarts, and her skill at turning herself from an impoverished orphan into tsarist Russia's premier actress surely tells one of the classic archetypal tales of self-transformation from the nineteenth century. Presaging the *Showboat* tune (1927) about "Life upon the Wicked Stage," she endured numerous character-building hardships but truly loved her work.[22]

[18] M. G. Savina, *Goresti i skitaniia: Pis'ma, vospominaniia* (Moscow: Iskusstvo, 1983).

[19] Quoted in I. I. Shneiderman's introduction to *Goresti,* 10.

[20] Savina, *Goresti,* 39.

[21] Schneiderman, introduction to *Goresti,* 11–12.

[22] "Life upon the Wicked Stage," music by Jerome Kern, lyrics by Oscar Hammerstein II. From *Showboat,* 1927, producer, Florenz Ziegfeld.

Then, in fine fairy-tale fashion, she was spotted by a producer when substituting one evening for the star. As it turned out, Savina was fortunate to be working the provincial stage rather than to have joined the more prestigious imperial company too soon. Whereas the monopoly regulated the theater in the two capitals until 1882, the ticket-buying public in the provinces could have more say in the selection of repertoires. Savina had to master numerous stage skills, playing vaudeville one night, operetta the next, and Ostrovskii over the weekend. Her repertoire came to include three hundred roles.[23]

Had Savina begun her career with the imperial company she would have most likely been typecast into a certain kind of part, changing her roles primarily with age. The two actresses who competed most publicly with Savina for the crown jewels of the Russian theater, Maria Ermolova and Vera Komissarzhevskaia, were both born into established theatrical families, daughters of a professional prompter and an opera singer, respectively. Ermolova attended the imperial theatrical training school, but Komissarzhevskaia had to spend a few years touring the provinces to develop her skills. Significantly, both excelled in a specific type of role and did not significantly expand their repertoires. History has remembered her competitors far more kindly than it has Savina because the other two specialized in roles that were politically radical in ways that hers were not, though neither Savina nor her fans would have predicted this upon her death.[24] Savina's commitment to playing "both a princess in a tragedy and a servant in a vaudeville with the same effort" showed her range.[25]

Commercial interests rather than luck brought P. M. Medvedev, one of the leading entrepreneurs of the provincial stage, to the theater in Nizhnii Novgorod in 1871 where Savina was performing during the national fair held annually in this commercial port on the upper Volga. As she retold the story, true to the genre of theatrical discovery, Medvedev was in attendance that evening to check out one of her male costars, and she was filling in for someone else. The troupe was surprised when Medvedev came back stage to take her back to Kazan under contract for 250 rubles per month.[26] She would also play two benefits per season. On these evenings she would pocket all the profits from ticket sales, and because her fans would know that this was "her" evening, they would bring tributes, often in the form of expensive gifts and jewelry. Savina's benefits provided unquestionable testimony to her popularity, and they enhanced her lifestyle

---

[23] *Gordost'*, 12.

[24] Catherine Schuler repeats the prejudices with her observation that "only Ermolova [as opposed to Savina] achieved the lofty status of national icon." *Women in the Russian Theatre: The Actress in the Silver Age* (New York: Routledge, 1996), 77.

[25] M. G. Savina, "Kak nashel menia P. M. Medvedev," in *Goresti*, 137.

[26] Ibid., 134–35.

Savina in costume (here and right). The sharp contrast in dress reflects the breadth of her repertoire.

М. Г. САВИНА   *19/92*   К. А. Фишеръ, Спб.

as she amassed well beyond what others could hope for.[27] The lists of extraordinary gifts her fans brought to her year after year included impressive annual contributions from the successive Romanov tsars.[28]

By the age of twenty Savina moved beyond Medvedev's Kazan troupe to a theater in Saratov at twice the monthly salary. She also began experiencing problems with envious costars, an occupational hazard particularly sharp among performers where competition ran as high as egos.[29] Savina was plagued more than most of her contemporaries with accusations of "intrigues," and not all charges were groundless.[30] When an actress whom Savina considered an inferior talent received an invitation to debut at the Alexandrinka, the ambitious Savina packed up to try her luck also in the imperial capital. In the mid-1870s, when the state theaters were still the sole legitimate stages in the two capitals, the plays being produced in private clubs provided an important venue to the theater world for aspiring hopefuls looking to be discovered. It is difficult to read her protestations of stage fright without the requisite grain of salt, but easy to swallow that success came immediately, even though the directors at the Alexandrinka, as she later complained, "exploited (her) disgracefully."[31] Regardless, they put the range of her talents to full use, which helped her career.

Savina's roles defined her persona and reflected her personality, despite a desire to be purely protean on stage. Not a great beauty, she gained fame for her technique. In the absence of film recordings of her work, it is difficult to tell precisely what this meant, but an analysis of the kinds of roles that attracted her can provide a few insights. Quintessentially a realist, she excelled in the social melodrama that staged contemporary issues and gave the leading female characters poignant scenes that allowed them to articulate in a manner that today would be considered excessive, making the character larger-than-life. Stanislavsky's naturalism, in contrast, asked actors to subdue their emotions, moderating their individualism in favor of the larger theme. The differences between Savina and Stanislavsky ran deeper than those of style and interpretation because Savina was at the center of a system where the actors themselves made critical decisions about performance. Stanislavsky, though, promoted the cardinal role of the director and ensemble acting.

[27] TsGIA, f. 468, op. 14, d. 786, l. 6. She collected three thousand rubles in 1892, one thousand more than her nearest competitor, the comedian Davydov.

[28] The list of Romanov gifts is in RGALI, f. 853, op. 2, ed. khran. 2. In 1913 Savina received a special jewel-encrusted medal, after years of diamonds and rubies. Notes on other benefits are in ed. khran. 56, l. 8, and ed. khran. 58, l. 119.

[29] M. G. Savina, "Saratov," *Goresti,* 98–99.

[30] Savina and Suvorin, the star and the publicist-cum-playwright, maintained a love-hate relationship for decades; she alternately took his roles and refused them; his newspaper was qualified in its support for her throughout. RGALI, f. 853, op. 2, d. 40, ll. 1–11.

[31] M. G. Savina, "Peterburg," *Goresti,* 104–5.

Chekhov provided the text that would best illustrate the division between realism and naturalism when the Alexandrinka first staged his *The Seagull* in 1896. Savina, who had triumphed in the role of actress *Tat'iana Repina*, now rejected the role of Nina Zarechnaia, Chekhov's actress-character and metaphorical seagull.[32] (The role of Nina went instead to the Alexandrinka's newest ingénue, Komissarzhevskaia, who would adopt it as her signature role when she left the imperial stage to start her own theater to counteract the artistic conservatism personified by Savina.) The play flopped, as Savina had anticipated.[33] This happened relatively late in Savina's career, but it serves the point here of illustrating what sort of actress she had become. Savina's interpretation of an actress's responsibility to her public reflected a political agenda no less sincere, or less meritorious, than that put forward by those who criticized her for her commercial success because they interpreted popular appeal to women as a sign of second-class art. For her part, Savina could not play Nina Zarechnaia because the fictional actress, having been victimized in the course of the play, did not *do* anything to regenerate herself, as Savina herself would have done.

In her memoirs Savina tried to downplay what she was best known for: her ability to dominate any scene. She prided herself most for her ability to disappear into roles, to become the personality she was playing.[34] The fin de siècle was distinguished psychologically by the search for the individual personality, in Russian terms, "*svoe ia,*" and reviewers praised Savina especially for giving her characters their own individual selves.[35] Yet this idea of immersion in a role was delusional on her part as well as that of the critics. She was central to the creation of many starring roles for women from the 1870s; although she was less readily typecast than Ermolova or Komissarzhevskaia, both her comic and tragic heroines were distinguished by their independence.[36] Journalist Vladimir Mikhnevich, an accomplished social observer, explained her popularity with women: "Savina allows our women to love themselves; she is their pride, their dynamic defender, their most articulate attorney.... She is their idol."[37] *Grazhdanin* explained her attraction to men, which drew from the assertive sexuality she brought to the stage: "We men happily love such women—sweet, but with fire in their eyes, coquettish, childishly naive, but with a thousand

---

[32] Discussed in *Vera Fedorovna Komissarzhevskaia: Pis'ma aktrisy, vospominaniia o nei, materialy* (Moscow: Iskusstvo, 1964), 214–17.

[33] Chekhov was apparently happy with a fresh face, although his attitude toward Savina remained unclear. Ibid., 217.

[34] RGALI, f. 853, op. 2, ed. khran. 56, l. 10, from 1881, discusses her uncanny ability to "forget her *self.*"

[35] A discussion of this lies in her personal archive, RGALI, f. 853, op. 2, d. 56, l. 10.

[36] Svetaeva, *Mariia Gavrilovna Savina,* 112, discusses the "*zhenskii teatr.*"

[37] Ibid., 131.

contradictions in their souls. . . . In real life women as interesting as she are a rarity."[38]

Mikhnevich pinpointed an aspect of Savina's persona that connected her to the world of consumption, one that made her a model for self-presentation in society: her clothes. The issue of costumes was especially thorny because actresses were obliged to provide their own, which could be an expensive enterprise and supply motivation for limiting one's repertoire to characters who would repeat the same attire.[39] Savina recalled early problems with Medvedev when she dressed "like a maid rather than a heroine," decidedly not someone with whom a marquis would fall in love![40] She learned the importance of dressing appropriately to the character, but she also wanted to entertain those in the audience who had come for the fashion show. Playing so many modern women gave Savina the opportunity to show off the cosmopolitan wardrobe that female fans came to see.[41] Two of her most popular heroines, both from Krylov's reworking of Sardou comedies, *Madame Sans-Gêne* and *Let's Get a Divorce,* situated her in the kind of domestic settings where wives could assert their authority in the high style of Parisian gowns and extravagant hats. Later Savina became embroiled in several public debates about the role of costumes, to the point of criticizing Bernhardt and Duse for dressing out of character when it better suited them to promote their own personalities.[42]

Despite a range far broader than she customarily receives credit for, Savina made her indelible mark in a certain kind of role, that of the modern woman of the 1890s, whether in comical farce or melodrama. Her forte lay in what Richard Schechner has termed "aesthetic drama," that is, performances intentionally designed to transform the audience's perspective. Schechner tied Savina directly to her audience with the observation that "in aesthetic drama everyone in the theater is a participant in the performance while only those playing roles in the drama are participants in the drama nested in the performance."[43] Highly critical of the "innovators" in 1910, Savina questioned whether or not they remembered that the audience came "to have their hearts beat in unison with what is taking place on the stage."[44] When playing Ostrovskii's most famous character, the impressionable Katerina, bullied into suicide by her mother-in-law in *The Storm,* Savina played up the girl's lack of sophistication in dealing with the real world. This diverged from the traditional portrayal of Katerina as a

---

[38] Ibid.

[39] Schuler, *Women in Russian Theatre,* 31–35.

[40] Savina, "Kak nashel menia," 136.

[41] Press reviews mention this throughout her career. See especially an article in *Grazhdanin* from 1914, held in her archive, RGALI, f. 853, op. 2, ed. khran. 45, l. 143.

[42] RGALI, f. 853, op. 2, ed. khran. 45, l. 9.

[43] Richard Schechner, *Performance Theory* (New York: Routledge, 1988), 171.

[44] RGALI, f. 853, op. 2, ed. khran. 58, l. 99.

helpless victim of social circumstances, who lacked the inner strength to act on her own. Leonid Andreev, the gritty realist who began flirting with symbolism after 1905, almost persuaded Savina to star in one of his plays, but after more than thirty years perfecting what she understood her art to be, she resisted the winds of theatrical change with the assertion: "I am accustomed to reflecting life on stage, not symbols."[45]

Savina's career was linked inextricably with that of Krylov, the Russian Sardou. He was the dominant artistic force at the Alexandrinka when Savina moved there in the 1870s, and despite recurring storm clouds in their relationship, they fed off each other's talents.[46] Thirty of her three hundred roles were in his plays.[47] Although *Madame Sans-Gêne* was undoubtedly their best known collaboration, the pair worked together first in 1877 on I. S. Turgenev's *A Month in the Country*. Impressed with the way Savina accepted the secondary female role but then reinterpreted it to heighten some of the nuances of the situation, Turgenev began a correspondence with Savina that provided her with a few credentials to counter allegations of artistic banality.[48] But it was writers such as Krylov, dramaturges dismissed by intellectual history as second-rate, who created her stage persona.

One of the persistent critiques of the middlebrow culture with which Savina is identified, intensified by the female component of her audience, derives from the predominance of contemporaneous settings. Where Ermolova is remembered for attracting Moscow's student crowd with her politically inspirational rendition of Schiller's *Maid of Orleans*, Savina is known for inviting her audiences into her drawing room, into contemporary situations, some comical and others serious. In fact, Ermolova played in Krylov roles and other social melodramas, just as Savina played Shakespeare to Ostrovskii. But their images were built according to the politics of how their audiences chose to view them. Dramatic situations that develop out of present-day circumstances can quickly become outdated, whereas high art supposedly reaches instead to address universal truths. In response to the perpetual association of highbrow culture with men and middlebrow culture with women, feminist literary critics have illustrated how assumptions about "ahistorical truths" have invariably been affected by exterior social and cultural changes.[49] The presentism of Savina's primary repertoire therefore provides the cultural historian with indispensable insights into the era: her most popular roles offered social commentary on the concerns of Russia's middle-class women.

---

[45] RGALI, f. 853, op. 2, ed. khran. 58, ll. 123–27.

[46] Shneiderman, introduction to *Goresti*, 64–66.

[47] Ibid., 63.

[48] M. G. Savina, "Moe znakomstvo s Turgenevym," *Goresti*, 137–47.

[49] Jane Tompkins, *Sensational Designs: The Cultural Work of American Fiction, 1790–1860* (New York: Oxford University Press, 1985), 3–4.

73.

Savina as Katerina in *The Storm*

Savina's dramatic representations of the modern woman's tribulations reinforce Felski's argument that although modernity has commonly been depicted in essentialized masculine images, the "analysis of modern femininity brings with it a recognition of the profoundly historical nature of private feelings."[50] Emotional stability appeared more difficult for women to obtain because they were presumed to lack the capacity for rational thought that would allow them to balance their lives. No Jeanne d'Arcs leading the people against political tyranny, Savina's heroines were hysterical women, adulterous and suicidal, melodramatic rather than classically tragic figures. The contemporary critic who praised the realism of Savina's hysteria as quintessentially female behavior was arguably ahead of his time intellectually for applauding the artistic contributions of the hysterical heroine.[51]

The ultramelodramatic *Tat'iana Repina* gave Savina a signature dramatic role in 1888.[52] Suvorin's only bona fide hit, and based on a true event, it told the story of an actress who, spurned by her lover for a wealthy widow, decides to poison herself on stage during a live performance.[53] In the title role, Savina spent the entire last act in death throes. Even the spectators played a dual role: watching Savina, they knew that Repina was dying, but those who found themselves caught up with Repina's performance could suspend their disbelief and confuse actress with character.[54]

Dying on stage was an especially feminine action. Ever since Marguerite Gautier, the consumptive courtesan of Alexandre Dumas's (*fils*) *La Dame aux camélias,* coughed her way into theater history in 1851, the stage heroine could accent her life statement with a lingering death.[55] These staged deaths were coded by the dominant morality: sexually innocent women did not perish in this manner. Another of Savina's trademark roles, *Ol'ga Rantseva,* was a particularly shameless adventuress. In fact, author Boris Markevich had trouble passing the censors because of its immoral heroine.[56] Bored in her marriage, Ol'ga is discovered dining out with her lover by her kind-and-decent husband. Divorce does not end their complicated relationship; when she later prepares to marry again, the ex-husband materializes to expose her as an adulteress. Yet he is also by her side at the end,

[50] Felski, *Gender of Modernity,* 3.

[51] RGALI, f. 853, op. 2, ed. khran. 67a, ll. 42–43.

[52] She reported that it had "consumed her." Interview in *Peterburgskaia gazeta,* December 3, 1901, no. 332.

[53] Kadmina, a provincial opera star, had done this several years earlier, stirring an obvious sensation.

[54] The reviews from the popular Petersburg press, which are generally more favorable to the actress than to the playwright, including Suvorin's own *Novoe vremia,* are in her personal archive, RGALI, f. 853, op. 2, ed. khran. 45, ll. 66–87.

[55] Savina had played the character of Marguerite, to the author's approval. His review appeared in *Le Figaro,* maintained in RGALI, f. 853, op. 2, ed. khran. 56, l. 1.

[56] Ibid., ll. 42, 47.

when she lies sick with consumption in a Moscow garret, finally dying in his arms.[57] Anyone in the audience who might have been censorious in the first act had plenty of time to come around: one reviewer noticed how Rantseva "took a long and agonizing time to die on stage."[58]

The intersection of Savina's public and private selves is particularly interesting for what it suggests about her fans.[59] Medvedev had proclaimed her his perfect ingénue, but if Savina had ever truly enjoyed the luxury of innocence, she had lost her sexual naïveté before her first marriage at sixteen to N. N. Savin, an actor. Not surprisingly, Savina romanticized her affairs in terms of love rather than sex: "in my eyes he was a knight in shining armor," she said of her first lover, the company's director and a man twice her age.[60] But she married the ne'er-do-well Savin, who had forfeited his promising naval career because of an embezzling incident in Buenos Aires. With his refined manners and ability to do a French accent, Savin could command seventy-five rubles a month, better pay than he could have garnered in state service.[61]

Newlywed bliss soured quickly, and Savina countered his womanizing with a "protector," a prince who tried to buy off her husband while Savina also carried on a five-year affair with a second abusive nobleman, N. N. Vsevolozhskii, who pressured Savina to give up the stage to tend to life on his provincial estate.[62] She played up their social distance initially for sympathy, acting the part of the loving wife upon whom her husband's circle looked down. In truth, he needed the money she could earn on the stage to rescue him from bankruptcy. They divorced in 1891. Her third marriage, almost six years later, to wealthy businessman A. E. Molchanov, a director of the Russian Society for Shipping and Trade and a member of the board of directors of the imperial theater, lasted until her death. She used the title of an Ostrovskii play, "it lights but it does not warm," to describe their relationship: their marriage owed its success in part to the fact that the spouses maintained separate lives. Savina lived by her own salary, though this husband demonstrated a devotion lacking in the first two by establishing a museum to her memory.[63]

Significantly, Savina's love affairs were no secret to her audiences. Her memoirs, first published in 1898, illustrate how the conflation of "public"

---

[57] The reviews for the 1888 premier of *Ol'ga Rantseva* are in RGALI, f. 853, op. 2, ed. khran. 45.

[58] The review appeared in *Novosti,* maintained in RGALI, f. 853, op. 2, ed. khran. 45, l. 58.

[59] The sociologist Erving Goffman would have characterized an actress like Savina as "a model for, not a model of," social behavior. *Frame Analysis: An Essay on the Organization of Experience* (New York: Harper and Row, 1974), 41.

[60] M. G. Savina, "Pervaia liubov'," in *Goresti,* 51.

[61] Shneiderman, introduction to *Goresti,* 10.

[62] M. G. Savina, "Moe zamuzhestvo," 73–87.

[63] Shneiderman, introduction to *Goresti,* 18.

women, actresses with prostitutes, centered around perceptions of a more open sexual life than would be tolerated among average women of whatever social background. The point here is not about Savina's personal morals but rather about a reputation that hindered neither her artistic nor her social opportunities. The sort of self-confidence mandatory for performing nightly before strangers strengthened not only Savina's private resolve but also her persona on stage. Her ease at crossing the boundary between public and private persuaded her female fans to welcome her as a role model rather than to see her as a potential threat to their domestic economies. This was especially vital late in the nineteenth century, when women regularly found themselves caught between the conventions of femininity and the politics of feminism in the quest for a means to exercise authority. Trapped by a legal system that denied them independence in the public sphere, they maneuvered creatively to carve out spaces around the restrictions.[64] Savina, ladylike on stage and assertive in life, could offer the fundamentals of both. Feminine and feminist presented two sides of the same coin, on which "the figure of woman . . . as a powerful symbol of both the dangers and the promises of the modern age"[65]— opposite sides, but still the same coin.

Savina would hardly have called herself a feminist, which in turn-of-the-century Russia evoked images of obstreperous British suffragettes. Nor would she would have had patience with the socialist position that sex must be subsumed under class. Despite an unwillingness to ally with gender politics, she spent much of her life asserting her personal independence, staking a place in the theater where business and artistic decisions were made. She was a so-called "new woman," that one who "experimented with new forms of public behavior and new gender roles."[66]

Savina moved into one public space where women could make their mark by involving herself in numerous theatrical charities.[67] Many provincial performers testified to her altruism; she gave from her own pocket, and she toured with them in the summer, a generous gesture from someone who had no need to supplement the highest salary paid at the Alexandrinka.[68] In 1883 she helped to organize the Russian Theatrical Society in

[64] Roshanna Sylvester, "Crime, Masquerade, and Anxiety: The Public Creation of Middle-Class Identity in Pre-Revolutionary Odessa, 1912–1916" (Ph.D. diss., Yale University, 1998), 318–21.

[65] Felski, *Gender of Modernity*, 2–3.

[66] Glenn, *Female Spectacle*, 6.

[67] Sylvester, "Crime, Masquerade, and Anxiety," 166–72. See also Adele Lindenmeyr, *Poverty Is Not a Vice: Charity, Society, and the State in Imperial Russia* (Princeton: Princeton University Press, 1996).

[68] RGALI, f. 853, op. 2, ed. khran. 45, l. 56. She also organized benefits to raise money for provincial actors. RGALI, f. 853, op. 2, ed. khran. 6, l. 3. Svetaeva also discusses her incredible generosity with both her time and her money (*Mariia Gavrilovna Savina*, especially 224, 249).

The dominant actress fends off the storm gathering behind the curtain.

an effort to raise the level of professionalization; she later chaired that organization. She also promoted the First All-Russian Congress of Stage Performers in 1897. Perhaps her most valuable legacy was the Home for Aged Performers she founded in 1896 and, with an obvious nod to her own childhood, her refuge for children of the theater. Nor was her public-spiritedness limited to theatrical colleagues; she devoted time to the Red Cross during the Russo-Japanese War and worked for an imperial charity during the Great War.[69]

In her final years Savina faced more theatrical changes than she proved capable of handling. Advanced age did not prevent her from attempting roles such as *Anna Karenina*, whom she had grown too old to portray.[70] Appointed to the Alexandrinka in 1908, director-*terrible* Vsevolod Meierkhol'd brought with him the unwelcome avant-garde, challenging Savina's dominating presence. She prevailed over him, buttressing claims to her continued extraordinary appeal with complaints that the only place she could study her lines was in her carriage because her phone was ringing off the hook with proposals for new shows.[71] Past her prime when she made this extravagant claim, she had by then become a Russian institution. For forty years Savina exercised great influence on notions of what styles and behaviors would be appropriate and attractive. If the culture hawks objected to her commercialization, to her willingness to succumb to commodification, in the context of late imperial Russia she was as empowering as she was powerful.

The Wrestler

The hypermasculine sport of wrestling epitomized the masculinity of industrialization triumphant, the strong body needed on the factory floor and the agile mind needed in the office.[72] Produced by the movement to improve health and hygiene in order to combat the evils of industrialization in the 1880s, the wrestler triumphed because of his conditioned strength and cleverness. As Richard Dyer points out, "The built body (is) the body made possible by . . . natural mental superiority. The point is after all that it is built, a product of the application of thought and planning."[73] Highly competitive but emotionally controlled and not violent, the wrestler personified the synthesis of Greece's classical hero and the emergent mechanical order.

[69] Information about her participation in various charities is maintained in RGALI, f. 853, op. 2, ed. khran. 20.

[70] Svetaeva, *Mariia Gavrilovna Savina*, 289–308.

[71] Interview in *Peterburgskaia gazeta*, December 3, 1909, no. 332.

[72] Peter Stearns, *Be a Man! Males in Modern Society* (New York: Homes and Meier, 1990), 54, 159. Allen Guttmann discusses the Marxist critique of bodybuilding for these purposes in *The Erotic in Sports* (New York: Columbia University Press, 1996), 146–47.

[73] As Richard Dyer pointed out, "The built body might seem a problematic signifier of the natural body, and certainly it is not the body white men are born with; it is, however, the body made possible by their natural mental superiority. The point is after all that it is built, a product of the application of thought and planning." Richard Dyer, "White Men's Muscles," in *Race and the Subject of Masculinities*, ed. Harry Stecopoulos and Michael Uebel (Durham: Duke University Press, 1997), 310.

In England and the United States, boxing emerged as the sport that encoded masculinity at the turn of the century.[74] But in Russia, boxing could not shake its image of peasant brutality, and the Russian Ministry of Internal Affairs never approved organized fisticuffs.[75] Boxing recalled the rural activity known as "the wall," where villages entertained themselves by going at each other in hand-to-hand combat.[76] Forbidden by law from 1832 onward, these fights not only continued in the countryside but also spread to the factory workers of the cities. The tsarist government's prohibition of professional wrestling until 1894 was likewise based on anxieties about the physicality of the lower classes.[77] Wrestling did not become professionalized until the bodybuilders in the amateur athletic societies adopted the Greco-Roman style, which encouraged discipline over the brawn associated with the circus.[78] The wrestler struggled with his dual personality, half village strongman and half disciplined patrician, until he successfully combined elements of each to appeal to an audience that combined elements of both.[79]

In his at times outrageous deconstruction of wrestling, Roland Barthes lent the legitimacy of critical theory to an activity that cultural critics had disparaged on the basis of prejudicial assumptions about mass culture.[80] Avoiding the highbrow/lowbrow binary, Barthes instead focused on how wrestling generates a system of signs meaningful to its audience. He emphasized how wrestling above all privileges bodies, offering a "the euphoria of men raised for a while above the constituent ambiguity of everyday sensations."[81] The Russian audience, composed primarily of the male "petty

---

[74] Elliott Gorn, *The Manly Art: Bare-Knuckle Prize Fighting in America* (Ithaca: Cornell University Press, 1989).

[75] One particular enthusiast, M. O. Kister, a member of Kraevskii's original circle, thoroughly dominated the brief history of Russian boxing. M. N. Lukashev, *Slava bylykh chempionov* (Moscow: Fizkul'tura i sport, 1976). See also Foma Balagur, *Udaloi moskovskii kulachnyi borets Potap Butylkin: Ego pokhozhdeniia po kulichnym boiam, stenkam na stene* (Moscow: A. D. Sazanov, 1908).

[76] See, for example, the article by A. Pash., "Bor'ba v Mikhailovskom manezhe," *Artist i tsena*, no. 4 (1910): 14–15. Although opera bass Fedor Shaliapin romanticized about the unwritten rules of "wall" combat, e.g., never hitting a man who was down or hiding heavy objects in gloves, police reports and official body counts after such contests painted a much more violent picture. Fedor Shaliapin, *Stranitsy iz moei zhizni* (Moscow: Iskusstvo, 1959), 41–42.

[77] I. V. Lebedev, *Istoriia professional'noi frantsuskoi bor'by* (Moscow: Teatr-Kino-Pechat', n.d.), 31.

[78] I. V. Lebedev, "Vospominaniia o doktore V. F. Kraevskom," *Illiustrirovannyi zhurnal atletika i sport*, nos. 1–2 (1905): 12.

[79] Nikolai Razin, *Polveka nazad. Vospominaniia bortsa* (Moscow: Fizkul'tura i sport, 1963), 5–11. See also B. V. Gorbunov, "Narodnye vidy sportivnoi bor'by kak element traditsionnoi kul'tury russkikh (XIX–nachalo XX v.)," *Sovetskaia etnografiia*, nos. 4–16 (1989): 90–101.

[80] Roland Barthes, "The World of Wrestling," in *Mythologies*, trans. Annette Lavers (New York: Hill and Wang, 1972), 115–25.

[81] Ibid., 125.

bourgeoisie, the shopkeeper," but also including the Ribop'ers and seductive society ladies alongside "hairdressers and hooligans," with students and coquettes scattered throughout, found pleasure in wrestling's symbolic reenactment of the masculine struggle in everyday life.[82]

Wrestling's professional promoters circulated its imagery widely through the mass-oriented media. For example, the Miniature Library Series published a cheap history of wrestling in a run of ten thousand in 1908, and M. Solov'ev's *How to Become a Wrestler/Athlete* proposed to teach the skills to ambitious young men. Impresario Lebedev, "Uncle Vania," had something of a mini- publishing empire, including his own bimonthly magazine, *Gerkules* (Hercules) from 1911 to 1917. He anticipated Charles Atlas by writing pamphlets on bodybuilding, and in 1917 he fed the contemporary fascination with the wrestler's body in a book with portraits of 375 "gladiators of our times." By making use of his work as master of ceremonies in his publications, Lebedev "bridge[d] the gap between bodily spectacle and the voice of textual authority."[83] Posed portraits of wrestlers also circulated on postcards, enhancing the power of popular culture to produce and disseminate some of these evolving notions of masculinity.

Whereas Savina stood out among the actresses of the era for the longevity of her popularity and the variety of her roles, Poddubnyi faced stiffer competition among his fellow wrestlers for national predominance, handicapped as he was by the reality that athletes have shorter careers. Twice crowned world champion in Paris, Poddubnyi merited the reputation that sustained him through the Soviet era and even carried him into the post-Soviet years when he became a posthumous spokesperson for the milk industry. If Poddubnyi did not dominate the ring to the extent that Savina did the stage, he must nonetheless be considered a first among equals. His biography explains the phenomenon of wrestling best when read together with the life stories of some of the other champions from the arena. The great stature of the wrestler in late imperial society emerges from the mosaic of personalities whose shared passion for the sport eclipsed differences that would have separated them in an earlier age.

Hailed as the contemporary incarnation of Russia's mythical strongman Ilya Muromets, Poddubnyi came from a family of Zaporozhian Cossacks. Born in 1871 in a peasant village in Poltava Province (present-day Ukraine), he alleged that his father and grandfather (who reputedly lived to be 125) were both stronger than he. Young "Vania" and his father entertained local villagers by fighting each other in such contests as fisticuffs (*na kulakh*), or the peasant version of wrestling that required men to grab

[82] N. N. Breshko-Breshkovskii discusses the audience in *V mire atletov* (St. Petersburg: A. V. Koreliakov, 1908), 42.

[83] Michael Budd, *The Sculpture Machine: Physical Culture and Body Politics in the Age of Empire* (New York: New York University Press, 1997), 45.

World champion Ivan Poddubnyi

each other by the belt and try to put the other on his back (*na poiasakh*). The foreman on the estate where his village was located, a former migrant worker himself, persuaded Vania to strike out for distant horizons, because someone with his strength would be eminently employable. At twenty, Poddubnyi left home.[84]

Striking out in the decade when Russia began its commitment to industrialization, the country boy became an emblem of the virtues of modernity. Poddubnyi washed up first in the port cities along the Black Sea as a longshoreman for a Greek shipping firm, first in Sevastopol and then Feodosia. In the urban environment, he became caught up in the already widespread fashion of bodybuilding. In 1897 a traveling circus brought another rising wrestling star, Georg Lurikh, into town. As part of a typical show, the circus's professional wrestlers would call out challengers from the audience. Poddubnyi earned his first money from wrestling by beating Lurikh at "belts," but when he lost to another professional, he gained the more valuable insight that his strength alone would not suffice, that he would have to develop both physical and mental agility.[85]

Once he developed some of the skills involved in wrestling, Poddubnyi found the sport easier and more profitable than unloading cargo ships. In 1900 he moved to Odessa, and then to Kiev where he signed a contract with the Nikitin Brothers Circus, one of the largest and most successful entertainment enterprises in Russia. Showman Akim Nikitin persuaded him to grow a thick mustache so that he would *look* the part of the Cossack that he was. Circus wrestlers walked a thin line between pure entertainment and athleticism, and Poddubnyi began performing with the Nikitins at that propitious moment when Lebedev was spearheading the drive to legitimize wrestling, using its classical heritage as the basis of his appeal. The Poltava villager found himself sought out by some of Kiev's leading citizens, who wanted to work out with him in their gyms. Dr. E. F. Garnich-Garnitskii induced him to take up the "French" style, highly skilled wrestling based on the conventions from ancient Greece, as opposed to peasant "belts" or the rougher "catch-as-catch-can" technique that predominated in America.[86]

In Kiev, Poddubnyi also made contact with a writer and sportsman active in local athletic clubs who was influential in getting name recognition for athletes at least on the periphery of the *intelligentsia*, Leonid Andreev. Poddubnyi's true professional break came when his name reached the ears of

[84] V. Merkur'ev, *Ivan Poddubnyi*, 2d ed. (Krasnoiarsk: Krasnoiarskoe knizhnoe izdatel'stvo, 1976), 6–8.

[85] Ibid., 10–11.

[86] A popular French history of wrestling appeared in Russian in 1903, written to dispel the image of wrestlers as "fairground clowns" and "to restore the dignity from ancient Greece." Leon Ville, *Bor'ba i bortsy* (St. Petersburg: F. I. Mitiurnikov, 1903).

sportsman Ribop'er, who invited him to Petersburg and then dispatched him to Paris to participate in his first international competition in 1903. The Soviet sports journalist Chesnokov accused Ribop'er of treating the athletes he sponsored much as he did his thoroughbred horses.[87] Although at times the peasant Poddubnyi probably felt out of place in a group that could easily include sports enthusiast Grand Duke Vladimir Aleksandrovich, Ribop'er always used the polite form of "you" with the wrestler and spent his life creating a fraternity based on athletic interests rather than social estate.[88] Legendary German strongman Eugen Sandow was also welcomed into a circle that included Sir Arthur Conan Doyle and the Marquess of Queensberry.[89]

It would be an exaggeration to present the professional wrestlers and their noble sponsors as an idealized community enjoying a social equality, but their relationships did reflect a genuine reshuffling of some of the past criteria for stratification. Ribop'er and others like him who wanted to associate with athletes appreciated that the latter offered a new space for homosocial bonding based literally on the strengths of masculinity rather than the weaknesses more commonly associated with it, such as drink and cards.[90] Training, athletic prowess, and something of a meritocracy came into play in these relations. After the 1905 Revolution had generated fears about the violent potential of the lower classes, Poddubnyi and other peasant champions could display their physical self-control to soothe apprehensions.

One of Poddubnyi's attributes, perhaps more distinctive than his class, was his nationality: he was the first ethnic Russian to dominate the sport. The empire's first world champion, Vladislav Pytliasinskii, was from Warsaw, then the capital of Russia's Grand Duchy of Poland. The health and hygiene movement had moved eastward from France and Germany to Poland and then into the Baltic areas of the Russian empire before expanding into its two national capitals. Educated in Switzerland, Pytliasinskii had become involved in bodybuilding and traveled to Berlin and Paris to compete before wrestling had moved out of the fairground in Russia. He took his successes back to Petersburg, to Kraevskii's gym, where he trained the omnipresent Ribop'er and the future champion Ivan Zaikin.[91]

Estonia, a Baltic province of the Russian empire since the era of Peter the Great, provided the next source of Russian champions. Alexander Aberg was the first Estonian wrestler to acquire an international reputation. Russia's first world champion, crowned in Paris in 1901, Georg

[87] B. Chesnokov, "Bortsy dorevoliutsionnoi Rossii na mezhd. sorevnovaniiakh," *Teoriia i praktika fizicheskoi kul'tury*, no. 19 (1929): 866.

[88] Merkur'ev, *Ivan Poddubnyi*, 13.

[89] Budd, *Sculpture Machine*, 65.

[90] Eve Kosofsky Sedgwick, *Between Men: English Literature and Male Homosocial Desire* (New York: Columbia University Press, 1985), 1.

[91] A. Svetov, *Ivan Zaikin* (Moscow: Fizkul'tura i sport, 1957), 22.

Gakkenshmidt (Hackenschmidt), was an ethnic German from Estonia. This "Russian Lion" had come from a poor background in Revel (Tallinn) to hone his skills in Kraevskii's gym.[92] The geography was becoming familiar: subjects of the tsar closest to the West were picking up the significance of this new kind of sport and participating in it abroad.

Estonian Georg Lurikh, whom Poddubnyi had bested at "belts" at the beginning of both their careers, carved a special niche for himself in this sport. The son of a merchant, the sickly young Lurikh had, like Theodore Roosevelt, initially taken up wrestling in school to try to improve his health. As a teenager Lurikh broke what had long been considered a sports dogma: that wrestlers were not athletes. Still at the gymnasium he competed in numerous sports, setting twenty-one local records in a variety of competitions that proved his agility. He moved to Petersburg after graduation, where he worked out at Kraevskii's gym, mastering numerous styles of wrestling, from French to "belts."[93]

Lurikh was the first Russian wrestler to develop a persona, embodying the combination of circus showmanship and the respectability Lebedev sought to bring to the sport. Projecting himself as a gentleman and a scholar, Lurikh undoubtedly deserved his reputation as a ladies' man.[94] Embellishing his intellectual background and showing off a build that was muscular without being bulky, Lurikh advertised himself in publicity shots sporting at times a tuxedo, and in other photos naught but a fig leaf. Lebedev noted that even other wrestlers considered him a "god" because of his incredible agility and always had had high praise for this athlete, able to "ignite the public better than any other." Even Jewish fans claimed him as one of their own, rumoring that he had changed his name from Solomon.[95]

After Poddubnyi another peasant, Ivan Zaikin, rose to the top of the game. Ten years Poddubnyi's junior, this grandson of a serf left his village in provincial Simbirsk in 1899 and traveled the Volga as a migrant worker. Landing a job as a clerk in Saratov, he joined a local amateur weightlifting society. News of his potential reached Pytlianskii, who brought him to Petersburg to train in French-style wrestling at the Kraevskii gym. He then returned to the Volga region to wrestle for a circus in Tsaritsyn. In 1905 he was invited to participate in a championship at Moscow's Aquarium nightclub. His star continued its ascent, shining also in Paris where he became something of a regular in competitions.[96]

---

[92] I. V. Lebedev, *Bortsy* (Petrograd: Gerkules, 1917), 9.

[93] *Koe chto pro Georga Lurikha* (St. Petersburg: Pechatnoe delo, n.d.).

[94] A 1906 advertising brochure for an upcoming international competition at the Farce shows "Another of Lurikh's Famous Holds"—the wrestler in a woman's embrace.

[95] Lebedev, *Bortsy*, 11.

[96] Svetov, *Ivan Zaikin*. A personal archive also exists for Zaikin, f. 2347 of the Russian State Archive of Literature and Art (RGALI).

Georg Lurikh, cosmopolitan wrestler

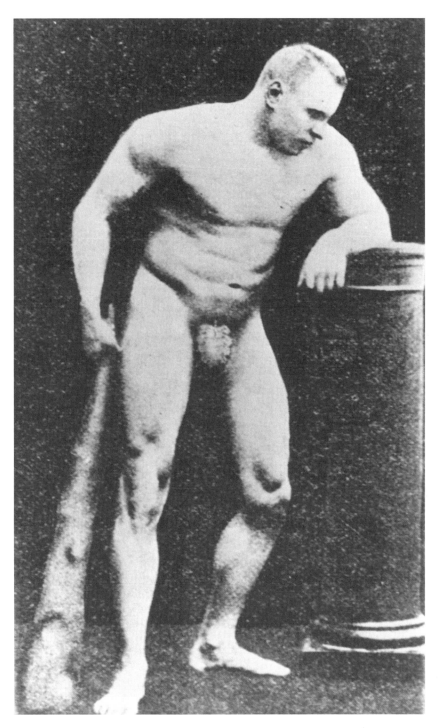

Lurikh shows off a few of his basic charms.

In the French capital Zaikin developed another interest that would affect his popularity—aviation. Flying became quite fashionable in the years leading up to the Great War, attracting, like wrestling, many from the European avant-garde.[97] Zaikin took lessons at the flying school established by pioneer Henri Farman, and his entourage included renowned sportsman Sergei Utochkin, Captain B. V. Matseevich, a pacesetter in Russian aviation, Giacomo, the popular clown from the Cinizelli Circus who was one of Andreev's closest associates, and the two Orthodox holy men who seemed to compete more for publicity than for souls, Rasputin and Iliador. Alexander Kuprin, another of the macho realists, was also a part of his crowd. Zaikin and Kuprin got the chance to prove their masculine mettle when the pilot-wrestler took the writer on a flight that ended in a nearly fatal crash. Kuprin recounted in harrowing detail the engine trouble, the crash, he and Zaikin barely jumping in time: "but during the fall, neither I nor the pilot experienced one moment of fear."[98] As one newspaper headlined the next day, "Zaikin Puts Even His Airplane on Its Back!"[99]

The sources are unclear on whether Zaikin was out of the country on tour in 1917 or left following the revolution. Regardless, he showed no inclination to return, spending his last professional years on the circuit in the United States and Cuba. He was promoted by Jack Curley, who milked the wrestler's persona as the Volga peasant who had escaped the Bolsheviks. One particularly inflated piece of publicity drew an image of prerevolutionary Russia that, although fallacious in detail, nevertheless captured the essence of the celebrity fraternity of the era. The New York press reported in January 1925 that another Russian émigré, Shaliapin, instead of singing at the Met would be ringside at the Armory, cheering on Zaikin, his boyhood pal. According to Curley, the two had joined forces in their youth with a third lad, Maxim Gorky, and the trio traveled the Volga like characters out of Mark Twain. Futurist poet and aviation aficionado David Burliuk actually did watch Zaikin perform in New York.[100]

Promoters everywhere needed fixed locations where they could pitch the competitions, as by the turn of the century wrestling enjoyed a stable fan base that could support it through ticket sales. When Lebedev staged Russia's first national championship at the Petersburg Farce in 1905, he was following western patterns of transferring wrestling from the circus to the nightclub, such as the Folies Bergérè in Paris and Berlin's Winter Garden. The nightclub setting invited a wealthier audience than would attend

---

[97] Robert Wohl, *A Passion for Wings: Aviation and the Western Imagination, 1908–1918* (New Haven: Yale University Press, 1994).

[98] Kuprin's account appeared in *Sinii zhurnal* in 1911, from which it was reprinted in other journals, including *Sportivnaia zhizn'* (Odessa), no. 11 (1911): 11–14.

[99] Svetov, *Zaikin*, 69–73.

[100] The clippings are in RGALI, f. 2347, ll. 13–14.

the circus, but not to the exclusion of the less well-heeled. It also begat the kind of sexy atmosphere that inspired Lurikh to picture himself as a bon vivant and that lured society ladies, and other women, ringside. In short, the nightclub arena confirmed the sport's versatility and adaptability.

When Lebedev transformed himself into "Uncle Vania," impresario extraordinaire, he tapped into the entrepreneurial side of the sport, becoming an example of its links to commercial capitalism. Lebedev had joined forces with the premier Russian showman of the day, P. A. Tumpakov, owner of the Bouffe. Their first staged championship was a bust, attracting only what Tumpakov sneered at as "the buffet crowd," the suckers to whom this "Russian Barnum" hesitated to give an even break. Tumpakov decided to whet the public's appetite by sending out a notice that "the government has refused to approve the performance." In 1905, when Russians were demonstrating their unwillingness to obey state directives, such a ruse sparked interest. After three days Tumpakov smirked that he had filled all his tables. Lebedev estimated that Tumpakov netted over forty thousand rubles in profits that season, and criticized him for underpaying his athletes out of a mere 35 percent of the receipts.[101] Wrestling, though, proved lucrative for all involved.

Despite the extra compensation they received as athletes, wrestlers remained performers who depended on showmanship for the sport to turn a profit. Lebedev himself had known only moderate success on the canvas, and he joked that crowds originally called him a "professor of athletics" because he often competed like a scholar rather than an athlete. A dandy (*frant*) with handlebar mustaches, he embellished his reputation through attire, which combined the traditional peasant blouse, high boots, and long-waisted coat (*poddevka*) with the peaked cap (*furazhka*) worn by students. Lev Tolstoy, Gorky, and Shaliapin were other celebrities who made a stylized peasant dress fashionable.

Uncle Vania realized that wrestlers needed individualized personalities in order to build up fan support. The tuxedoed Lurikh and the Cossack Poddubnyi, for example, formed an antipode of cultural types; and the Cossack held moral sway over the dandy in 1908 when Poddubnyi accused Lurikh of trying to bribe him to take a fall.[102]

After tenuring himself as a "professor," Lebedev played up images of wrestlers as intellectuals, a nice publicity ploy in the perennial brains-versus-brawn polemic.[103] The painter A. I. Kravchenko also wrestled professionally. A graduate of the Military-Surgical Academy fought under the name "Bul'denko" until his medical services were needed at the front dur-

[101] Lebedev, *Bortsy*, 5.
[102] Razin, *Polveka nazad*, 15.
[103] Iu. Embros, "Fakty i mysli," *Sportivnia zhizn'* (Odessa), no. 11 (1911): 9–10.

ing the First World War, and "public favorite" Al'fons Shvartser, a "combination Adonis and Ulysses," exchanged a career on the canvas for one in medicine, specializing in venereal diseases. A. V. Znamenskii "looked like a mathematics professor" when he fought wearing thick pince-nez, an erudite image he accentuated by performing as "William Moor," an imaginary Englishman who supposedly spoke five languages.[104]

Others traded on less cerebral images. One, for example, took the name "Vanka Kain," after the eighteenth-century bandit who lived in folklore and chapbook literature. Another styled himself after "Anton Krechet," a fictional bandit-hero from the adventure stories serialized in Petersburg's "boulevard" newspaper, *Gazeta kopeika* (The kopeck gazette).[105] Moishe Slutskii billed himself as "the Jewish Sampson," although because of his slight build and great dexterity he was better known as "the son of rubber." One of the most original personalities was V. Avdeev-Bulatsel', or "Uncle Fatty" (*Diadia Pood*).[106] With the bulk of a Sumo wrestler, weighing in at almost five hundred pounds, Uncle Fatty at times depended on his legion of fans to help him out by dousing his opponent with water. An entertainer rather than an athlete, he ended up as an impresario and even made a few movies.[107]

Wrestling heroes also needed foes, personae who supplied contrasts for more than simply athletic skills. Race entered the ring here as an important ideological factor that asserted a distinctively Russian masculinity. The southern areas of the empire included the Caucasus and Central Asia, which brought in athletes identified by their dark skins, victims of Russian fantasies of cultural superiority. These foils, whether of African descent or from the southern part of the empire, flaunted a wild, debased masculinity that needed to be put under check. Perceived as jungle creatures, they showed off "the instinctive litheness of a wild animal," or "leapt and slithered like a panther, a dark bronze, glistening panther."[108] The two black wrestlers who performed most often for Russian audiences were always on their worst behavior. The Tunisian Murzuk offered a role model for Mike Tyson with his vicious and illegal use of teeth. Sal'vator Bambula, the stage name adopted by the "chocolate American" John Murphy, would sometimes fire a revolver at unruly fans.[109] In a particularly telling comical story in *Gerkules*, the author recounts his frantic search for a "Negro" to wrestle

[104] Lebedev, *Bortsy,* 7–8, 12.

[105] On the popular culture of bandits, see Jeffrey Brooks, *When Russia Learned to Read: Literacy and Popular Literature, 1861–1917* (Princeton: Princeton University Press, 1985), chapter 5.

[106] Foss, a similarly rotund wrestler, created a furor with his weight in Odessa in 1914. Sylvester, "Crime, Anxiety, and Melodrama," 185–88.

[107] Lebedev, *Bortsy,* 8, 16.

[108] Ibid., 108.

[109] Lebedev, *Bortsy,* 30; and Svetov, *Zaikin,* 37.

in the local competition and the subsequent disaster that occurred in the ring when his artificial African broke out in an allergic reaction to the makeup that had been used to darken his skin.[110]

Although such stereotyping awarded black wrestlers a behavioral license in the ring that increased their market value, it also made them the straw men who demarcated the boundaries of the integrity of the sport. Writ large against the backdrop of imperialism at the turn of the century, the civilized whites who bested the black barbarians in the ring were performing an explicit political message. To be sure, the barbarians had their own fans, voices of protest against the constraints imposed by civilization; the author in the *Gerkules* story had promised a "Negro" in his advertising posters because he knew how popular this would be. (Africans in a 1909 film travelogue were advertised for their "truly black skin, not Europeans in makeup!")[111]

Given the dearth of dark-skinned athletes in Russia, and their popularity with audiences, impresarios such as Uncle Vania had to improvise. In addition to those who blackened their bodies to change their identities, others found it easier to hide behind masks when they engaged in outrageous conduct. These masked wrestlers became racialized by breaking the rules of good sportsmanship.[112] All one summer Uncle Vania kept the crowds coming on the false promise that the "Red Mask" would reveal himself at some point.[113] Of course, he did not; it would have been as unacceptable for one of wrestling's heroic figures to pull off a piece of cloth and show himself capable of reverse behavior as for Poddubnyi to bribe Lurikh.

Gender Trouble at the Turn of the Century

Savina represented the "new" woman, and she encouraged other women to follow her into public spaces, which posed a potential threat to the balance of gender power. Brian Pronger argues that "one of the techniques for the subordination of women by men is a complex semiotic of masculine and feminine behaviors that communicate power."[114] The sheer phys-

---

[110] V. I. Riazanov, "Kak ia byl arbitom Provintsial'nogo chempionata," *Gerkules*, nos. 1–27 (1917): 17–23.

[111] Information from ads in *Vestnik kinematografov*, 1908.

[112] Donald Nonini and Arlene Akiko Teraoka argue that breaking the rules in wrestling is a form of protest against hierarchies. "Class Struggle in the Squared Circle," in *The Politics of Culture and Creativity*, ed. Christine Gailey (Gainesville: University of Florida Press, 1992), 147–68.

[113] Pash., "Bor'ba v Mikhailovskom manezhe," 14–15.

[114] Brian Pronger, "Gay Jocks: A Phenomenology of Gay Men in Athletics," in *Rethinking Masculinity: Philosophical Explorations in Light of Feminism*, ed. Larry May and Robert Strikwerda (Lanham, Md.: Rowman and Littlefield, 1992), 43.

icality of wrestling assured this sort of subordination because the scrupulously conditioned body functioned as a quintessential signifier of masculinity. The man in the ring was enhanced by his counterpart in fiction.
Real-life wrestlers and their fans found recognizable caricatures of themselves in the popular fiction of one of the most prolific writers from the
boulevard, Nikolai Breshko-Breshkovskii. Son of the fabled Socialist Revolutionary Ekaterina Breshko-Breshkovskaia, he had been raised by her parents after his mother was sentenced to Siberian exile. After finishing
school, he moved to Petersburg in 1893 for a job as an accountant in a tobacco factory. But by the century's end he enjoyed sufficient success as a
journalist that he took up the pen professionally, later becoming a scenarist in the nascent movie industry.[115] Breshko-Breshkovskii's work is remarkable for the gender politics that underlies his stories. For example, a
novel about the revolutions in 1917 blamed the degenerate liberals, whom
the author despised for what he perceived as their effeminacy.[116] The
threat of predatory feminization that pervaded his fiction underscored the
importance of the wrestler to the reconfiguration of masculinity.

Breshko-Breshkovskii's two most popular wrestling stories, "The World
Champion" and "Gladiators of Our Times" were published together as *In
the World of Athletes* in 1908. The book went through at least two editions
and was dramatized for the stage in 1909 as *Gladiators*. One reviewer commented that audiences who complained that there was not enough action
in the contemporary theater would have their demands satisfied in this
production, which he placed, with tongue in cheek, "just after Ibsen,
Chekhov, and Maeterlinck."[117] But the middlebrow daily newspaper *Peterburgskaia gazeta* (The Petersburg gazette) noted with pride that members
of the artistic world were among the sellout crowds when it premiered.[118]

The attraction of the play, like that of his stories, was the thinness of the
disguises Breshko-Breshkovskii used. The main protagonist, Tampio, was
a blonde Estonian who had taken up wrestling to resolve chronic health
problems. His womanizing and preference for purchasing victories instead
of winning outright rounded out his resemblances to Lurikh. The old
trainer Lemmerman, a retired champion trying to instill the athletic principles of the French style in his young charges was easily recognizable as
Pytlianskii. The main heroes recalled Poddubnyi or Zaikin, ill-educated
boys who demonstrated their strength at traveling circuses and were then

---

[115] Biographical information about N. N. Breshko-Breshkovskii comes from B. Kassis's introduction in the republication of Breshko-Breshkovskii's *Dikaia diviziia* (Moscow: Moskov-
skaia pravda, 1991), 3–5.

[116] *Dikaia diviziia* and *Na belom kone: Iz zhizni dobrovol'skoi armii* (Berlin: Otto Krikhner,
1922). In Breshko-Breshkovskii's telling, Prime Minister Alexander Kerensky deteriorates
into cocaine addiction.

[117] "Gladiatory," *Obozrenie teatrov*, no. 913 (1909): 7–8.

[118] *Peterburgskaia gazeta*, November 29, 1909, no. 328.

A cartoon from *Gerkules* warns that "when records come, health goes"—stolen by the predatory female.

taken to Petersburg by Lemmerman for coaching. The quasi-fictional impresario was called a "professor of athletics" and costumed in a *poddevka* and a student's cap à la Lebedev. Ribop'er even appeared by name in one story, pouring cognac for the table of his companions—high society and athletes.

His known associations in the real world of athletes lent Breshko-Breshkovskii's fiction the authenticity of the sort of behind-the-scenes gossip that fed fan frenzy. Kuprin boosted Breshko-Breshkovskii's career with praise for his characterizations from the world of wrestling, and the two writers collaborated on a film starring the clown Giacomo.[119] Breshko-Breshkovskii also wrote the libretto and starred with Lebedev in the 1913 film *The Wrestler behind the Black Mask.* Symbolist poet Alexander Blok, known for his great fascination with popular culture became interested in Breshko-Breshkovskii on Kuprin's recommendation. Russia's modernist avant-garde painters became absorbed with the perfect (male) body represented by the wrestler, who had shorn his class image and offered in its place a modern, muscular masculinity.[120] These heady associations, among others linking the boulevard to the avant-garde, made plain the importance of wrestlers as masculine ideals.

Breshko-Breshkovskii constructed a cultural masculinity in large measure from his keen antipathy toward women—avaricious consumers of men, sapping crucial reserves of male sexual and financial vitality. Adulterous wives deceive hardworking husbands and exhort money from them to buy gifts and champagne for the men whose hard bodies they crave. In a story likely drawn from local gossip, a cuckolded bureaucrat is denied a promotion because his wife's scandalous public pursuit of a wrestler reflects poorly on the decent husband.[121]

Betraying all the vices associated with conspicuous consumption, these women see only commodified bodies and expect that they are for sale. The wrestlers, in contrast, are characterized with much of the same innocence about human nature as heroines in a melodrama, even though they enjoy greater sexual license. After occasionally surrendering to seduction, the men develop the consciences necessary to maintain the ethics of the sport. One typical fictional hero found himself frustrated between an aunt who wanted his money and an ingénue at the local theater who was after his body. For Breshko-Breshkovskii, women who went out in public were "public women"; several of his stories included female artists' models (*natur-*

---

[119] S. Felitsyn, "Literaturnyi pasport pevtsa areny," *Vestnik literatury,* no. 3 (1911): 69. Kuprin's review appeared in *Sinii zhurnal,* no. 8 (1911).

[120] John Bowlt, "Body Beautiful: The Artistic Search for the Perfect Physique," in *Laboratory of Dreams,* ed. John Bowlt and Olga Matich (Stanford: Stanford University Press, 1996), 37–58.

[121] N. N. Breshko-Breshkovskii, *V mire atletov* (St. Petersburg: A. V. Koreliakov, 1908).

shchitsy), who were understood to have sidelines in prostitution.[122] One such character, who pilfered from the artist to spend her ill-gotten gains on a wrestler, came across as more degenerate than the men who commodified her body.[123] Although wrestlers also posed, usually nude, they escaped the stigma of selling either body or soul because of the imagined origins of their nudity in classical antiquity.[124] This reversion to antiquity provided the necessary illusion that permitted scantily clad men embracing each other to escape accusations of pornography.

The malevolence of the women who invade Breshko-Breshkovskii's wrestling world underscored the need for a homosocial space to which they could escape. By pricing the costs of sex with women so high, he raised doubts about the desirability of intimate relations with them. Portraying women as predators rather than as prey, he reversed the traditional roles of the two sexes in public places. This had ideological implications because it suggested that men found themselves at peril when women went out in public. Vampires, these women implicitly drove men to one another.[125]

Setting greedy women loose on honest men raised the question of who would be available to rescue the men. However, retreat to a world from which women were excluded inevitably raised the specter of another "sexual species" currently under construction: the homosexual.[126] The word itself was coined to describe a specific category of person, developing in conjunction with the modernization that was making gender-based social assignments.[127] Homosexuality surfaced as a public issue in Russia at the turn of the century, when legislators were attempting to rewrite aspects of the legal code so that it could accommodate social and economic changes. Significantly, same-sex relations were considered a legal issue only when men were involved; lesbianism was dismissed as a psychological problem. Compared to western countries—especially England after the passage of the Labouchiere amendment in 1885 that put Oscar Wilde on trial a decade later—imperial Russia has been portrayed as relatively tolerant of homosexuals.[128] One of Tsar Alexander III's younger brothers did not feel obliged to hide his orientation, and several openly homosexual aristocrats

[122] Laura Engelstein, *The Keys to Happiness: Sex and the Search for Modernity in Fin-de-Siècle Russia* (Ithaca: Cornell University Press, 1992), 393.

[123] Breshko-Breshkovskii, *V mire atletov*, 102.

[124] Tamar Garb, *Bodies of Modernity: Figure and Flesh in Fin-de- Siècle France* (London: Thames and Hudson, 1998), especially chapter 2.

[125] Bram Dijkstra has argued persuasively that these fictional vampires played a critical role in the creation of a muscle-bound male ideology at the turn of the century. *Evil Sisters: The Threat of Female Sexuality and the Cult of Manhood* (New York: Alfred A. Knopf, 1996).

[126] Foucault, *History of Sexuality*, 43.

[127] Weeks, "Discourse, Desire, and Sexual Deviance," 82.

[128] See, for example, Simon Karlinsky's discussion of this in his introduction to *Out of the Blue: Russia's Hidden Gay Literature*, ed. Kevin Moss (San Francisco: Gay Sunshine Press, 1997), 15–26; and Engelstein, *Keys to Happiness*, 58.

not only enjoyed protection from the tsar but maintained high positions in government, including at the Ministry of Foreign Affairs.[129] The behavior of these men could be excused as aristocratic decadence.[130] As John D'Emilio, Kenneth Plummer, George Chauncey, and others have argued, capitalism has more ideological reason than aristocracy to censure homosexual relationships.[131] Stretching the basic Foucauldian position that the new social discourse written by liberal politics is still repressive, just in different ways, this argument parallels points made by Laura Engelstein in her study of Russia's fin-de-siècle sexuality. As Engelstein points out, "the power hierarchies of the Western liberal order depended as much on gender as on class, as much on sexual discipline as on social norms."[132] The mass circulation of images of wrestlers indicates that the new masculinity would not permit sexual relations between men, but men still needed to bond with each other if they were to maintain hierarchies and manage businesses.

The pictorial homoerotica of wrestlers, especially prevalent in *Gerkules*'s pictures of seminude men embracing each other, suggests that the homosexual identity was being co-opted by an evolving heterosexual masculinity. These photos emphasized the male body in a politically significant way. R. W. Connell's argument that "true masculinity is almost always thought to proceed from men's bodies"[133] became personified nightly in the ring. As Chauncey pointed out, "bodybuilders . . . sought to defend a particular social arrangement of gender by investing it with the timeless authority of the body itself."[134] Lebedev sexualized these images, waxing poetically that "crowds in the twentieth century love the power and the lines of the body."[135] One fan remembered from his boyhood that "I could almost swoon as I gazed at the broad shoulders of the Estonian demi-god under the arc-lights . . . his whole body dusted with powder that gave his skin the tint of Carrara marble."[136]

In his analysis of the American equivalent of *Gerkules*, *Physical Culture*, Greg Mullins argued that the journalism of the physical culture movement

---

[129] K. K. Rotikov's gossipy *Drugoi Peterburg* (St. Petersburg: Liga Plius, 1998).

[130] Evgenii Bernshtein, "The Russian Myth of Oscar Wilde," in *Self and Story in Russian History*, ed. Stephanie Sandler and Laura Engelstein (Ithaca: Cornell University Press, 2000), 169–75.

[131] John D'Emilio, "Capitalism and Gay Identity," in *The Gender/Sexuality Reader*, ed. Roger Lancaster and Micaela di Leonardo (New York: Routledge, 1997), 169–78; Kenneth Plummer, "Homosexual Categories: Some Research Problems in the Labeling Perspective of Homosexuality," in *Making of the Modern Homosexual*, ed. Plummer, 53–75; and George Chauncey, *Gay New York* (New York: Basic Books, 1994), especially chapter 4.

[132] Engelstein, *Keys to Happiness*, 422.

[133] R. W. Connell, *Masculinities* (Berkeley: University of California Press, 1995). 45.

[134] Chauncey, *Gay New York*, 121.

[135] Ibid., 26.

[136] Quoted in Sylvester, "Crime, Masquerade, and Anxiety," 184.

of this era operated as "a well muscled closet."[137] The primary audience for these magazines was the heterosexual male, and they sent an ambiguous message when they contrasted pictorial images with written texts that contradicted the implicit homoerotica. Thus they focused on the homosociability found in the wrestling world, where men could create a hegemonic masculinity that was also racialized by the ethically superior ethnic Russian.

Homosocial exclusionary policies were reinforced by the images of ladies preying on men's bodies because these consuming women were asserting their specifically female demands on men to produce sexually. The female fans were indeed rapacious; a journalist described the women at a wrestling match thus: "they completely lost their heads ... and unashamedly applauded their favorites loud enough for the whole circus to hear." Women also threw personal objects into the ring.[138] Virility had become a commodity. A cursory scan of the advertisements for patent medicines in commercial journalism revealed that masculinity was perceived to be weakening and in need of restoration. Patent medicines promised to cure impotence, a reminder of the demands the new woman made of even the nonathletes. Ads promising to cure baldness emphasized the need for an outward appeal. Others promised to cure alcoholism, the target of the ad being invariably the man who had destroyed his family through drink. The attacks on liquor cut both ways because although they upheld the work ethic and the family, they also threatened to deprive men of a time-honored homosocial activity. Novelist Jack London, for example, whose works were widely popular in Russia, too, exuded a masculinity that sought to ward off social reformers with fiction that encouraged virile behavior, including strong drink.[139]

The threat did not come from organized feminism, which was too weakly developed in Russia to pose a menace.[140] The femininity that converted women into sexual beings with a new list of demands was more frightening. Stress, or "neurasthenia," became a middle-class male disease in the 1880s in Russia as well as in the West.[141] Added to this, the increased opportunities for education generated commensurate ambitions among women for meaningful employment and access to public life in general,

---

[137] Greg Mullins, "Nudes, Prudes, and Pigmies: The Desirability of Disavowal in *Physical Culture,*" *Discourse* 15, no. 1 (1992): 28.

[138] Sylvester, "Crime, Masquerade, and Anxiety," 184.

[139] Joe L. Dubbert, *A Man's Place: Masculinity in Transition* (Englewood Cliffs, N.J.: Prentice-Hall, 1979), 84–86, discusses American ideas of masculinity and the social reform movement of the era.

[140] Linda Edmondson, *Feminism in Russia, 1900–1917* (Stanford: Stanford University Press, 1984).

[141] Stearns, *Be a Man,* 64. The popular press contains numerous ads for patent medicines promising to cure Russian men of neurasthenia.

even in the domesticated areas of charities and related social reform movements, such as those in which Savina participated.

As Michael Kimmel has pointed out, the industrialization that "reduced the importance and visibility of masculinity" was the true enemy, not women per se.[142] On Russia's factory floors, Taylorism and the time/motion studies that attempted to rationalize productivity led to worker alienation.[143] Moreover, the Russian wrestling fan faced threats to his masculinity beyond those experienced by his western counterpart. Russia's autocratic patriarchy subverted the authority and autonomy of its male subjects almost as much as it did the females. The image of masculinity projected from the Winter Palace by Nicholas II offered little of social utility in the modern world; the tsar's outmoded vision of his role as paterfamilias of the empire contradicted the political demands of capitalism.[144] Each *verst* of railway laid and each factory built eroded the hegemonic patriarchy of the tsar and the village elders who impersonated his authority. Nicholas's half-hearted effort to enfranchise a small portion of male Russians following the 1905 Revolution satisfied few needs. More important were the Stolypin Land Reforms of 1906 that finally freed peasants from their legal obligations to the commune, prompting tens of thousands of them to move to the cities and participate in the continuing industrial takeoff. Professional wrestling matches provided a social site for many of these urban immigrants to learn some of the new rules of conduct in the city, including self-control in competition and spectatorship.

Bending the Gender and Patrolling the Borders

Savina and Poddubnyi personified the identities of male and the female most competent to carry Russia into the future. Gender stability, though, was an ideal rather than a social maxim. Public performers also appeared in the liminal area between male and female, cross-dressers who reminded their audiences that not everything was as it seemed, that certain choices that might seem carved in stone were in fact negotiable.[145] The signifi-

---

[142] Michael Kimmel, "The Contemporary 'Crisis' of Masculinity in Historical Perspective," in *The Making of Masculinities,* ed. Harry Brod (Boston: Allen and Unwin, 1987),146.

[143] Heather Hogan, *Forging Revolution: Metalworkers, Managers, and the State in St. Petersburg, 1890–1914* (Bloomington: Indiana University Press, 1993), 222–29.

[144] Richard Wortman, *Scenarios of Power: Myth and Ceremony in Russian Monarchy,* vol. 2 (Princeton: Princeton University Press, 2000), part 3.

[145] As Marjorie Garber has argued, in the nineteenth century "transvestism was the specter that rose up—both in the theater and on the streets—to mark and overdetermine this crisis of social and economic change.... *Transvestism is a space of possibility structuring and confounding culture:* the disruptive element that intervenes, not just a category crisis of male and female, but the crisis of category itself." *Vested Interests: Cross-Dressing and Cultural Anxiety* (New York: Routledge, 1992), 17.

ОЛЬГА АЛЕКСАНДРОВНА

ДУЛЕТОВА

НЕПОДРАЖАЕМАЯ
ИСПОЛНИТЕЛЬНИЦА

РУССКИХЪ
БЫТОВЫХЪ
ПѢСЕНЪ.

АДРЕСЪ: ВЪ БЮРО Р. О. А. В. И Ц.

СЕНТЯБРЬ, ОКТЯБРЬ — ОМСКЪ.

Female cross-dresser Olga Duletova

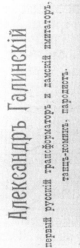

Transformator Alexander Galinskii, in full regalia

cance of cross-dressing is not that it imitates a "true" gender, but, according to Judith Butler, that it simulates the very structure of gender and therefore provides insights into how a society constructs its identities of gender.[146] The clothes a person wears, like Savina's extensive wardrobe and Poddubnyi's scant one, is one way in which power is exercised in social life, and those who dress across genders are appropriating power for those groups left outside the female/male binary. Cross-dressing and gender-bending routines became staples on vaudeville circuits.[147]

Alexander Galinskii, Russia's premier female impersonator, or "*transformator,*" pictured himself in drag in his advertising posters. The multitalented Galinskii also billed himself as a comic dancer, a parodist, and playwright, author of, for example, *The Cuckold.* Although the Moscow Arts Theater never produced any of his works, the competition for light fare in any city's theater district, where features changed weekly, brought him royalties and kept the sexual repartee going on stage. One of his acts, "Contemporary Stars," mimicked popular songstresses and actresses. He also appeared as a geisha, signifying how the war with Japan had piqued more than just military interest. Playbills document that sex impersonators were not at all uncommon, and women also crossed gender on the Russian stage, following the professional success of the extremely popular British performer Vesta Tilley.[148]

Cross-dressers ironically patrolled the borders of normative gendered identities personified by Savina and Poddubnyi. Through performance and objectification, the actress and the wrestler used their public personae to establish cultural stereotypes of femininity and masculinity in late tsarist Russia. These personae reflected the institutionalization of sex roles, gendered identities, and the growing culture of consumption. Politically and epistemologically, the stereotypes took shape in response to the needs of the changing society, and therefore they reflected facets of both its hopes and fears. Men had to be strong and controlled, protectors not only of the fair sex but also of each other from those predators from the female sex who were trying to shed its "weaker" image. Women assumed their role as

[146] Judith Butler, "Lana's 'Imitation': Melodramatic Repetition and the Gender Performative," *Genders,* no. 9 (fall 1990): 1–17.

[147] The history of men performing as women dates back to antiquity, when women were not allowed on stage. Roger Baker, *Drag: A History of Female Impersonation in the Performing Arts* (New York: New York University Press, 1994). On the American scene, see Joe Laurie Jr., *Vaudeville: From the Honky-Tonks to the Palaces* (New York: Holt, 1953), 87–95. *Transformator* Sergei Lazurini played Maksim's in Moscow, also appearing at the Nizhnii Novogorod Fair in 1916. Sylvester, "Crime, Masquerade, and Anxiety," 320, discusses these performers in Odessa.

[148] Boyish rather than butch, Tilley styled herself as a young man about town, complete with swagger, tilted hat, and small cigar. The male fan who commented that "you just felt like going up on stage and kissing her" let more than Freud slip in expressing this desire. Laurie, *Vaudeville,* 93.

consumers with heightened expectations of wielding power in the domestic economy, looking for roles that might be separate but potentially equal.

The personae fostered by Savina and Poddubnyi lent themselves well to the popular fictions that were formulaically gendered to assign social roles: Horatio Alger taught boys to pull themselves up by their pluck, but Cinderella told girls to endure abuse until that day when a prince would rescue her from circumstances over which she had no control. Poddubnyi perfectly fits the bill of the boy who worked his way from rags to riches, earning respect along the way and never dependent on luck alone to change his circumstances. Likewise, Savina's career can be read as an updated version of the Cinderella story. With the democratization of social structures and the entrance of women into the workforce, the formulaic plot of the working girl who finds happiness ever after in the arms of a protective male came to serve a whole new cultural function. Although Savina's accomplishments were certainly no less the result of hard work than were Poddubnyi's, she presented herself in life as she did on stage, as the symbol of feminine need for a stronger, guiding presence, a talent rather than a worker. Ironically, when the prince appeared in the form of Molchanov, she had become sufficiently self-reliant to use him as a prop, a stand-in to signify the happy ending that she had achieved on her own.

The outbreak of the Great War made the question of masculinity paramount and sharpened both femininity and feminism with the roles the war assigned to women. The advent of the war also coincided with and inspired the growth of the most potentially powerful medium yet of communicating cultural images to mass audiences: the motion picture. Russia's silent movies, discussed in the final chapter in this book, show the gender conflict deepening as femininity and masculinity struggled to find cultural norms during the years of chaos.

The Russian Tourist at Home and Abroad

Nikolai Leikin, a journalist from the merchant estate who enjoyed terrific popularity among his own kind for his burlesques of their often confused contacts with modern life, parodied a group of Russia's *nouveaux riches* on a tour of the European continent in 1892. Some of the characters in *Where the Oranges Ripen* had appeared two years earlier in Leikin's *Our People Abroad*, visiting the World's Fair in Paris. Uncomfortable in fashions that did not suit them, served dishes that only soured their appetites, and in constant distress for cross-cultural gaffes, Russia's merchant tourists had reason to question why they should imitate the nobility and make the de rigeur Grand Tour of the continent. Armed only with foreign vocabulary words for "hotel room" and "liquor" and fearful of anything served to them other than beef, Leikin's characters made an important discovery: that home is best. Like their redoubtable Cockney counterpart, the fictional tourist Mrs. Brown on the Bridge of Sighs in Venice, they found the place had "no size at all."[1] Like Mark Twain's *Innocents Abroad*, Leikin's hapless wayfarers tell much about their own society through their reactions to the places they visit.

In the eighteenth century, Europe's young noblemen embarked on tours of the continent, stylized sentimental journeys, more for purposes of self- than scientific discovery.[2] When Russia's merchant-tourists set out a

---

[1] Quoted in James Buzard, *The Beaten Track: European Tourism, Literature and the Ways to Culture, 1800–1918* (New York: Oxford University Press, 1993), 117. An innocent abroad on several fictional Cook's tours, Mrs. Brown, created by George Brown, entertained British readers from the 1870s.

[2] Thomas Nugent's *The Grand Tour*, published in 1749, made the trip to the Continent, es-

century later, following similar routes, they were after the patina of so-phistication that had rubbed off on the Continental tour. These tourists were determined to accrue some of the cultural capital that, as Pierre Bourdieu has argued, would provide an essential socially convertible com-plement to their financial resources.[3] Sensitive to the relationship between sophistication and power, many Russians took advantage of improved transportation and communication to expand their literal and figurative horizons. During the rapid industrialization of the late nineteenth century, when personal fortunes ebbed and flowed with the tides of industry, tourists had very practical reasons for accumulating cultural as well as fi-nancial capital.

In caricaturing his tourists as yokels, Leikin was playing on the irony that they were in fact protagonists of modernity. The development of tourism as a commercial industry paralleled the emergence of a middle class, and the influence of capitalism on modes of, and motivations for, travel proved paramount. Capitalist principles affected all aspects of tourism, beginning with the transportation revolution that facilitated commercial travel. On the psychological front, tourists dealt with a new concept of time, the idea of the vacation as an intermission in the work cycle. As James Buzard has noted, a vacation promises a "time or imaginary space out of ordinary life for the free realization of (an) otherwise thwarted potential."[4] This free-dom, though, would be fixed by time and wages. Time now had to be prop-erly structured so that transportation schedules could be met, and specific amounts of it must be apportioned to be able to follow the recommenda-tions of the commercial guidebook. The nascent tourist industry leaders learned from commercial capitalism how to package and sell experience. Financed by advertising, tourist-oriented publications promoted the com-modification of adventures into souvenirs when the trip ended. The in-sightful travel letter became the hastily jotted postcard;[5] the timepiece and the guidebook, essential to the tourist, would have had no place in the trav-eler's knapsack.

Tourism evolved as a means through which the Russian middle classes developed an identity that paradoxically combined cosmopolitanism and conservative nationalism. It begins with the conversion of the noble "trav-eler" into the bourgeois "tourist," with all the implications of social change implicit in this movement from elitism to commerce.[6] Although Harvey

---

pecially to sites from classical antiquity, an essential part of the education of young men with ambitions.

[3] Pierre Bourdieu, *Distinction: A Social Critique of Judgment,* trans. Richard Nice (Cambridge, Mass.: Harvard University Press, 1984), 64–69.

[4] Buzard, *Beaten Track,* 102–3.

[5] Marsel Prevo (Marcel Prevot), "Iazyk otkrytok," *Prekrasnoe daleko,* no. 3 (1912): 16–18.

[6] James Clifford has written that "I hang onto 'travel' as a term of cultural comparison,

Levenstein has demonstrated how this dichotomy depends on a fantasized notion of "traveler" at the expense of that "despised word tourist," it makes a useful social distinction between educational and recreational travel.[7] As the tourist industry developed, it found itself deeply enmeshed in the conflation of discourses of nationalism with those of imperialism, as the Russian state expanded to incorporate its borderlands. Tourism played a significant role because the most attractive spots for tourists were the spas and seacoasts in the non-Slavic territories in the east and the south.

The cultural appropriation of geographical names was a first step in this process, facilitating the creation of what Edward Said termed "imaginative geographies."[8] As Mary Louise Pratt has observed, renaming was one way in which the "discoverer" transformed local knowledge into that of the conqueror.[9] For example, Catherine the Great's tour of the Crimea in 1787 absorbed the peninsula with a panache lacking in the formal treaties, emphasizing the exotica of the Orient that Russia had now absorbed as a part of its own identity.[10] She Russified it by restoring the ancient place names, attempting historical revision by writing out the region's Tatar past, especially its Muslim heritage. Catherine's primary purpose was to connect the peninsula to ancient Greece, which in its later incarnation as the Byzantine Empire had been the source of Russia's Orthodox Christianity.[11] The Tatar Gezlev, for example, reverted to the Greek Eupatoria (Evpatoria in Russian), and it became a leading tourist attraction after the Crimean War because a major battle had been fought there. Custom had a way of prevailing, though, and not even Catherine's efforts to restore the peninsula's first historical name, Taurida, could win out over the Turkish Krym, or Crimea.[12]

Russification through translation extended cultural conquest. In the Caucasus, Piatigorsk, which the Russians initially called "hot waters," acquired the name that translates loosely as "five mountains" from the orig-

---

precisely because of its historical taintedness, its associations with gendered, racial bodies, class privilege, specific means of conveyance, etc." "Traveling Cultures," in *Cultural Studies*, ed. Lawrence Grossberg, Cary Nelson, and Paula Treichler (New York: Routledge, 1992), 110.

[7] The "despised word tourist" is a quote from Henry James. In Harry Levenstein, *Seductive Journey: American Tourists in France from Jefferson to the Jazz Age* (Chicago: University of Chicago Press, 1998), ix–x.

[8] Quoted in Arturo Escobar, *Encountering Development: The Making and Unmaking of the Third World* (Princeton: Princeton University Press, 1995), 9.

[9] Mary Louise Pratt, *Imperial Eyes: Travel Writing and Transculturation* (New York: Routledge, 1992), 202.

[10] Larry Wolff, *Inventing Eastern Europe: The Map of Civilization on the Mind of the Enlightenment* (Stanford: Stanford University Press, 1994), 128. See also Andreas Schonle, "Garden of Empire: Catherine's Appropriation of the Crimea," *Slavic Review* 60, no. 1 (2001): 1023.

[11] Grigorii Moskvich, *Putevoditel' po Krymu*, 27th ed. (Petrograd: Putevoditelei, 1915), 4.

[12] On historical aspects of the changing terminology, see K. Kogonashvili, *Kratkii slovar' istorii Kryma* (Simferopol: Biznes-inform, 1995).

inal Persian word for the area, Besh-Tau.[13] Tbilisi, the Georgian name for the capital of its former kingdom, became Russianized as Tiflis. The new conquistadors of the Caucasus also named places after themselves. At Borzhom, which would earn the reputation of "the Russian Vichy," the commander of the Russian forces in 1845 named the two mineral springs for himself and his daughter, whom he had brought with him for her health.[14] On the Baltic, when the area where the Narva River flows into the Gulf of Finland began attracting summer tourists in the 1870s, local leaders changed the name Peter the Great had given them, Gungerburg, or "Hungertown," to the more appealing Ust'-Narva, or "Mouth of the Narva."[15] Thus by redrawing the map did Russians rewrite their imperial history.

The geographical sites might be Russified, but the reverse held true when it came to naming the places where tourists would seek respite after a day trekking through culture and history. Seemingly, the first hotel to go up in almost any Russian city was called the European (*Evropeiskaia*), an indication of the level of service guests were supposed to be able to anticipate. Other popular names included Russian transliterations of the Bristol, the Grand Hotel, the Bellevue, and even the San Remo. Moscow's Slavic Bazaar, which had grown into one of the second capital's favored hotels, complete with a fine restaurant, stood out for marketing its local identity. The extent to which the Russian hotels maintained the standards of the places whose names they bore undoubtedly varied and improved over time. Although western guidebooks hardly used Russian norms as a unit of measurement, one written in 1912 applauded "the service and cuisine of the hotels in (Russia's) chief cities [which] cannot be excelled."[16]

In addition to its growth as a modern industry, tourism is analyzed here as a discursive construct of modernity. Whatever the contemporary debate about the relative benefits of modernity, the first tourists were active agents on its behalf. Even Freud analyzed tourism; for him the escape from the family, especially the father, made travel psychologically beneficial.[17] The sociologist Dean MacCannell has argued that "the empirical and ideological expansion of modern society (is) intimately linked in diverse ways to . . . tourism and sightseeing."[18] John Urry has discussed how in the nine-

---

[13] Susan Layton, *Russian Literature and Empire: Conquest of the Caucasus from Pushkin to Tolstoy* (Cambridge: Cambridge University Press, 1994), 36.

[14] *Borzhom: Spravochnaia knizhka* (Tiflis: Ia. I. Liberman, 1903), 11–13.

[15] In the Soviet era this acquired the Estonian spelling, Narva-Iyesuu. E. Krivosheev, *Narva-Iyesuu* (Tallinn: EESTI RAAMAT, 1971), 13–14.

[16] Ruth Kedzie Wood, *The Tourist's Russia* (New York: Dodd, Mead, 1912), 3. She also noted that the internal transportation system was both good and the least expensive in Europe.

[17] Paul Fussell, ed., *The Norton Book of Travel* (New York: Norton, 1987), 13.

[18] Dean MacCannell, *The Tourist: A New Theory of the Leisure Class* (New York: Schocken, 1976), 2.

teenth-century various institutions, technologies, and ideologies constructed a "tourist gaze," a specific way of incorporating new contacts into a previously held worldview.[19] How the locals returned this gaze is another story, not told here. However, the Russian at home caught in the gaze of the western tourist finds a place in this story because of how the western gaze established the basis for comparative modern identities.

The Russian Traveler

The quintessential Russian traveler would be Peter the Great, who journeyed to western Europe to find not only himself but, more to the point, to find the nation that he embodied. The requisite trip West for the elite among the nobility then began under Peter as a form of state service. The diaries of one such noble, Peter Tolstoy, sent to Italy in 1697, show him to be more appreciative of cultural differences than Leikin's merchants, but just as needful of an appropriate vocabulary.[20] In this, as in many other matters of forced westernization, Russians were imitating rather than duplicating experiences. As Andreas Schonle has pointed out, this substantially distinguished the works produced by Russians from those written by their continental counterparts, because Russian writers had to educate their readers about cultures already familiar to most other European readers at the same time that the Russians were also searching for self-identity.[21] Not surprisingly, two of the writers most influential in the creation of a Russian literary language, Nicholas Karamzin and Alexander Pushkin, were also crucial in the development of the genre of travel writing. Through their stylistic and psychological innovations they taught Russians to articulate themselves into their changing imperial surroundings. Although both Karamzin and Pushkin felt the heavy hand of European literary structures and fashions, they Russianized them so thoroughly as to give their fellow nationals a vocabulary and a context for imagining themselves in a larger, more diverse world. They created for readers what eighteenth-century American traveler John Ledyard called "philosophic geography," that is, the redrawing of the physical within predominant philosophical boundaries.[22]

Describing his 1790 journey through Germany, Switzerland, France, and England (his particular favorite), Karamzin traced the Englishman Thomas

---

[19] John Urry, *The Tourist Gaze: Leisure and Travel in Contemporary Societies* (London: Sage, 1990).

[20] *The Travel Diary of Peter Tolstoi: A Muscovite in Early Modern Europe,* trans. Max Okenfuss (De Kalb: Northern Illinois University Press, 1987).

[21] Andreas Schonle, *Authenticity and Fiction in the Russian Literary Journal, 1790–1840* (Cambridge, Mass.: Harvard University Press, 2000), 210.

[22] Quoted in Wolff, *Inventing Eastern Europe,* 6.

Nugent's seminal *The Grand Tour* (1749). He made Russia's first contribution to the current style of travel writing popularized by Laurence Sterne's *A Sentimental Journey* (1768). This native of provincial Simbirsk's *Letters of a Russian Traveler*, serialized in *Moskovskii zhurnal* (The Moscow journal) shortly after his return, mixed descriptive reportage with imaginative self-reflection.[23] Writing in the first person and addressing his "dear friends" as though his readers walked alongside him, Karamzin blurred the distinction between reading and traveling.[24] He wrote, "At this point, would you like to look at the most famous buildings in Paris with me? No. Let us leave that for another time. You are tired, and so am I."[25] His *récits de voyage* told Russians to make themselves, not science, the objective of their travels.

Karamzin was Russia's most prominent proponent of sentimentalism, a genre that encouraged travel because it held that knowledge accumulates through sensory experiences.[26] Highly emotional in his descriptions, Karamzin made internal connections to the external world. Upon his return to Russia, landing at the naval base just outside Petersburg, he wrote, "I stop everyone I meet, I ask questions only to speak Russian and to hear Russian people. . . . You know it would be difficult to find a more miserable town than Kronstadt, yet it is dear to me!"[27] Moreover, as Karamzin grew increasingly self-confident, he became Russia's first important historian, providing new texts for Russians to inscribe themselves into their geography.[28]

Pushkin, in contrast, never realized his dream of visiting Europe because the autocracy, for political reasons, refused him a passport. But having studied French, English, and the classics at his lyceum, he was familiar with European literature. A nominal state servitor in Odessa and Kishinev, he became a travel writer through his poetry. He took readers to the new imperial frontiers in Piatigorsk in *The Prisoner of the Caucasus* (1821), to the Crimea in *The Fountain of Bakhchisarai* (1822), and to Bessarabia in *The Gypsies* (1824). He also described in prose the campaigns along the Turkish-Caucasian border in *Journey to Arzrum* (1829).

Pushkin wrote from extremely limited personal experience, having jour-

[23] On Karamzin's style, see Yuri Lotman and Boris Uspensky, *Pis'ma russkogo puteshestvennika* (Moscow: Nauka, 1984), 535–40.

[24] Layton, *Russian Literature and Empire*, 23. See also Michael Butor, "Traveling and Writing," trans. John Powers and K. Lisker, *Mosaic* 8 (fall 1974): 1–3.

[25] Nikolai Karamzin, *Letters of a Russian Traveler, 1789–90: An Account of a Young Russian Gentleman's Tour through Germany, Switzerland, France, and England*, trans. and abr. Florence Jonas (New York: Columbia University Press, 1957), 187.

[26] Roger B. Anderson, "Karamzin's *Letters of a Russian Traveler*: An Education in Western Sentimentalism," in *Essays on Karamzin, Russian Man of Letters, Political Thinker, Historian*, ed. J. L. Black (The Hague: Mouton, 1975).

[27] Karamzin, *Letters*, 340.

[28] As Schonle writes, Karamzin "hoped that his self-fashioning would . . . enable Russia to participate in the advance of world civilization toward enlightenment" (*Authenticity and Fiction*, 210).

neyed to the Caucasus for only two months in 1820 and again in 1829. His landscapes, like his heroes, were imagined more vividly than reality would have allowed. Critics have explored the influence of England's Romantic idol Lord Byron over Pushkin because of the common theme of the disillusioned hero who has rejected civilization and sought the meaning of society among the peoples outside its borders.[29] Despite his intention of turning his back on society, the hero indulges his fantasies of superiority and refuses to be assimilated by the outsider community with whom he seeks refuge.[30] Through their highly idealized contacts with the Other, Pushkin's heroes inspired travel by presenting exotica as attainable. Equally telling, his works masked the violence with which the frontier had been conquered by depicting a fierce Other who is at heart eager for assimilation into the superior culture.[31] Pushkin's poetry provided an immediate psychological connection to place, in this case to the borders of empire.[32]

The Romantic travel writers inspired many to follow their paths literally.[33] Ironically, both Byron's and Pushkin's bodies were posthumously transformed into tourist attractions. Byron's untimely death in Greece brought his fellow countrymen there in droves, hoping to re-create the poet's experience. Pushkin, too, died the death of one of his protagonists, and not only did the site of his fatal duel at Chernaia rechka in St. Petersburg become a shrine, but so did every place he ever lived or worked. An advertising appeal made in 1912 for the profitable tourist industry in the Caucasus used the pitch that Russians "raised on Pushkin have dreamed since childhood of visiting that area."[34] Almost two hundred years after his birth the excursion around Pushkin's old haunts remains a pilgrimage of sorts, a journey intended for the discovery of both the self and Russia, whatever its current political or geographic guise.[35]

[29] Stephanie Sandler, *Distant Pleasures: Alexander Pushkin and the Writing of Exile* (Stanford: Stanford University Press, 1989).

[30] Layton, *Russian Literature and Empire,* 104, argued that in Pushkin's "The Gypsies," the author "suggested that a civilized outsider's intrusion into a primitive society merely sows discord and destruction."

[31] Layton, *Russian Literature and Empire,* 158–59, discusses a later form of "the myth of regenerative violence."

[32] Buzard, *Beaten Track,* 120, discusses how British travelers and tourists carried Byron's poetry to Greece with them. Pushkin had a similar effect. See also Layton, *Russian Literature and Empire,* 24–27.

[33] Ruth Kedzie Wood noted that in 1909 "Bakshisarai was a favorite wedding journey for Russian young people." Ruth Kedzie Wood, *Honeymooning in Russia* (New York: Dodd, Mead, 1911), 295.

[34] G. G. Evangulov, "Glavnyi komitet pooshchreniia turizma na Kavkaze i ego zadachi" (copy of an official report with no publishing information).

[35] Andrei Sinyavsky (Abram Tertz), *Strolls with Pushkin,* trans. Catherine Nepomnyashchy and Slava Yastremski (New Haven: Yale University Press, 1993). An intellectual rather than a geographical stroll, Sinyavsky's still captures the Pushkin's influence on the Russian imagination.

Karamzin and Pushkin differed in both style and substance, the sentimentalist in Europe and the Romantic along the southern fringes of the empire. But each in his own way made clear how significant travel had become to the development of the evolving sense of self. Karamzin emphasized the experience that others might enjoy vicariously through his *Letters,* and then he wrote the history that provided the framework for Russia's geopolitical position. Pushkin provided imagination and the motivation necessary for Russians to visit other parts of *their* empire in images that inflamed the Russian feelings of superiority. Romantic writer Mikhail Lermontov stood out among the many of Pushkin's heirs who continued to take their readers on these poetic journeys.

Karamzin's quote that "the individual with the pack on his back and the staff in his hand is not responsible to either officialdom or academics" made a popular epigraph in subsequent travel writing.[36] Count D. I. Khvostov, a minor poet and translator, published his *Travel Notes* on a trip "from St. Petersburg along the Tikhvinskii road to various cities of the empire" in 1818.[37] He described some of the oldest, and hence holiest, cities of ancient Rus', including Yaroslavl and Suzdal, whose Orthodox monasteries date from the thirteenth to fourteenth centuries of Christianity in Russia and remain a foremost tourist attraction today. Khvostov mixed details of travel with those of history, and population figures with poetry. A second edition of his *Travel Notes* appeared in 1824, supplemented with correspondence from readers. Khvostov's publisher came out a few years later with a chattier, more casual *Wanderers' Journal,* with socializing and conversations between two travelers, recorded as a diary, although the author's identity was never determined.[38]

State servitors began camouflaging the official objective of their travel in purple prose imitative of Karamzin's. In 1828 State Councilor Gavriil Gerakov published an account of some of his travels through provincial Russia.[39] Gerakov's travel diary is especially valuable because of how he used the narrative of self-discovery to open up the territory he was visiting.[40] In Nizhnii Novgorod he weeps at the grave of "the eternal Minin," the local butcher credited with organizing a national army that drove out the Swedes and Poles during the Time of Troubles in 1612. Gerakov successfully used the emotional experience of being at the site to connect him-

---

[36] Schonle states that by 1816 Russians had 105 books, including translations, from which to choose with the title *Journey to . . . , Authenticity and Fiction,* 6.

[37] Graf D. I. Khvostov, *Putevye zapiski* (Moscow: M. N. Makarov, 1824), III.

[38] *Zhurnal peshekhodtsev ot Moskvy do Rostova i obratno v Moskvu* (Moscow: M. N. Makarov, 1830).

[39] Gavriil Gerakov, *Putevye zapiski po mnogim rossiiskim guberniiam, 1820* (St. Petersburg: Tip. Imperatorskogo Vospitat. Dom, 1828).

[40] Gerakov dedicated his travelogue to "the venerated fair sex," whom he assured that "I am happy and satisfied with only your smile and your approval." Ibid., n.p.

self to Russia's past, accentuating the need to be an eyewitness in order to authenticate the experience.[41]

Gerakov traveled as far as Simferopol in the Crimea. Sprinkling history onto verbal portraits of the peoples and terrain he encountered, he introduced the Tatars, Georgians, and Cossacks as exotic co-subjects with Russians of a shared geography. The "foreigners" in this travelogue are the western Europeans who came to the Crimea for the mineral waters.[42] Gerakov was equally innovative in his emphasis on issues fundamental to the activity of traveling: roads, meals, and lodgings.[43] These very basic problems had to be resolved before the singular traveler, out for self-reflection, could be replaced by the horde of tourists, out for a holiday. As Pratt has pointed out, the new tourist was an economic pragmatist rather than a romantic, out to overcome logistical rather than military obstacles.[44] The first places capable of accommodating casual visitors were the major cities. In 1837 the first of several editions of a pocket guide appeared, steering readers from Moscow to Petersburg and to houses whose proprietors would feed and lodge paying customers. Not quite hotels, these establishments foretold that the days were numbered when travelers had to presume on acquaintances or the local peasantry to put them up.[45]

Describing his excursions in *Travel Notes and Impressions of Eastern European Russia* in 1851, Iosif Berlov walked the figurative borderline between traveling and touring.[46] A transitional figure, his constant allusions to economizing make plain that he was no member of the idle rich. The sheer variety of his lodgings reflected Russia's changing profile: the nobles in rustic Perm welcome the outsider as a link to Moscow, but on the road he must stay in the squalid huts of the coach drivers. Generally contemptuous of the habits of the Muslims and other Asian subjects of the Russian tsar, he enjoys a brief interlude with one Tatar family. For longer layovers, Berlov provides useful information about inexpensive furnished rooms in Moscow and Kazan. As tourism became increasingly popular, hence profitable, entrepreneurs around the empire opened *pansiony*, or "pensions," economical lodgings especially well suited for tourists who wanted to stay longer than a few days.

Berlov, though traveling solo, mentions encountering other groups on tour, which included women growing as anxious as men to discover them-

[41] Ibid., 19.

[42] Ibid., 98.

[43] Pushkin's novella *The Station Master* captured life on the road before the advent of provincial hotels, when travelers stayed at the postal stations.

[44] Pratt, *Imperial Eyes*, 148.

[45] I. Dmitriev, *Sputnik ot Moskvy do Peterburga* (Moscow: A. Semen, 1841). This is the second, updated edition of the 1837 original.

[46] Iosif Berlov, *Putevye zametki i vpechatleniia po vostochnoi evropeiskoi Rossii* (Moscow: A. Semen, 1851).

A *pansion* in the Crimea

selves in their travels.[47] Berlov includes the obligatory history lessons, but his keen eye for ethnic differences in the empire, especially the Tatar population in Kazan, stands out. Keeping his distance as a neutral observer, Berlov uses travel as a means of incorporation of peoples from "the Great Wall of China to a French province" into Russia.[48] He looked about with an ethnically specific gaze "that survey[ed] and catalogue[d] other races while remaining unmarked and unseen itself."[49] His distanced mode of observing and use of historical snippets established a Slavic presence atop the political hierarchy of this kaleidoscope of peoples and anticipated a corollary "tourist gaze," a structured way of looking that would allow the viewer to locate him/herself in unfamiliar surroundings.

The autocracy gave Russians both reason and opportunity for travel in launching the Great Reforms: the expanded meaning of citizenship gave people reasons for wanting to insert themselves into the broader imperial mission, and the ensuing industrialization added the commerce and technology that increased opportunity. Information had to be made more readily available; the Englishman John Murray III pioneered in guidebooks marketed for the tourist in the 1840s. Murray's success was quickly improved upon by German Karl Baedeker, who ultimately dominated this

[47] Edmund Swinglehurst, *Cook's Tours: The Story of Popular Travel* (Poole, Dorset: Blandford Press, 1982), 35, pointed out that "ladies were to be the mainstay of Cook parties throughout the century."

[48] Berlov, *Putevye zametki*, 79.

[49] This is how Vicente Rafael describes the U.S. colonizers watching Filipinos in "White Love: Surveillance and National Resistance in the United States' Colonization of the Philippines," in *Cultures of United States Imperialism,* ed. Amy Kaplan and Donald Pease (Durham: Duke University Press, 1993), 200.

business because he appreciated the commercial aspects and published travel guides in many languages. Russians, though, had to turn first to the Imperial Geographical Society, founded in 1845, which published books that covered the geographical terrain but without the personal information. Later, ethnographers began producing a multivolume series of textbooks on what they referred to as the "homeland" (*otechestvovedenie*) rather than the "empire," another source of information that scripted the new lands into the empire for potential travelers, who were now metamorphosing into tourists.[50] Heralding the arrival of the tourist in 1875, a newssheet with information about hotels in both Russian capitals, financed completely by advertisements, appeared in Petersburg and circulated in major European and Russian cities.[51]

Organized Travel and the Development of Tourism

The Englishman Thomas Cook is generally recognized as the founder of commercial tourism in the middle of the nineteenth century because of the subsequent effects of his organizational innovations on travel. Secretary of the Leicester Temperance Society and committed to "leveling upward," Cook began his business by organizing outings for the local working classes so as to divert them from drink. Arguing, not always successfully, that workers should be given time off and encouraged to travel for educational purposes, Cook relied on the principles of the industrial revolution to convey more than 150,000 tourists from the British Midlands to London to visit the spectacular Crystal Palace exhibit in 1851, England's dazzling monument to the future. Cook realized that the railroad offered an opportunity to rethink many of the fundamentals of travel, just as he saw how practical organization and mass production could streamline efficiency and reduce costs. The tourist's financial investment in the journey could be easily rationalized on the grounds of self-improvement.[52]

Cook devised a formula that would translate the ideas behind "vacation" and "disposable income" into what would eventually become the world's largest industry.[53] He brought together people of various backgrounds by

[50] See, for example, D. Semenov, *Otechestvovedenie. Rossiia po rasskazam puteshestvennikov i uchenym issledovaniia* (Uchebnoe posobie dlia uchashchikhsiia), vol. 4, *Vostok i zapad,* 2d ed. (Moscow: S. Orlov, 1879).

[51] *Peterburgskii listok dlia gostinnits. Ezhednevnaia spravochnaia gazeta ob"iavlenii* (St. Petersburg: n.p., 1875–76).

[52] Much has been written on Thomas Cook and his agency. See, for example, Swinglehurst, *Cook's Tours.*

[53] In 1990 the tourism industry employed over 101 million worldwide, with gross sales surpassing $2 trillion, or 5.5 percent of the world's GNP. *World Travel and Tourism Review: Indicators, Trends and Forecasts,* ed. Frank Go and Douglas Frechtling, vol. 1 (Wallingford: C-A-B International, 1991), ix.

removing some of the psychological impediments that had intimidated the less sophisticated. As Edmund Swinglehurst pointed out, tourists who signed on with Cook "felt [as if] something of the gloss of their social superiors descended on their shoulders and, as many of them were the teachers, doctors and clergy who served the upper classes, they reasonably hoped that in the course of time the closing of the cultural gap would lead to the bridging of the social gap as well."[54] Cook packaged tours with multilingual guides, arranged for lodging in advance, and helped with currency exchange and customs at border crossings. The art critic John Ruskin, who hoped to use his aesthetic influence to reclaim agrarian Romanticism from the depredations of industrialization, deplored this tendency for people to "treat themselves like parcels, moving speedily between destinations."[55] But Ruskin was a traveler in an age when tourism had denuded travel of its elitism, and it was precisely this capacity for packaging that allowed so many to accrue what Ruskin-the-critic was turning into the cultural capital they craved.

The organizational model Cook pioneered was easy to duplicate, and other agencies began recruiting tourists. Although in Russia no Cooks or Baedekers emerged, Russians founded numerous smaller agencies capitalized by dues-paying members and joint-stock companies that facilitated tourism both within the empire and, less frequently, abroad. The first major such company, the Russian Society of Shipping and Trade (ROPT) recognized what Ruskin had so despised, that people were commercial objects, too. Chartered in Odessa in 1857, ROPT benefited from government subsidies in the push to industrialize. The shipping company then joined with the developing network of railroads, carrying passengers as well as freight.[56] By 1897 forty-seven—almost half—of ROPT's fleet accepted passengers, including two cruise ships designed for tourist travel.[57] In most years, barring such natural and social disasters as the famine and cholera epidemic of 1892 and the 1905 Revolution, the company showed a healthy profit.[58] Pilgrims to the Holy Land, even though they tended to buy the cheap tickets, traveled in sufficient numbers to provide ROPT one of its most profitable sidelines.[59] By 1915 it boasted connections to numerous national and international lines, and organized discounted excursions for groups of twenty or more. Students and school teachers could also travel

[54] Swinglehurst, *Cook's Tours*, 34.

[55] Quoted in Buzard, *Beaten Track*, 33.

[56] *Istoricheskii ocherk piatidesiatiletiia uchrezhdeniia Russkogo obshchestva parokhodstva i torgovli, 1857–1907* (Odessa: Tip. Akts. Iuzhno-russkogo ob-va pechatnogo dela, 1907).

[57] *Putevoditel' po Chernomu moriu* (Moscow: ROPT, 1897).

[58] This is based, in addition to the above-cited history, on the company's annual *otchety* after 1903, published by E. Arnol'd.

[59] *Zamechanie F. K. Fontona na obshchem sobranii aktsionerov 11 iunia 1913 g.* (St. Petersburg: Tip. Arngol'da), 2.

at reduced rates.[60] Headquartered in St. Petersburg, ROPT maintained bureaus in all major cities and in seacoast resort areas.

The enterprise that claimed to be Russia's first tourist agency was founded in Petersburg by Leopol'd Lipson, who began organizing tours of Italy and Spain as early as 1867. Lipson's advertising strategy was to emphasize ease of travel. Borrowing from Cook's system, he promised to assume "all the worries about spiritual and physical comfort . . . all the annoyances associated with tickets, baggage, guides, transportation, and tips." What distinguished him from his competitors was that his tours moved slowly, giving customers time to appreciate the people and country so that they could take home "memories to last a lifetime."[61]

Replicating relations in the modern city, members of his tour met as strangers, and he welcomed both sexes. Significantly, he made proper social behavior a condition for joining one of his groups. Because success depended upon the compatibility of the group, for example, he advised against discussions of religion and politics. To maintain a hierarchy of authority, he insisted that complaints be made directly to the leader, and never in front of the others. Anyone caught trying to bring contraband across international borders would embarrass the whole group. Significantly, forty years later organizers were continuing to emphasize the importance of behavior on tours, an indication that tourism still functioned for many as a medium of socialization, a source of cosmopolitanism.[62] Lipson's prices in 1885 ranged from 350 rubles for three weeks in Finland and Sweden to 2,500 rubles for a three-month voyage that included Paris, Italy, and Egypt. These arrangements would have been affordable to newly moneyed Russians, who would need Lipson's organizational skills to compensate for their lack of experience in such matters.[63]

The data on Russia's commercial agencies are hopelessly scattered; the most solid conclusion to which they point is that several existed and enjoyed sufficient success to stay in business for at least a few years. Motivated presumably by similar corporations trying to set up resorts, a group of investors established a joint-stock company in 1903, Turist. The slender sources do not enlighten on the extent of Turist's success or failure, but its charter reflects the issues central to the growing industry. Although Turist solicited members at a minimal cost of three rubles per annum, the primary funding was to come from agents who invested at a rate of five thou-

---

[60] Groups would receive 25 percent off for second-class tickets, 50 percent off for third-class. Advertised in *Ekskursii po Krymu, Kavkazu, i zagranichei* (Odessa: ROPT, 1911).

[61] Leonol'd Lipson, *Pervoe v Rossii predpriiatie dlia obshchestvennykh puteshestvii, 1885–86* (St. Petersburg: Kene, 1885).

[62] *Obshchestvo "Maiak": Programma letnykh ekskursii* (St. Petersburg: Tip. Glav. Up. Udelov, 1910).

[63] Ibid.

sand, three thousand, or fifteen hundred rubles, depending on their degree of responsibility; all would share profits proportionally. The organizers understood the significance of volume to their enterprise and explained that "we do not want to enter into agreements with shops or petty enterprises." They also recognized that the underdeveloped provinces could not always accommodate tourists, so they promised to find adequate housing and eating arrangements. A push to recruit multilingual agents indicated a desire to bring in foreign tourists. Essentially, though, the founders of Turist had recognized what Ruskin had disdained: tourism kept people and products in circulation. The company negotiated to produce and sell commodities essential for tourism, from soap to postcards, in railroad stations around the country. It may well have failed, though, because it also honored the capitalist principle of exploiting labor: those agents who were saddled with the most work earned the least.[64]

Russians, however, seemed to prefer officially chartered societies to the private agencies. Alpine clubs, for example, brought amateur mountain climbers together in the Caucasus and the Crimea from the 1890s onward. Like other voluntary associations, such as the numerous sports clubs, these societies did not have to turn a profit because they could solicit outside funding from those sympathetic with their objectives. Many were also chartered to sponsor fundraising events. Moreover, in their charters these societies emphasized their commitment to using tourism as a medium of education, especially about health. Many published their own journals, and in addition to such official organs, several commercial journals audiences began publication, *Puteshestvennik* (The traveler) in 1905 and *Prekrasnoe daleko* (The beautiful faraway) in 1912. Whereas the first tried to mount an educational platform by mixing scientific information with sensational stories, the latter capitalized heavily on contributions from readers. The brisk prose and objective eye of the new tourist differed markedly from the travel writer's emotionalisms of old.

The Russian Society of Tourists became the largest of these associations. Based in Petersburg, it grew out of the Touring Club of Bicyclists-Tourists, founded in 1895. Bicycling was an appropriate activity from which to begin this agency for two reasons, the most obvious being that cycling was a comparatively inexpensive mode of travel. In addition, regulations relevant to cyclists varied from city to city and the requirements at customs for taking bikes across borders were sufficiently complex to warrant such a centralized organization. The cyclists had begun organizing excursions and coordinating with similar organizations in other cities. Their journal, originally entitled *Velosiped* (The bicycle), was rechristened *Russkii turist* (The Russian

---

[64] *Instruktsiia agentam akts.-ogo obshchestva "Turist"* (St. Petersburg: A. F. Shtol'tsenburg, 1903).

tourist) in 1898.[65] In 1903 it boasted 2,153 members.[66] Annual dues were set at two rubles, but later dropped to one. The ubiquitous Ribop'er lent moral support by paying fifty rubles for a lifetime membership.[67]

The new name switched more than the image of the tourist as a cyclist. Although it continued to use *russkii*, which implied ethnic Russian, in the title of its journal, the society adopted the more inclusive *rossiiskii*, which held an insinuation of empire, for its official title. It maintained representatives in other major cities, plus agents positioned in towns and villages throughout the empire. By 1910 the society boasted more than one hundred representatives and twenty-five larger committees in major urban areas.[68] *Russkii turist* published the names of some of these agents, and a partial list in 1899 denoted the diversity of tourism: agents included a postmaster, a village doctor, a Lutheran pastor, and a prince.[69]

Russkii turist peddled images of the open road, but for all the reports on trips to Italy or walking tours of China, most excursions were considerably more modest. Primarily, local agents organized day trips to points of interest in their locales, at a cost of ten kopecks. Moreover, these trips helped to activate the concept of "weekend," filling the time away from work with pleasurable projects for self-improvement. A day trip to a Moscow candy factory, captured for memory by a Kodak (a company that advertised in the magazine) converted a Saturday into an experience.[70] The Tula branch initiated what would today be called "Tolstoy Tours," arranging for visits to the great man's estate at Iasnaia Poliana.[71] Members in Rostov-on-Don arranged picnics at the estate of N. I. Pastukhov, the former bar owner who had made millions publishing Moscow's most successful tabloid, *Moskovskii listok* (The Moscow sheet), and had then retired to his provincial birthplace.[72]

The Tourist Society gave lessons in sophistication, underscoring the notion that one reason to be a tourist was to acquire cultural skills that could bridge social divisions. For example, it explained how to use automatic ticket machines being installed in train stations around the turn of the century.[73] The advertisements in its journal indicated the extensive commer-

---

[65] *Russkii turist*, no. 1 (1899): 2, 4.

[66] The charter is published in *Russkii turist*, no. 6 (1903): 188–90. See also *Russkii turist*, no. 3 (1904): 85.

[67] *Ezhegodnik. Rossiiskoe obshchestvo turistov za 1903. (Bezplatnoe prilozhenie k zhurnalu Russkii turist)* (St. Petersburg: Izd. Ross. ob-tva turistov, 1903), 10.

[68] *Russkii turist*, no. 1 (1910): 1.

[69] *Russkii turist*, no. 1 (1899): 12.

[70] *Russkii turist*, no. 4 (1904): 104–6. A photo accompanying the article showed the approximately thirty tourists hoisting their flag in front of the factory.

[71] *Russkii turist*, no. 1 (1899): 11.

[72] *Predstavitel'stvo rossiiskogo obshchestva turistov. Spravochnik i programma ekskursii* (Rostov on Don: n.p., 1910).

[73] *Russkii turist*, no. 7 (1903): 213.

cialization of the industry. Just as the society could arrange for group passage across borders, so could it negotiate discounts for hotels or tourist-related paraphernalia, such as cameras. Merchants would arrange with the society's local representatives to offer bargains for members on tour. Thus did the official badge awarded for the initiation price of two rubles have a negotiable cash value. In addition, the society offered members a quasi-political outlet, as when it mobilized groups to complain to the authorities about the inadequate maintenance of Russian roads.[74]

The Moscow branch of the Russian Tourist Society declared its independence in 1910 in order to expand its agenda.[75] Echoing Cook's original creed of "leveling upwards," it arranged educational tours for those on the lower socioeconomic rungs, such as schoolteachers, students, and subordinate medical personnel, whose jobs evidenced that they were interested in self-improvement. Significantly, tourism was being recognized not only as something everyone might *want* to do, but something that they *should* do. The *Vestnik znaniia* (Herald of knowledge) group of self-styled "people's *intelligentsia*" joined the fray in 1910, publishing its own guidebook and hoping to organize tours for the journal's subscribers.[76] Given the embarrassingly unprofessional nature of the guide, it is unlikely that this group managed to organize anything so detailed as an excursion. For example, they refused to bore readers with train schedules, focusing instead on philosophical issues. Nevertheless, they sought to incorporate the slogan "learn your native land" into their motto "learn and teach."[77] This reflected shifting attitudes toward and opportunities for tourism, which would prove crucial to the inclusion of access to tourism on the list of worker demands, and government favors, after 1917.[78]

The Moscow Society kept helpful records. For example, it published the salary figures for 363 members who participated in excursions in 1911. They fell into a range of less than 300 to more than 600 rubles annually, with a median between 300 and 420 rubles.[79] These salaries would include skilled workers, teachers, shopkeepers, and low-level bureaucrats—the lower levels of the nascent middle classes who could identify themselves as such in part by participating in tourism. The prices for the various excur-

[74] *Russkii turist,* no. 12 (1899): 323–25. The road problem became all the more acute after the zemstvos were freed from mandatory upkeep in 1891.

[75] *Moskovskoe otdelenie Rossiiskogo Obshchestva turistov.* Otchet kompanii za 1911 (Moscow: Pechatnoe delo, 1912), 3.

[76] On this group's cultural ambitions, see Jeffrey Brooks, "Popular Philistinism and the Course of Russian Modernism," in *Literature and History: Theoretical Problems and Russian Case Studies,* ed. Gary Saul Morson (Stanford: Stanford University Press, 1986), 90–110.

[77] V. V. Bitner, *Sputnik ekskursanta* (St. Petersburg: Vestnik znaniia, 1910).

[78] Dr. D. M. Gorodinskii, *Chto nuzhno znat' pri poezdkakh na kurorty Kryma i Kavkaza* (Leningrad: Dvigatel', 1926).

[79] *Moskovskoe otdelenie Rossiiskogo Obshchestva turistov.* Otchet kampanii za 1911 (Moscow: Pechatnoe delo, 1912), 21.

The guidebook, or *Sputnik,* published by *Vestnik znaniia*

sions ranged from 55 to 115 rubles, depending on destination (all were within the empire, from Finland to the Caucasus) and length of stay. The society turned to several of Moscow's best-known philanthropists for supplemental funds, including the merchant patronesses Iu. T. Krestovnikova and M. K. Morozova, three from Moscow's Riabushinskii family, and the generous Countess S. V. Panina.[80]

Experience improved the quality of the tours, which likewise increased numbers of participants and lessened the need for patrons. In 1912 the society showed a slight profit when, although they had planned for seven hundred tourists, more than eight hundred signed up for their expeditions.[81] The organizers slowed the pace, offering more time for relaxation during the outings. Even in the early, more problematic years, 84 percent of those polled expressed satisfaction. Presumably the person who drowned during the trip to the Caucasus was enjoying himself at the time.[82] In response to a post-tour survey, village schoolteachers granted a reprieve from the stultifying life in the countryside spoke their gratitude in one voice, condensed here: "Living all year in the godforsaken village, without a close group of friends to whom I can pour out my heart, my soul exhausted . . . after the school year thirsts for rest, entertainment. . . . They dream of this all year, and then suddenly, Oh happiness! The dream comes true."[83] The ambitious organizers planned several future European trips, but this was in 1913, not long before the Great War closed international borders.

The Spas: Empire as Nation

It would be impossible to calculate whether tourists thought first about fortifying their bodies or their souls, but by the twentieth century the physical and mental were not so clearly distinguished that tourists would be making a conscious choice. People treating a specific illness differed from those who had adopted the notion that they needed a break from work to restore lost energy and to re-create themselves. Taking care of the body required a specific type of site and mineral waters, with their restorative powers, had been fashionable destinations since antiquity. The spas built around them offered recuperation to those under stress or in otherwise poor health.[84] The development of tourism as an industry led to the transformation of the spa into a vacation resort, catering to the middle-class

[80] Ibid., 29.
[81] Ibid., Otchet kampanii za 1912, 1, 9.
[82] Ibid., Otchet kampanii za 1911, 13–14.
[83] Ibid., 20.
[84] Layton, *Russian Literature and Empire,* 54–56, describes the popularity of Russia's first spas in the 1820s.

family and offering a variety of entertainments to complement the mineral and mud baths.[85] To be sure, even before it had been absorbed by the tourist industry, spa culture had involved much more than simply taking the cure. It offered possibilities for romance with mysterious strangers and with the even more mysterious peoples who lived along the borderlands, where the most popular spas were located.

Spas appeared frequently in pre-tourism travel literature. Russian theater audiences attending Prince A. A. Shakhovskoi's enormously popular 1815 comedy *The Lipetsk Spa* knew that these mineral springs in Tambov Province provided an ideal setting for the play, which developed around its subtitle, *A Lesson to Coquettes*. The dominant male characters were, appropriately, officers recovering from the Napoleonic wars, but the main character was a scheming young widow. The spa provided a serviceable backdrop because it brought transient characters together for short periods of time, analogous to the setting of the hospital in television soap operas. Alexander Bestuzhev-Marlinskii, whose participation in the Decembrist uprising in 1825 landed him in Siberian exile, joined Karamzin and Pushkin as a literary travel writer with his *Letters from Dagestan* (1832) and set two novellas in the 1820s, *An Evening on the Bivouac* and *An Evening at a Spa in the Caucasus,* at these sites. The most famous work of Russian literature set at a spa, though, would be Lermontov's *A Hero of Our Time* (1841).[86] Lermontov, whose checkered military career had seen him banished twice to outposts in the Caucasus, also found himself dispatched for reasons of health to a spa in Piatigorsk in 1841.[87]

The romantic Caucasus, where Pushkin and Lermontov stimulated wanderlust with tales of passion and dark eyes, were sprinkled with mineral waters. The other regions in the empire so blessed by nature included the Crimea, especially along the Black Sea littoral, and the Baltic coast. Thus spa culture developed as an offshoot of imperialism, tourists following the troops, so to speak. Because of the custom of sending officers to spas to recuperate, the tsarist government often inadvertently accelerated the development of this branch of tourism.[88] Establishing spas at the mineral springs in the Caucasus represented a rearguard action of cultural appro-

---

[85] As Swinglehurst, *Cook's Tours,* 183, has pointed out about British tourists of the era, "visitors to these watering places disguised their true motives for being there by a pretended concern for their health."

[86] Simon Karlinsky, *Russian Drama from Its Beginnings to the Age of Pushkin* (Berkeley: University of California Press, 1985), 232. On Bestuzhev-Marlinskii's travelogues, see Layton, *Russian Literature and Empire,* 175–91.

[87] Tatiana Aleksandrovna Ivanova, *Lermontov na Kavkaze* (Moscow: Iskusstvo, 1968).

[88] On the systematic creation of faux national borders, see Benedict Anderson's seminal *Imagined Communities: Reflections on the Origins and Spread of Nationalism,* rev. ed. (London: Verso, 1991). On some ways in which frontiers were artificially created in Russia, see Ronald Suny, *The Revenge of the Past: Nationalism, Revolution, and the Collapse of the Soviet Union* (Stanford: Stanford University Press, 1993).

priation in the long and costly conquest of the mountainous region.[89] Piatigorsk, the most famous spa because of its literary guests, was the first to be officially recognized in 1803, although serious construction of the resort did not begin for another twenty years. Essentuki, one of the largest of the mineral spa areas with its twenty springs, began as a military outpost but became a resort in 1839. Borzhom, its ultimate rival in popularity, began receiving soldiers in the 1820s.

Borzhom's history encapsulates that of the area's development. Buildings and baths began going up in the 1830s. In 1845, when General E. A. Golovin brought his daughter down to partake of the cure, he expedited the official transfer of the waters from the military to civil authorities. Located approximately 130 miles from Tiflis, Borzhom could grow only as quickly as transportation to the area would permit. The 1859 capture of Shamil, the Islamic tribal leader who had kept Russian forces at bay in the northern Caucasus for over forty years, facilitated development of the entire region. Royal family members established estates there, which upped its desirability. Nicholas II's sickly younger brother Georgii lived and died there. In 1901 the number of ethnic Russian inhabitants (2,031) outstripped the native Georgians (1,424) for the first time—an indicator of development, if not necessarily of progress.

Tourism would also have been encouraged by the Society for the Restoration of Christianity in the Caucasus, founded in 1860 and armed with the objective of erasing differences in ways that would make the Russian tourist more comfortable, more at home in the region.[90] The mineral waters were now being bottled for export, and Borzhom shed its hospital image of quartering invalids for a new reputation as "the kingdom of the hearty appetite." Climbing and horseback riding competed with bathing, and orchestras and touring stage companies played during the summer season. By 1903 advance reservations quickly filled the available hotels, dachas, and rental apartments.[91] Russians, no less than the western Europeans Buzard described, did not so much "wish to cast off the familiar and experience the native, but rather have the familiar recreated in a new environment."[92] The tourist boom in the region paralleled the proliferation of images of the Caucasus in popular urban culture, which suggests that the two fed each other.[93]

---

[89] V. Perevalenko, *Abastumanskie i Urabel'skie mineral'nye vody* (Tiflis: Guliiants, 1851), for example, discusses the relationship of the military to the development of some Georgian spas.

[90] Austin Jersild, "Faith, Custom, and Ritual in the Borderlands," *Russian Review* 59, no. 4 (2000): 520. Jersild does not discuss tourism, but the connections are likely because of their coincidence in both time and purpose.

[91] *Borzhom: Spravochnaia knizhka.*

[92] Buzard, *Beaten Track*, 8.

[93] Thomas Barrett, "Southern Living (in Captivity): The Caucasus in Russian Popular Culture," *Journal of Popular Culture* 31, no. 4 (1988): 85–88.

Russia's seacoasts also offered regions for tourism. Combining health with recreation, the beaches could accommodate thousands more tourists than the spas. The Crimea, with its beautiful beaches, mountains, and temperate climate, would become the nucleus of Russian tourist development.[94] When the railroad finally connected the peninsula to the two capitals in the 1870s, possibilities for economic development turned into probabilities. The spark for tourism came when the court physician S. P. Botkin "sent his august patient to Livadia," a settlement close to the port city of Yalta where the Romanov dynasty had maintained an estate since 1834.[95] Regular visits from the Romanovs turned nearby Yalta into the first genuine resort area on the Black Sea: "it grew not by days but by hours."[96] The first luxury hotel, the Rossiia, came with the railroad, and the construction of it illustrated aspects of tourism's modernizing impact. First, the hotel required plumbing, which entailed revamping the water supply system. The local Tatar population could not furnish the requisite construction workers, so Russian peasants were brought in from surrounding provinces, and many of them remained. Bazaars with Tatar, Jewish, and Greek sellers gave way to permanent shops.[97] The tourist boom had begun.

A physician who prescribed bathing in the Black Sea for patients, and treated his own ailments thus, wrote a guidebook in 1873. Odessa, site of some of the first sanitoria, was long the only spot on the seacoast accessible by train.[98] The doctor noted, though, the ill effects of the urbanization that had nearly doubled the population since the Crimean War; and the dirty air of the city and the torturous climb down the famous steps to the beach diminished the health benefits.[99] Costs ran high because many locals inflated prices, exploiting the sick. The ROPT, however, was making its move into tourism with scheduled trips to the spots that would become famous vacation areas: Evpatoria, Sevastopol, Alupka, Feodosia, and the jewel in the royal resort crown, Yalta. The good doctor's personal favorite was Feodosia, which, although lacking the natural beauty of Yalta, com-

[94] At the time of the Russian annexation in 1783, however, the air was described as "unwholesome, the waters poisonous." Wolff, *Inventing Eastern Europe,* 124.

[95] Dr. V. N. Dmitriev, *Ialta. 25 let tomu nazad* (St. Petersburg: Tip. Doma prizreniia maloletnykh bednykh, 1892), 1. Dmitriev was an active member of the local climbing society and organized numerous excursions over the years.

[96] Ibid.

[97] Ibid., 7–10. Demands for lodging rose faster than the building could keep up with it, allowing the locals to gouge visitors for a spot on a balcony or in a basement when the Romanovs were in town.

[98] *50 let sushestvovaniia gidropaticheskogo zavedeniia vracha L. Shorshtein* (Odessa: Iug.-rus. Obshchestvo pechatnoe delo, 1898). See also P. K. A-in, *Mineral'nye vody voobshche i tselitel'nost'vody i griazei Odesskikh limanov* (St. Petersburg: V. K. Nakhimov, 1880).

[99] In 1858 the population was 104,493; in 1873 it was 193,513. Frederick W. Skinner, "Odessa and the Problem of Urban Modernization," in *The City in Late Imperial Russia,* ed. Michael Hamm (Bloomington: Indiana University Press, 1986), 212.

Гостинница „РОССІЯ" въ ЯЛТѢ. ✢ Hôtel de „RUSSIE" à Jalta.

Имѣющая 150 номеровъ, по своей чистотѣ и комфорту смѣло можетъ быть сравнена съ лучшими гостинницами за границей.

ЦѢНЫ НОМЕРОВЪ: Съ 1-го Ноября по 1-ое Августа отъ 1 р. 50 коп., а съ 1-го Августа по 1-ое Ноября отъ 2 р. 50 коп.

Арендаторъ Г. КАУБИШЪ.   *Arendator G. KAUBISCH.*

Yalta's first luxury hotel, the Rossiia

pensated for this with greater peace and better waters. His recommendations for life after one has restored one's health (which happened "not by the day but by the hour") demonstrated Feodosia's transformation into the tourist resort: he counseled visitors to dance to the strains of the Czech orchestra that played in the public garden rotunda on Sundays and Thursdays.[100]

Another doctor describing the Black Sea littoral in 1881 rued the intrusion of entertainments because they attracted tourists out for a good time, whose boisterous behavior could upset his patients. He described another phenomenon, the conversion of private estates into resorts built for paying customers. The princely Golytsin family, whose estate in the region predated Peter the Great, anticipated Anton Chekhov's drama *The Cherry Orchard* by subdividing and selling off lots.[101] Prince Vorontsov, who owned Alupka, kept growth slow by forbidding restaurants or orchestras on the resort he built. Count Shuvalov's Miskhor offered complete quiet, but without a cook on site was less desirable. General Mal'tsev had built a miniature crystal palace as an attraction at his Simeis, and fountains in front of the rental cottages, but the rooms smelled bad. The doctor did manage to find "the only comfortable place on the whole south shore of the Crimea," Ivan Smelov's Limany. This entrepreneur had styled his *pansion* on the Swiss model, with comfortable rooms, good food, and a ballroom with a grand piano for socializing. His "desire to make his pensioners happy" had

[100] *Morskie kupal'ni Chernogo moria: Iz putevykh zametok vracha I. N. Lagogy* (Chernigov: Zemsk. tip., 1873).

[101] Dmitriev, *Ialta*, 11.

produced such success that he built a second wing.[102] At least two joint-stock companies were formed, one in 1899 and the other in 1901, to solicit private investment for development of resorts along the coast of the Black Sea.[103]

Within a few decades this intense development had victimized Yalta. Enlarging the port facilities had filled the coastline with debris and eroded the shore so severely that ships docked almost at the entrance to the once chic Rossiia hotel. The city's indeterminate population reflected the uncontrolled growth.[104] What upset the sanitation inspectorate, though, delighted promoters of the tourist industry. Chekhov, a native of southern Russia and a virtuoso at depicting social change, set his short story *The Lady with the Lapdog* (1899) at a Yalta spa, an environment with which he was especially familiar from his sojourns there to treat his tuberculosis. He once described Yalta as "a mixture of something European that reminds one of views of Nice, with something cheap and shoddy."[105] Twelve hotels and numerous *pansiony* welcomed guests year-round, including Europeans who wanted to explore the battlegrounds of the Crimean War.[106] The war had provided the dramatic connection between health and history, two of tourism's most important elements.[107] An American tourist to Yalta in 1912 described it as "the gayest, the most exclusive, and the most expensive Russian resort . . . the social capital of the Crimea."[108] The growth was both quantitatively financial and qualitatively entertaining.

Tourism to the Crimea continued its steady growth. In 1901 Prince Alexander Ol'denburg began turning much of Gagry, his family's large estate on the eastern shore of the Black Sea, into a luxury resort that also included accommodations for some who needed the health features but

---

[102] Dr. V. I. Guchin, *O klimatolechebnykh mestakh iuzhnogo berega Kryma*, no. 1 (Kharkov: Eduard Goppe, 1881).

[103] *Ob"iasnitel'naia zapiska po delu osnovaniia obraztsovogo kurorts v Chernomorskoi gubernii* (n.p., 1899). This company sold 6,000 shares at 250 rubles per share. See also *Ustav aktsionernogo obshchestva Chernomorskikh kurortov* (St. Petersburg: Tip. Ministerstvo finansov, 1901). This company raised 4 million rubles at 250 rubles per share.

[104] P. Rozanov, "Dvizhenie sanitarnogo i kurortnogo blagotvoritel'stva g. Ialty za poslednye 5 let," *Russkii vrach*, no. 49 (1903): 6–8.

[105] Quoted in Janet Malcolm, "Travels with Chekhov," *New Yorker*, February 21 and 28, 2000, 239.

[106] John Murray's popular guidebook devoted its longest section to the Crimean War. *Handbook for Travelers in Russia, Poland, and Finland, including the Crimea, Caucasus, Siberia, and Central Asia*, 4th ed. (London: John Murray, 1888).

[107] For example, a Russian guidebook of 1909 featured the battlegrounds, *Prakticheskii spravochnik v kurortakh Kryma* (Sevastopol: S. M. Brun, 1909), as did one that had been published in regular editions since 1888, G. Moskvin, *Putevoditel' po Krymu* (St. Petersburg: Putevoditel', 1915). See also *Istoricheskii putevoditel' po Sevastopoliu* (St. Petersburg: Tip. Min. Udelov, 1907).

[108] Wood, *Tourist's Russia*, 212–13. When first visiting Yalta in 1909, she appreciated the absence of foreign tourists, noting that it "is a resort of the Russians, for the Russians." *Honeymooning in Russia*, 303.

could ill afford steep prices. Gagry offered a private family zoo, donkey rides for children, two hotels with telephones even in the least expensive rooms (rates ranged from one to thirteen rubles), restaurants "better than the first-class (ones) in the two capitals," a grand piano for guests, an orchestra, and even a stage for amateur and summer stock companies. On weekends Ol'denburg opened the grounds to picnickers who rode the train down from Novorossisk. The beach was segregated for male and female swimming, as were the other public beaches.[109] Gagry could remain open year-round because the other side of the estate was rife with game for hunters. It was sufficiently popular that the ROPT kept an agency on site.[110]

The improved lines of transportation (which like all else in the industry grew "not by the days but by the hours")[111] permitted the conversion of a small fort on the coast into Sochi, the first resort specifically constructed on the beach and designed to compete with the French Riviera for foreign as well as national tourists—which it did, if not as briskly as the investors had hoped. New docking facilities and paved roads made it accessible. Public parks, an esplanade, hotels and *pansiony* for a variety of budgets, and warm weather year-round turned Sochi into the largest resort in the Soviet era. Two of Petersburg's millionaire publishers, A. S. Suvorin and S. N. Khudekov, built villas here. Several other smaller, less expensive resorts also began going up. The commercial influence was such that by 1912 a guidebook to the Crimean resorts appeared that anticipated *Consumer Reports* in that its publisher refused to accept ads.[112] By 1913 one could travel quickly from the two capitals on the Black Sea Express or purchase rail passes that saved the time of having to buy a specific ticket for each leg of a journey, which made possible spontaneous tours around the area.[113]

The Baltic coast provided a quite different site of intensive tourist development, its popularity intimately connected with Petersburg. Even the casual visitor to the imperial capital in any season would quickly appreciate the toll that the marshy climate takes on the human organism, and the pressures of urbanization were adding approximately fifty thousand new

[109] Dr. A. S. Kraevskii, *Morskie kupan'ia v Batume* (Batum: P. L. Lobko, 1886). This forty-kopeck brochure explained some of the new bathing etiquette. Apparently men were still permitted to swim naked but women, never.

[110] *Gagry. Klimaticheskaia stantsiia na Chernomorskom poberezh'i* (St. Petersburg: Suvorin, 1905).

[111] Vasilii Sidorov, *Volga: Putevye zametki i vpechatleniia ot Valdaia do Kaspiia* (St. Petersburg: A. Katanskii, 1894), iii. See also, Dr. P. N. Andreev, *Illiustrirovannyi putevoditel' po iugo-zapadnym kazen. zh. dorogam* (Kiev: S. V. Kul'zhenko, 1898), which includes a history of the growth of the southwest railroad.

[112] V. L. Sokolov, *Sputnik-putevoditel' po kurortam Chernomorskogo Poberezh'ia* (Moscow: A. D. Drutman, 1912).

[113] *Zheleznodorozhnyi sputnik po kurortam . . . Po Peterburgskomu vremeni* (Rostov on Don: Aktsionernaia pechatnia, 1913).

residents a year from 1890 onward.[114] Once the Baltic became a day's ride away and the economy in the capital could support thousands of residents with discretionary income, a summer rental on the seashore became preferable for some to a dacha in the city's suburbs.

Tourism here repeated the familiar formula: it followed the royals, who came to bathe in the 1860s, and then the railroad.[115] A guidebook for the coastal area in 1892 revealed the ironical chauvinism of Russia's imperial presence on the windowsill of the West.[116] Beginning with the admonition that it was not necessary to vacation abroad, the author appeared pleased that foreigners, especially Germans, would come to Russia. He considered Riga "one of Russia's prettiest cities,"[117] and he had much to say about the local language problem. First he tried to amuse the reader with the locals' poor translations into Russian, but then his frustration became apparent in criticisms of signs that appeared in German and local languages. He also noted with disgust that Russian tourists "become quickly Germanized" by falling into the obnoxious habits of these foreigners.[118] He estimated that summer bathers in the Gulf of Riga, inexpensive when compared to places closer to Petersburg, numbered up to sixty thousand.[119]

The two major resorts built on the Baltic seacoast were Ust'-Narva and Druskeniki, both of which remain active today. Ust'-Narva, in present-day Estonia, became "the pearl of the region by the end of the nineteenth century."[120] In the 1870s a local entrepreneur, A. F. Gan, recognized the possibilities for developing this small port area at the mouth of the river. He persuaded other local industrialists to finance the reconstruction of the area into a summer retreat. Gan also solicited support from the city council, who gave money for a road, essential for bringing people to the dachas, hotels, and *pansiony*. Connected by both shipping and rail lines, Ust'-Narva was welcoming fourteen thousand summer tourists by 1914. Moreover, it served the artistic elite from the imperial capital much as Palm Springs developed from the Hollywood crowd seeking respite from Los Angeles. The list of famous vacationers included, among others, the stage stars Maria Savina and Konstantin Varlamov, the writers Nikolai Leskov, Fedor Sologub, and Konstantin Bal'mont, and Fedor Dostoevsky's daughter Liubov'.[121] The common vacationers might thus hope to associate with the

[114] James H. Bater, "Between Old and New: St. Petersburg in the Late Imperial Era," in *The City in Late Imperial Russia*, ed. Hamm, 51.

[115] Dr. O. F. Veber, *Pribaltiiskii morskoi kurort "Libava"* (Libava: M. Uksting, 1911), 3–4.

[116] *Putevoditel' po kurortam i morskim kupan'iam Baltiiskogo poberezh'ia* (St. Petersburg: V. K. Simanskii, 1892).

[117] Ibid., 47.

[118] Ibid., 49.

[119] Ibid., 56.

[120] Krivosheev, *Narva-Iyesuu*, 15.

[121] Ibid., 21.

famous, sharing the same resort area. And who knew who might be spotted out on a promenade?

Where Ust'-Narva was the result of a specific entrepreneurial vision, Druskeniki boasted the finest natural springs in the area. Located in present-day Lithuania and inland from the Baltic, Druskeniki served the Polish area of Russia. When the railroad finally connected the resort to the major lines in 1908, the number of those coming for the waters immediately doubled from eight thousand to sixteen thousand.[122] A joint-stock development company showed profits of almost twenty thousand rubles in 1909.[123]

A tourist to Druskeniki during the summer of 1912, Evgenia Lovitskaia, published memoirs from her excursion.[124] A single woman traveling alone, she registered no qualms about her solitary position. Looking to get out of Petersburg, but unwilling to go too far away, Lovitskaia settled on Druskeniki over the objections of her doctor and friends, who thought she should seek out one of the more fashionable German spas. In her opinion, though, their fears betrayed ignorance of this region, whose natural beauty was matched by the peace and quiet it afforded. Throughout, she described happily how much the local environment had been adapted to accommodate customers such as herself; for her, imperialism was a pleasant and rewarding experience.

Like most others who came for the entire season, Lovitskaia planned to stay in a hotel only until she could find less expensive lodgings. Not thinking to make advance reservations, she had problems upon arrival but eventually found a suitable room. Exploring the town, she discovered the need to purchase tickets for everything from the baths to entrance to the park if she wanted to listen to the orchestra. The system of ticketing, described in other guidebooks as well, was designed more as a medium for maintaining order than to gouge the tourist's ruble. It was intended as a means to keep potential predators away from tourist prey. At the train station, for example, Lovitskaia had met a young man who complained about how much more fun Druskeniki had been before all the new regulations. Lovitskaia's problem with the tickets was that they represented the precision with which everything operated. In the old days she could have lingered in the baths, but now someone else had a ticket and could take her cabin at the top of the hour. Staying on until the season ended in September, she departed with the thought that, although it might not compare to the fa-

---

[122] Dr. S. Konverskii, *Otchet o deiatel'nosti Druskenikskogo kurorta za 1907–1911* (Vil'na: n.p., 1911), 10.

[123] *Otchet aktsionernogo obshchestva Druskeninskikh mineral'nykh vod za 1909* (Vil'na: Iosif Zavadskii, 1910), 27.

[124] Evgeniia Lovitskaia, *Na dache-kurorte (v Druskenikakh)* (St. Petersburg: Vausberg i Gershunin, 1913).

Partaking of the mud baths in Druskeniki

mous European resorts, here one can find "all the peace, loveliness, therapy, and at an affordable price!"[125]

Other indicators of the growth of the tourist industry illustrate how pervasive the idea of a vacation was becoming. Russia's network of rivers, for example, began to offer more than routes connecting travel destinations.[126] An 1894 guidebook attempted to turn the attention away from the Crimea to Russia's other natural wonders, in this instance, the Volga.[127] In 1900 a Saratov publishing firm began publishing an annual *Guidebook of the Volga and Its Tributaries,* so filled with advertisements for cruise ships, hotels, and restaurants along the rivers as to indicate a tremendous appetite for this sort of tour. The building of the Trans-Siberian Railroad eased transportation for those living in Russia's Far Eastern provinces and contributed to the commercialization of the Anninskie mineral waters after 1900. A boat from Kharbin ferried tourists more cheaply than the train.[128] In fact, the resorts going up distant from the metropolitan areas

[125] Ibid., 39.

[126] The ROPT advertised its tours especially along the Volga. *Putevoditel' po Volge,* 5th ed. (Nizhnii Novgorod: Tip. Gubernskogo upravlenii, 1889).

[127] Sidorov, *Volga: Putevye zametki.* Wood, *Tourist's Russia,* 154–82, describes tours of the Volga for potential western tourists.

[128] *Kurort Anninskie mineral'nye vody arend.* Dr. V. M. Porvatova i Ko. (Vladikavkaz: R. E. Shtreitman, 1912).

Enjoying the new fad of roller skating, a popular pastime at resorts

advertised their economical rates and served a more localized population than the Black Sea resorts. Where once the Caucasus mountain range had substituted for the Alps,[129] with the completion of the railroad Russia now found its Switzerland in Siberia.[130] In 1911 a series of fifteen booklets on "Russians Abroad" anticipated/copied the Berlitz method of language acquisition, including pronunciation, "in the shortest possible time, without previous training, and without a teacher."[131]

The Tourist's Gaze

The travel literature, guidebooks, and periodicals that promoted various forms of travel provided the starting point for structuring the tourist's way of looking, or gaze, in such a way that they prompted the reader to see him/herself fitting into unfamiliar surroundings. Buzard has emphasized the function of tourism as a medium that "fundamentally engages and tests cultural *representations.*"[132] In setting the focus, travel literature normalized differences between the seer and the seen and made it appear that what the tourist was observing fell quite naturally into place and was not the result of haphazard incidents or controlled government policies.[133] Bourdieu has argued persuasively that tourists misrecognize social reality in such a way as to "[maintain], by naturalizing, [their] advantages."[134] These *meconnaissances,* or willful misrecognitions, helped tourists to adapt by re-creating the familiar in a strange environment. Arguing that "other regions give back what [the visitor's] culture has excluded from its discourse," Michel de Certeau has suggested that tourists also go to look for something denied them at home.[135] This might help to explain why people strike out to "discover" new worlds, but it glosses over the extent to which the tourist demands to have enough of the familiar re-created to provide an anchor. A Russian guidebook to Palestine published in 1890, for example, provided a detailed tour of sites around the Holy Land, but it managed to script both Catholicism and Judaism out of the geography.[136] This example underscores a key point of commercial tourism: politics are in the eye of the beholder.

[129] Layton, *Russian Literature and Empire,* 39–46, discusses the Caucasus as the Russian Alps in the literary imagination.

[130] V. P. Aleksandrov, *Illiustr. putevoditel' po Borovomu* (Tomsk: Katsenelenbogen, 1913).

[131] The booklets were edited by M. M. Mikhailovskii, published by the *Peterburgskoe uchebnoe magazin* and cost thirty kopecks.

[132] Buzard, *Beaten Track,* 13.

[133] Ibid., 11.

[134] Quoted in Buzard, *Beaten Track,* 83.

[135] Michel de Certeau, *The Practice of Everyday Life,* trans. Steven Rendall (Berkeley: University of California Press, 1984), 50.

[136] *Putevoditel' v Palestinu po Ierusalimu, sviatoi zemle i drugim sviatyniam vostoka* (Odessa: Afinskogo Sv. Andreevskogo skita, 1890).

Tourists abetted the political mission of imperialism by the way in which they appropriated the peoples in the borderlands areas they visited. The politics of imperialism mandated that ethnic Russians come not simply to conquer but also to improve the lives of the other peoples being incorporated into the empire. As Pratt has argued, "It is the task of the advance scouts for capitalist 'improvement' to encode what they encounter as 'unimproved' . . . available for improvement."[137] Travel literature charted Russia's civilizing influence, highlighting integration, as opposed to conquest. Living like a Tatar in 1873 meant sleeping on an uncomfortable floor, as in a stable. A visiting doctor to the "underdeveloped" Crimea worried that healthy people would get sick here rather than vice versa. He observed that "one can eat shashlik, but you need the stomach of a Tatar to digest it."[138] Less than a decade later, an 1881 guidebook noted that Tatars clean by burning, which can result in foul air, but it was generally possible to rent rooms in their homes, which could be preferable to a hotel because they are often good cooks.[139] After 1900 perhaps the clearest impression of cultural imperialism can be found in the numerous restaurants throughout the empire advertising that they served the ethnic cuisines from around the empire.

The guidebooks record just as readily Russian detachment from local customs. A 1913 guidebook to Borzhom commented on the difficulty of finding good female help, without any recognition that this might be a reflection of local gender relations. Fortunately for Russian tourists, though, male servants were reasonably competent. The closest village, Rebiatishki, was described as "rather clean for a poor Georgian village. Their dwellings are rather like peasant huts, indigent and unpleasant on the inside."[140] The march of modernity can be traced through the attempted domestication of the empire's ethnic minorities as they appear in the travel literature: from Pushkin's erotic Circassians, to Berlov's unhygienic Tatars, to the Bashkirs who are particularly poor at building roads because "they do not like physical labor in general or compulsory work in particular."[141] The guidebook thus helped to establish standards for both difference and hierarchy.

The Russian as Object of the Western Tourist's Gaze

Russian tourists used travel to structure an identity that helped them to function in their changing world, but they were also the objects of a touris-

---

[137] Pratt, *Imperial Eyes*, 61.
[138] *Morskie kupal'ni Chernogo moria*, 25–27.
[139] Guchin, *O klimatolechebnykh mestakh*, no. 1, 2, 21.
[140] *Borzhom: Spravochnaia knizhka*, 139, 246.
[141] *Russkii turist*, no. 12 (1899): 325.

tic gaze that saw them differently from how they imagined themselves. Buzard's observation about tourism as a medium that "engages and tests cultural representations" underscores how western tourists problematized Russia's place in the concert of great-power nations. A quick take on the Russians as the object of the gaze offers another slant to the argument that tourism structures realities in ways that domesticate the unfamiliar and distort cross-cultural communications.

The autocratic political system provided the primary point of contrast between Russia and the West. After that, westerners looked for creature comforts and entertainments analogous to what they enjoyed at home. Like the Russians at the health spas, they wanted their exotica maintained within a setting to which they enjoyed cultural access. As Larry Wolff has illustrated so meticulously, western travelers during the Enlightenment "invented" an Eastern Europe as "a paradox of inclusion and exclusion, Europe but not Europe . . . an intellectual project of demi-orientalism."[142] Borrowing from Edward Said's seminal analysis of the enervating political agenda behind western investigation of eastern societies, *Orientalism,* Wolff argued persuasively that western Europe used the differences that it found in the East to construct its own philosophical image, an image that depended on differences capable of constructing a hierarchy that privileged West over East.

In *Orientalism,* Said assumed the Foucauldian position that texts produce knowledge, which the producers then wield as power. Travel literature and guidebooks structured a gaze and produced a knowledge that bolstered this hierarchy. For example, the publication of the travel diaries kept by the Marquis de Custine of his adventures in Russia in 1839 reinforced some of the most odious stereotypes of autocracy and Russian barbarity.[143] The next widely influential piece of travel literature to describe Russia to westerners came from the pen of American George Kennan, who journeyed to Russia in 1865 as a member of the Russ-Am Telegraph expedition. Staying on to explore Russia's Wild East, he returned and published *Tent Life in Siberia,* with numerous parallels to the United States' taming of its own expansive West. It was when he went back in 1885, though, to study the political exile in Siberia that Kennan's ideas garnered more critical attention. Published first in the popular mass-circulation magazine *Century,* Kennan's sensational series assured that politics would dominate even a travel agenda. Moreover, Kennan lectured widely in support of the Russian revolutionary movement, which he read as liberal rather than socialist in

---

[142] Wolff, *Inventing Eastern Europe,* 7.

[143] Marquis de Astolphe Custine, *Journey for Our Time: The Russian Journals of the Marquis de Custine,* ed. and trans. Phyllis Penn Kohler, with an introduction by Walter Bedell Smith (Chicago: H. Regnery, [1951]). Translation is based on the third French edition of *La Russie en 1839.*

its opposition to autocracy.[144] The sympathetic depictions of Russians who opposed their government that appeared in the U.S. popular press can be traced loosely back to Kennan.[145]

Two personal western views of Russia published not long after Kennan's pieces on Siberia, told from very different perspectives, nonetheless intersect at key points. Placed against the impersonal backdrop of a Murray guidebook from the same era, Russia emerges as an exciting fairground, a theme park with wolves and colorful revolutionary characters. Peter Heath and Elizabeth Champney, typical of the Americans now joining western Europeans as instant authorities on eastern Europe,[146] each contributed a travelogue, set in Russia and blending fact with fiction, to a travel-oriented series: Heath's *A Hoosier in Russia* (1888) was one of the Lorborn Series by American Writers; and Champney's *Three Vassar Girls in Russia and Turkey* (1889) was a continuation of the escapades of these fictional heroines who showed that women, too, indulged in adventurous travel.

Unable to leave his Protestant work ethic in the hotel room, for fear that even *that* would be stolen, Heath painted a picture of Russia that differed little from de Custine's indictment of the prereform era. He promised readers not to bore them with descriptions of palaces but to give them the real story. Government agents abounded everywhere, even at his hotel, exercising a nocturnal reign of terror. Only thieves appeared to outnumber spies. Heath quoted an old Russian proverb to illustrate the lack of religious conviction that encouraged such an atmosphere: "Our Savior would rob also if his hands were not pierced."[147] The basic lawlessness of the place permitted sympathy for the nihilists, he intimated, and the lower classes had cause to revolt against the examples set for them by the upper classes. Still, the Russian wild held an allure, and Heath's penchant for hyperbole was most entertaining in his description of an attack on his iron-covered sled by a pack of five hundred wolves.[148]

Champney's Vassar students fought Turks rather than wild animals. Against the backdrop of the Russo-Turkish War of 1876, these young ladies, who had previously survived the Franco-Prussian War of 1871 in Paris, provided personal insights into Europe's most precarious political system. Christianity, revolutionary politics, and orientalism surface continually as subthemes. One of the girls was on her way to study medicine

[144] George Kennan, *Tent Life in Siberia, and Adventures among the Koraks and Other Tribes in Kamtchatka and Northern Asia* (London: S. Low, Son, and Marston, 1871); and his *Siberia and the Exile System*, 2 vols. (London: J. R. Osgood, McIlvaine, 1891).

[145] Frederick F. Travis, *George Kennan and the American-Russian Relationship* (Athens: Ohio University Press, 1990).

[146] Maria Todorova, *Imagining the Balkans* (New York: Oxford University Press, 1997), 102.

[147] Peter Heath, *A Hoosier in Russia*, Lorborn Series by American Writers (New York: Lorborn, 1888), 51.

[148] Ibid., 58.

in Petersburg, but upon her arrival she found her Russian friend in prison because a nefarious police agent had marshaled false evidence against her. Another character whom the girls met on shipboard is an orientalist scholar, whose narrative function is to explain the many ethnicities in Russia, as well as the unwelcome presence of the Turks in southeastern Europe. The girls ended up volunteering for the Red Cross to aid the Russians wounded during the war. But the Christianity that had made for a more natural alliance than simply sharing space on the European continent fell victim to Russia's quest for revenge following its victory. Russia's Orthodox church, like its political system, lay beyond the parameters of civilization marked by the West.[149]

The Murray guidebook separated the various parts of the empire, with chapters for Poland, Finland, the Crimea, and the Asian regions that reminded readers of the great diversity in the Russian lands. All guidebooks offered historical blurbs, and this one charted the expansion of the tsarist state without overt editorial comment, although the various regions were noted for maintaining their cultural identities. The longest historical section detailed the battle sites of the Crimean War, of obvious interest to the target audience. Writing with primarily well-heeled Londoners in mind, Murray noted that "travelers with letters of introduction will find the *salons* of St. Petersburg as brilliant as those of Paris, but they are unfortunately not as numerous."[150] A few Moscow sites "for men only" suggested that at least one form of romance remained on the tourist's agenda. The tourist attractions that received the most space were Petersburg's Hermitage Museum and the sport of hunting all sorts of prey, although Murray's wolves were considerably less intimidating than Heath's. Like a responsible tour guide, Murray left religion and politics out, concentrating instead on where to have a good time.

The turn of the century increased tourism to Russia because the industry as a whole was booming. Switzerland was the most popular European destination.[151] In 1904 the International League of Tourists, based in Belgium, celebrated a decade of growth and a membership of eighteen thousand.[152] One million people checked into Berlin hotels in 1906, and even more visited Baden-Baden and other German spas.[153] Europeans also found armed conflict a tourist attraction, and not just the postwar battlefields; British groups visited Paris in 1871 to witness the skirmishes be-

---

[149] Elizabeth Champney, *Three Vassar Girls in Russia and Turkey* (Boston: Estes and Lauriat, 1889).

[150] *Handbook for Travelers in Russia*, 78.

[151] Two and one-half million tourists visited Switzerland in 1904, and they spent more than two million francs. *Russkii turist*, no. 4 (1904): 98–99.

[152] *Russkii turist*, no. 7 (1904): 214.

[153] Peter Fritzsche, *Reading Berlin 1900* (Cambridge, Mass.: Harvard University Press, 1996), 66.

tween the troops and the communards.[154] During its 1904 war with Japan, European Russia attracted record numbers of western tourists. Apparently the numerous visitors wanted more jingoism than could be found among the natives, who were largely disaffected by the tsar's war; the manager of one of Petersburg's luxury hotels complained that his guests disapproved of what they saw as Russian apathy.[155]

Tourists visiting Russia, no less than Russian tourists themselves, sought to explain cultural differences by putting the places visited within a framework that measured according to their own expectations. Ruth Kedzie Wood, a real-life American with the adventuresome spirit of the Vassar girls, spent her honeymoon in Russia in 1911. Like her predecessors, she found herself involved with citizens who opposed the autocracy, especially teachers and university students. Despite the government, she developed a genuine affection for the people, whom she considered more eastern than western, even in the two capitals. She followed her first book with *A Tourist's Russia* (1912), which purported to provide the kind of personal information not included in official guides. She characterized "the temper of Russia" as "Oriental rather than European," a recurrent analytical motif.[156] Her observations resembled the picture painted by the most authoritative international guidebook to Russia in 1914, Baedeker's.

Like Wood, Karl Baedeker presented Russia as an eastern civilization, lumping it with Teheran and Peking.[157] He assured his readers that in major cities visitors could find accommodations "little inferior to Western ones" with multilingual service personnel. Hotels in provincial towns, however, "satisfy as a rule only the most moderate demands."[158] Because hunting remained high on the list of tourist objectives, many would undoubtedly have to adjust to the "unsatisfactory" conditions. The Baedeker forte was to provide the specifics of travel, details so precise as to impart an aura of scientific accuracy. Wood herself preferred the "silent red Baedeker" to her human museum guide.[159] But Baedeker did not content himself with describing only the physical layout, and his insights into the mentalité of the local populations appeared scientific when presented alongside the precise travel data. The guidebook explained the "want of organization, the disorder, the waste of time which strike the western visitor to Russia" thus:

[154] Levenstein, *Seductive Journey*, 140. During the Great War, agencies also organized a few tours of the trenches. Ibid., 217.

[155] The original story was from the daily newspaper *Birzhevye vedomosti*, reprinted in *Russkii turist*, no. 8 (1904): 235.

[156] Wood, *Tourist's Russia*, 1. Throughout, she uses the term "oriental" to describe people of various ethnicities.

[157] In contrast, in 1758 William Coxe had included Russia with "the northern kingdoms of Europe." Wolff, *Inventing Eastern Europe*, 5.

[158] Baedeker, *Russia*, xxvi.

[159] Wood, *Honeymooning in Russia*, 41.

[Russians] are easily disciplined and so make excellent soldiers, but have little power of independent thinking or of initiation. . . . Even the educated Russian gives comparatively little response to the actual demands of life; he is more or less the victim of fancy and temperament, which sometimes lead him to a despondent slackness, sometimes to emotional outbursts.[160]

Russians, like children, sought to satisfy their immediate needs without thought to moderation, responsibility, or consequences. Wood also commented on "childish Russian traits" and observed that someone "who pleases a Russian pleases a generous child."[161]

Returning to Said's argument about the potential influence of texts, Baedeker's and the other guidebooks that were perceived to lie outside of politics because they did not engage in political debates nevertheless constructed images that were put to use in nuanced but powerful ways.[162] As Pratt has argued, such critique is "integral to social exploration as a political practice."[163] Although the West did not colonize Russia as it did Egypt and the other Biblical lands in Said's study, it insisted on the dominant position in an analogous hierarchical relationship with respect to Russia for essentially the same reason that it did vis-à-vis the Orient: because it could.

The western travel writers denied the tsarist empire its longed-for spot in the concert of western nations, placing it instead in an Orient that they had constructed to fit their own needs. Inherently critical of a political system that stifled their own brand of liberalism, westerners could only see Russians as self-indulgent and indifferent to the repercussions of their actions.[164] Certainly the sympathy for their rebellious Russian acquaintances did not translate into an endorsement of socialism, much less its Marxist version. By decoding Russia in the terms of liberalism, and then recoding it in those of infantilism, the westerners who introduced the tsarist empire to tourists were inspiring the latter to "live widely" as the Russians themselves were perceived to be doing—that is, indulging in the moment with no thought to the consequences.[165] Imitating behaviors of their predecessors, such as the international gigolo Giovanni Casanova, who had helped himself to a thirteen-year-old slave girl during his visit to Russia, western tourists could release themselves in Russia without being subject to the same social conscience that ruled at home.[166]

[160] Baedeker, *Russia*, xlii.

[161] Wood, *Tourist's Russia*, 20, 36.

[162] Edward Said, *Orientalism* (New York: Random House, 1979), 9, distinguishes the *pure* from *political* knowledge, as the terms were understood in the nineteenth century.

[163] Pratt, *Imperial Eyes*, 160.

[164] Said cites an analysis of Arab behavior written as late as 1972 that makes the same sort of patronizing generalizations about "normality" that the Baedeker guide did. *Orientalism*, 48.

[165] Baedeker, *Russia*, 277, for example.

[166] Wolff, *Inventing Eastern Europe*, 50–59, on Casanova. He describes other such libertine attitudes throughout his study.

Russians tried to defend themselves, but they lacked an authoritative guidebook in their arsenal. One Russian bemoaned the bad manners of Europeans in Russia, citing a tourist in Ust'-Narva who felt free to spit on women and throw cigarette butts from his balcony because he's "in our house" (*u nas*).[167] Personalized views written by Russian travelers to Europe after 1905 tried to reverse some of the same negative stereotypes westerners had used against them. A Russian guide to Europe from that era noted that in train travel, "Belgians are not known for courtesy."[168] *Prekrasnoe daleko*'s tourist-contributors found easy fault with France, which was too noisy for relaxation and where a request for clean linen was met with a contemptuous "what you have is clean enough."[169] Someone repeating the Grand Tour in 1912 made the same sorts of negative observations about western European countries that others had made about Russia, beginning with fear of rough treatment at the German border. It seemed that no one who had ever visited the Caucasus could ever fully appreciate the Alps, which by comparison "were not as high, and not covered with the wild forests that cover the western slopes of the mountains."[170] This sort of nationalism might boost the local tourist industry, but without a Baedeker, Russians were simply writing for each other.

The West's "orientalizing" of Russia, then and now, depends upon an understanding of Russia posited on paradox: politics represses public initiative, but spontaneity reigns in social life. Authentic experience? This could make a prime example of de Certeau's notion that other regions offer up issues that the visiting culture has excluded from its own discourse. However, it should be borne in mind that tourists were not supposed to reconstruct that excluded discourse after they returned home. The image of Russia as a place where one could toss hygiene and responsibility to the wind did not bode well for a cerebral acceptance of this land of visceral childhood fantasies as a partner in any modern venture.

The Tourist Industry during the First World War

Russian relations with the West became increasingly complex as a result of such attitudes, but the drive to keep the Russian tourist within the borders of empire was stimulated as much by economic as nationalist reasons.

---

[167] V. N. Petrusevich, *Ust'-Narvskii priboi* (St. Petersburg: Trud, 1911), 121–22.

[168] P. P. Kuzminskii, *Kur'er. Prakticheskii putevoditel' dlia russkikh po gorodam i kurortam zapadnoi Evropy i po Egiptu* (St. Petersburg: Suvorin, 1912), 203. This author also advised readers quite soundly to seek out the nonsmoking cars everywhere because they were likely to have more empty seats, vii.

[169] "Po severu Frantsii na avtomobile (Zhenskie vpechatleniia)," *Prekrasnoe daleko*, no. 3 (1912): 9.

[170] "Za granitsei. (Iz putevykh vpechatlenii)," *Prekrasnoe daleko*, no. 16 (1913): 2.

For example, by the 1880s industry promoters were asking why Russians crossed the borders of their empire to visit "foreign," meaning "European" in this case, spas, such as the ultrafashionable resorts at Carlsbad and Baden-Baden. Better accommodations, which included medical attention as well as lodging and entertainment, seemed the best answer.[171] However, as one doctor pointed out, inadequate local arrangements forced many Russians to go to western spas when they would have preferred to remain home, at ease with the culture and language. This observer also noted Russia's national inferiority complex vis-à-vis the West, but without demonstrating any awareness of the irony that Russia's premier tourist areas differed significantly in language and culture from the ethnic Slavic tourists.[172] Leikin's tourists would certainly have savored the chemical comparison of water from Borzhom to that from Vichy in 1896, which proved the superiority of the former. The analyst concluded somewhat prematurely that "the days of us drinking foreign waters are over."[173]

The drive to ensure that Russian tourists would spend their rubles at home was greatly abetted by the outbreak of World War I. *Pace* Lenin's theory that imperialism had pushed capitalism to the next stage, international business interests seemed to have rendered national borders quite porous. But war proved good for some elements in the economy and good for nationalism; this felicitous combination had much to offer the local tourist industry. With the routes to Baden-Baden closed, Russians who would have otherwise headed west had to look in other directions.

A congress held in Odessa in 1915 on "How to Improve National Health Sanatoria," called to address treatment for the war wounded, proved an ideal gathering for the discussion of tourist spas.[174] Ol'ga Solov'eva, the proprietress of a resort on the Crimea's southern coast, outlined in an impassioned speech the industry's needs and opportunities. After traveling abroad to study resorts, she had opened her own in 1903. Ten years later, her efforts had been rewarded with several national prizes and a visit from Nicholas II. She boasted all the requisite comforts, including a newly built casino. Presumably the war could only increase her success, with the added influx of vacationers. Indeed, her three hundred rooms were always occupied and she was adding another two hundred. This was commensurate with other economic booms during the war years.[175]

---

[171] See, for example, *Krymskie mineral'nye griazi v derevne Saki, i morskie kupan'ia v gorode Evpatorii: Iz vospominanii priznatel'nogo patsienta A. N. N-na* (St. Petersburg: n.p., 1883); and O. A. Khaletskii, *Kavkazskie mineral'nye vody, v meditsinskom otnoshenii* (St. Petersburg: n.p., 1883).

[172] Guchin, *O klimatolechebnykh mestakh*, no. 1, 33.

[173] Prof. G. Zakharyn, *Borzhom i Vishi* (St. Petersburg: Suvorin, 1896).

[174] Much information about this is in the guidebook *Odessa kurort* (Odessa: Tip. "Odesskie novosti," 1915).

[175] *Doklad vladelitsy kurorta Suuk-su na iuzhnom beregu Kryma O. M. Solov'evoi, prochitannoi na*

The explosive growth made past inadequacies all the more apparent. Most important, the region needed a commitment from the government to improve transportation in the region. Basing her demands on finance, she argued that Russians had been pouring two hundred million rubles annually into the West without even knowing their own country. Moreover, she complained that resort owners like herself were now having to satisfy customers who would have preferred to go to Europe. The issue was not, she argued, that Europe was naturally superior, just that it was better organized.[176]

Others leapt to Solov'eva's bandwagon, blaming the inadequate infrastructure for driving Russians abroad. They impressed upon the government the need to increase its investment and support for the private initiative that could turn Russia's "Riviera" into another France or Italy.[177] The privately operated Russian Society for Tourism and Study of the Native Land opened its doors in 1916 to tap the flow of tourist rubles no longer flooding west. The founders appealed on the grounds that "our spacious fatherland includes in its territory many places that, in terms of natural beauty and historical, cultural, and economic importance not only do not stand second to western Europe's, but often surpass them."[178]

The figures for the gold pouring into Baden-Baden and the other German health resorts seem inflated, and could easily have been pulled from the thin mountain air, because they were not officially documented in these reports. In 1900, though, concern about the amount of money Russians spent abroad had prompted an inquiry from the Ministry of Internal Affairs.[179] Regardless of whether the figure actually approximated two hundred million rubles, the exaggerated numbers would bolster the case for heavy government investment. The proximity of an enemy across the Black Sea in Turkey did nothing to dampen the capitalist enthusiasm of those intent on building up the Russian coastline.[180]

Odessa stood poised to explode as the center of the tourist industry in 1917. The port city was particularly well positioned to handle the restructuring of tourism because the government was expending considerable sums to help the city deal with the war wounded. Improvements made for

---

s"ezde (7–11 Ian. 1915) po uluchsheniiu otechestvennykh lechebnykh mestnostei (Petrograd: n.p. 1915), 5–6.

[176] This problem reappeared after the collapse of the Soviet Union in 1991, when Russians who could afford vacations preferred to travel abroad. Colin McMahon, "Black Sea Resort Sees Better Days," *Chicago Tribune*, August 23, 2001.

[177] "Neotlozhnye zadachi kurortnogo dela," *Russkaia riv'era*, nos. 1–2 (1915): 3–4.

[178] *Russkoe obshchestvo turizma i otchiznovedeniia* (Petrograd: A. M. Mendelevich, 1916): 1.

[179] Article in *Rossiia*, August 17, 1900, no. 471. The ministry found that the Russians spent less than other foreign nationals, so it decided against the levels of investment that developers wanted.

[180] *Russkaia riv'era*, nos. 1–2 (1915): 3.

soldiers could later be used by tourists. Moreover, as the largest city in the Jewish Pale of Settlement, Odessa's population included a major ethnic group that had largely been excluded from Russian resorts. Solov'eva raised this sticky issue: the exclusion of Jews from most Crimean resorts had forced them to spend their money in other locales, proving her point with a list of Jews abroad when the war erupted.[181] As she argued, tourism could not prosper on out-dated conventions any more than it could on the present railroad lines.[182]

Conclusion

In the last years of the imperial era, Russia's tourists represented progress, modernity, and a multicultural nationalism driven by a capitalist engine that would not be stalled by traditional prejudices. Annually, by the tens of thousands, they sought cosmopolitan and adventurous identities through the multiple opportunities for contrast offered by travel.[183] Gender barriers were also toppling, exemplified by advice in 1913 to women joining hiking or riding excursions that they should "dress in the masculine spirit."[184] The accumulation of cultural capital through tourism offered the possibility of canceling the social divisions of the past, while creating a new sense of self derived from issues of nationalism and imperialism. Striking out, guidebook and Kodak in knapsack, in the summer of 1914 Russia's tourists could look out on a positively brilliant horizon.

[181] Local Jewish communities had long before established a sanitorium for their needy brethren, but those with money took it elsewhere. See, for example, *Otchet po soderzhaniiu Boiarskoi sanatorii dlia bednykh bol'nykh evreev g. Kieva za 1899* (Kiev: A. O. Shterenzon, 1900).

[182] *Doklad vladelitsy,* 2, 3, 10.

[183] In 1903 almost 75,000 Russians visited mud and mineral baths. Those numbers rose yearly, to over a hundred thousand by 1913. *Kratkie statisticheskie dannye o russkikh lechebnykh mestnostiakh i ikh posetitelei. Doklad Dr. S. A. Novosel'skogo* (St. Petersburg: I. N. Kushnerev, 1913), 3–5.

[184] V. P. Aleksandrov, *Illiustrirovannyi Putevoditel' po Borovomu* (Tomsk: Katsenelenbogen, 1913), 30.

CHAPTER SIX

"Steppin' Out" in the Russian Night at the Fin de Siècle

Although the capitalist cliché that makes time synonymous with money calls to mind first the culture of work, it can refer just as handily to play. Such an economy puts coins in the pockets of those who work in it, and the way in which it standardizes the hours of the workday has reciprocal implications for playtime. The burgeoning strata of middle-class Russians earning money at their jobs were also accumulating leisure hours, and they needed places to spend both. In commercialized societies the knotty concept of "disposable" income is intimately connected with that of leisure, because the earnings not needed to maintain the household become themselves commodities to be disposed of—that is, exchanged for pleasure in leisure time. The notion of "free" time turns out to be a contradiction in terms.

As work is to play, so is night to day in the entertainment world. Night marks the coordinates not just of time but also of space, according to Michel de Certeau's interpretation of the latter as "the effect produced by the operations that orient it, situate it, temporalize it, and make it . . . *a practiced place.*"[1] Peter Fritzsche saw nighttime as "an intriguing terrain because it relocated, juxtaposed, and heightened the contrasts of the industrial city."[2] Financed by discretionary income, nightlife fashioned a distinctive cultural fare as exciting and variable as the terrain itself. The night was a "heterotopia," characterized by Michel Foucault as "a place

[1] Michel de Certeau, *The Practice of Everyday Life,* trans. Steven Rendall (Berkeley: University of California Press, 1984), 117.

[2] Peter Fritzsche, *Reading Berlin 1900* (Cambridge, Mass.: Harvard University Press, 1996), 111.

where all the other real sites that can be found within a given culture are simultaneously represented, contested, and inverted."[3]

Before the commercialization of nightlife, the evening was separated according to notions of "public" and "private" spheres. Evening liberated most employees from work, dispatching them back to domesticity. But when they had some place other than home to go, many refused to stay put. Increasingly steeped in the culture of consumption, they realized that they could change their identities as readily as they did their clothes. Commercializing nightlife precipitated a minor revolution by taking what had formerly been considered private out in public, which transformed both spheres. At night, social, gender, and ethnic relations could play according to different rules than during the day. With its emphasis on consumption, the stimulation of evanescent desires, the new nightlife lent substance to much that made the world "modern."

Initially, sexual segregation gendered the night as it did the day. In the evening women might either attend private functions or venture into public as far as the legitimate theater, where well-established rules for decorum regulated reputations. Those women who broke the rules were deemed "public," creating a synonym for prostitute that spoke volumes about the gendering of the night space. Indeed, the anti-rape slogan of the end of the twentieth century "Take Back the Night!" reveals the extent to which this remained contested terrain from the beginning of the century when women began assuming a place there. The females who first entered the traditionally male night spots, though, do not usually figure as heroines in the narrative of women's liberation. For them, equality entailed dancing rather than voting, and they made themselves quite literally the victims of fashion when they straitjacketed themselves into corsets to attract the male gaze. Yet when women walked into restaurants and nightclubs, they were taking subversive action by liberating their sex from gendered ideas about proper behavior.

Another cliché holds that business can be a pleasure, when the reverse is more often the case, that pleasure is a business. Russia's restaurants and nightclubs grew out of two very different entertainment enterprises: private clubs and public fairs. Spaces for fun, both were also spaces where social relations could lose some of the rigidity assigned by estate. The introduction of commercial principles as fundamental to the structure of these entertainments created a new set of personal dealings—triangular relationships among managers, customers, and service personnel. Nightlife had been considerably more personalized from the late eighteenth century onward; various interest groups in the major cities, such as the En-

---

[3] Michel Foucault, "Of Other Spaces," *Diacritics* 16 (spring 1986): 22–27.

glish and German expatriates, and the better-heeled nobility and merchantry, had founded clubs where they could take their families, guests, or just themselves for meals and entertainment. While the ban on private theaters was in force, the clubs evaded the restriction by staging what they claimed to be noncommercial, members-only productions. In addition to dramatic plays, the casts of which often included members of the imperial theaters accepting money under the table, singers and comedians performed at clubs.[4]

At the other end of the entertainment spectrum lay the public festivals, or *narodnye gulian'ia,* that epitomized premodern urban spectacles. Magnified by Tsaritsa Anna's magnificent "holiday on ice" in 1742, these festivals brought all elements of a city's population together into a common space. Two major developers of nightlife, Mikhail Lentovskii and Aleksei Alexeev-Iakovlev, also directed *gulian'ia.* Associated principally with religious holidays, especially the *Maslenitsa* (Butter Week) that precedes Lent, these fairs were sponsored by official elites but deeply rooted in popular culture. They featured some of the music, marvels, and performed humor that would be brought indoors, into the nightclubs by century's end.[5] The primacy of the city over the countryside became apparent when the congestion that accompanied rapid urbanization forced the government to ban fairs in the city centers in 1896.[6]

In 1918, watching all that he knew come unglued by revolution, former theater censor Baron N. V. Drizen waxed nostalgic about the public amusements of his boyhood. Tracing a gradual movement away from the grand holiday celebrations to the night spots on Krestovskii Island, Drizen was mourning his loss of privilege, which he saw then as society's loss of innocence.[7] Drizen and others exaggerated when they blamed market forces for removing an idealized "folk" spontaneity from performance.[8] The entrepreneurs of the new culture industry did more than simply shelter customers from the elements: they created permanent places, but with fluctuating entertainments, which allowed for continual experimentations unrestricted by seasonality.

[4] I. F. Petrovskaia, "Raznye stseny tsentra i okrain," in *Teatral'nyi Peterburg. Nachalo XVIII veka—Oktiabr–1917 goda. Obozrenie-putevoditel'*, ed. I. F. Petrovskaia (St. Petersburg: RIII, 1994), 344–46.

[5] A. F. Nekrylova, *Russkie narodnye gorodskie prazdniki, uvesoeleniia i zrelishcha* (Leningrad: Iskusstvo, 1988).

[6] *Russkie narodnye gulian'ia po rasskazam A. Ia. Alekseeva-Iakovleva* (Moscow: Iskusstvo, 1948), 99.

[7] Baron N. V. Drizen, "Staryi Peterburg," *Ves'mir,* no. 10 (1918): 8–12.

[8] In typical Soviet/populist fashion, M. V. Douzhinskii expressed the sad loss of "people's culture" at the *balagany* in his *Vospominaniia* (Moscow: Nauka, 1987), 19–20.

Restaurant Culture

The connection between food and pleasure dates back as far as spices, but as dining developed into a cultural practice that varied across societies, it accrued political significance because of how it mirrored social relations. In Europe, as absolutist monarchies evolved into representative governments, Norbert Elias has argued that changes in dining at the court table proved central to "the civilizing process," a dubious metaphor for movement out of the Middle Ages and into modernity as other social groups began to appropriate court customs.[9] As Elias demonstrated through colorful illustrations of human excretions at the premodern table, new modes of etiquette required a mutual respect for oneself and one's neighbors, a respect that underlay the move toward individualism that characterized the Enlightenment. Russia's tsars, like their western European counterparts, excelled at "sharing (their) table as a mode of cultural performance."[10] Russia kept its court until 1917, and the challenge by social groups who wanted to participate in politics was also expressed through "cultural performances," such as dining out in public.

The etymology of the French "restaurant," the word that Russians used also (*restoran*), derived from eighteenth-century medical discourse, the term referring to a type of cuisine concocted to "restore" a weakened body. Public dining before this captured the sense of feeding the livestock, with people eating at the same table, at a set time, often from the same dish, possibly even with the same utensils. As ideas about diet and hygiene worked their way into other social discourses, both time and table followed suit and allowed for flexibility in selection and service.[11] The diner became individualized by his or her choice. Ironically, the French, those people most closely associated with cuisine-oriented culture, borrowed from the Russians the style of serving individual portions served in sequence, differentiating "dining *à la russe*" from "dining *à la française*," where all the food was served together.[12] Moreover, restaurants operated according to one of the paradoxes of mass consumption: on one hand, with their set prices and portions, they played on the forces of rationality; on the other, they also depended on the stimulation of irrational desires for their profits.

Public dining assumed its private dimension gradually, when patrons be-

---

[9] Norbert Elias, *The Civilizing Process: The History of Manners,* trans. Edmond Jephcott (New York: Urizen Books, 1978).

[10] Darra Goldstein, "Russian Dining: Theatre of the Gastronomic Absurd," *Performance Research* 4, no. 1 (1999): 56.

[11] On the origins of restaurant culture, see Rebecca Spang, "A Confusion of Appetites: The Emergence of Paris Restaurant Culture, 1740–1848" (Ph.D. diss., Cornell University, 1993), especially chapters 1 and 2.

[12] Joanne Finkelstein, *Dining Out: A Sociology of Modern Manners* (Oxford: Polity Press, 1989), 41.

gan drawing imaginary lines between their own tables and those nearby, respecting the privacy of those whose conversations could be overheard with little effort.[13] Restaurants made possible extensive social mingling, with distances understood rather than legislated. As Rebecca Spang has pointed out, "we need to think of the restaurant not solely as a place to 'eat,' but also as a social space and a cultural institution."[14] By the 1890s restaurants in Russian cities were turning gendered tables as well, as women could dine in restaurants without losing respectability.[15] When in 1911 a Moscow judge ruled that only if customers were in a state of obvious inebriation could they be denied entrance to restaurants, he undercut the authority of the system of estate-based privilege.[16]

The ability of diners to imagine that they were holding forth privately in public places was part and parcel of one of the most significant psychological transformations associated with urbanization: strangers had to learn to share urban spaces, which required behavior modification. Manners taught the newly private individuals how to negotiate in the new public spaces, which were becoming increasingly important to social interaction. Many, though, still found it difficult to cross the border between public and private. Pavel Buryshkin, the perceptive autobiographer of Moscow's merchant estate, noted that many from the old guard, raised in traditions of generous hospitality (*khlebosol'stvo*), considered it rude to be entertained in a restaurant rather than at home precisely because this violated customary dealings, which did not distinguish the business from the interpersonal.[17]

A singular attraction of the private home lay in its ability to hide alcohol consumption from official eyes. In addition to the private clubs, which served alcohol, Russia's restaurant culture evolved from the taverns that prospered with the sale of alcohol. Known in Russia as *kabaki* and introduced in the aftermath of the Mongol conquest, the history of these taverns tells as much about politics as culture.[18] Although the stretch from restorative broths to wines fortified for medicinal purposes is not especially far, hard liquor changed the stakes of public alcohol consumption. Official debates about what kinds of alcohol could be served in public underscored that the state's own interests were conflicted: spirits provided a needed source of revenue, but their negative influences cost the state in

---

[13] Rebecca Spang discusses how this evolved from Enlightenment principles in "Rousseau in the Restaurant," *Common Knowledge* 5, no. 1 (1996): 92–108.

[14] Spang, "Confusion of Appetites," 14.

[15] A. V. Amfiteatrov, *Deviatidesiatniki*, vol. 2 (St. Petersburg: Prometei, 1910), 127.

[16] *Restorannoe delo*, no. 1 (1911): 5.

[17] Pavel Buryshkin, *Moskva kupecheskaia* (New York: Chekhov, 1954), 153–54.

[18] I. T. Pryzhov, *Istoriia kabakov v Rossii* (Moscow: M. O. Vol'f, 1867), 45. This volume was reprinted in 1991 in Moscow by Booth Chamber International. See also David Christian, *Living Water* (Oxford: Clarendon Press, 1990), especially chapters 1 and 4.

other areas. To a certain degree the *kabaki* anticipated restaurants, characterized as they were by the camaraderie of people of all estates (*vsesoslovnye*), men and women, mingling over mugs of beer or mead.[19] The *kabak* almost fell victim to church piety in 1652 when the tsarist government outlawed it, but public discontent and empty treasury coffers forced its return eleven years later.[20] On the eve of the Great Reforms, which would include the repeal of the state's monopoly on alcohol in 1863, Russia had over ten thousand *kabaki*.[21] As late as 1910 the State Duma was continuing the centuries-old debates by trying to decide which restaurants could serve alcohol and how late they could remain open. At that time the government set the close of the commercial night by ending the sale of alcohol at 5 A.M.

Alcohol may have been central to bringing people together socially, but it was the food that grounded restaurants in the domestic economy and proved most pivotal to change. Originally, supping with strangers was directly related to travel. In addition to inns, or *traktiry*, travelers would seek their board often where they found their rooms, in people's homes, or the huts in local villages. The idea of actively seeking pleasure in such dining arrangements would have seemed startling to pre-touristic travelers, but once accommodations began improving, so did the food, and, of course, the wine. When in 1897 Stanislavsky and Nemirovich-Danchenko struck their historical bargain to inaugurate the Moscow Arts Theater at the Slavic Bazaar, a fashionable Moscow restaurant, they assured it a place in cultural history. But this restaurant also rates the attention of social historians, who should think about why the two met in that sort of location.

At the turn of the century, restaurant culture appeared so natural that its role in providing a venue where history can happen was taken for granted. Russian etiquette manuals, however, betray the degree of effort expended in integrating restaurants into the process of socialization. An invaluable source of information for charting changes in the rules of the social game, these manuals gave much needed advice for developing the personal comportment necessary for urban living: dining in public required mastery of the new rules. Before the middle of the nineteenth century, the manuals indicate that social interaction, from business to balls, took place largely in private. The underlying theme of these primers in behavior was to explain how to make a positive impression on new acquaintances. This self-creation of a public persona who understood restraint and decorum was essential to modern identity, because, as the texts warned, "even the most intelligent people routinely react on the basis of first impressions."[22] The manuals

---

[19] Pryzhov, *Istoriia kabakov*, 46–126.

[20] Christian, *Living Water*, 38–39.

[21] Ibid., 100.

[22] *Ruchnaia i vspomogatel'naia kniga dlia molodykh i pozhilykh osob oboego pola* (Moscow: V. Got'e, 1849), 10.

taught respect without confusing it with social sycophancy: "The courteous person shows everyone proper deference, never forgetting one's own self-esteem."[23] By internalizing the new codes of conduct, people developed the skills necessary to live in the city.

In the second half of the century etiquette manuals began to include separate sections on conduct in restaurants.[24] Echoing advice given in other areas that stressed consideration for the people around the protagonist of the melodrama of manners, the section on restaurant etiquette admonished that "the well-bred person conducts himself the same everywhere . . . in a restaurant as in high society."[25] The specifics of the advice suggest that people tended to make themselves a bit too much at home. Admonitions against boisterous conversation and striking matches on the wallpaper spoke to confusion about place. Cautions against taking personal liberties with the service personnel reflected confusion about commerce in this environment: waiters were employees, not servants. Patrons had to learn that the price for the meal did not include a license for rude behavior; the well-bred man eschewed the contemporary and reprehensible attitude that "it's *my* money" (*za svoi den'gi*).[26]

Humorist I. I. Miasnitskii, one of the most astute observers of social change in late imperial Russia, often placed his hapless characters in restaurants or nightclubs because he recognized how appropriate these sites were to survey the practice of everyday socialization. A typical short story, for example, "The Provinces in Moscow," recounted the adventures of a backwater (*chernobolotinskii*) merchant and his nephew in the Big City. The nephew, hoping to show off his sophistication, took his uncle to a restaurant where the latter managed to break every rule in the etiquette manuals. Noisy, suspicious of the need to check his coat, irritated by the prices, and lost in the French on the menu, the uncle longed for his home town until, predictably, it was time to return to the backwater.[27] The kinds of trouble in which Miasnitskii's characters habitually landed, and their abilities to extricate themselves, complemented the etiquette texts.

Restaurant culture rewarded those who modified their behavior and adapted to an atmosphere where literal consumption entailed far more than caloric sustenance, as Miasnitskii's merchants learned. It would be misleading, however, to assume that restrained decorum marked the only acceptable restaurant manners. On the contrary, as Darra Goldstein has illustrated, Russia's merchant diners became notorious for carrying out the excesses identified with the tsar's table once they began frequenting

---

[23] Ibid., 35.

[24] Finkelstein, *Dining Out*, 13; S. Mennell, *All Manners of Food* (Oxford: Basil Blackwell, 1985).

[25] K. N. Meshcherskii, *Rol' muzhchiny v svete*, 2d ed. (Moscow: A. A. Levinson, 1885), 126.

[26] Ibid., 127.

[27] I. I. Miasnitskii, *Provintsiia v Moskve* (Moscow: Sytin, 1903).

restaurants, a measure of rising wealth and social status. Nikolai Leskov, another humorist popular with the merchantry he lampooned, told the same story in "Devil Be Gone!"[28] As Goldstein argues, in the nineteenth century "mealtime escapades . . . shifted to the self as hosts . . . project[ed] their desired public image on to a metaphorical stage."[29]

An early example of such a "stage" was Moscow's Strel'na—founded in 1859 by I. F. Natruskin; financed by N. S. Bakhrushin, scion of one of Moscow's prominent merchant families, it was named for a small palace built by Peter the Great. In the first years the restaurant's doors opened modestly into a single dining hall with only two private rooms, *kabinety*, for smaller, intimate dining experiences.[30] When P. D. Boborykin, the "Russian Zola," used the Strel'na as one of the settings for social interaction in his 1882 novelization of the Moscow merchantry, *Kitai-gorod*, he chronicled its transformation into a cultural landmark. By the time of its fiftieth anniversary, the restaurant boasted summer and winter gardens and luxurious decor accentuated by tropical palms. It could seat five hundred comfortably. A poem in the theater journal *Zritel'* in 1881 celebrated this "garden of delights" with its palm trees and banana plants.[31] The addition of a floor show then took some getting used to, and patrons who went for the performance futilely expected diners to remain seated and quiet throughout.[32]

Russia's evolving restaurant culture integrated the empire into an international phenomenon. The Strel'na formed the eastern point of a constellation of restaurants that began with Delmonico's in New York. These restaurants did more than simply cater to sophisticated tastes; their managers actively sought to create dining as a pleasurable and respectable social experience.[33] The menu itself was a revolutionary text, a "map of desirable fictions" that liberated victuals from their prosaic descriptors; and dining required new literacy skills to interpret the menu's exotic lists, choices, and prices.[34] The big restaurants expanded the venue beyond food and drink, adding floor shows, orchestras, dancing, and other entertainments, so that the headline entertainment could become as famous as the food. The gypsy choruses that incited the "gypsy mania" (*tsyganovshchina*) that engulfed Russia from mid-century began as floor shows,

[28] In Leskov's "Chertagon'," the protagonists begin their night of drinking at the Iar. The story is in his collected works, vol. 6 (Moscow: Gos. Izd. Khud. Lit., 1956), 302–14.

[29] Goldstein, "Russian Dining," 61.

[30] "Strel'na: 50 iubilei," *Sinii zhurnal*, no. 7 (1911): 15.

[31] M. Iar-on, "Strel'na," *Zritel'*, nos. 23/24 (1881): 4–5.

[32] The theater journal *Iskusstvo* editorialized, in no. 25 (1883): 293, against the boorish behavior of some diners during the show.

[33] Lewis Ehrenberg, *Steppin' Out: New York Nightlife and the Transformation of American Culture, 1890–1930* (Chicago: University of Chicago Press, 1981), chapter 2.

[34] Spang, "Confusion of Appetites," 260–61.

A typically crowded evening at the Strel′na

as did the dancers who inspired the "tango mania" after 1910. Technology aided prospective diners who could not afford the best restaurants; the inventions of the phonograph and the player piano, inexpensive substitutes for live music, permitted them to dine to the strains of pleasant music.[35] In 1908 the gramophone music pouring out of the smaller Petersburg *kabaki* and restaurants was deemed so loud that city officials had to intervene.[36]

The choruses, orchestras, or even solo musicians who serenaded diners fed the notion that eating should be considered an event. Many restaurateurs added attractions, rearranged menus, and developed identities that would entice customers to leave their homes. The Strel′na soon faced competition across town with the revival of the Iar, a former *kabak* named for an eighteenth-century pavilion for *gulian′e,* that had "served exclusively as the base for the impious among the merchantry."[37] By 1887 legendary proprietor S. S. Sudakov had purchased the Iar from the heirs of original

[35] "Vliianie muzyki na restorannyiu torgovliu," *Restorannoe delo,* no. 6 (1911): 4.
[36] Article in *Peterburgskaia gazeta,* November 22, 1909, no. 321.
[37] Iks. Luch., "Iar," *Artisticheskii mir,* no. 1 (1912): 10.

owner A. Aksenov and redecorated it, adding the dining room walled with mirrors that would become its trademark. The famous mirror-lined walls allowed people to see images of themselves in a new setting, reflected next to others with whom they would not have previously imagined themselves.[38] In tenor with the times, people out to be seen could see themselves being seen.

Such dramatic flair helped Sudakov to lure customers from the Strel'na. As one roué remembered, "It would be more sinful to visit Moscow and not dine at the Iar than to go to Rome and not see the pope."[39] One of the most popular tunes of the late imperial era hurried a coachman to the Iar, where romantic adventure waited. Another sang of "Crazy Nights, Sleepless Nights" at the Iar.[40] In 1916, during the war, the Iar was deemed still "cleaner, better, and more attractive than the rest" when the city government commandeered part of it for a temporary hospital, despite its lack of indoor plumbing.[41] An evening on the town typically included visits to both restaurants, which made this duo simply integral to prerevolutionary Moscow's nightscape.[42] As one journal reported in 1912, "the laurels and successes enjoyed by the Iar and the Strel'na are giving others insomnia, resulting in the establishment of fabulous new restaurants, such as the Apollo and the Golden Anchor."[43] A favorite haunt of Siberian mystic Grigorii Rasputin when he stayed in Moscow, the Iar profited heavily from his notoriety.

The "mad monk," like other celebrities, probably entertained his party in one of the *kabinety*, small rooms for private parties. Offering seclusion in the midst of festivity, the *kabinety* enjoyed the benefits of dining-room service. Patrons tipped the discreet waiter and sometimes negotiated for exclusive performances by the featured entertainers. As Spang observed, the door to a *kabinet* "hinted at communication between two separate spheres while it defined the boundaries of those worlds."[44] Predictably, these were the hot spots in any restaurant. For every married couple celebrating an anniversary or business meeting conducted in confidential surroundings, *kabinety* hosted an equal number of less proper assignations.[45]

[38] Rebecca Spang discusses mirrors in restaurants in this era in *The Invention of the Restaurant: Paris and Modern Gastronomic Culture* (Cambridge, Mass.: Harvard University Press, 2000), 55.

[39] Luch., "Iar," 10.

[40] Egor Poliakov, "Istertyi grif," *Tsirk i estrada*, no. 5 (1928): 6.

[41] *Var'ete i tsirk*, no. 6 (1916): 6.

[42] Alexander Serebrov (A. N. Tikhonov), *Vremia i liudi (Vospominaniia, 1898–1905)* (Moscow: Khudozhestvennaia literatura, 1955), 109–10. See also A. Sumbatov-Iuzhin's *Dzhentelmen*, act I, scene v, for a discussion of the popular gypsy romances, and the play *Raby*, by I. S. Platon (St. Petersburg: Teatr i iskusstvo, 1904), 34.

[43] *Var'ete i tsirk*, no. 1 (1912): 5.

[44] Spang, "Confusion of Appetites," 270.

[45] Singers were warned against accepting expensive tokens from those who engaged them

Coachmen waiting outside the Iar, memorialized in a popular tune

The mirrored splendor of the Iar

Homosexual liaisons were also held in the privacy of these intimate rooms.[46] Thus the *kabinet* created a liminal zone for expressing the most extreme emotional actions, from Rasputin's putative orgies to the suicides reported frequently in the popular press. Although organized restaurateurs worried that the suicides were bad for business, in part because the point was to shoot oneself *before* paying the bill, these private rooms essentialized the social novelty of the restaurant.[47] The *kabinety* entered urban lore as a setting of potential danger, but one ensconced within a larger, protective environment.

Newspaper advertisements chart the expansion of restaurants in all urban areas, and the indicated prices make plain that those who could ill afford the tonier places could still enjoy a night on the town. Two nationally circulated professional journals, *Restorannaia zhizn'* (Restaurant life) and *Restorannoe delo* (The restaurant business), appeared after 1905 and testified to the growing popularity of dining out. Like their patrons, restaurants had to develop distinctive identities that set them apart from the others. The most effective way of distinguishing the restaurant was through the cuisine, and the names of many reflect both Russia's uneven relationship with the West and its imperial mission. The Samarkand, a small Petersburg restaurant of the 1870s, was one of the first of many that sought to incorporate Central Asia gastronomically into the empire. Capitalizing on the romance of conquest, by the turn of the century all major Russian cities had at least one dining spot named for somewhere in the Caucasus or Central Asia. However, the Caucasus Restaurant in Rostov-on-Don served more as an employment agency than an outpost of Georgia on the Don River. Regional artists and impresarios congregated regularly at certain restaurants, looking to hire and be hired.[48] Moscow's Filippov Cafe enjoyed the reputation of a "Babylon" during its early morning hours of operation because of who congregated there.[49]

Even when a restaurant's name was not synonymous with its fare, it conveyed something about atmosphere. Moscow's Prague Restaurant furthered pan-Slavism in an upscale environment, one of several so-named dining spots in Russia. In fact, Moscow's Prague offered a sanctuary from the "gypsy mania" with a menu that offered to aid recovery from a hangover.[50] The transformation of Peterburg's Beograd into the Skutari in

---

for private performances, because "gentlemen" by daylight were prone to decide that they had been robbed of such trinkets. "Podarki v kabinetakh," *Artisticheskii mir*, no. 1 (1912): 3.

[46] Dan Healey, "Masculine Purity and 'Gentlemen's Mischief': Sexual Exchange and Prostitution between Russian Men, 1861–1914," *Slavic Review* 60, no. 2 (2001): 248.

[47] *Restorannoe delo*, no. 3 (1912): 12.

[48] Advertisement in the Kharkhov edition of *Artisticheskii mir*, no. 1 (1909). The ad promised "a local agent always present."

[49] *Var'ete i tsirk*, no. 5 (May 1916): 2.

[50] Egor Poliakov, "Istertyi grif," *Tsirk i estrada*, no. 5 (1928): 6.

"Hello, operator? I was trying to call the Aquarium, but you connected me with the home for unwed mothers. That was not very tactful, and besides, it was premature." *Strekoza,* no. 29 (1906): 4.

1913 seemed to jump from newspaper headlines about the recurrent Balkan wars. The two Russian capitals themselves regularly had restaurants named for them in provincial cities, because by invoking the capital cities, proprietors were intimating a certain glamour. The capitals responded in kind with predominantly small places named for provincial cities, such as the Tver and the New Iaroslavlets, a bow toward nationalism. Western, especially French names, insinuated elegance, imagined or otherwise. Petersburg's Vienna Restaurant took the flair if not the waltz from the Austrian capital. A place where the genuine literati gathered, on a clear night at the Vienna a patron could spot Decadents at one table and Realists in another corner—just as tourists could later gawk at French Existentialists at Les Deux Magots in Paris. Although it is not clear that Alexander Blok and Leonid Andreev actually conversed when at the Vienna, the reality that they could be found sharing the same menu and atmosphere prompted a book, *A Night at the Vienna,* "a depiction of Petersburg's literary life."[51] Roshanna Sylvester has catalogued a similar phenomenon in turn-of-the-century Odessa, where the Café Robina topped the list of fashionable spots.[52]

Social observers in the late twentieth century make cuisine an indication of globalization, the pervasive Indian restaurants in London signaling a kind of reverse colonization.[53] But restaurant culture has long invoked nationalism and the related impulse of imperialism. It could, for example, provide evidence of Russia's superiority, just as the internationally renowned French fare gave that country a patina of sophistication. Always quick to disparage Germans as "sausage eaters," for example, Russians learned more about comparative cuisine from Count Amori, the eponymous pseudonym assumed by Ippolit Rapgoff, a writer of pulp fiction who managed to find a niche for himself in almost every aspect of popular culture. Amori's critique of Germany's eating establishments described interesting aspects of culture in the self-congratulatory tone indicative of the years leading up to the Great War. Anyone who has spent time in Russia can appreciate Amori's surprise at finding "something green" on the plates and can just as easily recognize the Russian customers who ate the meat but sent the garnishes back. Noting how restaurants were becoming big business in Berlin, financed by joint-stock companies, Amori could only be disappointed by the tiny portions of meat and alcohol: "It's very expensive to eat in Berlin, if you want to eat Russian style."[54]

[51] Oskar Norvezhskii's *Noch' v V'ene* was reviewed in *Vestnik literatury,* no. 4 (1908): 82–83. Ads taken out in the periodical press billed it as "a rendezvous for writers," which may well have driven some of them away as the publicity increased.

[52] Sylvester, "Crime, Masquerade, and Anxiety," 200.

[53] Doreen Massey, "Power-Geometry and a Progressive Sense of Place," in *Mapping the Futures: Local Cultures, Global Change,* ed. Jon Bird et al. (New York: Routledge, 1993), 59.

[54] Count Amori's series on "Foreign Restaurants" ran in *Restorannoe delo,* nos. 2–3 (1912).

The alternative would be to take Russia to the rest of the world. Encouraged by the popularity of the restaurant featured at the Russian exhibit at Glasgow's international trade exposition in 1901, the Ministry of Trade and Industry promoted the building of others in Europe, an export that would allow Europeans to cultivate a taste for Russia. The ministry's plans called for such nationalist kitsch as waiters dressed as Cossacks and samovar service.[55] Ironically, this was the sort of restaurant émigrés opened abroad after fleeing the Bolsheviks in 1917.[56] Evoking nostalgia for an imaginary Russia, for an imitation vodka-and-caviar nobility without cares or responsibilities, the "Russian" restaurants fostered the sort of behavior that would run up the bill.[57] During the Cold War, when the Soviet Union served as an antonym for style and taste, New York's Russian Tea Room could successfully disguise the politics of the Old Regime behind a menu designed for historical forgetfulness—which, of course, fulfills a restaurant's charge: to manufacture an atmosphere.

Masters of ambience, Sudakov and Natruskin reached the top of an entrepreneurial ladder climbed by many other restaurateurs. Like other branches of commercial culture, restaurants depended on the imagination of men eager to begin new traditions because they had no stake in the old ones. The typical path trod by the successful restaurateur began in the provinces and led to the cities through a job in a minor branch of the food industry. V. G. Epifani, proprietor of several restaurants in Petersburg, including the Crimea, the Transvaal, and the Golden Birch Tree, began as a baker. In 1893, at the age of thirty-three, he borrowed money to purchase a small hotel, from which he expanded into restaurants.[58] M. V. Lebedev, who had left his village to serve in a *traktir*, had put together a mini-empire of small hotels and restaurants, spanning global appetites from his Tver to his China before his fortieth birthday.[59] The most famous entrepreneur to begin in restaurants, P. V. Tumpakov, worked as a waiter in the summer garden at the zoo before applying his genius to nightclubs.

Restaurateurs and their enterprises played a unique political role after the 1905 Revolution. Numerous restaurants nationwide had provided a locale for the so-called "banquet campaign" that immediately preceded the revolution, when liberal groups used the essential liminality of the restau-

---

[55] *Restorannoe delo*, no. 6 (1912): 6.

[56] The most famous of these restaurants in the United States, New York's Russian Tea Room and Romanoff's in Beverly Hills, were actually founded by Jewish émigrés cashing in on nostalgia for a lifestyle that would have held scant sentimental value for them. Nina Burleigh, "Champagne Wishes and Caviar Dreams," *New York Magazine*, October 18, 1999.

[57] The nostalgia generated by the Russian restaurants is one, to use Susan Stewart's words, "enamoured of distance, not of referent itself." Quoted in Svetlana Boym, *Common Places* (Cambridge, Mass.: Harvard University Press, 1994), 284.

[58] *Restorannoe delo*, no. 11 (1913): 14–17. This journal ran a series of biographies of prominent restaurateurs; their stories consistently repeat each other.

[59] *Restorannoe delo*, no. 8 (1913): 12–13.

rant to camouflage their none-too-secret political meetings. After 1905 the tsarist government increased its toleration of private social organizations, and in 1908 restaurant owners formally founded a professional society that worked in practice as a proto-lobby to the national parliament, the Duma. In fact, their interests touched on the most pressing social and political issues of the day, including the length of the workday, the alcohol question, and the gendering of public space.

Officially, the government tiered restaurants according to the rules that governed the serving of alcohol and hours of operation. The system, which used menu prices as the basis of the hierarchy, was designed with social control in mind: the cheaper the menu, the more restricted the hours and service of alcohol. Yet by the time the society was organized, dining had changed so much that clienteles could not be stereotyped so readily. As elsewhere, alcoholic drinks were rated according to the percentage of alcohol in the contents, "hard liquor" (*krepkie napitki*) forming the most problematic category. Women were forbidden from working in establishments that sold hard liquor, an official policy that denied them employment on the basis of outdated assumptions about women in public. The third-tier restaurants were prohibited from selling any spirits, and those at the second level faced limitations in the times that it could be served. The first tier, such as the Iar and the Strel'na, enjoyed a privileged official attitude because of equally outdated presumptions about a connection between wealth and refined behavior.

Rather than dividing along the same political lines as their presumed class-based clientele, though, the proprietors were savvy enough to recognize the importance of speaking in a single political voice. For example, the Duma's attempt to restrict alcohol sales at the second tier on evenings before holidays threatened all establishments because of how the Duma was flexing its muscle to legislate social concerns. In 1912 the restaurant owners' society hosted the first all-Russian conference to discuss "the needs of those who manufacture and sell wine and beer." With the outbreak of World War I in 1914 the government laid down the law of prohibition, a futile gesture at social control that disconcerted social life.

What Duma representatives saw as social concerns, the society's members read as their particular economic interests: the worker question loomed as large as the alcohol problem in this regard. Perhaps because so many proprietors had themselves come up through the ranks, they idealized the system as one in which energetic hard work would be rewarded. Or perhaps, like the old nobility, having reached a position of authority they had become patriarchal. Regardless, they did not want the Duma to intervene in their relations with their employees. The remarkably contradictory combination of old attitudes and new strategies comes across in an article on how the society had mustered its forces to prevent approval of a

1913 Duma bill that would reduce the workday from fifteen to twelve hours. Members who had striven to defeat the bill were congratulated for maintaining "such an unimaginable work tempo, such an enormous expenditure of energy, and crowned with such sparkling success!"[60] Following their logic, waiters were not to be confused with factory workers because the long, slow period between meals gave them a break in the workday.

The society had a valid point in that a simplistic pitting of employers against employees masked other legitimate concerns about the nature of work.[61] Service primarily for tips (*chainiki*) could not be determined by the workers' relationship to the means of production. In 1911 the populist Ivan Shmelev re-created the life of a waiter in the short story "The Man from the Restaurant," published in the quasi-leftist journal *Znanie* (Knowledge).[62] At least four film versions were made of this popular story. Although the protagonist appears one-dimensional and the action predictable, reading the story alongside the articles by and about waiters in *Restorannoe delo* makes it clear that Shmelev sketched accurate details of restaurant life.

The waiter of the title, Skorokhodov (whose name connotes "moving quickly"), saw himself as refined as his clientele, taking pride in his appearance and service. Deeply conservative politically and religiously, employees shared management's patriarchal attitude because they appreciated being rewarded for their respectful conduct. The vignettes of the diners' odious behavior intended to inspire contempt among *Znanie*'s readers were, if anything, more benign than much actual behavior. In real life, as opposed to short-story pathos, for example, a prince scarred the face of a waiter who had refused to serve him because of past unpaid bills.[63] Skorokhodov has a son who, in the leftist narrative of the times, becomes a revolutionary and expresses contempt for his obsequious father. Management fires the father when the restaurant's name appears in the press in connection with the son. Perhaps Skorokhodov should have taken the advice of one Petersburg's most frequent diners, S. N. Atava, and retired to write his memoirs: as Atava advised a favorite waiter, whom he knew to be privy to numerous scandalous secrets, "you would get rich."[64]

In August 1917 Moscow's waiters demonstrated that service was indeed an industry. They joined other workers and struck to disrupt a right-wing conference, forcing the out-of-town delegates to forage for food.[65] In Pet-

---

[60] *Restorannoe delo*, no. 4 (1913): 11.

[61] *Restorannoe delo*, no. 9 (1911): 5–6.

[62] "Chelovek iz restorana" appears in I. S. Shmelev, *Povesti i rasskazy* (Moscow: Gos. Izd. Khud. Literatury, 1960).

[63] *Restorannoe delo*, no. 12 (1913): 16.

[64] A. Pleshcheev, "Vakhanaliia," *Stolitsa i usad'ba*, no. 42 (1915): 21.

[65] Alexander Rabinowitch, *The Bolsheviks Come to Power* (New York: Norton, 1976), 111.

rograd's Tourist Restaurant, though, an alternative style of dining had just been introduced, the so-called "Finnish Table," or smorgasbord inherited from Sweden.[66] Modern in its emphasis on practicality, the smorgasbord undercut both the service and the cultural performance that made dining an entertainment.

Trippin' the Night Fantastic

Consumption of food in the ambience of restaurants stimulated other nocturnal appetites, and nightclubs further challenged traditional hierarchies. At the turn of the twentieth century, the nightclubs moved to the rhythm of the city, keeping up a fast pace, like the streetcar, and regulating their audiences as the latter did its passengers. They also cultivated the same sort of social commingling: even though moderate, the price of a ticket would restrict the very poor, just as the very wealthy could afford more refined transportation and entertainment. But the people in between could be serviced, and those at the socioeconomic extremes would occasionally venture into the mainstream; nightclubs symbolized how urban boundaries were never as fixed as some residents might desire. Like the "boulevard" press, they performed the moment, as disposable as the income that audience paid for a table.[67]

The nightclub has many historical antecedents: the *commedia dell'arte*, with its pantomimes and harlequinade; the *burla*, or practical-joke interlude born of the *commedia;* the *skomorokhi*, Russia's version of medieval wandering minstrels-cum-jesters; vaudevilles, which in Russia referred to a short performance on the legitimate stage between acts; the Sunday strolls set to music in the public parks, often located at imperial residences; the growth of secular music; the loosening of social codes that allowed men and women to embrace each other on the public dance floor; and the influence of French fashions throughout Russia's nineteenth century. The multiplicity of origins precludes the possibility of defining a nightclub precisely. Many of them hovered between the restaurant and the theater, spilling out into the parks in the warm evenings of the summertime. Following the era of the Great Reforms, when comparative economic prosperity was spurring urban growth, Russians had more reason to go out at night, more motivation to splurge on pleasure.

By the 1870s commercial pleasure gardens (*uvesitel'nye sady*) were springing up, modeled loosely on Copenhagen's Tivoli and the Konigsgarten in Berlin. Most evolved along the same lines as Petersburg's first im-

---

[66] Advertised in *Sportivnyi listok,* 1915, as "where to go after the races."

[67] Nightclub performances underscore Peter Fritzsche's point that "commerce was at once an economic foundation and a sensory experience." *Reading Berlin 1900,* 107.

portant equivalent, the Demidov Gardens. Part of what had once been a highly prestigious noble estate, located in the city, these gardens had hosted public concerts earlier in the century. In the 1860s the entrepreneur E. N. Egarev leased a section which he turned into an entertainment complex. Although he named it the Russian Family Gardens, it was known colloquially as the "Demidron." The social observer V. O. Mikhnevich described it as "the most stylish, the most dazzling pleasure garden in the city," and the French cancan enjoyed its Russian premier here.[68] Most of these nightclubs changed ownership and names every decade or two, with the advent of new fashions. In the 1880s, for example, V. A. Linskaia-Nemetti, one of tsarist Russia's few female entrepreneurs, took over the Demidron.

Egarev's principal innovation had been to build an *estrada,* or small stage for light entertainment.[69] Central to the creation of the nightclub, the *estrada* positioned the performers close to the audience, where the limited space fostered the crucial rapport between the two. Also called the "open stage" (*otkrytaia stsena*) to distinguish it from the legitimate stage, the addition of an *estrada* converted the main dining hall of the upscale restaurants into something more than an eating establishment. In Russian, the adjectival form of *estrada, estradnyi,* is used to denote a nightclub setting, marking off those areas in restaurants as well as the individual clubs.

The central downtown areas, public gardens, and some regions bordering the cities' limits all offered spaces for night spots. To use Petersburg as an example, the islands that dotted the imperial capital, especially Krestovskii, Aptekarskii, and Elagin, offered ample space for pleasure gardens and competed with the central urban artery of Nevskii Prospekt as nucleuses of fun. Like the Demidovs, other noble estates leased park areas for commercial entertainment. The Stroganov's Mineral Waters had provided a public park setting since the 1850s, becoming a popular night spot in the 1860s. Egarev opened the exotic Alhambra here in 1873, a nightclub of pseudo-Moorish design.[70] Russia's first public skating rink opened at Iusupov Park in 1865. Merchant E. Rost founded the Zoological Garden in the 1870s, showcasing almost more entertainments than animals. As more and more city dwellers leased summer dachas, they also wanted to amuse themselves in the parks and entertainments expanded accordingly. In the 1890s, with the expansion of working-class neighborhoods, nightclubs began springing up in those areas to siphon off some of the newly disposable income.[71] Petersburg's Lesnaia district, for example, with its

---

[68] I. F. Petrovskaia, "Chastnye antreprizy," in *Teatral'nyi Peterburg,* ed. I. F. Petrovskaia, 165.

[69] Evgenii Kuznetsov, *Iz proshlogo russkoi estrady: Istoricheskie ocherki* (Moscow: Iskusstvo, 1958), 120–21.

[70] Petrovskaia, "Chastnye antreprizy," 165.

[71] Kuznetsov, *Iz proshlogo,* 231.

mixed population, had numerous nightclubs.[72] Renowned chronicler of the night N. V. Nikitin estimated in 1903 that Petersburg's most popular nightclubs, including the Bouffe and the Aquarium, collected more than one thousand rubles on evenings during the summer season. He also estimated that several thousand strollers visited the gardens daily.[73] The international influence came with the Luna Park, a full-scale amusement park named for the popular original on New York's Coney Island, opened where Egarev's had been and operated by prominent merchant K. S. Eliseev. In addition to rides, it offered restaurants and an open stage.[74]

In Moscow, Petrovskii Park and nearby Sokolniki, areas spacious enough for the hippodrome and other athletic fields, were also prime places for pleasure gardens. Most began modestly. The Saks Garden, for example, founded in 1867, initially had only a military band playing on Sundays and holidays. The theatrical entrepreneur P. M. Medvedev, who had signed Savina to his provincial company, kept a base in Moscow with his Family Garden. Later a Tivoli sprouted in Sokolniki. Major cities and minor towns followed the same pattern, if on a smaller scale. These parks initially offered more activities for the daytime, too, with gardens for strolling, orchestra music in the background, and ponds that hosted great theatrical reenactments of historical events. The *balagany*, or fair booths that dominated at *gulian'ia*, could not compete with the Moorish or Chinese architectural exotica—which like the French dances transformed traditional into cosmopolitan, to the delight of most.[75] The Olympia in Moscow in 1908 typified these entertainment complexes: "a large garden with a summer theater, a restaurant, and an orchestra pit."[76]

The cancanesque joviality of France's Second Empire began to be felt in Russia in the 1860s, soon after it had debuted in Paris. The *café-concerts*—proto-nightclubs that moved indoors or out, depending on the season, and usually offered table service for drinks to keep audiences seated—were making their way into Russian cities.[77] Abbreviated as *café-concs,* these establishments were wealthier cousins to the *café-chantants,* another form of smaller nightclub in a more intimate surrounding. Russian vocabulary did not usually distinguish between the two, usually identifying both as *shantany*. As the numbers and types of acts increased, Russians also applied the

[72] Petrovskaia, "Raznye stseny tsentra i okrain," in *Teatral'nyi Peterburg,* 340–43.

[73] N. V. Nikitin, *Peterburg noch'iu* (St. Petersburg: Trud, 1903), 100.

[74] Al'bin Konechnyi, "Shows for the People," in *Cultures in Flux,* ed. Stephen Frank and Mark Steinberg (Princeton: Princeton University Press, 1994), 121–30.

[75] Information on Moscow parks can be found in the archive of the Bakhrushin Museum, f. 543, d. 1.

[76] G. M. Iaron, *O liubimom zhanre* (Moscow: Iskusstvo, 1960), 22.

[77] François Caradec and Alain Weill, *Le café-concert* (Paris: Hachette, 1980). See also Charles Rearick, *Pleasures of the Belle Epoque* (New Haven: Yale University Press, 1985), chapter 4.

term "variety" (*var'ete*); a survey in 1912 trying to distinguish a "variety" from a "restaurant" indicated considerable overlap.[78] The names of Russia's *shantany* bespoke the French conquest: Monplezir, Orfeum, Shato-de-fler, and, of course, Petersburg's own Foli-Berzher. The poorly conceived official prohibition against "programs that include conversation and singing, that charge admission and that advertise on billboards"[79] inspired creative entrepreneurs to take advantage of the French connection. Playing on the political angle of the prohibition, they argued that nothing subversive could be understood when songs were sung in foreign languages.

Those who frequented the nightclubs constituted Russia's most conspicuous consumers, people positioned to negotiate some of the new forms of social relations in leisure spaces. The entrepreneurs who founded these clubs set examples with their own ambitions, and the most successful not only remade themselves, they remade society. One of the most respected and successful entrepreneurs, F. F. Thomas, owner of the Arcadia, a skating rink, and Moscow's Maxim's restaurant, was a black man from Great Britain.[80] Two of the dominant figures in prerevolutionary entertainment remain virtually unknown today, lost in the transformation from commercial to official culture: M. V. Lentovskii and P. V. Tumpakov. Their personal biographies connected them to many of their customers. Lentovskii's name shows up in footnote references to activities that were really secondary to his major accomplishments, and he warranted a biography on the same basis.[81] Tumpakov's name disappeared seemingly without a trace after 1917, despite a richly deserved reputation as "the Russian Barnum" because of his entrepreneurial chutzpah. Both deceased by 1917, the moguls shared the same fate as victims of an indifferent historiography, and they deserve to return to the *estrada* of history.

Lentovskii's reputation barely survived 1917 because of the company that crossed his many theatrical paths. Born in provincial Saratov in 1843, the son of an impoverished serf musician, and brought to Moscow on an impulse by the great serf actor Mikhail Shchepkin, he then toured the provinces as a bit player with the great British-African actor Ira Alridge, and developed some entrepreneurial skills touring with Medvedev. Back in Moscow he joined the Malyi's company as a character actor in operettas and enlisted in Ostrovskii's Artistic Circle, anxious to overturn the official prohibition against private theaters. A better scout than a performer, he put several future stars on his stage early in his career, including Savina, and singing stars Vera Zorina and Alexander Davydov, plus the young Fe-

---

[78] *Vare'te i tsirk*, no. 2 (1912): 2–3.

[79] The decree is quoted in Kuznetsov, *Iz proshlogo,* 120.

[80] See the article about him in *Var'ete i tsirk*, no. 1 (1912): 6.

[81] Andrew Donskov, *Mixail Lentovskij and the Russian Theatre* (East Lansing, Mich.: Russian Language Journal, 1985).

dor Shaliapin. Architects Karl Val'ch, later of the Bol'shoi, and Franz Shektel', who worked to redesign late imperial Moscow, built sets for his productions.

That some of his ideas were enlisted in the debate about what constituted *public* entertainment ensured Lentovskii his historiographical footnote. His career illustrates the middle-class struggle with the cultural hegemony exercised by the *intelligentsia,* including the middle class's ambivalent desire for inclusion on the *intelligentsia*'s agenda. In 1897 both he and Stanislavsky presented plans to Moscow's city fathers to found a theater for the "people." The problem, though, lay in the extent to which the Russian word *narod* was culturally freighted. Although it translated as both "the people" and "the public," in the postemancipation period it signified "the peasantry," who hovered in elite imaginations as a protean Other, without agency and vulnerable equally to negative or positive influences.[82] The signature works of these two men, Moscow's most intellectually prestigious theater and its most popular nightclub, mark the extreme positions over the definition of public culture.

Lentovskii would find himself essentialized in the politicized vocabulary of the *narod.* As he described his ambitions for the "people," he declared an objective that theater be "accessible by price as well as by repertoire to the average viewer" (*srednyi zritel'*).[83] He himself specified his target audience: bureaucrats, merchants, students, and working people.[84] Although the *narodnoe gul'iane* had translated culturally as "public amusements," the commercialization of leisure had introduced the money element that mediated entrance to the new entertainments. Now officials decided that ticket prices would determine whether or not an amusement was aimed at the *narod,* and they made political decisions accordingly about what could be staged.[85]

Although he always enjoyed performing, whether as a vaudeville-style comedian between acts or as none other than the Prince of Denmark, Lentovskii found his vocation when he moved behind the curtain to run the show and to write the occasional routine. In 1878 he began the project that would make his reputation, redesigning and furbishing the theater and gardens at the Hermitage, a rundown estate whose past owners had included the illustrious names of Pushkin and Rimsky-Korsakov.[86]

---

[82] Lentovskii's personal archive is in Moscow's Bakhrushin Theatrical Museum, f. 144. This information is from d. 842, 6.

[83] Ibid., d. 842, l. 3.

[84] Lentovskii noted that these, the neither wealthy nor elite, needed a place to spend their money on family entertainments in his detailed prospectus for public entertainment, submitted to the Moscow city fathers in 1897. Included in his personal archive in its printed form but not catalogued, ll. 4–6.

[85] Donskov, *Mixail Lentovskij,* 49.

[86] Ibid., 29.

More than simply rebuilding the *estrada* of a small theater, Lentovskii cleaned the ponds and replanted the gardens, constructing a pleasure garden that outlasted the tsarist regime; in the post-Stalin thaw of the 1950s, big band leader Eddy Rosner, released from the prison camp in Magadan, re-created swing here.[87] In 1882 Lentovskii added "The Theater of the Fantastic" (*fanticheskii teatr*) to the complex. Therein lay his forte: novelty, fantasia, and pleasing the crowd. That year he was also appointed to direct the *narodnoe gul'iane* to celebrate the coronation of Alexander III, personifying the link between the *gul'iane* and the nightclub.

Lentovskii expanded his empire to the imperial capital. His first Petersburg enterprise, the Arcadia, opened to enthusiastic reviews with popular songbird Vera Zorina, the "Presnaia Patti," in 1881. But within the year it had burned to the ground.[88] Rebuilt, the Arcadia became a marvelous pleasure garden with both a closed theater and an open stage, though not of Hermitage proportions. Lentovskii revitalized the former Livadia, named for the Crimean resort, renaming it first the Kin-Grust' and then the Petersburg Hermitage, but it never truly developed into a hot spot.[89] In the 1890s he tried again with a garden theater called the Chicago, but irregularities with the deed forced an early closure.[90]

Buoyed by the possibilities for entertainment once the government repealed its ban on private theaters, Lentovskii expanded quickly. Too quickly. Overall, he managed eleven different enterprises. He added a legitimate stage to his Muscovite empire, the Skomorokh, and other nightclubs, including one in Nizhnii Novgorod operational during the annual national fair. His showpiece, the Hermitage, depended on infusions of the profits from his other enterprises, but it was a great cultural success; like the Iar, it became a fixture in Moscow's nightlife, made familiar through newspaper articles and light fiction by the most perceptive social observers of the era—V. A. Giliarovski, I. I. Miasnitskii, and Anton Chekhov. In 1909, after Lentovskii's death, his promotional legacy lived on in a journalistic lampoon, a newspaper framing all news stories around an upcoming extravaganza at the Hermitage.[91]

Lentovskii spent all the rubles necessary to build a complex that offered a panoply of entertainments priced according to which section one en-

[87] Although the Hermitage was no longer a single complex, even the Soviets created an advertising booklet for it: *Ermitazh* (Moscow: Mosk. otdel. teatral. zrel. kass, 1958). On Rosner, see S. Frederick Starr, *Red and Hot: The Fate of Jazz in the Soviet Union, 1917–1980* (New York: Oxford University Press, 1983), 194–205, 225–27.

[88] Kuznetsov, *Iz proshlogo*, 126.

[89] I. F. Petrovskaia, "Raznye stseny tsentra i okrain," in *Teatral'nyi Peterburg*, ed. I. F. Petrovskaia, 351.

[90] Bakhrushin Museum, f. 144, d. 946, ll. 11–12. See also Konechnyi, "Shows for the People," 126–27.

[91] The crime column, for example, reported a woman stabbing her husband for refusing to take her to a ball there. "Teatr Ermitazh" (Moscow, 1909).

tered and where one sat. The complex included the Opera-Bouffe, the gardens, and the Antheum, remodeled from the former Theater of the Fantastic to resemble Greek ruins. Operettas would be staged at the Bouffe, fireworks and acrobats in the garden areas. Savina performed favorite scenes here, and Ermolova worked for his Nizhnii Novgorod enterprise occasionally. Zorina and Davydov made their reputations here, and their heirs on the popular concert stage, Anastasia Vial'tseva and Mikhail Vavich, later headlined at the Hermitage. Lentovskii toured Europe regularly to ascertain that his productions kept up with the latest trends.

The historical significance of Lentovskii's career lies in his success at bringing a variety of social groups out into the commercialized night. His legitimate stages, the Skomorokh and the Antheum, allowed him to offer what the critics would consider serious culture, which he alternated with spectacular fare. His first great success at the Skomorokh was a production of Jules Verne's *A Trip to the Moon,* complete with earthquake and volcanic eruption, set to the music of Jacques Offenbach and starring an amazing electric moon.[92] A play about the national hero General Skobolev, *The White General,* reconquered the Turks on stage with its lavish sets and costumes, a slightly smaller version of the historical dramatizations in the Hermitage's gardens.

The playbill for a typical season at the Skomorokh favored the sensational, but it would be unwise as well as unfair to assume that these lacked intrinsic social or political values.[93] *The Murder of the Merchant Osipov's Daughter* intrigued the audience with its title, which suggested that it combined sensationalism with social estate and played on the increasing vulnerability of women who moved out into public. Russian history mounted the stage in *Stenka Razin, Iurii Miloslavskii, Ermak Timofeevich,* and with another popular general in *Suvorov in the Village.* Melodrama resounded in other productions: *The Thief of Children, Broken Dreams,* and *A Mother's Blessing.* The censors removed Miasnitskii's *The Bandit Churkin* from the bill in 1884 as part of the crackdown against the public lionization of this local thug.[94] Intermixed with these were a few that would be considered classics, especially Gogol's *Inspector General* and various Ostrovskii pieces.[95] Instead of separating the so-called classics from those that never made it beyond Russia in the 1880s, though, it makes more sense to see in the worlds of Gogol and Ostrovskii what a typical Lentovskii audience did: slapstick comic and melodramatic elements. Like American composer John Philip

---

[92] Bakhrushin Museum, f. 144, d. 1076, ll. 6, 23.

[93] Donskov, *Mixail Lentovskij,* 41.

[94] Jeffrey Brooks, *When Russia Learned to Read: Literacy and Popular Literature, 1861–1917* (Princeton: Princeton University Press, 1985), 124. "The Bandit Churkin" has been translated in *Entertaining Tsarist Russia,* ed. James Von Geldern and Louise McReynolds (Bloomington: Indiana University Press, 1998), 221–30.

[95] For example, the list for the 1888 season: Bakhrushin Museum, f. 144, d. 683.

Sousa, another impresario of the turn of the century relegated to the middlebrow, Lentovskii sought to cater to the many rather than the few.[96]

Lentovskii's ideas about entertaining the masses lacked the crucial didactic element that characterized the *intelligentsia*'s mission to create the idealized common culture. Sensitive to the discourse about the *narod* and wanting to offer decent amusements to those on a limited budget, he educated by entertaining through demonstrations of electricity, homing pigeons, panoramas of the conquest of Siberia, bicycle races, and testing fate on a wheel of fortune.[97] Lentovskii showed profound faith in the possibility of pluralism, and his sense of the lowbrow did not deflate it to pessimistic appraisals of either its contents or its potential audiences.[98] Persistent objections to his ideas about "people's" entertainments grew out of fears that he would manage them as he did the Hermitage—that is, provide operetta at the expense of opera, diversion at the expense of enlightenment. Open to the public, comparatively cheap, and responsive to the tastes of his fans, Lentovskii's enterprises offered fundamental cultural democracy.

For all his astute entrepreneurial savvy about what people enjoyed, Lentovskii made a patently poor businessman. His tremendous emphasis on spectacle undoubtedly cheered set designers Val'ch and Shektel', before they moved on to greater prestige and deeper pockets. In an innovative publicity move, Lentovskii advertised his budgets to assure his audiences that he had spared no expense. In 1884 he stalled his creditors, even taking a local newspaper to court on charges of slander because the paper had reported him "insolvent." He lost the case, but this did not deter him from building and rebuilding.[99] The Hermitage hemorrhaged as much as sixty thousand rubles when it opened, until by 1894 an entrepreneur with a better head for business, Ia. V. Shchukin, took it over.[100] On the up side, Lentovskii had a reputation for paying his performers well, but on the down side, none were there for him when he died in poverty in 1906.[101] The talented dreamer never learned that to continue, he would at least have to break even.[102]

Shchukin, another *desaparecido* from the prerevolutionary nightscape,

---

[96] Quoted in Lawrence Levine, *Highbrow/Lowbrow: The Emergence of Cultural Hierarchy in America* (Cambridge, Mass.: Harvard University Press, 1988), 237.

[97] Lentovskii's detailed prospectus for public entertainment, submitted to the Moscow city fathers in 1897, is included in his personal archive in its printed form, not catalogued.

[98] The biographical information comes from notes left by his sister Anna. Bakhrushin Museum, f. 144.

[99] Ibid., l. 23.

[100] Some of the annual financial statements from Lentovskii's enterprises remain in his archive at the Bakhrushin. The 1880s appear to have been profitable, in part because he did not spare expenses.

[101] His obituary is in Bakhrushin Museum, f. 144, dd. 829–31.

[102] Kuznetsov, *Iz proshlogo*, 230.

revitalized what Lentovskii had begun but without the necessary nod to the *narod*. Sniffed at for his "lackey" background, one of the "new type of bourgeois entrepreneurs" motivated by money, he expanded the gardens and called it the "new" Hermitage.[103] He paid his bills by consistently booking the extremely popular Saburov Farce Company, familiar for such routines as "You can't go out, You're undressed!"[104] In 1896 he demonstrated for visitors the latest technological marvel, the Lumière brothers' cinematography, just as Charles Aumont was doing in his Petersburg nightclub, the Arcadia. And like Tumpakov, he had moved out of the peasantry by finding work in a hotel, followed by a stint waiting tables.[105]

Tumpakov, in sharp contrast to Lentovskii, died an extremely wealthy man, mourned in the sort of extravagant funeral generally accorded state dignitaries. Some of the great names of the stage, including Varlamov, attended his service. The sum of his endeavors ranked lower than Lentovskii's, but Tumpakov turned out to be much the better businessman. Tumpakov celebrated novelty for the ruble that it could potentially turn, and his credo mandated that "if you've got something good, no need to look for anything better."[106] Also born into the peasantry, Tumpakov kept his village in Yaroslavl Province dear to his heart, but not the *narod* as a whole. Self-educated, he moved from waiting tables to working as an assistant to the comptroller at the Nobles' Society in St. Petersburg, where he established his operations. Rising to replace his boss, Tumpakov decided to work for himself. He quit to open his first restaurant, the Swan, where he suffered his only business failure. Forced back to the Nobles' Society briefly, he found a partner to help him finance his next venture, a nightclub that he renamed the Variety. With another partner, a chef, he opened a small pleasure garden, soon becoming sole proprietor of the Izmailovskii Gardens. Later, he added the Alcazar to his flourishing magic kingdom. His trademark establishment, though, became the Bouffe, open year-round and offering quality fun without any pretense to an underlying agenda of public betterment.

Situated on Nevskii Prospect, in the heart of the imperial capital, the Bouffe had been one of the first of the popular *café-chantants* from the 1860s. Anna Judic and other stars from the Paris operetta had delighted Petersburg residents, as the Bouffe became "the most fashionable spot for all sorts of wheeler-dealers, the heroes of the bourgeois epoch of great financial success stories."[107] In 1873 a songbook of tunes made popular at

---

[103] Ibid., 229.

[104] In 1912 Saburov was estimated to take in a twenty-thousand-ruble profit from his run at the Aquarium, which had reaped one hundred thousand rubles. Reported in *Utro Rossii,* September 2, 1912, no. 203.

[105] Shchukin's daughter wrote a history of her father's business: Bakhrushin Museum, f. 543, d. 1.

[106] *Dachnyi kur'er,* no. 1 (June 21, 1908): 4.

[107] Kuznetsov, *Iz proshlogo,* 123.

the Bouffe was published, making it possible to re-create, if on a smaller scale, the ambience of Petersburg's hottest spot.[108] The Bouffe found itself mocked by poet-*intelligent* Nikolai Nekrasov and romanticized by the avaricious Glafira in Ostrovskii's *Wolves and Sheep*.[109] An ideal establishment for an ambitious entrepreneur, the Bouffe became the best place in the imperial capital to enjoy two of the dominant diversions: operetta and wrestling.

Miniature Theaters

Not even the many nightclubs and pleasure gardens could keep pace with the changing tastes, especially after the 1905 Revolution had whetted appetites for greater freedom of expression on numerous levels. Modernity had ignited a mini-revolution in the high arts, exemplified by the Moscow Arts Theater. At the level of the nightclub, this resulted in the birth of the cabaret, which began "as informal grouping of artists . . . to mock and deride the values and cultural monuments of a society they condemned as hopelessly bourgeois and philistine."[110] Borrowed from the French, like the *café-concs*, but translated into Russian through performance, the elitism of cabaret culture keeps it beyond the purview of the present study, but its middlebrow analogue, the "miniature theater," used a similar theatrical form of vignettes to explore more than to satirize city life. Liudmila Tikhvinskaia estimated that in 1912, even before their explosion during World War I, the two capitals combined had 125 cabarets and miniature theaters.[111] Flowing out into the provinces, by that year "correspondents from all corners of the country were writing in about them."[112] By 1916 they had become so prevalent that the owner of Moscow's prestigious Maksim's opened one alongside the dining room, featuring bigger stars than the typical small theater could afford.[113]

Described by one entrepreneur as "micro-farce, micro-bouffe, micro-drama," the miniature theaters condensed, repackaged, and sold at cheaper prices entertainments to be found elsewhere. Some of the directors of these miniatures, including Tumpakov, Saburov and S. A. Pal'm, came straight from nightclub farces. At least two names associated with cabaret, Nikolai Evreinov and Vsevolod Meierkhol'd, also ventured briefly across the culture border into miniatures. These theaters differed from

[108] Ibid., 125.
[109] Ibid., 124.
[110] Harold Segel, *Turn-of-the-Century Cabaret* (New York: Columbia University Press, 1987), xiv.
[111] Liudmila Tikhvinskaia, *Kabare i teatry miniatiur v Rossii, 1908–1917* (Moscow: Kul'tura, 1995), 5.
[112] Ibid., 180.
[113] Ibid., 338.

nightclubs primarily in what they borrowed from the legitimate stage, acts written with a more coherent narrative storyline than the usual *estrada* routine. But they also could offer song, dance, and comedy. The speed and brevity of a "miniature" routine captured the pace of urbanization, just as such songs as "Marusia Poisoned Herself," a tearjerker about a young typesetter abandoned by her lover, captured one of its bitter flavors.[114]

Russia's first important, though ultimately unsuccessful, miniature theater was copied directly from France's "Grand Guignol," or theater of horrors. The Liteinyi, named for the Petersburg thoroughfare on which it was located, was opened in 1908 by V. A. Kazanskii, a provincial actor turned impresario, who converted it from a skating rink.[115] The three acts on its first bill showed the taste for blood: they included a psychiatrist raping his hypnotized patient; a prostitute murdering a rival in a seedy bar; and journalists investigating treatments at an insane asylum, losing several of their body parts in the process.[116] The theater became an immediate sensation, causing one critic to deplore that "shrouds have become the most fashionable dress, and corpses the stars of the season."[117] Despite a wild first two months, enthusiasm for the horrors wore off with the novelty, and by 1909 the same critic could write that "corpses can now return to their graveyards."[118] The forum, however, was there to stay.

The Liteinyi underwent several name changes after this, including a claim to "Intimacy" that spoke to capacity and "Mosaic" that reflected the variety in the playbill, while retaining the "miniature" format, that is, one-act topical comedies, often interspersed with music. Two of the best known contemporary satirists, A. A. Averchenko and N. A. Teffi (Buchinskaia) wrote sketches for these theaters, which also presented scenes from controversial symbolist or decadent plays currently being staged at the experimental theaters. Audiences could also become acquainted with the latest tunes and dance steps, and with the gender-bending performances of "*transformatory*," or male and female impersonators.[119] Those who performed regularly in these theaters were primarily deserters from the operetta, the farces, and *shantany*. By 1913 the miniature theater was officially recognized as a unique institution, and proprietors contracted with artists accordingly.[120] At least one multitalented performer, E. A. Mosolova, became a star identified with this venue.[121] Other celebrities, including the

---

[114] Ibid., 202. This song is translated in *Entertaining Tsarist Russia*, ed. von Geldern and McReynolds, 290–92.

[115] I. F. Petrovskaia, "Liteinyi teatr," in *Teatral'nyi Peterburg*, ed. I. F. Petrovskaia, 323.

[116] Tikhvinskaia, *Kabare*, 137–38.

[117] Ibid., 139.

[118] Ibid., 143.

[119] Ibid., 147.

[120] Ibid., 181.

[121] Petrovskaia, "Liteinyi teatr," 323–27.

singers Alexander Vertinskii and Iurii Morfessi, and the dancer Elsa Kriuger also performed on these venues, as did *faux* gypsies with ties to the Iar.[122]

The typical crowd at a miniature theater suggests that one reason they attended was to familiarize themselves with the modern city. Described as a conglomeration of "painted coquettes, nannies with their charges, the soldier with the cook, active and retired generals, students with models and with other students, shopkeepers and skilled workers, petty-bourgeois women in kerchiefs and rich women in expensive furs," audiences ran the gamut of urban citizenry.[123] Notably, this would also have described the usual gathering at a movie theater, with which miniature theaters were compared as new forms of urban-oriented entertainment.[124] Commonalities were numerous. The two media often shared the same building, and at times "miniature" presentations were staged between the showing of films. They also shared personnel, as numerous performers at the evening theaters held day jobs at film studios across town.[125] Both media exploded with the world war, the result of a combination of factors that included new money in circulation and massive immigration to cities, compounded by the psychological desire for stimulation when disaster portended.

Conclusion

Tumpakov's quick fade from Russian history says as much about the cultural debates over public entertainment as does Lentovskii's lingering shadow. Tumpakov, too, found common cause with Sousa, who could not stomach the pretentious demands of high culture: "Longhaired men and shorthaired women you never see in my audience. And I don't want them."[126] This reverse snobbery reflected a refusal to be co-opted by a politics that sought to devalue the contributions from the middle classes because they were tainted by commercialism. To be sure, the ticket buyers could and did express the kinds of sexist and racist attitudes that excluded groups from the larger public culture and that prompted the elites to want to control access to potentially negative influences. And Tumpakov, like Barnum, was not adverse to prevarication in his publicity, as when he capitalized on antigovernment feelings to mislead the public into believing that his wrestling tournament had met with official disapproval. So the public did not enjoy unlimited information or choices when it bought tickets.

[122] Tikhvinskaia, *Kabare*, 334.
[123] Ibid., 176.
[124] Ibid., 153.
[125] Ibid., 337.
[126] Quoted in Levine, *Highbrow/Lowbrow*, 238.

But choices they had. Somewhere in the mix of censorship, European imports, the *intelligentsia*'s impulse to hegemonize culture, performances both brilliant and disastrous, terrific talent, and absolute ambition, the commercial nightscape took shape from people's choices. Hungarian bandleaders, all-girl orchestras, "Miss Pearl Hobson, the Mulatto Sharpshooter," and a seemingly limitless variety of novelty acts and crooners, soubrettes and comedians, filled the playbills. A century before American funnyman Adam Sandler adopted the role, Russians burlesqued the wedding singer as a cheap imitation of popular entertainers.[127] Cultural politics emerged in the contents of the shows and the personalities of the performers. Once they became properly situated in restaurants, nightclubs, and pleasure gardens, the writers, producers, and performers helped to create and circulate social values responsive to audience needs and interests. Food and drink offered one sort of enjoyment, one sort of sustenance, but the floor show, the subject of the next chapter, provided quite another.

[127] Kuznetsov, *Iz proshlogo,* 180.

"In the Whirlwind of a Waltz": Performing in the Night

Nightclubs and pleasure gardens provided heterotopian contexts for bringing diverse audiences together, but the songs and comic routines provided the texts, the material sources of information for viewers about contemporary social situations. Russian censors who permitted certain plays to be published but not performed had deduced the potential influence of the performers to mediate between text and audience. As Veit Erlmann has pointed out, performing a text integrates it within a context in ways that render the meaning of the song, act, or joke "always emergent, relational."[1] In other words, performativity expands beyond its primary function as entertainment and helps to establish social identities; or to use the simpler phrasing of professional showman E. F. Albee, "the public had to be educated by vaudeville."[2] Although only a small portion of the songs and comedy routines from this era were recorded for posterity, the published versions reveal much about how they mediated social changes. Moreover, what we know about *who* was popular helps to explain *why* certain motifs captivated audiences.

Performing in a nightclub differed significantly from acting out a scripted work on the legitimate stage or the opera. Some entertainers enjoyed careers on both the legitimate stage and the *estrada*, or "small stage" in a nightclub, because they could combine the prestige of the former with the liberating potential of the latter, which permitted them to emphasize

---

[1] Veit Erlmann, *Nightsong: Performance, Power, and Practice in South Africa* (Chicago: University of Chicago Press, 1996), 16.

[2] Quoted in Henry Jenkins, *What Made Pistachio Nuts?* (New York: Columbia University Press, 1992), 81. This Albee is the father of the famous playwright.

their own personalities over characters created by others. Often actors would develop nightclub acts composed of favorite scenes from various plays, which had the advantage of suspending the need for sets and other actors. Entrepreneurs argued that showing snippets was an economically prudent medium of spreading high culture by cultivating tastes gradually. For example, Sarah Bernhardt found an easier and more profitable second career on the international nightclub circuit, giving millions the opportunity to "see" her without having to suffer through a longer play of little appeal.[3]

By removing particular scenes from their broader frameworks, critics charged performers with undermining the integrity of what was intended as a whole art. More to the point of capitalism, these showcases privileged the consumer: everything could be reduced for sale, including the Prince of Denmark, by the aging and wooden-legged Bernhardt. By no means apologetic for their tastes, fans flocked to a Lentovskii vaudeville that played on the social prestige involved in the efforts to score tickets to one of Bernhardt's Russian tours.[4] But this forum was not unique to the middlebrow nightclub; Shchepkin had performed skits at local clubs, just as Shaliapin circulated much more efficiently in concerts than in the ponderous Russian operas suited to his voice.

Gender had become an important issue relevant to nightlife as increasing numbers of women entered restaurants and clubs. And it seems that where gender goes, so goes ethnicity, because the two discourses find themselves linked by virtue of the complementary roles they play in the establishment of hierarchies of power. Women and ethnic minorities have both found themselves in subordinate positions, but even when they share the common goal of moving up, their means of ascent as well as the way in which power is defined for them can vary to the point of contradiction. As women inched out into these evening heterotopias, they found many of Russia's ethnic groups on stage, using this unique forum to reinvent themselves, to accommodate their "otherness" within the larger frame of Russian imperialism. Nightclub performers often found themselves conflicted between the desire for resistance to a structure that subordinated them and the safer path of assimilation. Without a proscenium arch to separate them, or strict rules of etiquette to manage behavior, audience and performer used the night to experiment on themselves and with each other.[5]

---

[3] On Bernhardt, see Susan Glenn, *Female Spectacle: The Theatrical Roots of Modern Feminism* (Cambridge, Mass.: Harvard University Press, 2000), chapter 1.

[4] M. Lentovskii and L. Guliaev, "Sarra Bernard, ili bel'etzh No. 2" (Moscow: Razsokhina, 1891). Translated in *Entertaining Tsarist Russia*, ed. James Von Geldern and Louise McReynolds (Bloomington: Indiana University Press, 1998), 186–97.

[5] Erving Goffman, *Frame Analysis: An Essay on the Organization of Experience* (New York: Harper and Row, 1974), 126.

In appearing on the public stage, performers assumed personas that allowed them to make palpable some of the tension between resistance and containment that pervaded the agenda of modern nationalism. As "steppin' out" bore witness to the prosperous transformation of the cityscape, those who enjoyed the advantages of this could indulge in a fantasy of the dark that lay behind it. They listened to the "cruel romances" and coupled to dance the tango and apache dances that romanticized the violence of the Other side, the night.

The crowds whose goal was to be seen seeing "La Grande Sarah" turned upper-case Culture into lower-case culture by establishing their own social rules and rituals, with the *estrada* providing the focal point of interaction between diners and performers. The commercialization underway enhanced rather than debased the value of the performances because it intensified the personal elements inherent in the interaction. The more the nightclub distanced the crowd from the universal, the more it could tell about the quotidian.

"Can I Be in the Show?"

The first true star of Russia's nightclub circuit was the French performer "Grendor" (*Grain d'Or*), whose costumes and mannerisms did not require fluency in French to interpret in the 1860s. "Kadudzha," a mezzo-soprano mulatto from one of France's African colonies, brought exotica. One of the most popular performers of the imperial era, Anna Zhiudik (Judic) appeared regularly in Petersburg after headlining in the Parisian *café-concert* Eldorado.[6] In Russia, she deserves more credit than anyone else for charging the atmosphere of the night: she sang hit tunes from popular operettas, danced the cancan, and recited suggestive couplets.[7] As one critic wrote, "She even *sings* between the lines."[8]

The international cast of performers gave a semblance of cosmopolitanism to the nightclubs. In the 1870s the Milanese dancer Enrico Cecchetti introduced the latest steps. The German magician Rudolph Becker had petitioned successfully that his silent act did not violate the theatrical ban, and when the wings of his doves caught fire in the footlights while delivering chocolates to the audience, it was civil society, in the guise of the Society for the Prevention of Cruelty to Animals, rather than the repres-

---

[6] François Caradec and Alain Weill, *Le café-concert* (Paris: Hachette, 1980), 159–60.

[7] Evgenii Kuznetsov, *Iz proshlogo russkoi estrady: Istoricheskie ocherki* (Moscow: Iskusstvo, 1958), 122–23.

[8] Caradec and Weill, *Le café-concert*, 160. Even Nekrasov wrote a poem to her celebrity: "The face of a Madonn-agaze of a cheru-Zhiudik-Incomprehensible!" Quoted in G. M. Iaron, *O liubimom zhanre* (Moscow: Iskusstvo, 1960), 8.

sive autocracy, that condemned him.[9] Nor did all "foreigners" come from abroad; former serf Ivan Rupin rechristened himself Giovanni Rupini to cash in on the fashion for Italian tenors early in the nineteenth century.[10]

The high profile of the European imports should not be read reflexively as evidence of Russia's alleged cultural inferiority complex. The censorship facilitated the singing of French songs, but Russian composers of popular music began coming into their own as nightclubs affected musical tastes. Russian symphonic and operatic music had come of age with the works of Mikhail Glinka in the 1830s, and it was about to enter its "Golden Age" through the compositions of the so-called "Mighty Handful." This group of five (Mily Balakirev, Alexander Borodin, Cesar Cui, Modest Mussorgsky, and Nikolai Rimsky-Korsakov) followed Glinka in using Russian national traditions to create internationally acclaimed artistic music—that is, complex structures that the untrained ear cannot fully appreciate.[11]

Less well studied, though, is the growth of Russia's tradition of commercialized music.[12] American musicologist Charles Hamm established criteria for "popular" music applicable to Russia in this era because they hinge on commercial influences: written to be performed by a single voice or small group; popularized on a secular stage and then consumed in the home; composed and marketed for profit; designed to be performed and enjoyed by those of limited musical training; and produced and disseminated in physical form, beginning with sheet music and later, the phonograph.[13] Although it would be premature to write in terms of the "industrialization" of music, the increased capacity to circulate songs that depended for their popularity on the ability of dilettantes to perform them and technology to distribute them contributed to the general restructuring of leisure underway.[14]

As the Mighty Handful's Cui himself observed, "Music lovers would find themselves in dire straits if they only had symphonies and operas."[15] The Russian songs that most closely conformed to Hamm's definition came under the rubric "romance," and although most of these celebrated some form of sexual encounter, others focused on love of country, especially during wartime. A popular theme combined the two passions, forcing sweethearts apart as the hero heads off to fight the Turks, Russia's most

---

[9] Kuznetsov, *Iz proshlogo*, 61, 120.

[10] Ibid., 61.

[11] Robert Ridenour, *Nationalism, Modernism, and Personal Rivalry in Nineteenth-Century Russian Music* (Ann Arbor: UMI Research Press, 1977).

[12] Carl Dalhous, *Nineteenth-Century Music* (Berkeley: University of California Press, 1989), 8–15, writes of the "twin styles" that competed in the era, personified by Beethoven at the highbrow end, to be listened to, and Rossini at the lowbrow, to be performed.

[13] Charles Hamm, *Yesterdays: Popular Song in America* (New York: Norton, 1979), xvii.

[14] Simon Frith, "The Industrialization of Popular Music," in *Popular Music and Communication*, ed. James Lull, 2d ed. (Newbury Park, Calif.: Sage Publications, 1992), 49–74.

[15] Ts. Kiui, "Ocherk pazvitie 'romansa' v Rossii," *Artist*, no. 45 (1895): 7.

Sheet music for the "original new salon dance, the Cake Walk"

persistent enemy throughout the nineteenth century.[16] Classical composers sometimes wrote romances with these simple themes. In fact, for years Cui shared an apartment with Viktor Krylov, whose reputation as a lightweight playwright made him an excellent partner to write verse to

[16] See, for example, "Rasluka," in the songbook *Minstrel'* (Moscow: Universitetskaia tip., 1833), 43–46.

Cui's romantic music.[17] Slighted by Cui as "not skilled in technique . . . too dilettantish," the musicians A. A. Aliab'ev and and A. E. Varlamov, father of the great actor,[18] set the early romantic trends.[19] Aliab'ev's "Nightingale" and Varlamov's "Red Sarafan" remain familiar tunes today.[20]

Classical composers differ from commercial tunesmiths primarily on issues of how they structure their pieces, and because popular music must be accessible to those with little musical training, those who write it must keep it simple. Thus Cui found most of the romances written by his artistic colleagues "banal," shaped by "ordinary" melodies, influenced by the "Continental style"—a code for denigrating the memorable melodies of the *café-chantant*. Many of the nineteenth century's classical compositions addressed larger cultural and political concerns, but the romances played on immediate social values. Through song, Russians confronted the most pressing issues of the day, including changing sexual relations, urbanization, and imperialism. Song writers such as Varlamov wrote with a finger on the social pulse, to borrow a cliché (as they would have been accused of doing).

Pocket-sized songbooks were already being sold early in the century, but these included only the lyrics, without the notes that would have been cost-prohibitive to publish. Either the tunes were already well-known or, more likely, the fairly simple rhythms were easily adapted to familiar melodies. An analysis of changing themes in Russian songs during the nineteenth century evinces their strong similarity to tunes popular in Europe and the United States—wherever the secular was displacing the religious, or "the folk" was shedding its musical authenticity with the same speed that it was changing its clothes for urban fashions. These themes include nostalgia for a pastoral innocence; the boisterous delights of alcohol; variations on the music of ethnic minorities in a partial homogenization of culture; and, most common, boy meets girl, boy loses girl—with the tempo determining the possibility of their reconciliation.[21] Through the dispersal of these songs, from public stages to private homes and back again, Russians developed a set of shared tropes, referential tunes that aroused emotions but did not require consensus of interpretation. For example, the musical version of poet-*intelligent* Nikolai Nekrasov's "Peddlers" (1861), popularized in the twentieth century by Vara Panina, hid the author's populist senti-

---

[17] Viktor Krylov, "Kompozitor Ts. A. Kiui. (Otryvok iz vospominanii)," *Istoricheskii vestnik* 15, no. 2 (1894): 472–81.

[18] The actor had never known his father, who had died playing cards while his mother was pregnant with him. K. A. Varlamov, "Istoriia moei zhizni," *Sinii zhurnal*, no. 5 (1911): 2–3.

[19] Kiui, "Ocherk," 7–8.

[20] Ibid. Kiui acknowledged the popularity of these two songs, while dismissing the skills of their authors.

[21] Jon W. Finson discusses these themes in *The Voices That Are Gone* (New York: Cambridge University Press, 1994).

ments behind spontaneous sex in a meadow. A sure sign of the commercialization of Russian music could be heard in the populist lament that the "authentic" village songs had become corrupted.[22]

Traditional tunes had become corrupted by new opportunities for social mobility, which found musical expression, and "Two Guitars" and "Endless Road" sang bitter-sweetly of distances from home. The afflictions of urbanization were sung in "Marusia Poisoned Herself." Familiarity with western fads inspired by black performers could be heard in "Little Creole Girl" and the farcical "Sarah Wants a Negro." The internationally cheerful "Ta-ra-ra-boom-de-ay" had a Russian version.[23] Love topped the charts, and lovers moved from desire to physical contact in the tempo of the times and the words of the songs. The sentimental waltz "White Acacias" signified the fin de siècle for Russians much as "After the Ball" did for Americans.[24] Dance crazes, especially the foxtrot and the tango, affected sexual mores and were learned first in nightclubs.[25]

These catchy melodies found a second medium beyond the *café-conc*, as Russians turned just as quickly and as happily as westerners to the theatrical genre born of the industrial boom's promises of prosperity, the operetta. Even when set against pseudohistorical backdrops, the operetta took stories from contemporary life and sang them in music that reverberated through restaurants and nightclubs, romantic waltzes and airy tunes with the power to rewrite every ending as a happy one. Russians borrowed this genre heavily from the Europeans. Although antecedents can be found in the opera-bouffe, or comic interludes in operas, the seminal works by Jacques Offenbach marked a fundamentally new medium of entertainment and were extraordinarily popular in Russia.

The French newspaper *Figaro* gave a birth date to the operetta: July 5, 1855, the day that Offenbach opened his first theater, the *Bouffes-Parisiens*.[26] Initially restricted by a Napoleonic edict limiting unofficial theaters to one act with four characters, the resourceful Offenbach remade nightlife just as he did himself, transforming Jakob Eberst, a Jewish cellist, into a Catholic Frenchman and one of the most influential composers of the nineteenth century.[27] When the ban was dropped in 1858, Offenbach

[22] V. Mikhnevich, "Izvrashchenie narodnogo pesnotvorchestva," *Istoricheskii vestnik* 3 (November 1880): 749–79; and Robert A. Rothstein, "Death of the Folk Song?" in *Cultures in Flux*, ed. Stephen Frank and Mark Steinberg (Princeton: Princeton University Press, 1994), 108–20.
[23] Donald Rayfield, "Chekhov and Popular Culture," *Irish Slavonic Studies*, no. 8 (1988): 47–49.
[24] Finson discusses this in *Voices That Are Gone*, 68–69, 153–54.
[25] Linda Tomko, *Dancing Class: Gender, Ethnicity, and Social Divides in American Dance, 1890–1920* (Bloomington: Indiana University Press, 1999), 24–29, discusses the gender significance of the new dances at the turn of the century.
[26] A. R. Vladimirskaia, *Zvezdnye chasy operetty*, 2d ed. (Leningrad: Iskusstvo, 1991), 14.
[27] Richard Traubner, *Operetta: A Theatrical History* (New York: Doubleday), 26–28.

ТАНГО

6

Испол. артистами
ОФЕЛЬ-БЕЦКОЙ и АНДРЕЕВЫМЪ.

Victims of "tangomania," circa 1912

had already established a style of light musical comedy that made for easy export. Offenbach's first large-scale operetta, *Orpheus in the Underworld* (1858), rewrote mythology to star a womanizing Orpheus who was reluctant to follow his wife into Hell and joyous to leave her there. His most stunningly successful work, *The Fair Helen* (1864), burlesqued Helen of Troy and the origins of the Trojan War with enough one-liners to make the story relevant to almost any political situation.

Where other countries translated and staged Offenbach as a prelude to developing their own national versions, Russians contented themselves for decades with borrowing, improvising through translation. A French touring company played Offenbach first in Russia at the Mikhailovskii Theater, where foreign-language productions were staged. The omnipresent Krylov returns once again to add his influence to yet another venture into the commercial night. In addition to Sardou's works, Krylov translated *Orpheus* (1859) and *The Fair Helen* (1868), and his renditions moved up Nevskii Prospekt to enjoy fantastic popularity at the Alexandrinka.[28] The Soviet critic who dismissed Krylov's versions as notable only for "drabness and mediocrity" echoed the tiresome sentiments of those unable to accept that the public could validate its own opinion.[29] *The Fair Helen* became such a phenomenon that Krylov wrote his own farce in 1872, *In Search of the Fair Helen,* the madcap adventure of a Russian provincial entrepreneur trying desperately to find a star for his production of the operetta.[30]

Offenbach made a superstar of his first leading lady, Hortense Schneider, and his operettas launched many another career. The first Russian Helen, Vera Liadova, moved from a career in the ballet, winning over Russian audiences by supposedly showing more refinement than the "erotic" Schneider, who played Russia in 1871.[31] That Krylov's version found a Slavic origin to Greek mythology no doubt abetted her triumph.[32] In the Alexandrinka's 1869–70 season, over 20 percent of all productions were by Offenbach.[33] The list of Russian dramatic superstars who began their careers in operetta included Savina, Komissarzhevskaia, Varlamov, and Stanislavsky.

After Paris, the capital of the operetta moved to Vienna. Johann Strauss II, already crowned the "Waltz King," increased the possibilities for dance in *Die Fledermaus* (1874), and then tapped into another vogue with *The Gypsy Baron* (1885). The historical animosity between Teutons and Slavs had been tempered in these years by a diplomatic alliance, and Strauss

[28] Vladimirskaia, *Zvezdnye chasy operetty,* 133–34.
[29] Quoted in Andrew Donskov, *Mixail Lentovskij and the Russian Theatre* (East Lansing, Mich.: Russian Language Journal, 1985), 21.
[30] V. Krylov, *V pogone za Prekrasnoi Elenoi* (St. Petersburg: Shreder, 1872).
[31] Vladimirskaia, *Zvezdnye chasy operetty,* 134–35.
[32] Ibid., 138.
[33] Iaron, *O liubimom zhanre,* 7. Of 256 productions, 60 were Offenbach operettas.

enjoyed tremendous popularity in Russia, touring regularly from 1856 onward. In his final visit, in 1886, he directed *The Gypsy Baron* at the Mikhailovskii and gave numerous other appearances around Petersburg.[34] Like Offenbach and other great composers, especially Franz von Zuppé, Imre Kalman, and the incomparable Hungarian Franz Lehar, Strauss generated musical careers for Russians as translators and performers.

Following Krylov, L. L. Pal'mskii and I. G. Iaron became the preeminent translators of operetta. An entrepreneur, Pal'mskii cultivated the genre throughout the provinces with his touring company. The Iaron name appears in several chapters on the history of Russian operetta, as his brother Mark became a director and his nephew Grigorii was one of the dominant personalities in Soviet operetta.[35] Despite the genre's tremendous popularity in Russia, though, only one important native composer wrote original operettas for local audiences, V. P. Valentinov.

Beginning his stage career as a comic performer, Valentinov began writing operettas after the successful staging of a comedy about the 1905 Revolution, *The Days of Freedom*, even before the barricades had been torn down. His first operetta, *One Night of Love*, premiered the next year. Though its theatrical longevity can be attributed more to the Russian setting and familiar themes than to the tunes, it played almost daily for two years and stayed in repertoires well into the Soviet period.[36] Set at the turn of the nineteenth century, the story evoked the era of Pushkin, but with fin-de-siècle sexual innuendos.[37] The reviewer who characterized Valentinov as "not an important author, but a talented individual,"[38] caught his ability to expropriate from other works and patch the bits together into a mosaic.

In the next four years Valentinov wrote three other operettas, *Moscow at Night* (1907), *Secrets of the Harem* (1909), and *The Queen of Diamonds* (1910). Because of his indiscriminate borrowing, it is difficult to speak of his works as an oeuvre, although they contain sufficient original moments to differentiate them from their French and Austrian competitors. Among them *Moscow at Night* stands out for the specificity of both locale and action; statues come alive, Gogol sings a contemporary song, and even contemporaneous politicians make appearances.[39] *Secrets of the Harem* drew upon the current fashion for the crumbling Ottoman Empire, and its subplots pile up around love triangles, revolutionaries, and the eunuch in charge of the

[34] Vladimirskaia, *Zvezdnye chasy operetty*, 62–63.

[35] Grigorii Iaron's memoirs, *O liubimom zhanre*, provide colorful behind-the-scenes anecdotes critical to understanding the genre in the Soviet era.

[36] Ibid., 27. Advertisements for *One Night of Love* can be read in the provincial press, featuring the grand stars of the era on tour: Vavich, Shuvalova, and Monakhov.

[37] Ibid., 28, reported that when Soviet companies performed it, they had to clean it up.

[38] *Obozrenie teatrov*, no. 256 (1907): 16–17.

[39] V. P. Valentinov, *Moskva noch'iu* (Moscow: Mirnyi trud, 1907).

harem who has not actually lost his male member.[40] It obeyed the standard structuring of an operetta plot, with fraudulent identities generating comic confusion. One critic praised it for its "Russian citizenship" in the genre.[41]

The Queen of Diamonds, perhaps musically Valentinov's most original work, put a Russian spin on a story plotted around love triangles. Parting company with western heroines, Tat'iana, the queen in the title and a concert soprano, trades her young Italian paramour for a tired old capitalist, surrendering true love for creature comforts. One of the hit tunes from the show, "In the Whirlwind of a Waltz," captured the gaiety, a prewar moment of Russians at play.[42] However, unlike her more popular contemporary on the stage, *The Merry Widow,* this *Queen of Diamonds* did not live happily ever after.

One reason for the enormous success of operetta everywhere was that individual songs could be extracted from the plot and sung separately. As a result, operetta spilled out into restaurants and nightclubs. Serafima Bel'skaia, the "Russian Judic," began in this medium and, like her namesake, appeared on the *estrada*. The Saburov Farce Company also produced operettas, launching the career of E. M. Granovskaia. Vera Shuvalova trained at the Petersburg Conservatory but found her fame in operettas, just as a few classically trained actresses made career moves to motion pictures. A. E. Bliumental'-Tamarin organized an operetta company in Kharkov that featured his wife Maria, who accrued national renown. Later, the gramophone gave singers a significantly wider audience. One of the most popular male vocalists of the prerevolutionary era, Mikhail Vavich, made his name in the Russian premier of *The Merry Widow* in 1906.[43] The second great tenor of the age, Iurii Morfessi, moved from operetta to *estrada* and back again, cutting records and selling sheet music in between live performances.

The brightest star of imperial Russia's nightclub galaxy was its consummate *Fair Helen,* Anastasia Vial'tseva. Born in peasant poverty in 1871, she remade herself into a glamorous role model, much admired by imitative fans. Discovered singing in Moscow's Aquarium, the ex-chambermaid's role as mistress to a wealthy Odessan did not prevent Vial'tseva from later marrying a colonel in a guards' regiment and being a guest in the homes of the socially elite. Surviving recordings betray her somewhat reedy singing voice and explain how, although she aspired to the grand opera, she found her niche in its diminutive. Vail'tseva had something more sig-

---

[40] V. P. Valentinov, *Tainy garema* (Moscow: Mirnyi trud, 1909).

[41] *Artist i tsena,* no. 1 (1910): 7.

[42] *The Queen of Diamonds* has been translated in *Entertaining Tsarist Russia,* ed. von Geldern and McReynolds, 198–202.

[43] Iaron, "O liubimom zhanre," 33.

The cast of V. P. Valentinov's *Queen of Diamonds*

234

Репертуаръ Театра „Буффъ" въ С.-Петербургѣ.

Пѣснь о Качеляхъ

Schaukel-Lied

исполняемая артистомъ

М. И. Вавичемъ

въ опереткѣ

Веселая Вдова.

музыка

В. Голлендеръ.

Цѣна 50 коп.

М. И. ВАВИЧЪ.

Собственность издателя.

Н. Х. ДАВИНГОФЪ

Гостинный Дворъ, № 12 (по Невскому). С.-Петербургъ.

Mikhail Vavich, heartthrob in *The Merry Widow*

235

Anastasia Vial'tseva, Russia's consummate "Fair Helen"

nificant to the era than being another soprano: personality. Newspaper columnist Vlas Doroshevich commented that "a serious critic, of course, cannot write that she is a great artist, but she herself is something of an art. Charming! An event in herself!"[44] Vial'tseva established herself nationally by touring many cities and cutting a number of records. Her premature

[44] I. V. Nest'ev, *Zvezdy russkoi estrady* (Moscow: Sovetskii kompozitor, 1970), 63.

891
ШУВАЛОВА.

Operetta star Vera Shuvalova

death from a blood disease in 1913 prompted a nationwide outpouring of grief, befitting her celebrity status. More than 150,000 people followed her funeral cortege, with a carriage drawn by six white horses, through the streets of St. Petersburg.[45]

If operettas can be considered primarily foreign in musical origin, Russia did boast a genre that—although not unique in its popularity to the tsarist empire—nonetheless set off a singular cultural phenomenon there: "gypsy mania." Fascination with an idealized image of the seemingly rootless Romany dated back to the singers and guitarists who played at the *kabaki* early in the century. Romantics Alexander Pushkin and Mikhail Lermontov transformed Gypsies poetically into a type of noble savage. Captivating the imaginations of bureaucrats with echoes of a fantasy life enjoyed in a work-free camp, where the only responsibility seemed to be to exact revenge against an unfaithful lover, Gypsy songs offered a rhapsodic escape.[46] Songs about "the darkest of eyes and whitest of breasts" encouraged listeners to "drink to the bottom and life will seem fine."[47] The novelist Alexander Kuprin wrote nostalgically about how "gypsy mania" had a "secret fascination unlike any other, a bewitching, savage charm."[48]

Of the hundreds of Russian romances written before 1917, one stands out for the longevity of its popularity, intensified by its haunting melody, and for the multiple discourses of popular music that its lyrics pull together: "Dark Eyes." Still played as background music to evoke the mythical "Russian soul," the song has been crooned from every forum available to popular music and inspired a movie version in 1916. Written in 1843 by the Ukrainian Evgeny Grebenka (Jevhen Hrebinka), "Dark Eyes" met all of Hamm's criteria for "popular." Grebenka's tune glamorized the people with the dark eyes and deep desires in his lyrics: "Oh, your dark eyes, eyes too passionate, eyes that burn through me. . . . Everything fine in life that God gave to us, I have sacrificed to your fiery eyes."[49]

As Alaina Lemon has successfully argued, Russia's gypsy culture reflected its own desires rather than those of the ethnic group whose life story Russian consumers were rewriting to respond to their own cultural needs. As Russians imagined Gypsies, these dark and passionate nomads

[45] Louise McReynolds, "'The Incomparable One': Anastasia Vial'tseva and the Culture of Personality," in *Russia, Women, Culture,* ed. Helena Goscilo and Beth Holmgren (Bloomington: Indiana University Press, 1996), 273–94.

[46] As Richard Stites writes, Gypsies, homeless themselves, "excelled in evoking a favorite Russian mood, *toska*—ineffable longing for something lost or far away." *Russian Popular Culture: Entertainment and Society since 1900* (Cambridge: Cambridge University Press, 1992), 13.

[47] "Rasposhel, a Gypsy Romance." In *Entertaining Tsarist Russia,* ed. von Geldern and McReynolds, 174. Alexander Davydov made this song popular.

[48] I. V. Nest'ev, *Zvezdy russkii estrady* (Moscow: Sovetskii kompozitor, 1970), 7.

[49] "Dark Eyes" is translated in *Entertaining Tsarist Russia,* ed. von Geldern and McReynolds, 109. V. I. Vavich's popular recording can be heard on the compact disc that accompanies the anthology.

embodied "elemental free will" (*volia*), as opposed to "the structured liberty from social law" (*svoboda*).[50] In this selfish appropriation of a subordinate culture, Russia's "gypsy mania" bears cultural resemblances to the contemporaneous popularity of blackface minstrelsy in the United States. Both took their versions of the borrowed/stolen culture to the stage, where they performed an illusion that had social consequences. Although a critical difference separated the two forms of entertainment from each other—namely, that ethnic Russians did not darken their skin with greasepaint in what could be a savage imitation of the Gypsy "Other"—Russians misrepresented Gypsies by domesticating them in nightclubs. One former member of a chorus recalled that the directors made his group change their clothes to dress in what had become the recognizably "authentic" fashion associated with certain Romanian Gypsies.[51]

In his study of blackface minstrelsy, Eric Lott emphasized the ambivalence that underlay these productions, and his argument has implications for other forms of intercultural performances. In *Love and Theft,* the title he specifically chose to underscore their ambiguity, Lott argued that blackface routines "worked to facilitate an exchange of energies between two otherwise rigidly bound and policed cultures." Moreover, the fascination that white audiences held for the minstrel was "less a sign of absolute power and control than of panic, anxiety, terror, and pleasure."[52] Like African Americans, Gypsies made better symbols than individuals. As late as 1886, a theater critic objected to a Gypsy male embracing a Russian female in the show at the Arcadia.[53] The first legitimate stars of the genre, Vera Zorina and Alexander Davydov, were not ethnically Gypsy, though the dark-complected Armenian Davydov could have passed. The redheaded Vial'tseva with the high soprano sang gypsy romances; no repertoire could exclude them, and ethnic authenticity was of no consequence.

The only true Gypsy to achieve celebrity status was Vara Panina, and the points that distinguished her from others who performed in the genre reflect the degree of desired domesticity for gypsy singers. Beginning in a chorus at the Iar, she moved out as a solo act and became a headliner, but one whose talents came off best in the intimacy of a *kabinet*.[54] Referred to simply by a diminutive of her first name, "as Gypsies do," she was denied the polite form of Russian address, which would include her patronymic. Moreover, in voice, body language, and dress, she was considered masculine. But because her repertoire included numerous numbers that were

[50] Alaina Lemon, *Between Two Fires: Gypsy Performance and Romani Memory from Pushkin to Postsocialism* (Durham: Duke University Press, 2000), 36.
[51] Egor Poliakov, "Istertyi grif," *Tsirk i estrada*, no. 5 (1928): 6.
[52] Eric Lott, *Love and Theft: Blackface Minstrelsy and the American Working Class* (New York: Oxford University Press, 1993), 6.
[53] *Obozrenie teatrov*, no. 8 (June 21, 1886): 1.
[54] Nest'ev, *Zvezdy russkoi estrady*, 41.

not Gypsy in origin, she escaped the chorus at the Iar and became wealthy enough to indulge her passion for diamonds. Identification as a Gypsy might have precluded her from singing the lighthearted melodies from madly popular operettas, but Vara excelled in the third musical category of the era, the "cruel romances" that lamented the failures of urbanization.[55]

Two other enormously popular singers who appeared in the final years of the old regime stand out for what they took into emigration with them, and how they represented the end of the era: Nadezhda Plevitskaia and Alexander Vertinskii. Plevitskaia, who also sang operetta and gypsy numbers, did not become a major figure until she took the nationalist turn and specialized in stylized renditions of folk songs. In 1910 she signed a contract for an unheard-of fifty thousand rubles; at those prices, ordinary entrepreneurs advertised "Plevitskaia imitators" because they could not afford the real thing.[56] Costumed as a pre-imperial *boiarina*, she played heavily upon a nostalgia for Russian exceptionalism, a heady theme especially during the First World War. True to the temperament of her persona, in Parisian emigration she involved herself in hopeless intrigues to restore the autocracy.[57]

After an early career singing such risqué fare as "Cocaine Girl," Vertinskii's persona moved in the opposite direction, toward a future more melancholy than the past. His fame increased dramatically during the war years, when with a style as saturnine as his persona, he powdered his face white and sang dressed as the harlequin Pierrot. Wildly popular, he even appeared in several movies. After years abroad, playing to a dwindling émigré community, Vertinksii returned for a second career in Soviet Russia, playing upon nostalgia in this incarnation.[58]

Comedy Tonight!

The nightclub forum accelerated the evolution of stand-up comedy because the celebration of the moment led to an emphasis on topical issues. Because words are constantly kept in play, eluding definition, the performer and audience must communicate through a shared symbolic language that would include slang and gestures. Emerging from clown acts and routines that played upon the universal human comedy, from pratfalls

---

[55] On Panina, see, for example, her obituary in *Artist i tsena*, no. 11 (1911): 7–8.

[56] *Artist i tsena*, nos. 18/19 (1910): 1.

[57] Nest'ev, *Zvezdy russkii estrady*, 66–102. He also includes excerpts from her memoirs, 109–76. Plevitskaia spent a short time in jail for spying.

[58] B. A. Savchenko, *Kumiry russkoi estrady* (Moscow: Znanie, 1992), 17–20; and Stites, *Russian Popular Culture*, 14–15.

Gypsy legend Vara Panina, from I. Rom-Lebedev, *Ot tsyganskogo khora k teatru "Romen"* (Moscow, 1990), 57

to domestic situations, stand-up comedy became an identifiable genre when it became simultaneously personal and political: personal, in the sense that the performer engages his or her audience on a level of familiarity, and political to the degree that this engagement involves satirical social commentary. As Henry Jenkins argued of American vaudeville comedy in this era, "Jokes . . . tend to cluster around points of friction or rupture with the social structure . . . (they) allow the comic expression of ideas that in other contexts might be regarded as threatening."[59] Both the persona adopted by the performer and the jokes were recognizable for their immediacy. As one critic pointed out, a joke for a nightclub routine must originate in the morning newspaper.[60]

Like song and dance, nightclub comedy developed as a form of individualized expression that grew out of established traditions. The fairground comedians, or *raeshniki*, enjoyed freedom of self-expression, but their primary purpose was to attract strollers into their booths.[61] Stand-up comics began as fillers between acts of a play and sometimes appeared as sideline characters in opera-bouffe, then operettas, to keep the mood light and the audience from leaving. The growth of nightclub culture provided comics with a new forum, the *estrada,* and generated an atmosphere that heightened the possibilities for interaction between performer and audience.

The increasing heterogeneity of the audience intensified the need for humor to mediate among social groups. Sigmund Freud, the era's most famous analyst of anxiety, found in humor a means of negotiating between the conscious and the subconscious.[62] Freud's ideas about the use of humor to uncover individual neuroses carry over into an analysis of nightclub comedy, especially to the degree that the latter is structured around points of social angst. The Viennese analyst and the stand-up comics intersected at the point of "identity," a fundamentally new way of looking at the self and integrating that self into the larger social whole. Ethnicity, social standing, and sexuality formed the core components. Each of these was far less fixed by century's end than at its beginning, and comedy alternately released or redirected the anxiety that resulted from this elasticity.[63]

The first nightclub comics did not enjoy free rein over performance, not in imperial Russia—or anywhere else, for that matter. Where government

---

[59] Jenkins, *What Made Pistachio Nuts,* 251.

[60] Kuznetsov, *Iz proshlogo,* 160.

[61] A. F. Nekrylova, *Russkie narodnye gorodskie prazdniki, uveseleniia i zrelishchia* (Leningrad: Iskusstvo, 1988), 99.

[62] Sigmund Freud, *Jokes and Their Relation to the Unconscious,* trans. and ed. James Strachey with an introduction by Peter Gay (New York: Norton, 1960).

[63] A clinical psychological study of jokes bore out much of Freud's "common sense" about the use of jokes to mask or deny anxiety. Thomas A. Burns, *Doing the Wash: An Expressive Culture and Personality Study of a Joke and Its Tellers* (Norwood, Penn.: Norwood Editions, 1975).

censors blocked some kinds of material, social censors blocked others. Tony Pastor, for example, is credited with turning American vaudeville into a genuinely mass culture because he cleaned out the dirty jokes in the 1880s to bring in more paying customers.[64] Undoubtedly the Russian censorship removed a bounteous source of humor when it declared the autocracy off-limits, but by pushing comics to other sources for material, tsarist officials encouraged the use of comedy to accentuate the politics of personal life.

The predominant style of nightclub comedy in Russia was the rhyming couplet, performed by the *kupletist*.[65] The couplet grew out of Russia's poetic tradition, capturing both the musicality of the language and the established use of poetry as a political vernacular. Couplets appeared in Russia's first vaudevilles; the genre's history parallels that of the legitimate stage and includes the same names among both authors and actors. A foreign influence could be felt here, too, as some of the satirical songs of the popular French entertainer Jean-Pierre Bérenger were translated and transformed into couplets in the 1840s. The verses were often sung, although simple recitation later took precedence over musical presentation. Often considered the city version of the traditional village satirical rhyme, the *chastushka,* the difference between the two became increasingly blurred through urbanization.[66]

Usually, a couplet had a refrain repeated between verses, easy for the audience to pick up. In Moscow V. I. Zhivokini dominated from the 1830s, and his Petersburg counterpart, N. O. Diur, wrote and collected from others enough material to fill three volumes of couplets.[67] Several influential members of the *intelligentsia,* including the literary critic Belinskii and the poet Nekrasov, took advantage of the genre's latitude in political commentary. Even the actress Ermolova occasionally recited couplets on the *estrada*.[68]

The next important source of nightclub humor came from the satirical journals that began sprouting in the 1850s, as the national mood began to lighten even before Tsar Alexander II had put quill to the emancipation decree. The original *Iskra* (The Spark), a humor magazine from the prereform years, put a comic touch on both the political and social changes underway. The rise of nightclub culture complemented this, and the two forms of entertainment joined forces when comedians began performing

---

[64] Lewis Ehrenberg, *Steppin' Out: New York Nightlife and the Transformation of American Culture, 1890–1930* (Chicago: University of Chicago Press, 1981), 67–69. See also Jenkins, *What Made Pistachio Nuts,* 38, on cleaning up vaudeville to bring in more customers.

[65] The most informative general history of the genre is G. Terikov, *Kuplet na estrade* (Moscow: Iskusstvo, 1987).

[66] Ibid., 53, discusses the *chastushka*.

[67] Terikov, *Kuplet na estrade,* 20–21.

[68] Kuznetsov, *Iz proshlogo,* 130–46.

the couplets published in the journals.[69] The reigning *kupletist* star of this era, I. I. Monakhov, is considered Russia's first professional stand-up comic because this became his only performance activity. He established himself at the Alexandrinka, reciting largely from *Iskra* between acts, especially jokes written by the master of comic verse V. S. Kurochkin.[70] The subsequent proliferation of inexpensive joke books and humor magazines encouraged private performances among friends, which presaged a commercial alliance between popular performance and mass publication of material.

Evgenii Kuznetsov, the accomplished Soviet historian of imperial Russia's nightlife, commented that Monakhov's material became "less literary" in the 1870s.[71] Following traditional historiography, he blamed the political crackdown on freedom of expression following the first attempt on Alexander II's life, the so-called "white terror." As evidence, Kuznetsov contrasted a couplet from Monakhov's repertoire from the 1860s with one from the 1870s, both about commerce:[72]

> (1860s) The haughty magicians at the stock exchange,
> Play a terrible game,
> And lowering the prices of stocks,
> They propagate a swarm of beggars.
> (1870s) I respect honorable pawnbrokers,
> They always serve us well.
> But unfortunately, I don't know any,
> Where are the honorable sort around here?

Kuznetsov read the first couplet as an indictment of capitalism as a system and objected to the second one because the humorist was poking fun at individuals rather than the system itself. However, when he pointed to the changed venue for *kupletisti*, who had moved at this time from the imperial stage to the operetta and the pleasure gardens, he offered a more satisfying explanation for the difference. In these nightclubs, more members of the audience would identify with pawnbrokers than with the stock exchange. Following this development into the 1880s, an especially gloomy decade in traditional histories because of the reactionary Alexander III's presence on the throne, Kuznetsov disdained the humor that had begun "addressing primarily petty everyday occurrences . . . mothers-in-law . . . wandering husbands . . . crooked politicians."[73] What was anathema to the Soviet historian proved a boon to cultural studies, because it permitted the

[69] Ibid., 147–54.
[70] Terikov, *Kuplet na estrade*, 31.
[71] Kuznetsov, *Iz proshlogo*, 157.
[72] Ibid., 157–58.
[73] Ibid., 159.

re-creation of daily experience through the lens of the humor that tried to circumvent life's obstacles.

Alexander III has suffered reproach for his conservative politics, criticism not always sufficiently offset by equitable attention to the financial prosperity ushered in during his reign, 1881–1894. Characterized as the decade of "small deeds," in reference to the *intelligentsia*'s strategy for incremental political reform, it would be just as appropriate—and better representative—to call it the years of the "small stage," marking the moment when the *estrada* expanded its role in public life.[74] Those who disparaged the tsar's personal political views might not have found much mirth in the upsurge of "tra-la-la" routines such as "Gentlemen, guard your pockets!" or the dubious "The Jew will never disappear."[75] But these acts resonated with immediacy.

The express train, derailed into a ditch, became a popular topic in couplets, a sign of the liabilities of the railroad boom. And if the autocracy was off-limits, local self-government was not. Styles also changed, as some onstage performers began inviting audience participation. It became more common to recite than to sing couplets, but the balalaika continued to provide musical accompaniment to the singsong rhythms. *Kupletisty* began developing specific stage identities, the first of which was the *lapotnik,* or the peasant wearing *lapty,* bast sandals.[76]

A second Monakhov-*kupletist* appeared, N. F. (no known relation to I. I.), who became the darling of the *estrada* as the preeminent *lapotnik*. Debuting at the Petersburg Zoo in 1894, Monakhov later added a partner to his routine, P. F. Zhukov. They developed an act that played on the growing phenomenon of peasant immigration to the cities, Monakhov the naive villager and Zhukov the experienced older man.[77] Easy to caricature and prominent on the social horizon, the peasantry provided abundant material to raise comic questions about the pace and process of urbanization. The dominant acts in western vaudeville at this time parodied both ethnic and rural immigrants to the big city, who stirred comparable concerns about socialization. In the United States, the legendary comic duo of Weber and Fields, for example, brought down houses for years as heavily accented German immigrants learning the new ways. The Marx Brothers, too, began as comical ethnic stereotypes: an Italian (Chico), an Irishman (Harpo), and a German (Groucho). Because they were not *supposed* to be wise to those new ways, they easily deflected much of the laughter directed at them at the same time that they satirized by purposefully setting the wrong example.[78]

[74] Ibid., 159, discusses the growth of the entertainment complexes in the 1880s.
[75] Terikov, *Kuplet na estrade,* 37.
[76] Ibid., 40–43.
[77] Ibid., 43.
[78] Gunther Barth argues that America's vaudeville audiences "saw vaudeville as a school

The comic character who came to command Russia's boards developed from the peasant persona, with the added quality of the trickster who winked knowingly to the audience at his social miscues. The tramp, called in Russian the *rvanyi,* or "raggedy man" in reference to his ragged costume, was the classic outsider who had willingly severed his ties to the social order. Decades before Charlie Chaplin took advantage of the cinema to circulate the comic imaging of the tramp, Russian *kupletisty* had begun refining that persona. The vagabond made an ideal character in this context, simultaneously familiar and faceless, enviably autonomous to the extent that he evaded autocratic subjugation. Though soon to become more famous for his operettas, Valentinov introduced the type on the *estrada* around the turn of the century. He moved from playing the *rvanyi* on stage to writing comedies for others, from *Wedding by Misunderstanding* (1902) to the political *Days of Freedom,* produced at Tumpakov's Winter Farce in 1905.[79]

Valentinov's first big hit, couplets from *Days of Freedom,* were published and sold separately; even the celebrated clown duo Bim-Bom performed them at the circus.[80] One of the most popular rhymes compared life abroad with that in Russia, the refrain being "Here we have the opposite." For example, one verse told of how the butchers abroad slaughter cattle rather than students, but "Here we have the opposite."[81] In another, Valentinov rhymed French and Russian "synonyms":

> In French, "candidate" (*kandidat*),
> In Russian, "traitor" (*izmennik*).
> In French, "bureaucrat" (*biurokrat*),
> In Russian, "swindler" (*moshennik*).[82]

Valentinov also played with one of the standard comic couples of the *estrada,* the cook and the fireman, who made for ideal romantic pairing because of the double entendres available to them about heat. By situating them amid the 1905 Revolution, he could use their squabbling to ironize the new vocabulary—for example, by having them call each other "democrat" or "bourgeois." In one routine, the cook informed her insolent suitor that she did not need to hide from him behind a barricade, in obvious reference to the radicals' additions to urban planning during the uprising.[83]

---

of etiquette, intimately related to the satisfaction of their hunger for improvement as well as entertainment." *City People* (New York: Oxford, 1980), 216.

[79] As a contemporary pointed out, it was unusual for a Tumpakov production to be so explicitly political. "Benefis P. V. Tumpakova," *Obozrenie teatrov,* no. 65 (1907): 9–10.

[80] V. P. Valentinov, *Dni svobody* (Moscow: n. p., 1905).

[81] Ibid., 7.

[82] Ibid., 19.

[83] Ibid., 15.

Valentinov's shift to operetta was natural in that operettas include the light verse of comedy.[84] Both the Monakhov-*kupletisty* had also starred in operettas. Like Lentovskii, who included *kupletist* on his long list of theatrical pursuits, Valentinov ultimately found the *estrada* too small. His tramp persona became expropriated by one who would come to dominate the comic boards, Sergei Sarmatov.

Born in Ukraine, Sarmatov dreamed first of becoming a dramatic actor. Years on the provincial stage, though, with its erratic talents and even less reliable payment of salaries discouraged his ambitions. Southern Russia, to his advantage, was the empire's comedy central, the original "borscht belt." Odessa was "the factory of *kupletisty*." Kharkov enjoyed a comparably comic reputation hosting *kupletist* competitions; after establishing his fortune Sarmatov returned and built his own club there. He had established a career in comedy by 1900, selling his couplets for twenty-five kopecks, with the caveat that his works not be performed in public without his consent.[85] Such a caution stood small chance of enforcement, but mass circulation would make his style as recognizable as his name. By 1910 Sarmatov was one of Russia's top-grossing performers, earning approximately one thousand rubles per month.[86] Like other celebrities, he even made several movies, "talkies" with gramophone accompaniment.[87]

Despite the original popularity of *Days of Freedom*, national politics figured as only a minor subject in most routines. Even though censors allowed open season on the Duma, the national parliament was largely ignored by the public because of its nonrepresentative nature. *Kupletist* Iura Iurovskii joked about forming a party at the Arcadia nightclub to run against Moscow's deputy Alexander Guchkov, a conservative merchant, but the trivialization of the Duma was not of much interest.[88] Political humor tended to belittle the process in ways that reflected how few Russians felt they had a genuine stake in the system: "Your Excellency, don't you think . . ." "I *serve*, sir; I do not *think!*"[89]

Sarmatov made his name by choosing topics closer to the spirit of a night on the town: sexual liaisons, spent youth, and the empire's ethnic minorities. His tramp persona contrasted sharply with the tall, dark, and hand-

[84] Terikov, *Kuplet na estrade*, 55, gives examples of Russian performers adding couplets about the Russo-Japanese War in a local production of the un-Russian *Merry Widow*. This was common practice.
[85] Sarmatov published at least two installments of *Modnye kuplety i shansonetki* (Kharkov: I. M. Varshavchik, 1902). The first was *Eroticheskie pesenki*, the second, *Pikantnye motivy*. Purchasers were advised to go to the Tivoli Restaurant for the sheet music, thus tying the commercial elements together.
[86] The biographical information is from "S. F. Sarmatov," *Artist i tsena*, no. 2 (1910): 16.
[87] *Novosti teatra*, August 4, 1916, 4.
[88] One of his political couplets is reprinted in *Var'ete i tsirk*, no 1 (1912): 4.
[89] From the humor magazine *On, Ona, Ono*, no. 1 (1906): 9.

Kupletist S. F. Sarmatov, in his signature bum's attire

some lady-killers who figured prominently in his couplets, men to whom "our Sonias, Katias, and Mashkas are ready to give everything, even their chemises" (*rubashki*).[90] The collapsing of sexual mores could be heard in the nightclubs, where naive girls grew experienced quickly in couplets— and probably more than a few in the audience, too.

In Sarmatov's shtick as a bum lay his appeal, his license to critique the

[90] *Eroticheskie pesenki*, 5.

system taking shape from the shuffling of social relations. He played conspicuously on the cultural distance between highbrow and lowbrow:

> I rarely go to dramas,
> I can't stand the opera,
> Only the operetta
> Do I love with my soul.
> Only there I'm never bored,
> I forget the day's troubles—
> I sit and simply melt
> When they sing about the young Spanish girl,
> Lost in her passionate dance.[91]

The multiple paradoxes of contemporary life bounced back and forth in Sarmatov's rhymes. He joked about the latest fads, such as the craze for the "Cake Walk" and women's fashions better suited for spectacle than for dress. Yet the line was never too clear and one could be *had by* manners as well as *have* them. In one couplet Sarmatov mocked etiquette manuals, giving such gentlemanly advice as "use your vest to wipe your nose" and "blame someone else at the table for your mistakes."[92] Another couplet that spoofed excess in everything from clothes to sex winked at the audience through the refrain of "Present company excepted."[93] The ability to move inside the joke as well as outside of it helped the viewers to locate themselves across the moving social grids.

By aiding in this relocation, Sarmatov and his legion of copycat comics served a necessary cultural function. The nightclub gave them a place where they could perform the oppositions characteristic of social change but at the same time keep those oppositions under the control set by the parameters of the joke. The issue of this control is important because it allowed performers to manage the images being put up for public consumption. Issues of class and gender ricocheted back and forth, never secured, keeping identities negotiable.

Comedy has long provided one of the ever-changing battlefields for the eternal struggle between the sexes. A female *kupletist* played ironically with the problem of spousal abuse with her rhyming tale of treatment by her three husbands: the "handsome soldier boy / Always shouting / Always asking for new dishes" . . . the surveyor who "couldn't glance at me without whipping out his ruler. He'd get right to the task at hand / across my body laying it" and third, the doctor, "a pitiless butcher / He tried out all his chemistry / completely on me."[94] This routine complemented the

---

[91] Ibid., 15.

[92] S. F. Sarmatov, *Pesni, kuplety* (Kharkov: S. A. Shmerkovich, 1907), 9.

[93] *Pikantnye motivy*, 15.

[94] Varya Zimina, "Three Husbands," translated in *Entertaining Tsarist Russia,* ed. von Geldern and McReynolds, 280–81.

common attitude expressed by the joke "In Court" (1906): "You are accused of beating your wife." "Please, judge, don't take away the only pleasure I've enjoyed in fifteen years of married life!"[95] Significantly, these jokes can be interpreted as based on lower-class perspectives, which provided the middle-class audiences with the distance they needed to both laugh and feel superior. But it was just as much an issue of gender; more familiar with each other in public, men and women still needed time to become more comfortable with each other in their changing social roles.

Another identity that audiences had to negotiate was that of their ethnicity, as opposed to their citizenship, determining what it meant to be "Russian" in an imperial age. The nature of this humor suggested elevated levels of apprehension in the extent to which the non-Russian Other functioned as the butt of a joke and was deprived of opportunity for redress.[96] But because humor is by nature slippery, constantly evading fixed signification, it can unsettle the same hierarchies it has established. The two nationalities that appear most frequently in Russian humor were the *khokhol* and the Jew, invariably avaricious in jokes as in local prejudices. A pejorative for Ukrainians, "*khokhol*" made unflattering reference to a tuft of hair imagined to be sticking straight out, a caricature Americanized later by the child movie star Alfalfa. The *khokhol* was ignorant, unable to communicate because he had not mastered the language, and had become pacified into a "Little Russian." Although many Jews were performers, by billing themselves specifically as "Jewish *kupletisty*," when they told jokes about themselves they were "inside," which let them escape from being the butt of someone else's cultural anxieties.[97] Despite the fact that all of the top three *kupletisty*—Sarmatov, Iu. V. Ukeiko, and S. A. Sokol'skii—were from the Pale of Jewish Settlement, none was Jewish. Perhaps this was a reflection of emigration to the United States, where Jewish comedians have had a major influence over the evolution of popular culture.

A comic routine featuring both the *khokhol* and the Jew played upon the distinction between the two: "Three *khokhli* were asked to name the smartest man in their town. One came up with the tavern keeper, Chaim [a recognizably Jewish name]. Another responded, 'Oh, he's not the smartest man, he's the stupidest! He has all that alcohol, which he doesn't drink, but sells!' So the three agreed that Chaim was the most ignorant."[98] The listener has a choice of arranging the hierarchy: which goes lower, the

[95] From the humor magazine *On, Ona, Ono*, no. 1 (1906): 5.

[96] Barth, *City People*, 217, refers to "an ever-changing kaleidoscope of victims," without recognizing that certain groups did not find themselves targeted by cruel humor.

[97] Freud focused primarily on Jewish self-ironization in his work on the relationship between humor and sense of self. Elliott Oring, *The Jokes of Sigmund Freud: A Study in Humor and Jewish Identity* (Philadelphia: University of Pennsylvania Press, 1984).

[98] N. I. Krasovskii, *Kupletist-razskashchik. Repurtuar dlia stseny i doma* (Moscow: N. N. Bulgakov, 1902), 71–72.

khokhol who does not have the brains to get ahead, or the Jew, who controls both their liquor and their economy? The Russian stands securely outside this joke.

Among the other ethnic groups that appeared in Russian humor, the Armenians fared comparatively well; jokes revolved primarily around their role as merchants who did not speak the Russian language clearly, but the punch line seldom held them in ridicule or contempt.[99] Gypsies performed the same service in couplets as they did in song, symbolizing the passion and violence that responsibilities forced the audiences to repress. The couplet "Song of the Gypsy Lover" exhilarated that "there is no nation better than the Gypsies!"—a sentiment that breezed over the reality that the Gypsies would be performing rather than mixing in the audience.[100]

The mass circulation of Sarmatov's routines, coupled with the proliferation of humor magazines after 1905, turned parlors and social clubs, from the prestigious English Clubs to those organized by workers, into mini-nightclubs for those who lacked the money or the inclination to visit the more public commercial venues. These more private gatherings complemented the nightclub circuit, and they increased the possibilities for participation in the new styles of urban entertainments. The gramophone could bring in Vial'tseva and Morfessi, while the local talent could rework Sarmatov and others to play to community sensibilities. Unanimity of interpretation was not required.

Conclusion

Many questions of personal identity hit hard in July 1914, when Russians had to define themselves against a very real enemy on the battlefield. Social identity became further complicated by the political blurring of enemy lines, and predators seemed as dangerous on the home front as in battle. Germans replaced others as the target of humor that became increasingly less amusing as the body count mounted.[101] In 1916 the extremely popular Sokol'skii began churning out more serious fare, saying, "I have put couplets aside; in this terrible year, there is no place for jokes."[102] But in sacrificing humor, he surrendered the edge of ambiguity that had made couplets so powerful for thinking about identity. He chose simply to erase the mounting problem of class by denying that workers

[99] For a variety of translated ethnic jokes from this era, see *Entertaining Tsarist Russia,* ed. von Geldern and McReynolds, 203–11.

[100] Ibid., 77.

[101] Hubertus Jahn, *Patriotic Culture in Russia during World War I* (Ithaca: Cornell University Press, 1995), 50–62.

[102] Sergei Sokol'skii, *Pliashchushchaia lirika* (Petrograd: Tsentral'naia, 1916), 19.

were on strike, for example; and when he just as facilely returned women to a pedestal, he removed them from any context where they could exercise free agency.[103]

Despite the fact that much commercial culture boomed during these turbulent years, comedy too often found itself a political prisoner of war, imprisoned by the observation that nightclub humor must originate in the morning newspaper. When the headlines told of lost battles and lost lives, comedians could only try to reinvent humor in ways that were often not funny. The deprecating image of chubby Germans devouring sausages fell to the unhumorous reality of victorious Huns on the battlefield. A joke about Nicholas II after his abdication, in which he claimed "Now I understand how the Jews felt in the Pale of Settlement!" registered little levity.[104]

[103] Ibid., "Slovo pro Rossiiu," 37–42, and "Pesenka o damakh," 111.
[104] Quoted in *Entertaining Tsarist Russia*, ed. von Geldern and McReynolds, 203.

CHAPTER EIGHT

Tsarist Russia's Dream Factories

The moving picture images that flickered across the silver screen infused the vital element of reality into the magic lantern shows and other forms of conjured-up representations that had preceded them. When Thomas Edison and the Lumière brothers made it possible to photograph live action, they revolutionized all levels of the entertainment industry. Inexpensive, ubiquitous, and endowed with unimaginable potential to influence spectators' visions of themselves and their world, the movies rewrote the debate about the potential of commercial culture to shape society. All the leisure-time activities discussed in the preceding chapters struggled to find a place in the new industry, from stage stars threatened by the camera's closeness to wrestlers who found another venue for performance. Modernity's consummate blend of industrial technology and personal experience, movies made possible "the *dynamization* of space and, accordingly, the *spacialization* of time," to quote Erwin Panofsky.[1] Soon to tower above all others in the culture industry, they generated a new set of analytical questions in the study of how culture simultaneously reflects and reshapes the society that produces it. The first of these questions was posed about the medium's influence on the spectator's sense of self.

Motion pictures debuted in Russia, as elsewhere, in nightclubs as novelty acts in 1896.[2] An intertextual medium from the outset, the motion pic-

[1] Quoted in Thomas Levin, "Iconology at the Movies," in *Meaning in the Visual Arts: Views from the Outside,* ed. Irving Lavin (Princeton: Institute for Advanced Study, 1995), 316.
[2] Nadezhda Buchinskaia, "Teffi," had a satirical cabaret act: "At the Cine-Mato-Scopo-Bio-Phono-etc.-Graph," reprinted in Laurence Senelick, *Cabaret Performance,* vol. 1, *Europe 1890–1920* (New York: PAJ, 1989), 172–74.

ture spent its formative first decade trying to find its individuality while borrowing from other entertainments.[3] Because Russia did not have its own film industry until 1908, theater owners had to import, especially from the French companies run by the Pathé Brothers and Charles Gaumont, who owned several entertainment ventures in Russia and is credited with showing the first movies in his nightclubs.[4] Single-reeled, these first films were what Tom Gunning has termed the "cinema of attractions," a featured bit of trick photography on a vaudeville bill.[5] A typical such movie, *The Magic Lantern* (1903), paid comic homage to its predecessor by doing what the lanterns imagined for viewers: spitting real people out of the box.

A list of films playing at Petersburg's Renaissance movie house in 1908, all imports, offered the blend of exotica and erotica familiar from vaudeville: *The Female Samson; Venice and Its Fairytale Places; The Artist and His Model* ("very interesting!"); and *Help Me Fasten This Corset!*[6] As movies became a fixture on the cultural landscape, the Saburov Farce Company reversed the role of film as an entry on the playbill and recorded their routines as movies, complete with phonograph soundtrack, including the sexually suggestive *When Night Falls* (1912) and *The Mother-in-Law in the Harem* (1914). The Saburov Company missed the point, though, of film's potential for originality. By simply filming routines designed for the stage, they were ignoring the radically innovative developments in narration that had liberated movies from nightclub bills and allowed them to tell stories in an original medium.

It took several years, numerous discoveries, and the sheer genius of several experimental directors and camera operators to transform the novelty into the narrative. If the Russians came late to this particular table, they arrived with distinctive fare, even before the first Soviet generation who revolutionized film theory in the 1920s.[7] Through the gradual development of narrative strategies, movies evolved into significantly more than the escape valve that they were thought to offer; they became a medium for constructing an ideologically motivated narrative, a story that depended on the spectator to piece visuals together in the frame of social context. Moreover, narrative cinema took shape in a fundamentally capitalist ideological

---

[3] On the precursors to Russia's silent movies, see N. M. Zorkaia, ed., *Ekrannye iskusstva i literatura: Nemoe kino* (Moscow: Nauka, 1991).

[4] Neia [N. M.] Zorkaia, *Na rubezhe stoletii: U istokov massovogo iskusstva v Rossii 1900–1910 godov* (Moscow: Nauka, 1976), 24.

[5] Tom Gunning, "The Cinema of Attractions: Early Film, Its Spectator and the Avant-Garde," in *Early Cinema: Space, Frame, Narrative*, ed. Thomas Elsaesser and Adam Barker (London: British Film Institute, 1990), 56–62.

[6] *Vestnik kinematografov*, no. 3 (1908): 15.

[7] See, for example, Sergei Eisenstein, *The Film Form and the Film Sense*, trans. and ed. Jay Leyda (New York: Meridian, 1957), and Lev Kuleshov, *Kuleshov on Film*, trans. and ed. Ronald Levaco (Berkeley: University of California Press, 1974).

matrix, evident in the contents as well as the distribution patterns of movies.

The Evolution of the Newest Culture Industry

The novelty of the "cinema of attractions" was wearing thin by 1908, and producers revived what was a fading industry by creating a substantively different medium and attracting a much larger, more heterogeneous audience. In his history of narrative film, Gunning identifies this as the transformative year, the chronological point at which various strands of technology, social discourse, and business practices came together to move the film industry emphatically in the direction of longer stories, peopled with more psychologically complex characters.[8] On an international scale, from 1908 onward directors began experimenting with the camera, producers in search of profits encouraged styles that would increase the audience for a single film, and social critics lobbied for movies that would raise the cultural level of the lower classes who frequented them.

France's inauguration of its *film d'art* series in 1908 marked a great social effort to elevate the position of movies in the cultural landscape, which was to have the added economic benefit of expanding the audience by attracting more from the middle classes. French film makers began to make movies based on great books, historical events, and highbrow plays.[9] The Bible provided a ubiquitous source, but most of these films still had an identifiable nationalism. Stylistically, the early art films borrowed more from practices associated with tableaux, staging flat scenes in front of an immovable camera.[10]

In Russia, 1908 was also the year that native film producers stepped out on their own. Yet despite declarations of national independence, it would take years before Russian film companies could produce a supply capable of keeping up with the demand. Russian producers took their first cues from the French, with whom they had the most contact. Inspired initially by the nativist agenda implicit in the *film d'art* movement, they began cranking out movies with plots and characters specifically recognizable to Russians. Until 1912, when the approximately half-dozen major native studios began composing significantly original stories, historical and literary themes accounted for almost 80 percent of studio production.[11]

[8] Tom Gunning, *D. W. Griffith and the Origins of American Narrative Film* (Urbana: University of Illinois Press, 1991).

[9] Richard Abel, *The Ciné Goes to Town: French Cinema, 1896–1914* (Berkeley: University of California Press, 1994), 39–42.

[10] Ibid., 246–56.

[11] Denise Youngblood, *The Magic Mirror: Moviemaking in Russia, 1908–1918* (Madison: University of Wisconsin Press, 1999), 8.

In their first five years of production, 1908–13, Russia's studios produced fewer than four hundred movies.[12] In March 1914 the State Duma considered the protectionist measure of levying high duties on imports, but the outbreak of the First World War a few months later obviated the need for this.[13] Before the war the films themselves, the stars, and the production materials had crossed borders easily. With these borders now closed, the national companies were forced to become self-reliant.[14] Not only did quantity increase, with more than one thousand feature films made during the war, but quality also improved as Russia's producers and directors experimented with their own distinctive methods.[15]

The Russian adjective used to describe these first movies, *nemye*, translates best as "without speech," which characterizes them better than does the English word "silent." From the outset Edison had developed technology capable of recording sound on film, but he declined to use it because he feared it would undermine the ability of motion pictures to "achieve the illusion."[16] Although the characters on screen did not speak, sound was crucial to the showing of any movie because films were associated with, and accompanied by, music. As movies increased in popularity, so did the importance of the score, and some theaters trumpeted not just which films they were showing but also the orchestras that were playing. Singers and musicians advertised their specialties for the "talking and singing cinema" in trade journals. Even the tiny provincial theaters needed at least a pianist, or a gramophone, to accompany a film. These sound effects generated a supplementary labor pool, and movie houses held benefits to augment the salaries of pianists and projectionists, who averaged a modest thirty to fifty rubles per month in major cities.[17] Work hours grew proportional to audience demand for additional showings; a Petersburg pianist died on the job in 1910, reportedly from too many twelve-hour days.[18]

The symbiotic relationship between screen and song resulted in numerous movies inspired by fanciful interpretations of lyrics. The great fa-

---

[12] Veniamin Vishnevskii collected titles and information about production, including stars and studios, in his indispensable *Khudozhestvennye fil'my dorevoliutsionnoi Rossii* (Moscow: Goskinoizdat, 1945).

[13] Discussed in *Obozrenie kinematografov, sketing ringov, uveselenii, i sportov,* no. 162 (March 19, 1914).

[14] V. S. Likhachev, "Materialy k istorii kino v Rossii (1914–1916): Russkoe proizvodstvo i mirovaia voina," *Iz istorii kino,* no. 3 (1960): 37–103.

[15] Nikandr Turkin, "Zagran. shedevry," *Pegas,* no. 2 (1916): 53–54.

[16] Quoted from an interview in the *Times of London* in *Vestnik kinematografov,* no. 5 (November 22, 1908): 1.

[17] The benefits would be advertised in the trade journals, such as *Peterburgskie kinemoteatry.* The salary information is from surveys conducted by *Sine-fono,* no. 16 (1908): 5, and no. 1 (1913): 12.

[18] A. A. Chernyshev, *Russkaia dooktiabr'skaia kinozhurnalistika* (Moscow: Moscow University, 1987), 59.

miliarity with "Dark Eyes," not to mention its sexy theme, made it a natural for film. In the 1916 movie version of Grebenka's tune, the forlorn hero enjoyed a double social identity as "a merchant in the *intelligentsia.*" Moreover, he had a daughter to play domestic foil to the Gypsy, to whose fiery eyes he sacrificed all. The 1910 film version of Nekrasov's "Peddlars" had more of the drama of the popular song than the politics of the original poem.

In addition to music, at times actors would accompany a film being shown by reciting lines, voiceovers to what was being mouthed on screen. A filmed scene from a famous play, for example, could be enhanced by a reading of lines.[19] Every year studios produced "talkies" (*kinogovoriaushchie*), movies that required live performers speaking roles. This gave local thespians performance opportunities, and created a new job for "film-reciters" (*kinodeklamatory*).[20] Talkies included vaudeville routines, scenes from famous plays, and even monologues. Edison's Russian office produced at least thirty-seven sound (*zvukovie*) films, or movies that required specific records for gramophone accompaniment, including two of Sarmatov reciting his *kuplety.*[21]

The absence of spoken language proved fundamental to the wide circulation of *nemye* films on an international scale. Although international entrepreneurs had been producing films since Edison first licensed the technology, theater operators depended on one-reel shorts, especially those produced by the Pathé Brothers. When movies provided quick diversion instead of sustained engagement, quantity was paramount and the Pathé symbol, the Red Rooster, ruled the transcontinental cinematic roost.[22] The Scandinavian Nordisk Company joined the embryonic Italian and German film industries in producing films that circulated internationally, before Hollywood began its global domination following the First World War. Russia's imports greatly exceeded its exports, but the tsarist empire marketed some of its film culture abroad, from west to east, from Sweden to Japan.[23] Because theater owners had free rein with respect to musical accompaniment, they could shape the fundamental experience of viewing: African-Americans watched white actors in Harlem to the strains of a jazz band, just as Russians enjoyed Danish stars performing against a balalaika background.[24]

[19] On some of the Russian experiments with this, see M. Kushnirovich, "Russkii stsenarii—detstvo . . . otrochestvo . . . iunost' . . .", in Zorkaia, ed., *Ekrannye iskusstva i literatura,* 130–56.
[20] Yuri Tsivian, *Early Cinema in Russia and Its Cultural Reception,* trans. Alan Bodger, ed. Richard Taylor (New York: Routledge, 1994), 32.
[21] Vishnevskii lists them by year in *Khudozhestvennye fil'my dorevoliutsionnoi Rossii,* 142–55.
[22] Richard Abel, *The Red Rooster Scare: Making Cinema American* (Berkeley: University of California Press, 1999).
[23] Article in *Pegas,* no. 2 (1915): 109.
[24] Mary Carbine, "'The Finest Outside the Loop': Motion Picture Exhibition in Chicago's

CHAPTER EIGHT

Constructing the Narrative

The potential for movies to influence audiences more profoundly than other cultural media derives from how it positions them in the narrative. In his study of narrative film theory, David Bordwell explains how the activity of narration combines three principles: representation, structure, and process.[25] The spectator participates in all three, "prepared to focus energies toward story construction and to apply sets of schemata derived from context and prior experience."[26] The director situates the viewer in the story by establishing and arranging visuals into a fundamentally new language, one that "not only stages a new visual episteme, but simultaneously schools a new mode of vision."[27] It affected not just *what* the audience saw but *how* they saw it.[28] By adjusting the camera, the director can create intimacy through the close-up or, for the opposite effect, use a deep-focus shot that conveys simultaneous action. Dissolves and slow motion allow directors to shatter established perspectives of time and space.

Two contrasting directorial techniques combined the technological with the artistic and made significant breakthroughs for the development of narrative film at this juncture. The first, mise-en-scène—literally, those things "put in the scene"—used the arrangement of compositions within shots to advance the story. Directors who preferred this style juxtaposed characters and objects within the frame to make a point visually. The second dominant style was montage sequencing, or the intersplicing of scenes in such a way as to tell the story through the relationship of individual shots to one another. Mise-en-scène characteristically works most effectively in psychological dramas, and montage for action-oriented films. The first style is most closely associated with European film, including Russian films, and the second with the American cinema pioneered by D. W. Griffith.

A contrast between Russian and American versions of the same silent movie explains how directorial styles reflected meaningful differences in national cultures. Griffith's *The Lonely Villa* (1909) was remade by Iakov Protazanov as *Drama on the Telephone* (1914). The plot tells of a man who leaves his family in their country villa to go into town; thieves break in after he leaves, and the wife telephones her husband, hoping he can get back in time to save them. In the original, Griffith set new standards in montage

---

Black Metropolis, 1905–1928," in *Silent Film,* ed. Richard Abel (New Brunswick: Rutgers University Press, 1996), 234–62.

[25] David Bordwell, *Narration in the Fiction Film* (Madison: University of Wisconsin Press, 1985), xi.

[26] Ibid., 34.

[27] Levin, "Iconology at the Movies," 316.

[28] Miriam Hansen, *Babel and Babylon: Spectatorship in American Silent Film* (Cambridge, Mass.: Harvard University Press, 1991), 80.

to create suspense, cutting quickly back and forth between the villains breaking down the door and the husband driving furiously back to the rescue. Protazanov's remake uses mise-en-scène to generate tension, bringing ironic attention to the inadequacies of the advanced technology of the telephone to connect husband and wife in this particular situation.[29] Griffith's husband arrives in the nick of time, whereas the slower-paced Russian returns home too late. Both directors employed a specific cinematic technique that drove the film's narrative, determined the outcome, and reflected deep cultural differences.

Among prerevolutionary Russia's several exceptional and influential film directors, Evgenii Bauer stands out for his innovations in mise-en-scène. His critics have slighted his work for what they see as "formalism," unappreciative of how he used the forms within his shots to shape the narrative.[30] Bauer drew much from his pre-cinema careers, designing sets for nightclubs and working as a portrait photographer. Despite a reputation earned for the sumptuous, big-budget melodramas made at the end of his career, he started in 1913 working on the film celebration of the three-hundredth anniversary of the Romanov dynasty, developing his technique in more than eighty films, including *The Humpback's Terrible Revenge* (1913) and *The Female Impersonator: A Farce* (1914).

Famous for his use of columns and staircases to establish depth, and his spatial lighting to emphasize mood, Bauer seemed to have little need for intertitles, or the brief, written comments between scenes that explained action or supplied dialogue. His sets were always cluttered with articles of consumption, establishing an ambience of physical comfort from which moral questions could arise. The criticisms of Bauer show how much better he understood the new medium than those who judged him. Under the obvious influence of Stanislavsky's work on stage, one reviewer complained that Bauer sacrificed historical accuracy for the sake of atmosphere. As if anticipating and disparaging the *auteur* theory of directorial preeminence, this critic did not like it that Bauer asserted his own vision over that of the collective.[31] In response to what is commonly accepted as his magnum opus, *A Life for a Life* (1916), though, one critic applauded, "Thank God, that the external corresponds to the internal in this movie!"[32] Despite his favorable impressions of *Life*, though, Valentin Turkin, tsarist Russia's most professional movie critic, protested that "it is shameful that even the most independent directors cannot renounce . . . the demands of mise-en-scène."[33] Regardless

[29] No prints of the remake remain. The discussion is from M. Arlazorov's biography of the director, *Protazanov* (Moscow: Iskusstvo: 1973), 53–54.

[30] S. S. Ginzburg, *Kinematografiia dorevoliutsionnoi Rossii* (Moscow: Iskusstvo, 1963), 306–7.

[31] See Granitov's commentary in *Pegas*, no. 1 (1915): 93.

[32] *Pegas*, no. 4 (1916): 87.

[33] *Pegas*, no. 5 (1916): 50.

of Turkin's complaint, Bauer's ideas reverberated throughout the industry. Although the other great directors—including the first exclusively professional director of film Petr Chardynin, Vladimir Gardin, and Protazanov—would develop their own unique styles, their emphasis on sets and psychology can be linked with Bauer's pioneering influence.[34]

Narrative film required innovation from more than those who told the stories; those who watched them also had to develop fundamentally different viewing habits. The changing spectatorial point of view was equally critical to the new cinema. As Miriam Hansen has pointed out, the way in which narrative films positioned "the spectator in relation to the represented events . . . assumed the very notion of a spectator as an implicit reference point."[35] Movies situated the spectator in a space that was novel because of what it simultaneously required of and deprived of the imagination. Point of view changed from the early one-reelers, which by pretending to peek through a keyhole fixed the spectator's position on the other side of the door. The technological improvements that allowed a single movie to use multiple reels encouraged the development of more complex narratives, which in turn expanded the audience's role. Spectators found themselves positioned as omniscient observers, not just statically watching the action but now also receiving visual information that provided psychological insights into motivation. This central paradox of film viewing, the bestowal of omniscience and intimacy concurrently, made movies a powerful medium for influencing the spectator because they intensified his/her capacity to identify with the screen action.[36] Because movies took off in Russia during the particularly fractious interrevolutionary years, the special license that they enjoyed to affect viewers' perceptions of their place in the world has made them a critical source for analyzing cultural change.

Writing without Dialogue

Once the storytelling capacity of narrative film began to take shape, directors turned to published fictions as an obvious source of plots. In his invaluable compendium of movies produced in prerevolutionary Russia, Veniamin Vishnevskii includes an appendix of movies made from literary works.[37] Vishnevskii's list is especially striking because it does not separate the highbrow from the lowbrow, a segregation that would have been misleading because of the persisting qualitative mismatches between litera-

---

[34] Ginzburg, *Kinematografiia dorevoliutsionnoi Rossii* (Moscow: Iskusstvo, 1963), 310–13.

[35] Hansen, *Babel and Babylon,* 81.

[36] Gunning, *D. W. Griffith,* especially 15–34.

[37] Vishnevskii, *Khudozhestvennye fil'my dorevoliutsionnoi Rossii,* 157–60.

The director Evgenii Bauer used mise-en-scène to accentuate the distance between the adulterous wife (Vera Kholodnaia) and her bourgeois husband (Ivan Perestiani). *A Life for a Life* (1916).

ture and film adaptation. The first efforts to combine these two cultural forms privileged the literary over the visual, with predictably dubious results for the visually oriented cinema. Film and literature enjoyed a tangled relationship, beginning with the producers who wanted to make movies of classic books to uplift the audience, leading to the realization by certain directors that what they were doing was translating stories into a fundamentally different language.

A comparison of the two film versions of Alexander Pushkin's *Queen of Spades,* both intended to be serious works of art, illustrates how the evolution of cinema technology and style ultimately made it possible to translate Pushkin adequately into the new visual language. As the father of the Russian literary language, Pushkin's cultural stature made him an obvious choice, but it was feared that the screen would devour his genius by erasing his words. The first version, produced in 1910, displayed the technical limitations of the era. Filmed with a static camera, featuring several tableaux that suggested this was a recording of a staged play, the story had one decidedly cinematic moment: when the hero imagines seeing the face of an old woman on the card that brought him doom rather than riches. Trick photography from the days of the cinema of attractions made this scene effective. Six years later, the second rendition shows the strides cinematography had made in the intervening years. Mounting cameras on bicycles, for example, freed the characters to move through the sets. Lighting techniques, especially the use of shadows to convey mood, exposed the hero's psychosis.[38] A single facial expression, correctly lit, could connote as effectively as a stanza of poetry.

The pantheon of writers from Russia's Golden Age had passed from the scene, Lev Tolstoy being the last to go in 1910, so screening their works was left to the uneven talents of studio personnel. The two authors whose works were most often adapted for the screen, Pushkin and Tolstoy, also dominated highbrow and politicized culture. Movies enjoyed several distinct advantages over books for potential mass audiences: access to them was less expensive, and they also demanded a lesser commitment of time and did not require literacy skills. As a result, they could extend access to national cultural symbols, such as Pushkin's playing card. But the liberties that producers often took with these works gave the viewing public license to reinterpret them at will, as in the surprise screen sequel to a Tolstoy masterpiece, *Anna Karenina's Daughter* (1916).

Much of the literature for movies came from the fiction that circulated through the same urban spaces that movies did, especially along the boulevard.[39] Some of the writers were hacks, briskly churning out sensational screenplays, or "librettos," to use the Russian term. A. M. Pazukhin was one of several newspaper journalists who found a second career writing screenplays.[40] Mocked by one critic as "a tragedian" because "a tragedy offers up two or more murders," as in his librettos, Pazukhin jumped media easily because he made his home on the boulevard.[41] Someone else who moved from the tabloid to the silver screen was the omnipresent Count Amori, the pen-name persona of Ippolit Rapgoff, a self-styled moralist who lived in the heart of scandal.[42]

Authors who considered themselves artists with a social conscience, such

---

[38] Paolo Cherchi Usai, Lorenzo Codelli, Carlo Monanaro, and David Robinson, eds., with Yuri Tsivian's "Some Preparatory Remarks on Russian Cinema," *Silent Witnesses: Russian Films 1908–1919* (London: British Film Institute, 1989), 108–10, and 352–56.

[39] Zorkaia's *Na rubezhe stoletii,* published in 1976, remains the best source for connecting movies with literature, but Zorkaia adopts the perspective of the *intelligentsia* and does not apply film theory that could relate films meaningfully to each other.

[40] Among the authors listed whose works were translated in screenplays, Pazukhin ranks third, behind Pushkin and Tolstoy. Vishnevskii, *Khudozhestvennye fil'my dorevoliutsionnoi Rossii,* 159.

[41] "Bul'varnye tragedii," *Pegas,* no. 5 (1916): 77.

[42] Amori wore as his signature a red necktie, which, if Russians followed other fashions in coding, would have identified him as a homosexual. As Dan Healey pointed out, gay Russian men of this era "sported bright red cravats, a kind of homosexual uniform, and some have a bright red handkerchief blazing from the pocket." In *Homosexual Desire in Revolutionary Russia* (Chicago: University of Chicago Press, 2001), 40.

as Maxim Gorky, Leonid Andreev, Alexander Kuprin, and Mikhail Artsy-bashev, attempted to raise the stature of the boulevard by writing *about* it rather than *for* it. Some of them hoped to legitimize the city streets through film adaptation of their own works, either adapting their published stories or writing original librettos. Because they were writers first, it was not always easy for them to grasp the profound differences between word and screen image.[43] Kuprin, for example, disclaimed the film version of his *The Coward,* but as the movie's director pointed out, the author himself had written the libretto.[44] The more sensationally inclined Artsybashev, eager for publicity, precluded the film version of his *Jealousy* with a short publicity film of himself posturing.[45] Even middlebrow Alexander Amfiteatrov boosted the status of the lowbrow cinema, making headlines when he signed an exclusive contract to translate his books for a studio.[46] The demand for new material became so strong that by 1916 studio chief Alexander Khanzhonkov was holding contests for stories written exclusively for the screen, offering up to fifteen hundred rubles.[47]

Cinema and literature had the most profound impact on the emergence of female writers. The extensive presence of women in movie theaters, public spaces that welcomed them singly or in groups, goes far in explaining this connection. Two of the dominant authors at the fin de siècle, Evdokia Nagrodskaia and Anastasia Verbitskaia, carried their notoriety from print to screen because their works were eminently adaptable.[48] One member of the *intelligentsia* who took his self-appointed stewardship of the masses much to heart, Kornei Chukovskii, voiced concern in 1908 when the public seemed to prefer Verbitskaia to Tolstoy. Notably, Chukovskii belittled Verbitskaia's writing style for the very properties that made it film-worthy: her characters' emotionalism, registered on film in constant swooning and blazing eyes.[49]

Nagrodskaia's name appears almost more often in film than in literary history, invoked disparagingly in both cases. Despite having written several serialized criminal adventures for the boulevard press in the 1890s, she wrote librettos based on the serious fiction she produced later. Less flamboyant and more introspective than Verbitskaia's, Nagrodskaia's heroines

---

[43] The trade journal *Kino* interviewed several popular writers about their attitudes toward the movies. The closer the writer was to the avant-garde—e.g., symbolist poet Konstantin Bal'mont—the greater the appreciation of films. No. 88/8 (1914): 18.

[44] *Kino,* no. 91 (1914): 18.

[45] The censors blocked the filming of Artsybashev's most controversial novel, *Sanin.*

[46] Khanzhonkov announced the contract in *Pegas,* no. 1 (1916): 120.

[47] He advertised the contests in his journal, *Pegas.* Second prize was 750 rubles, third was 500 rubles, and fourth place netted 250 rubles.

[48] For a joint, and not flattering, review of movies made of their works, see "Kino-retsenzii," *Rampa i zhizn',* no. 37 (1915): 14.

[49] Jeffrey Brooks, "Young Kornei Chukovskii (1905–1914): A Liberal Critic in Search of Cultural Unity," *Russian Review* 33, 1 (1974): 50–62. See also Zorkaia, *Na rubezhe stoletii,* 96.

also struggled to disentangle themselves from the webs spun by socially constructed gender inequalities, typified by the artist heroine Tata in *The Wrath of Dionysus* (1915).[50] Among other women who wrote for the screen, Princess Ol'ga Bebutova had, like Pazukhin, established her reputation writing serial novels for the popular press. At least three movie stars also penned librettos: two, Anna Mar and Zoia Barantsevich, enjoyed marginally better screen reputations as writers than as performers. Vera Karalli, an enormously popular ballerina-turned-actress, decided (erroneously) that she was best suited to compose her own material.

The significance of the female screen writer did not lie in numbers, which was ever only a small fraction of the total. Rather, it lay in the cinema's unique cultural relationship with women, who composed its primary audience and who, in the social chaos the century's first decades, had the most to learn from movies. This phenomenon characterized all emergent national cinemas.

The Audience

"Absolutely everyone goes to the cinema," wrote Alexander Korianskii as early as 1907. Four years later Symbolist writer Andrei Belyi, himself a great aficionado of popular culture, described the audience: "aristocrats and democrats, soldiers, students, workers, schoolgirls, poets and prostitutes."[51] Important places for socialization, these motley assemblies had to learn a new etiquette. From the early years of merchants behaving "as if they were at home," bringing food and drink with them, by 1915 the average cinemagoer had "learned the new code of behavior among the cinema public," remaining quiet and respectful.[52]

Members of both sexes went to the movies, but film history and theory agree that movies were both more popular among and important to the female component.[53] This was a public entertainment women could attend alone, secreted by the dark. Even someone like Elizabeth Riabushinskaia, wife of one of Moscow's wealthiest and most influential merchants,

---

[50] On Nagrodskaia, see *Wrath of Dionysus*, trans. with an introduction by Louise McReynolds (Bloomington: Indiana University Press, 1998), vii–xxviii. On Verbitskaia, see McReynolds, "Reading the Russian Romance: What Did the 'Keys to Happiness' Unlock?" *Journal of Popular Culture* 31, no. 4 (1988): 95–108.

[51] Quotes from Tsivian, *Early Cinema*, 33, 35.

[52] Tsivian, *Early Cinema*, 32, 41.

[53] Yuri Tsivian, "Russia, 1913: Cinema in the Cultural Landscape," in *Silent Film*, ed. Abel, 198; Hansen, *Babel*, chapter 2; Shelley Stamp, *Movie-Struck Girls: Women and Motion Picture Culture After the Nickelodeon* (Princeton: Princeton University Press, 2000); Patrice Petro, *Joyless Streets* (Princeton: Princeton University Press, 1989), chapter 4; and Roy Rozensweig, *Eight Hours for What We Will: Work and Leisure in an Industrial City* (New York: Cambridge University Press, 1983), 197–202.

went to the movies as well as the MAT.[54] The relationship between females and mass consumption was key to the commercialization of motion pictures. As Miriam Hansen has argued about the early American cinema, the "film industry [was] less concerned with women's conformity to traditional roles than with their economic potential as consumers."[55] A Russian observer made a similar connection in 1917, noting that "it has become commonplace to give women the majority of movie roles"; the writer's chief concern about this was that women seemed primarily interested in the fashions actresses wore on screen.[56] The movie boom during the Great War, when women began moving into jobs as millions of men left for the battlefront, intensified the cultural connection between the female viewer and the cinema.[57] In all the belligerent countries it was melodrama rather than patriotism that dominated film production.

The female spectator played a central role in the development of the cinema as a particular kind of medium of communication. Quintessentially modern from the perspective of technology and distribution, movies intrinsically promoted mass consumption because they circulated as consumer objects. As Elizabeth Ewen has argued in her study of the immigrant female audience in the United States, movies prospered as "a way of turning people's attention to the consumer marketplace as a source of self-definition."[58] The movies "lay at the heart of commodity culture" after the turn of the century, and they encouraged their female audience "literally to act out the instability of gender identity, and thus to refashion themselves as women."[59] The successful targeting of women as models for mass consumption has been well established in the histories of other societies, but because consumption itself has been less well studied in Russia, the impact of women on it is less clear.[60] Tracing the evolution of a particular style of narrative cinema marketed for the female viewer therefore sheds light on the incorporation of women into the bigger picture of modernity,

---

[54] The Riabushinskii archive is held in the Manuscript Division of the Russian State Library (RGB), f. 260. Elizabeth's account books are in karton 15, ed. khran. 1.

[55] Miriam Hansen, "Early Silent Cinema: Whose Public Sphere?" *New German Critique*, no. 29 (spring/summer 1983): 176.

[56] *Obozrenie kinematografov, sketing-ringov, i teatrov*, no. 235 (January 15, 1916): 3.

[57] For example, the proportion of women employed in industry rose from 26.6 percent in 1914 to 43.2 percent in 1917. Alfred Meyer, "The Impact of World War I on Women's Lives," in *Russia's Women: Accommodation, Resistance, Transformation*, ed. Barbara Clements (Berkeley: University of California Press, 1991), 214.

[58] Elizabeth Ewen, "City Lights: Immigrant Women and the Rise of Movies," *Journal of Women in Culture and Society* 5, no. 3 (1980, supplement): 57.

[59] Mary Louise Roberts, "Gender, Consumption, and Commodity Culture," *American Historical Review* 103, no. 2 (1998): 843. Roberts is describing stage actresses at the end of the nineteenth century, but her analysis applies equally to movie stars.

[60] For example, Roberts, "Gender, Consumption, and Commodity Culture," and Elizabeth Wilson, *Adorned in Dreams: Fashion and Modernity* (Berkeley: University of California Press, 1985).

on screen and off. On the negative side, the cinema's female fans have been held responsible for keeping it an inferior cultural form, for example, as one aspect of the feminization of mass culture, a process taken ipso facto by its critics to be a form of degradation.[61] As Svetlana Boym wrote about Russia, "In turn-of-the-century culture bad taste often became synonymous with feminine taste."[62]

Movie Palaces

Well before the advent of the cinema, ambitious showmen were demanding separate spaces to demonstrate entertainments driven by technological innovations. Moscow's city governor granted permission to a French balloonist in 1804 to open a "phantasmagorical theater," to a "British citizen" in 1823 to show "moving pictures," and to a "foreigner" in 1857 for a "mechanical theater."[63] As movies were playing in nightclubs, "electric theaters" began appearing on the streets of major cities, and entrepreneurs drove movies around the countryside for village presentations

The comparatively inexpensive and pervasive motion picture precipitated a deluge of applications to open theaters where it could be demonstrated. Moscow administrators were flooded from 1907 onward for permissions to present movies in private houses, a situation indubitably repeated in administrative centers around the empire.[64] City fathers had more reason to be concerned about fires than censorship, and approval depended on examination of a building's wiring. But for every makeshift movie house that burned down, two sprang up in its place. Moscow boasted seventy-eight movie houses in 1917.[65] By 1910 the small projection rooms were being eased out in favor of the grand new theaters with modern lighting and seating capacities of a thousand and more. Although some would be located in socially specific neighborhoods, most would be concentrated along a city's central thoroughfares, the boulevards of mass culture. Prices varied according to both theater and seat location, so it would be an exaggeration to place the Riabushinkiis regularly alongside their help.[66] New theaters sprang up, designed to transform public space by attracting a

---

[61] Andreas Huyssen, "Mass Culture as Woman: Modernism's Other," in *Studies in Entertainment: Critical Approaches to Mass Culture,* ed. Tania Modleski (Bloomington: Indiana University Press, 1986), 188–208.

[62] Svetlana Boym, *Common Places* (Cambridge, Mass.: Harvard University Press, 1994), 59.

[63] Moscow City Archive, f. 46, op. 3, d. 407; op. 4, d. 420; and op. 21, d. 218.

[64] The paperwork for applications and investigations has been maintained in the Moscow City Archive, f. 46.

[65] Zorkaia, *Na rubezhe stoletii,* 84.

[66] Tsivian, *Early Cinema,* 32–33.

A catastrophe in a makeshift movie house, 1909

larger, more middlebrow audience without losing the established regulars.[67]

Petersburg's Cosmos was one of the first of the grand theaters, opening in 1908 with promises that it had the best technical equipment, "as in Berlin or Paris," and "an elegant public auditorium, with an electric organ and a fine piano."[68] It advertised, "Bring your wife and children!" Another theater in 1908 pledged quality through its name, As in Paris, and resolved the family issue by showing children's films during the day but changing the bill at night, inviting adults to watch *The Cake Walk* and *Amour and Psyche*. The Big Parisian Electrotheater in Moscow's Arbat district had an Egyptian motif, decorated with lions, desert, and pyramids.[69]

The flamboyant names bestowed on the movie houses testified to their owners' visions, or at least to their pretensions. The names repeated themselves, spreading from the two capitals throughout the empire. Foreign, predominantly French, vocabulary predominated: the Renaissance, the Soleil, the Odeon, the Coliseum. The Cascade advertised that it had opened an adjoining café, while the Café-Bristol in turn added a theater. The fancy titles might have been inspired by the fact that the movies themselves were

[67] Alexander Blok preferred the older, sleazier theaters to the new ones because of the clientele. Zorkaia, *Na rubezhe stoletii*, 60.

[68] *Vestnik kinematografov*, no 1 (1908): 5.

[69] Zorkaia, *Na rubezhe stoletii*, 82.

largely imported, but other names reflected an aura of progress, as in the Modern and the Progress itself. The trade journal *Vestnik kinematografov* (Cinematographers' herald) reviewed theaters as well as movies. Buildings originally designed for other entertainments, such as Petersburg's Sporting Palace and even Moscow's venerable Solodovnikov Theater, closed and reopened as movie houses. As further evidence of the degree to which movies had become respectable in civic life, in 1915 the Moscow city administration granted cinema personnel official status as a *sostoianie,* a social category that gave them the legal recognition they needed to act together on behalf of group interests.[70]

The numbers chart the movies' explosive growth: in 1907 Petersburg had an estimated one hundred theaters, though most seated fewer than seventy-five and were fire traps.[71] Three years later, 108 million tickets were sold in 120 movie houses around the empire, each one averaging 250 viewers per day.[72] The large theaters showed the new releases first, then rented them out at cheaper costs to the smaller theaters.[73] In 1913 the number of national theaters had skyrocketed to fifteen hundred; two years later, that number had increased by another thousand. In 1916 Russia boasted four thousand movie theaters that showed five hundred new movies to more than 180 million viewers.[74] Theaters that had previously had two or three showings per day doubled those numbers in 1916. Approximately 10 percent of the urban population, which was itself 20 percent of the national population, saw a movie every day in 1916.[75]

The film industry generated a spin-off business in journalism. Theater owners did not advertise in the mass-circulation dailies, whose editors for their part were slow to embrace movies. An incident involving a movie or its star, such as the furor surrounding *The Keys to Happiness* in 1913, Russia's first genuine blockbuster, might appear as news, but newspapers did not review movies as they did plays. Specialized journals, sold by subscription, stepped into this informational void. *Sine-fono* (Ciné-phono), a bimonthly that began publication in 1907 and cost six rubles annually, was the first and most successful. Part trade journal and part fan magazine, published in Russia's movie capital, Moscow, *Sine-fono* kept readers abreast of technical, legal, and social developments in the industry. Growing with

[70] Moscow City Archive, f. 179, d. 3533.

[71] *Sine-fono,* no. 9 (1908): 2–3.

[72] Chernyshev, *Russkaia dooktiabr'skaia kinozhurnalistika,* 78.

[73] Article in *Peterburgskaia gazeta,* December 7, 1909, no. 336. The author estimated that theater owners spent more than five hundred thousand rubles weekly renting films.

[74] B. B. Ziukov, *Vera Kholodnaia. K 100–letiiu so dnia rozhdeniia* (Moscow: Iskusstvo, 1995), 42; and Chernyshev, *Russkaia dooktiabr'skaia kinozhurnalistika,* 100.

[75] Figures are from Chernyshev, *Russkaia dooktiabr'skaia kinozhurnalistika,* 99; and Youngblood, *Magic Mirror,* 11. Boris Mironov estimated that in 1916 the urban population was just over 20 percent of the total. *The Social History of Imperial Russia, 1700–1917,* vol. 1 (Boulder: Westview, 2000), 468.

the movies, in later years the journal printed synopses of new releases, both foreign and domestic. Subsidized by advertisements from the studios, its publisher generated fifty thousand rubles in profits in 1913.[76]

Sine-fono remained a dominant journal, but its competition expanded with industry as a whole. Savvy entrepreneur Robert Perskii began his *Kine-zhurnal* (Cinema journal) in 1910 with a staff that briefly included avant-garde poets Vladimir Mayakovsky and David Burliuk.[77] This ultimately became the most widely circulated trade journal, and its one hundred thousand rubles in profits gave Perskii the financial leverage to open his own studio. The reverse scenario, producers moving into publishing, also occurred. Studio head Alexander Khanzhonkov began *Vestnik kinematografii* (The cinematography herald) in 1910, primarily to publicize his own productions but also to keep open discussions of industry-related issues. The Ermolaev Studio published *Zhivoi ekran* (Living screen) with a similar platform. In 1915 both studios aimed to elevate the quality of movie journalism by publishing more intellectually sophisticated monthlies with lengthy reviews and discussions of technological and artistic issues: Khanzhonkov's *Pegas* (Pegasus), named for the studio's trademark, and Ermol'ev's *Proektor* (Projector). Despite privileging their own studios' productions, these journals were not simply in-house publicity organs.

In all, at least twenty-seven specialized journals and forty-one cinema-oriented newspapers were published empirewide in prerevolutionary Russia, several of which enjoyed circulations in the tens of thousands.[78] The large, luxury theaters often distributed small papers with news of current fare and coming attractions. Other periodicals tied the movies into other entertainments, such as *Obozrenie kinematografov, sketing-ringov i teatrov* (The review of movie houses, skating rinks, and theaters). Fans found news and gossip about favorite stars, and business people in the industry found substantive news about technology, new theater openings, and personnel hiring.

The Movie Moguls

The "mass" qualities of movies—circulation and consumption—depended on another critical aspect of modernity, mass production. A Petersburg photographer, Alexander Drankov set that in motion when he opened the first Russian film studio in 1908. An entrepreneur of uncommon ambition, he pioneered first in photojournalism, serving both *The*

---

[76] Chernyshev, *Russkaia dooktiabr'skaia kinozhurnalistika,* 24.
[77] Ibid., 30.
[78] Ibid., 38. The book includes a valuable bibliography of these publications, 207–15.

Times of London and *L'Illustration* in Paris as their Russian correspondent.[79] Drankov mustered the considerable energy mandatory for a project so daunting as building a national film industry in a country that lagged behind in both technology and capital investments. As the local distributor of the Nordisk Company films, he was keen to the potential for an audience. Despite earning a poor reputation for the artistic quality of his products, Drankov was a true visionary. He harbored ambitions of professionalizing all aspects of the medium, aspired to open a conservatory to train the musicians who accompanied films, and even pressed for studies of the medical effects of the intensity of viewing.[80] After producing a spate of newsreels on specifically Russian topics, in October 1908 the Drankov Studio released tsarist Russia's first nationally produced fictional film, *Stenka Razin*, a sensationalized account of an historical outlaw. Filmed on outdoor locations, Drankov subdued Razin's seventeenth-century antiautocratic politics to the outlaw's ruinous sexual appetite. The Russian audiences loved the film, as well as the musical score commissioned especially for it. One reviewer praised the cinematography, complaining only that the movie was too short to do justice to the subject matter.[81]

Stenka Razin tells a simplistic tale: the title character gets drunk, believes his conniving crew when they tell him that his Persian mistress has been unfaithful, and throws her into the river. For all its cinematic naïveté, the film was remarkable for its symbolic activation of Russian moviegoers, transforming them from objects of French cameras and commercial interests into nationalists motivated to spend time and money watching their history, their lives on screen. The two other movies released by the Drankov Studio in 1908 reflected both the nationalism and confusion about the intertextuality inherent in the new medium. *Krechinsky's Wedding* was attempted as a "ciné-talking" picture; Drankov filmed a scene from the popular nineteenth-century play on stage at the Alexandrinka, starring V. N. Davydov. He then coordinated actors to hide from the audience behind the screen and lip-synch the lines.[82] The next release, *The Diligent Batman*, came straight from the vaudeville stage of sight gags and pratfalls, with the comic lead playing consciously to the camera.

Drankov had the proper ingredients but not the formula quite yet. He also had a cross-town rival, Alexander Khanzhonkov, a retired army officer who had established a film distribution company in Moscow in 1906, representing, among others, the Pathé Brothers. Khanzhonkov barely failed

---

[79] Without Drankov, "no one was buried. . . . The elements would not rage and monarchs would not meet." Quoted in *Silent Witnesses*, ed. Usai et al., 556.

[80] The critic who reported these proposals commented that Russia's film industry would not be hurt were Drankov to disappear. He was writing for Khanzhonkov's journal, *Pegas*, no. 5 (1916): 104–5.

[81] *Vestnik kinematografov*, no. 1 (October 25, 1908): 6.

[82] *Silent Witnesses*, ed. Usai et al., 54.

in his attempt to release a Russian film before Drankov, and his first movie, filmed on location, put Russia's "gypsy mania" on film: *Drama in a Gypsy Camp near Moscow.* As in *Stenka Razin,* sex overwhelmed cultural accuracy. When the two producers became successful, both organized joint-stock companies, a necessary financial action that made their products more commercial, and in so doing complicated the debate about the social role of the cinema.

Drankov and Khanzhonkov laid the groundwork for the studio system in tsarist Russia, a process that brought a rational business infrastructure to film production and distribution, underscoring the commodification of cinema. The French companies that had controlled the cinema in Russia, Pathé and Gaumont, responded by opening production studios in Moscow, making films for local consumption with the possibility of export. They maintained their distribution offices in Russia, but many of their local agents imitated Drankov and Khanzhonkov. Gaumont's representative in Moscow, Paul Thiemann, scion of a wealthy Baltic German family, procured financial backing from Moscow industrialists and in 1909 opened Thiemann, Reinhardt, and Osipov, which produced films locally and distributed foreign, primarily Italian, imports.[83] Three years later his studio absorbed the Pathé offices, and in 1913 he produced the hugely successful *Keys to Happiness,* based on the Verbitskaia potboiler. The proceeds from this triumph allowed him to refurbish his own factory and produce a higher quality of film.[84] A. G. Taldykin, who originally owned a costume firm and helped to bankroll Drankov, then moved to the production side by opening a studio.[85] G. I. Libken, the first producer from the provinces, built a theater chain and established himself as the top distributor for central Russia before moving into production, first in Yaroslavl and in Moscow. Another prospector, Dmitrii Kharitonov, struck gold first in a theater chain. His productions began moving up the quality chain when he began poaching from Khanzhonkov's prestigious studio by offering higher salaries in 1916.[86] Iosif Ermolaev, born into the conservative Moscow merchant estate, transformed himself into a genuine entrepreneur, first as a representative for the Pathé Brothers in Baku, from which he branched out to begin his own firm; on the eve of 1917 his financial and critical successes had inspired him to begin building a "cinema city," like the one Carl Laemmle was building for his Universal Studio outside of Los Angeles. Perskii, a latecomer to the field, opened a noteworthy studio from his background in cinema journalism.

---

[83] *Silent Witnesses,* ed. Usai et al., 588–90.
[84] So popular was this film that many theater owners could charge extra for tickets and run it around the clock. B. S. Likhachev, *Istorii kino v Rossii,* vol. 1 (Leningrad: Academia, 1927), 121.
[85] Jay Leyda, *Kino* (New York: Collier, 1973), 64.
[86] Youngblood, *Magic Mirror,* 27.

These men were the moguls among the many other aspirants. The number of studios jumped as the industry took off during World War I, from eighteen registered studios on the eve of war, to forty-seven by 1916. During the war the tsarist government had even established its own production company under the auspices of the official Skobelev Committee, which oversaw patriotism and propaganda. At least one classic in early animation, V. Starevich's *The Lily of Belgium,* came from this unlikely source for originality.[87] Most of these studios turned out to be as combustible as the nitrate film they used, but the successful ones had tremendous cultural impact during their few short years of operation, 1908–17.

Taking a page from the growing advertising industry, the moguls adopted symbols that would identify their products. Drankov upgraded the Pathé brothers' rooster with peacocks, and Khanzhonkov used Pegasus, the winged horse. Latecomer Ermolaev overwhelmed them with an elephant rolling film in his trunk, and Taldykin played upon nationalist images with a bear.[88] Effective advertising mandated that the symbol be connected to a specific product, and the studios had to carve distinctive niches for themselves as they sought to establish product identification.

The standard historical narrative polarizes Russian studios between Drankov at the lowbrow end and Khanzhonkov at the highbrow, with a concessionary nod to Drankov as the trailblazer who brought so many of the top talents into the industry, only to watch them jump ship to more respectable operations.[89] The problem with this binary view is that it underestimates Drankov's influence. True, these two dominant studio bosses had very different ideas about movies. Where Khanzhonkov clearly deserves commendations for artistic achievements, producing some of the most cinematically original films of the silent era in any country, Drankov made equally significant social contributions by expanding the base of moviegoers and connecting films more vividly to urban life.

Khanzhonkov produced *A Life for a Life,* the film greeted by critics as comparable to the best of the foreign movies. It put on screen all of his studio's best: director, acting talents, sets, and cinematography. A melodrama based on a popular French novel, *Life* featured the beautiful starlets Vera Kholodnaia and Lidiia Koreneva, the veteran character actors Olga Rakhmanova and Ivan Perestiani, the matinee idol Vitol'd Polonskii, and a compelling story of family betrayal that ends in murder. What distinguished *Life* from its plot, though, was the narrative strategy employed by Bauer, one of Drankov's early discoveries who had left for the creative freedom made possible by Khanzhonkov's bigger budgets and desire to create a distinctively artistic cinematic style.

---

[87] Ginzburg, *Kinematografiia dorevoliutsionnoi Rossii,* 159.

[88] The trademarks are reprinted in *Silent Witnesses,* ed. Usai et al., 536–37.

[89] Discussed in, for example, *Silent Witnesses,* ed. Usai et al., 554–58; and Youngblood, *Magic Mirror,* 25–28.

Matinee idol Vitol'd Polonskii

Drankov would never have bothered with detail or spent so much money on production design or on salaries for the big stars. His forte lay in speed of production and emphasis on sensationalism, "cheap films on vulgar subjects shot in exteriors."[90] Most emblematic of his productions were the sensational serials he produced, such as the *Moscow after Dark* series, typified by *In the Claws of the Yellow Devil* (1916). This series also bowdlerized Dostoevsky's *Gambler* (1915), producing a film that had the cultural benefit of bringing the great writer to the public about whom he wrote. The Drankov Studio's most notorious production, though, was the serial *Light-Fingered Sonka* (1915), about a real-life pickpocket who ended her life in exile on the island prison of Sakhalin. Those who identify Drankov by his sensational serial fail to mention a film that Bauer directed for Khanzhonkov in that year, *The Adventures of Shpeier and his Gang, the Jacks of Hearts,* which portrayed a famous swindler matching wits with that very same Sonka.

Drankov's lasting contribution to Russian cinema lay in *how* he did things differently from Khanzhonkov, Ermolaev, and the studios that defined themselves according to their creative ambitions. He enjoyed a reputation for stealing another studio's libretto and rushing an inferior version into production to shanghai the audience.[91] A man of the moment, Drankov moved quickly into and out of production, a skill that aroused the ire of critics but was popular with the fans and theater owners who depended upon rapid turnover. From his background in newsreels he recognized that writers themselves would be as film-worthy as their fiction, and he managed to capture both Lev Tolstoy and Maxim Gorky on film, over the irate protests of the latter, no fan of the movies himself.[92] This was Drankov at his best: a quick raid, rushed into production, and disbursed in a cannonade of publicity. It also earned him an invitation to Tolstoy's estate at Iasnaia Poliana, where the venerated author made his guests sit through multiple showings of himself on the silver screen.[93]

When the Romanov dynasty finally collapsed, both Drankov and Khanzhonkov raced to make a movie about a topic long denied film makers, Russia's revolutionary movement. The contrast between these productions reinforces the studios' stylistic differences. Khanzhonkov's *The Revolutionary* told a sentimental tale of a man growing old in Siberian exile, who then returns to celebrate the dawn of the free Russia with his grandson. Drankov's *Grandmother of the Russian Revolution* was based very loosely on the life of

---

[90] *Silent Witnesses,* ed. Usai et al., 558.

[91] Ibid., 556.

[92] Leyda, *Kino,* 40–44. Gorky anguished that characters in the black-and-white celluloid stories were "condemned to eternal silence and cruelly punished by being deprived of all of life's colours." Quoted in Tsivian, *Early Cinema,* 2.

[93] Article in *Peterburgskaia gazeta,* November 22, 1909, no. 321.

the infamous Socialist Revolutionary Ekaterina Breshko-Breshkovskaia (whose son Nikolai wrote the occasional libretto for Drankov). No sentimentalism here, as the title character moves as animatedly as Sonka, in and out of just as many jail cells. In one long scene she makes a mad, unexplained dash through woods, pursuers unknown. The first movie tells a poignant story with a political message, the second coordinates slapdash action shots; each producer influenced in his own way audience expectations of moving pictures.

Thiemann and Reinhardt's Golden Series of movies based on works of literature provides another example of how elitist cultural ambitions could be overwhelmed by the ingredients that would make a movie sell. The Golden Series fanned Chukovskii's fears because it did not distinguish between Tolstoy and Verbitskaia. Thiemann followed up *The Keys to Happiness* with *Anna Karenina* and *War and Peace*, plus another Verbitskaia novel, *Vavochka*. This series also presented current social fads, such as two films directed by Protazanov, *Tango* (1914) and *The Vampire's Dance* (1914).[94] Protazanov, who had worked on *Keys*, then undertook the Golden Series' most intellectually ambitious production, a film version of avant-garde director Vsevolod Meierkhol'd's staging of *A Picture of Dorian Grey* (1915).

Protazanov is most commonly associated with the Ermolaev Studio, to which he moved from Khanzhonkov's in 1914. This director anticipated film noir with his dark psychological dramas, including the second *Queen of Spades, Satan Triumphant* (1917), and *Father Sergius* (1918). Set designer Vladimir Egorov and cameraman Alexander Levitskii contributed to this style which, like Bauer's, made extensive use of mise-en-scène. Although these macabre dramas gave the Ermolaev Studio its stylistic signature, the first moneymaker, which subsidized future artistic endeavors, was the crime serial *Sashka, the Seminary Student* (1915).

Those studios committed to quality, however nebulous that term, formulated a cinematic mode that was distinctively Russian. This technique developed on two corresponding levels, one of form and the other of content. Not only did they pace action more slowly than in western films, but Russian directors consciously filmed movies at a slower speed. The extended use of mise-en-scène, as opposed to the more action-oriented montage, to shape the narrative also decelerated the pace. Russian directors emphasized their characters' psychological development, preferring to let the camera linger instead of pushing it forward in abrupt close-ups. Bauer, Protazanov, and Gardin specifically choreographed the movement in certain scenes according to slow-motion dance steps, especially the tango.[95]

---

[94] "Vampire's dance" was a cultural alias for the tango. Yuri Tsivian, "The Tango in Russia," *Experiment* 2 (1996): 307–34.

[95] Tsivian, "The Tango in Russia," discusses this, 315–23.

Under the motto "film story, not film drama," they distanced themselves from the western schools.[96]

The tempo and the tone of Russian dramas directed storylines away from the "happy" endings characteristic of western cinema, where problems are resolved in the final reel. As one Moscow reviewer insisted, Russians "stubbornly refuse to accept that all's well that end's well. . . . We need tragic endings."[97] Occasionally Russian movies intended for export filmed two endings, unhappy for native audiences but happy for foreigners.[98] Rather than dismiss this attitude with a cliché about the Russian soul, it is important to bear in mind that movies captured Russian middle-class sensibilities that were distinctively different from their western peers'. Russia's cinematic style reflected society's ambiguous attitudes toward the status quo, which characteristically remained unrestored at the end of the movie: all did not end well after all.

Policing the Cinema

Both the tsarist government and many of its critics wanted to intervene in film production for purposes of social control, but the flickering images eluded their grasp. Russia's censors had an especially difficult time trying to interpret their mission, and no clear pattern of censorship developed. As defined by law, censors were to protect against insults to Orthodoxy, autocracy, and nationalist feelings and to prevent incitements of public disorder. Individual theater owners were supposed to have all films preapproved by local authorities, which made centralization impossible.[99] The loosely constructed moral borders censors had to patrol were rather pregnable. In 1881 the imperial censorship could force the publisher of a mass-circulation newspaper to kill off the bandit-hero in its serial novel, but after the 1905 Revolution, the censors' prerogatives were much less clear. The infamous bandit Churkin met a sorry demise in the press and ended his stage career in the 1880s, only to reappear in the movies, brought back to life by Pazukhin. Though censors tried to limit excesses of sex and violence on the screen, they could not extinguish them. In *The Scalped Corpse* (1915), for example, they cut out a scene of a "dagger blow," but the title gives pause about what censors left in the movie. In another case they prohibited *The Woman You Shouldn't Talk About* (1916), the story of a boy's inces-

[96] Tsivian, "Some Prepatory Remarks on the Russian Cinema," in *Silent Witnesses*, ed. Usai et al., 30–32.

[97] Ibid., 24.

[98] Ibid., 26. American movies also had to adapt to differing censorships across state lines. Paolo Cherchi Usai, *Burning Passions*, trans. Emma Sansone Rittle (London: British Film Institute, 1994), 19.

[99] These censorship issues are discussed in *Peterburgskii kinematograf*, January 9, 1911, no. 8.

tuous love for his mother, only after having approved Drankov's *The Fa-ther's Forbidden Passion* (1913), in which a father and daughter come within a moment of consummating their mutual attraction. During the First World War the Skobelev Committee threatened the lifeline of the cinema-oriented periodicals by taking away their right to accept advertising, a measure seldom enforced.[100] In 1916 the Ministry of Education investigated the idea of a government monopoly over the cinema, but such an extreme measure would have to wait for the next political regime.[101]

The relatively free access to the cinema that the lower classes enjoyed posed particular problems. As Anne Friedburg has pointed out, the concerns of film censorship "stem from the position that the cinema encourages imitation/mimetic incorporation of the harmful, illegal, or immoral actions of character, actor, or star."[102] Imitation of popular characters is by no means unique to the cinema, but the combination of photographic verisimilitude and the viewing practice that allowed the spectator to locate him/herself in the narrative has long made films appear to have special powers. A social debate arose around the early Russian cinema that continues to plague policy makers everywhere: because storylines are dominated by sex and violence, will watching movies spawn a criminal generation?

Sensational crimes jumped from city streets onto the screen almost before the pistols had a chance to cool. When the question about whether life imitated art, or if the reverse held true, came from the police blotter, the jury of social critics found the movies guilty of inspiring imitations in real life. Tsarist Russia suffered no shortage of scandals. For example, the murder of socialite Zinaida Prasolova by her estranged husband at Moscow's Strel'na, his family successfully petitioned to prevent further showings on local screens.[103] The vodka tsar Peter Smirnov paid a movie producer eighteen thousand rubles in extortion money to rename the characters in a movie version of a scandal in his family.[104]

An analysis of the repertoire of Russian films in 1912 discovered that crimes of greed and vengeance dominated the plots of seventy-six out of every hundred movies. Thieves and criminal gangs appeared in almost one-third of the films, and sexual intrigues in over half of them. In only 10 percent of Russian movies was love presented as "lofty, capable of inspiring noble sentiments and self-sacrifice."[105] As Pazukhin's career made

---

[100] Chernyshev, *Russkaia dooktiabr'skaia kinozhurnalistika*, 114.

[101] S. Nikol'skii, "Gor'kaia deistvitel'nost'," *Pegas*, nos. 9–10 (1916): 130–34.

[102] Anne Friedburg, "A Denial of Difference: Theories of Cinematic Identification," in *Psychoanalysis and Cinema*, ed. E. Ann Kaplan (New York: Routledge, 1990), 45.

[103] *Obozrenie kinematografov, sketing-ringov, i teatrov*, no. 238 (February 10, 1917): 8.

[104] *Silent Witnesses*, ed. Usai et al., 284.

[105] Chernyshev, *Russkaia dooktiabr'skaia kinozhurnalistika*, 67, discusses this research.

plain, the sensational serials that sold newspapers moved easily to movies. Originating in France in 1913 with the cunning criminal Fantomas, who matched wits with his equally clever foil, the Detective Juve, serials became a cinematic staple. *Fantomas* played well in Russia, the format enkindling a local version of the genre in which criminals carried on personal battles against society and the police. Unlike American serial heroine Pearl White, who overcomes stereotypical gender victimization by asserting herself in the Pathé-produced *Perils of Pauline*,[106] the queen of Russian serials was based on a real-life figure—the pickpocket, prostitute, and suspected murderess Sofia Bliuvshtein, better know by her sobriquet "Light-Fingered Sonka." The male protagonist who kept Russians returning to see what he was up to was *Sashka, the Seminary Student*. Despite the title, paralleling the career of future dictator Joseph Stalin, this cold-blooded thug had abandoned a future in the Orthodox Church for one in crime.

Only fragments of these serials remain, more of *Sonka* than of *Sashka*. Not enough is left of either to piece together a coherent storyline, but remaining reels of action shots show an excess of theft, armed robbery, and flashing pistols. Sonka was also a firebug. Nina Gofman, who portrayed the pickpocket, attested that she had been trained for her role by local thieves. She claimed that in one episode she successfully lifted the pocket watch of the actor playing her lawyer.[107] As Gofman remembered thirty years later, she moved to a rival film company to make two more episodes, in which Sonka died a poor, miserable old woman.[108] In the final segment still available for viewing, *Sonka the Detective*, she switches sides and goes undercover for the police to catch another criminal. Sashka's fate remains unknown.

Sonka and Sashka predictably raised a fury among social observers. A 1916 farce, "I Want to Be Light-Fingered Sonka," placed the pickpocket at the heart of mass culture thirty years after the factual Sonka's imprisonment. Not only did Sonka and Sashka lower the cultural standards of the cinema itself, they stood accused of inspiring imitative behavior. In 1915 two men who brutally murdered the women they had picked up that evening, not identified as prostitutes, claimed the ingenious "Sashka" defense, protesting that the movies had incited their behavior.[109] The trial jury was not swayed, but members of the industry felt pressured to defend the crime serials, the most inglorious of their products, because of the implied threat of censorship.[110]

---

[106] On the gender significance of the American serials, see Stamp, *Movie-Struck Girls,* chapter 3.

[107] *Silent Witnesses,* ed. Usai et al., 294. This scene is preserved in the film archives, and each viewer can judge for him/herself the veracity of Gofman's claim.

[108] Ibid., 296.

[109] "V zhurnalakh i gazetakh," *Pegas,* no. 1 (November 1915): 73.

[110] Ibid., 74.

The Stars

The most effective connection between film production and consumption came in the person of the movie star, the individual who lived in the ambiguous territory between the fantasy on the screen and the real world it was understood to represent. In his analysis of the social function of movie stars, Richard Dyer locates their origins in an economy that depended on mass circulation and social mobility: the star had to be equally accessible to everyone on the same basis.[111] Actors and actresses become "stars" because they are able to personify on screen the dominant social and political concerns of their audience, and therefore they generate a bond between the persona that they have become and the public that uses their images to work vicariously through its own issues.[112] Stars fit the studio's business practices because they have "tangible features which could be marketed" and subsequently stereotyped for sale.[113] Movie stars are products, manufactured by the combined efforts of the performers themselves, the studio, and the public.

Not the first celebrities, movie stars nonetheless differ in more than magnitude from the most popular performers on the legitimate stage, sports, and nightclubs.[114] National tours could not bring other public performers anything close to the exposure that movies made possible. More important, though, was the difference between the camera that rearranged spatial relationships and the other forums of presentation that distanced performer from spectator, such as the proscenium arch or the playing field. Audiences for personal performances could participate in the action by extending or denying applause, but movies allowed for more personalized identification despite greater actual distance. As the increasingly sophisticated motion picture began manipulating the spectator's point of view, the star's ability to generate a dynamic identification between the central character and the viewer intensified the cultural power of the cinema.[115]

The first genuine movie stars in tsarist Russia were both foreigners, the French comic Max Linder and the Danish dramatic actress Asta Nielsen.

---

[111] Richard Dyer, *Stars* (London: British Film Institute, 1998), 7–8.

[112] Or in the words of Barry King, "By embodying and dramatising the flow of information, the stars promote depoliticised modes of attachment (i.e. acceptance of the *status quo*) in its audience." Quoted ibid., 27.

[113] The words are Hortense Powdermaker's, quoted ibid., 11.

[114] Barry King, "The Star and the Commodity: Notes towards a Performance Theory of Stardom," in *Cultural Studies* 1, no. 2 (1987): 145–61.

[115] Of the literature on audience identification, see especially Andrew Tudor, *Image and Influence* (New York: St. Martin's Press, 1974); and Christian Metz's Lacanian argument in his *The Imaginary Signifier: Psychoanalysis and the Cinema,* trans. Celia Britton, Annwyl Williams, Ben Brewster, and Alfred Guzzetti (Bloomington: Indiana University Press, 1982).

Their extraordinary celebrity should not be interpreted as an example of Russians preferring western fashions, because both Linder and Nielsen enjoyed superstar status on the pan-European market. Linder made a triumphal tour of Russia's two capitals in 1913, but Nielsen did not visit her fans there. The appeal of both can be attributed to the stock character each played, combined with their individual skills at mastering performance styles appropriate for the new technology.

A minor stage actor, Linder became a bit player in films in 1905. By 1910 he had developed an identifiable persona, the lazy bourgeois dandy, the *flaneur* who had lost his dominion over the city streets and was consequently victimized by his own pretensions. Equally important, though, by 1910 Linder had become sufficiently proficient in the new medium to write and direct his own material. He quite literally constructed his comic genius through the arrangement of camera shots.[116] In other words, he generated identification on two levels: with a character who reenacted for laughs the anxieties of the world in which the majority of his fans lived, and by the way in which he used visuals to pull his audience in with him.[117] Russian A. P. Kozlov pirated Linder's publicity and billed himself as "Max's double" in a series of shorts that never competed well against the originals, and across the ocean many critics noticed Linder's influence on Charlie Chaplin's style. This character was exemplified best in Russia by the comic *Antosha* series, with A. Fertner as a deceptively solid citizen in continual trouble for his chicaneries.

Asta Nielsen's trajectory also began in 1910. Although she soared as high as Linder, she flew in the opposite cultural direction. Linder represented the lighter side of social change, a man so foolish that his servants could hypnotize him and indulge momentarily in his lifestyle. Nielsen portrayed its dark side, the woman victimized by her ambitions in a repressive society, as in *The White Slave Trade* (1911).[118] The striking gender difference between Linder's and Nielsen's personae points to modernity's undercurrent of sexual tension, exacerbated by the increased presence of women in public and often vociferous in their claims for equal access to the public sphere. Nielsen's small frame and huge, expressive eyes gave her an advantage when the camera moved in for a close-up. Personifying the androgyny implicit in the New Woman, she alternated "between sexual mobility and emotional pathos . . . destabiliz[ing] the polarized opposition between masculine and feminine identities."[119] At times Nielsen's androgyny was physical, as when she dressed like a man on screen; like Bern-

---

[116] Abel, *Ciné*, especially 236–45.

[117] Charles Ford, *Max Linder* (Paris: Seghers, 1966). Linder died of a nervous breakdown in 1925.

[118] Stamp, *Movie-Struck Girls*, discusses white slave films in chapter 2.

[119] Petro, *Joyless Streets*, 153.

hardt, she played Hamlet, caught in a homoerotic triangle with both Ophelia and Horatio. Her androgyny could also be implied, as in playing *The Suffragette* (1913), when her character demanded the traditionally male political role in society. One Russian reviewer waxed eloquently, "Asta's talent is democratic; for a modest fee, simple people can see great art. Although people do not applaud at movies, when the lights go on, you see tears in everyone's eyes, the candid tears of the viewer who has shared her soul."[120] A range as broad as hers was uncommon for the first generation of screen actresses, and although this helps to explain her extraordinary success, the sources do not indicate which of her roles Russian audiences liked best.

As studios were set up on native soil, Russian producers had to search out local talents. The established stage stars initially held movies in contempt and had little concept of the different modes of performance required for the new medium. Typically, the Malyi magnate Sumbatov-Iuzhin refused to approve movies as an art form until he saw the operatic bass Fedor Shaliapin on screen.[121] Unlike Bernhardt, Savina and Ermolova did not make movies, though Savina appeared on screen once as herself. Few luminaries made the transition smoothly. Varlamov, the Malyi's leading comic and an avid movie fan, made two successful melodramas with E. A. Smirnova, a ballerina turned movie star, and the theater that premiered their work touted the fifteen-piece orchestra hired to accompany the screening.[122] Another corpulent performer moved over from the wrestling ring. The impresario "Uncle Fatty" made several topical comedies, such as *Uncle Fatty's Dacha Romance* (1913) and *Uncle Fatty in Luna Park* (1916). Two other celebrated singers, the concert star Plevitskaia and Vavich of operetta fame, broadened their audiences through movies.

The great corps of movie personalities, though, came from the pool of talent that had prepared for the stage but saw the handwriting on the silver screen. Ol'ga Preobrazhenskaia, trained at the Moscow Arts Theater, graduated from the provincial stage for a screen career that included playing the heroine in both Verbitskaia's and Nagrodskaia's most important novels, *The Keys to Happiness* (1913) and *The Wrath of Dionysus* (1914), respectively. Already thirty when she played younger women on the screen, Preobrazhenskaia found a second career as the first important female director after 1917. Two of Russia's top ingénues, Ol'ga Gzovskaia and Lidia Koreneva, heavily publicized their training at the prestigious Moscow Arts Theater. This promotion reflected the advertising considered necessary to legitimize their migration to a medium that many intellectuals disdained,

---

[120] E. Nearonov, "Asta Nil'son," *Peterburgskie kinemoteatry*, no. 20 (March 20, 1913): 2–3.
[121] Reported in *Pegas*, no. 1 (1915): 91–92.
[122] The first, *The Ballerina's Romance*, was written by N. N. Breshko-Breshkovskii.

Comic wrestler turns comic movie actor in *Uncle Fatty in Luna Park* (1916).

but that would give the actresses undreamed-of exposure.[123] And money: Gvozkaia signed a three-picture deal in 1915 for twenty thousand rubles, outstripping even what Savina commanded in her heyday.[124] Ballerina Vera Karalli enjoyed fantastic success in the movies, often playing a dancer.

Among male movie stars, the romantic idol Vladimir Maksimov had a better theatrical pedigree than most leading men. After parting with his family over his choice of careers, moving from law to the theater, he had worked at the Malyi and then the MAT. As early as 1911, however, he signed with Thiemann and Reinhardt, while other actors still doubted the artistic credibility of the screen.[125] Iurii Iur'ev later moved from the Malyi, although both film stars continued to appear in stage productions as well. Two of the brightest stars, Polonskii[126] and Andrei Gromov, came to the cinema from considerably more modest theatrical backgrounds.

These popular personalities typified others that could easily be included in the Russian constellation because they were sufficiently young and at-

[123] Tsivian, *Early Cinema,* especially 8–10.
[124] Youngblood, *Magic Mirror,* 52.
[125] Ziukov, *Vera Kholodnaia,* 47–51.
[126] Polonskii's daughter became more famous than he in many circles because of her passionate liaison with suicidal poet Vladimir Mayakovsky.

Ol'ga Preobrazhenskaia in *The Keys to Happiness* (1913). Reproduced by permission RGALI, f. 1042.

Ol'ga Preobrazhenskaia in *The Wrath of Dionysus* (1914). Reproduced by permission RGALI, f. 1118.

Ballerina-turned-movie star Vera Karalli, in *Burned Wings* (1915)

tractive to inspire empathy and romantic attachment. Without their good looks and aptitude for the new medium they could never have become screen idols, but it was the roles they played that made them stars—that is, personifications of the larger social and ideological issues from which narrative film had sprung. Because one of the most important of these issues was the different social roles assigned to gender, a contrast between the two most popular Russian stars of the era, Ivan Mozzhukhin and Vera Kholodnaia, will explore the messages sent to each sex.

The son of well-to-do peasants from Penza, Mozzhukhin joined a list of theater people dating back to Ostrovskii who abandoned Moscow University for a more interesting life in the theater. Not prominent on stage, he went to movies from the Korsh Theater, by way of the provinces.[127] Although Mozzhukhin could play comedy, his specialty lay in the dramas that allowed him to weep his famous "Mozzhukhin tears," such as two 1914 tear-jerkers with Karalli: *Chrysanthemums: A Ballerina's Tragedy* and *Do You Remember?* He began with Khanzhonkov, his first big part being Napoleon III

---

[127] M. I. Volotskii, ed., *Migaiushchii sinema* (Moscow: Novosti, 1995), 247–52.

Iurii Iur'ev, one of the few who managed actings careers on both stage and screen

Ivan Mozzhukhin, the sensitive star best known for his tears in Russia's first major multireel feature, *The Defense of Sevastopol* (1911). He made other historical dramas, but was cast most often in adaptations from literature, from Tolstoy's *Khas-Bulat* (1912) to Shmelev's *Man from the Restaurant* (1912). In one of the most notorious incidents of Ermolaev luring away talent with lucrative contracts, Mozzhukhin jumped Khanzhonkov's ship in 1915. Mozzhukhin insisted that he left to work with Protazanov, who enjoyed a solid reputation as an "actor's director."[128] Gossip had it that he left Khanzhonkov because Bauer refused to cast him in the coveted role of *Leon Drey: The Lady-Killer.* The gossip might well have been true, because Bauer would have had to cast him against type, as Mozzhukhin's specialty lay in playing ineffectual men.[129] Protazanov did not transform Mozzhukhin into a heroic leading man but added the fatal flaw of psychosis to his already weakened masculinity. His most memorable performances include the unscrupulous gambler who went mad in *The Queen of Spades;* the suicidal, pedophile rapist in *Little Ellie* (1918); and a pastor quite literally possessed in *Satan Triumphant* (1917).

Not a romantic idol in the same style as Polonskii or Maksimov, Mozzhukhin was predominantly a hero for the male audience. As a principal male figure, what stands out is the Mozzhukhin character's incapacity to restore order when tragedy befalls his loved ones. When given a wife, as in *The Daughter-in-Law's Lover* (1912), he permits his own father to rape her; in *Life in Death* (1914), he murders his wife and then fetishizes her corpse. In his ineffectiveness Mozzhukhin parallels the screen lovers who might have gotten the girl in one reel but usually lost her by the last. The male movie stars embodied the impotence of a society that had lost confidence in the political patriarchy and had not succeeded in replacing it with something more satisfying. The hapless Linder and his successor comics made perfect foils to this emasculation. When presented seriously, however, this situation offered few smiles. Capitalism had not fulfilled the liberal promises it was thought to have made elsewhere, and Russia's history and culture, which provided the sources for myriad movie roles, did not supply screenwriters with many fulfilled promises. Russian male movie stars were more likely to lie dead at the dramatic finale, victims of females running amok because the status quo could not confine them.

Enter the woman: Vera Kholodnaia had the eyes and the sighs to wrest fans from Nielsen, but not the androgyny that gave the Danish star her unique stature. The Kholodnaia phenomenon, short-lived because of the actress's death from flu in 1919 at the age of twenty-six, had an exceptionally far-reaching cultural impact. The brightest star in the Russian pleiad, male and female alike, the intensely private character she por-

---

[128] Ibid., 255.
[129] *Silent Witnesses*, ed. Usai et al., 580.

Vera Kholodnaia, the peerless product of Russia's dream factories

288

trayed on screen had public implications because of how deeply her fans identified with her circumstances.[130] Dividing her audience according to (hetero)sex, she created two levels for identification, sending a different version of the self-destructive message to each.

Before being discovered by Nikandr Turkin, head writer for the Khanzhonkov Studio and Russia's first professional film theorist, Kholodnaia had acted only in amateur productions.[131] With her barrister husband, Kholodnaia exemplified the smart set, enjoying tennis and auto racing until he was drafted to fight the First World War. When her husband was badly wounded in Poland, she became the sole support of a family of five women and went looking for work in the movies. The only surprise in her biography was that her name—*Kholodnaia*, which means "cold"—which suggests the frigidity that underlay her signature roles, was genuine rather than a publicity stunt dreamed up by the studio.

Kholodnaia left many a dead man in her wake, usually by his own hand. However, no one, least of all she, exercised the power to resolve the situation that had led him to suicide. Men were helpless against her, although not because she was trying to master them. On the contrary, they usually wanted to step in and take over because she could not control herself. They died because they were weak, not because she had sucked them dry, as corrupting heroines did in western movies.[132] Typical movie titles, such as *Song of Love Triumphant* (1915) and *Tale of Love So Dear* (1915), underscored the romantic passion of her persona, but they also belied the tragic denouement that awaited her. Although she made only six of her twenty-two movies under Bauer's direction, Kholodnaia was most closely associated with him: he had trained her, and their cooperative efforts resulted in the classic *Life for a Life*.[133] He designed the sets, arranged the lights, and moved her between foreground and background—heavy breathing up close, immobile in the distance, projecting through her body the story of a woman who cannot stop herself from having an affair with her adoptive sister's husband, played with smarmy cynicism by Polonskii. The girls' mother can save what is left of her family only by killing Polonskii and faking it as suicide.

In another of her widely circulated movies, *Mirages* (1916), based on a novel by the popular writer Lydia Charskaia and directed by Chardynin at the Khanzhonkov Studio, Kholodnaia lay dead in the last scene, having taken her own life. Her two lovers, played by Gromov and Polonskii, com-

---

[130] Kholodnaia inspired identification by "promot[ing] a privatisation or personalisation of . . . a mass consciousness in the audience." Barry King, quoted in Dyer, *Stars*, 27.

[131] Ziukov, *Vera Kholodnaia*, 12–18. She had a bit role as the Italian nanny in "Anna Karenina."

[132] On the American femme fatale, see Bram Dijkstra, *Evil Sisters* (New York: Knopf, 1996).

[133] In 1916 Bauer made *The Queen of the Screen* but starred V. Iureneva in the title role. A waltz of this title, though, was named for Kholodnaia and featured her on the sheet music.

peted for the two halves of her soul. The student Gromov wanted an intellectually companionate marriage, but the wealthy Polonskii tempted her away by showering her with *things.* Her "mirages" were daydreams, fantasies of a world where she could escape such choices. In a last desperate attempt to save herself she wrote to her mother, played by Rakhmanova, as in *Life:* "Please come quickly. I'm not responsible for my actions." Mother arrived too late; Kholodnaia lay the victim of her daydreams.

If they left the theater with essentially the same message, men and women had watched Mozzhukhin and Kholodnaia differently. Because audiences typically identify more closely with the star of the same sex, conversely they will objectify the star of the opposite sex.[134] And although each spectator would have experienced the films on an individual level, the range of possibilities for empathy and identification would have been restricted by social circumstances. The various prototypes embodied by the stars would have been stereotypical of a recognizable set of social relations, and movies provided an important source of images for those who felt constrained by, as well as comfortable with, the extant relationships.[135] If at the most fundamental level shop girls wanted to make themselves up like Kholodnaia, at a deeper level they were receiving highly equivocal messages about her actions.

Movies' plots reflect angles and aspects of the societies that produce them, so the way in which situations are resolved on screen can suggest possibilities for social change. One way to accomplish this is through rewarding or punishing certain types of screen behavior. The refusal of Russian directors to script every ending as happy, to reward destructive behavior and to punish the good, mirrored doubts about the direction society was taking. Kholodnaia showed females that self-indulgence could be perilous to personal fulfillment, but it could also be an end in itself. She offered her male viewers no confidence that they could construct a domestic patriarchy. Mozzhukhin, whether degenerate or merely impotent, did not insinuate to his male fans that they had much chance of becoming masters of their own destiny, and his inability to keep his women safe did not bode well for patriarchy.

Conclusion

Russia's movie studios manufactured dreams that audiences in other cultures would have considered nightmares. But dreams they were, from the

---

[134] Leo Handel, *Hollywood Looks at Its Audience* (Urbana: University of Illinois Press, 1950), 144. See also Tudor, *Image and Influence,* especially chapter 4.

[135] Richard Dyer, *The Matter of Images: Essays on Representations* (New York: Routledge, 1993), chapter 3.

aesthetic visions crafted by Bauer to the criminals dashing madly through a Drankov serial. Commercial enterprises, Russian studios nonetheless sent mixed messages about commerce in the persona of the object-oriented, destructive heroine. These ambivalences were also the direct result of many factors: the political weakness of the autocracy; the *intelligentsia*'s hegemonic qualms about the commercialization of culture; and the social instability that rapid industrialization had left in its wake. Russia's silent movies testified to the growing number of women gaining access to modernity, and many of these movies revealed just how complicated their entrance into public life was.

Before establishing itself as the quintessential artifact of mass culture, the motion picture had to spend its first decade staking out territory, establishing its legitimacy while selling to everyone. Whether in the Riabushinskii mansion or the peasant village, movies changed not just what people could know but how they would know it. If the message was ambiguous, the medium was not. Exemplary of modern technology, movies cut across all social and intellectual categories and opened up new public spaces. Those who could not come to terms with the modern world embraced by the cinema would be left on the cutting-room floor.

Epilogue

The Bolshevik victory in 1917 put a Marxist government in power, and the bourgeoisie it confronted was better defined by cultural institutions than political ones. Adhering to the theoretical dictates of Marxism, the new regime argued that culture could not be an autonomous zone, for in any society culture is shaped by and representative of the economic base. But because the Bolsheviks had taken power in the name of the workers before the bourgeoisie had completed its historical mission, the new regime found itself on a crash course to assemble the economic base appropriate to its political philosophy. On the cultural front, too, the Bolsheviks were obliged to improvise. Isolated at home and abroad and realizing they could not wait for the social base to evolve according to the "natural" logic of historical materialism, they elected to jerry-build a new Soviet culture before the appropriate economic base was fully in place.

As part of this process, the regime reworked commercial leisure-time activities so as to render them politically and economically dependent on the revolutionary state. The various enterprises discussed in this book endured mixed fates after 1917, each harnessed in some way for state purposes to cultivate the consumer's identification with the state. Once the government nationalized the commercial market, it influenced the structure and content of leisure-time activities much more directly than the consumer had in the past. To cite one example, after the state had assumed publication of all periodicals, it limited the public discourse that had been so important to specialized and professional journals. The hefty price tag of government intervention proved cost-prohibitive to the freedom of choice on which commercialism had depended. In the 1930s, when Stalin's government trumpeted the creation of its own *massovaia kul'tura,* or mass culture, it was employing the technology of mass production and distribution but serving up content in its own self-interest. Once the Soviet "culture industry" had joined other industries as state monopolies, it developed significant potential to market the values promulgated by its governmental producers.

In this book I have argued that changes in leisure-time activities permitted Russians who partook of them to develop a new sense of self that allowed for personality shifts according to circumstances. In the final decades of tsarist Russia, when commercial culture was moving toward modernity faster than were political organizations, many of the tsar's subjects were developing desires for personal autonomy and self-fashioning. The applied Marxism of the Bolshevik regime, however, elevated the socialist collective above the individual. The new government sought to produce an equally new individual, homo Sovieticus, whose fundamental identity would derive from his or her relationship to the state, which was defined in the vocabulary of social class.

Homo Sovieticus was to be a product of both work and play. In one of several paradoxes born of the need to modernize rapidly, during the formative years of Soviet rule an affinity between the cultural avant-garde and political revolutionaries developed because both devalued the liberal individualism associated with capitalist consumption. Once again, the stage entered decisively into these politically informed cultural debates about Russia's future; as Katerina Clark has pointed out, "Intellectuals saw theatrical revolution as the midwife of the political."[1] With its tremendous potential to expand mass participation, the theater was engulfed by the enthusiasm of would-be thespians using their class status to land starring roles on local stages.[2] Commissar of Enlightenment Anatolii Lunacharskii, a Bolshevik *intelligent* with jurisdiction over theater, shuddered at the speed with which his colleagues were pressing forward. Favoring a more gradual process, Lunacharskii was silenced by the cultural revolution at the end of the 1920s. On the stage, Ostrovskii was one of the few to survive the stultifying politicization of culture through the enforced doctrine of socialist realism, in large measure because his plays could be co-opted by Dobroliubov and the *intelligentsia,* who read criticism of merchants into them. A more nuanced reading of Ostrovskii suggests another reason for his abiding popularity: because the social and economic issues he staged had yet to be resolved, his plays struck a responsive chord in Soviet audiences.

Whereas the stage restricted individual expression, sports celebrated in-

[1] Katerina Clark, *Petersburg, Crucible of Cultural Revolution* (Cambridge, Mass.: Harvard University Press, 1995), 75.

[2] Lynn Mally, *Revolutionary Acts: Amateur Theater and the Soviet State, 1917–1938* (Ithaca: Cornell University Press, 2000).

dividual achievement by connecting it directly to state power. The murder of the track star Victor Kotov in December 1917 illustrates how the public role of the athlete changed. In response to Kotov's brutal beating the bourgeois press suggested that irrational violence had deluged Moscow since the Bolsheviks had assumed control: Why kill an athlete, who was not, after all, a political figure?[3] The rigor, control, and disciplined training which had characterized the runner's life were now being defeated by a barbarism which threatened the civility that had been fostered by organized competition in the first place.

The new regime, however, had a keener appreciation than did its predecessor of how organized athletics could be used as an engine of modernization, and how athletes could be feted as embodiments of state power. Throughout the civil war major cities continued to host football championships. In 1920 the Council of People's Commissars established the first Institute of Physical Culture, imparting official status to that which the "professors" of athletics had long sought, the idea that education included the physical as well as the mental.[4] Sport was officially touted as "a weapon of culture, a means of education, and a way to organize the cultural leisure time of the masses."[5] Numerous athletes, including "outlaw" soccer star Chesnokov and "Uncle Vania" himself, enjoyed high official standing in Soviet Russia. The state coopted the athlete by using sports as the umbilical chord between self and society, privileging the social and economic status of athletes as a form of remuneration for appropriating their status as individuals.

Public and individual ambitions also blurred in the nascent Soviet tourist industry. Combining the organizational strategy of capitalism with the positive discourses of nationalism and health, official tourism policy funded travel for many who could not have afforded vacations in the past. Replacing the market as the mechanism that determined who went on vacation and who stayed home, the new government presented temporary escape from the drudgery of the workplace as a proletarian prerogative. Moreover, tourism continued to offer an especially effective medium of imperial conquest; Soviet leaders understood readily what postmodern studies of tourism would later discover: that tourism makes an effective political weapon in the battle to colonize the cultures of the borderlands. For example, in the 1920s the newly founded Society of Proletarian Tourism, the Society of Tourism and Agriculture, and the Society of Tourism and National Defense all made explicit the government's agenda, which transformed tourism from the re-creation of the self to the re-creation of the

---

[3] *Ves' mir,* no. 52 (December 1917): 29.

[4] B. M. Chesnokov, "Ot bor'by 'dikarei' s 'atristokratami.' K olimpiiskim pobedam," *Sportivnaia zhizn' Rossii,* no. 12 (1960): 18.

[5] Quoted in Robert Edelman, *Serious Fun: A History of Spectator Sports in the USSR* (New York: Oxford University Press, 1993), 55.

nation as socialist. As a result, the proletarian tourist became "the medium to take all that is new and cultured into the far corners of the Union."[6]

The new regime set up two agencies that promoted another political agenda, one intended to segregate Russians from visitors who might offer alternative visions of the world: Turist regulated domestic travel and Inturist dealt with international tourists.[7] Turist continued the efforts of those prerevolutionary developers who had emphasized both the economic and political value of tourism within the national borders. Inturist crudely attempted to control the foreign tourist's gaze and ended up piling so many of Bourdieu's *meconnaissances* on one another that the foreign tourist could find little more than political images of Soviet "authenticity." Inturist also made it easy for foreign travelers to repeat the adventures of their prerevolutionary forebears; on the one hand, the guides' efforts recreated the orientalist stereotypes of oppression, while on the other, the government's need for the tourist's hard currency generated a subculture of self-indulgence. The flow of inexpensive vodka once again allowed westerners to suspend rules of behavior they would have followed at home.

Of all the commercial leisure industries, restaurants were hardest hit by Bolshevik policies because of the contradictory discourses into which they fell. The paradox that had given dining out its raison d'etre—the desire for a private experience in a public place—disappeared when all space was declared public, a dictum that dispatched diners back to the privacy of the domestic sphere. The working conditions that had generated such sympathy for Shmelev's ill-fated waiter were reversed by a policy that abolished the notion of service as an industry. Shmelev's story had inspired four bathetic movie versions in the prerevolutionary era that spotlighted the tragic father, but when Protazanov refilmed it in 1928, he told a more aggressive story of the exploited proletariat reaching political consciousness.

Ironically, though, waiters were now envied because their job brought them into contact with one of the scarcest commodities in the Soviet state: food. By invoking the principle of food as sustenance as opposed to entertainment, the Bolsheviks severely limited the potential of restaurants to combine literal consumption with its figurative counterpart, the consumption that fed desires rather than basic needs. Restaurants had not become depoliticized but repoliticized according to the new hierarchies and uses of public space. In 1912 the American tourist Ruth Kedzie Wood had noted that "the great number of large restaurants in the principal cities causes one to wonder if the Russian ever lunches or dines at home."[8] In

---

[6] *Turist-aktivist,* no. 1 (1929): 7. Tourism was described as "a weapon in the cultural revolution."

[7] Z. Mieczkowski, "Foreign Tourism in the U.S.S.R.: A Preliminary Investigation," *Geographical Survey* 3, no. 2 (April 1974): 99–122.

[8] Ruth Kedzie Wood, *The Tourist's Russia* (New York: Dodd, Mead, 1912), 34.

later years, scores of tourists at undersupplied *Inturist* establishments would wonder just the opposite, why anyone would *ever* eat out. The negligible culture of public dining that developed in the Soviet era depended on personal connections for access to restaurants, which in essence returned dining to the private sphere.

The other evening entertainments, especially nightclubs, fell under attack initially because of their quintessentially bourgeois qualities.[9] At the same time, however, Soviet nationality policies gave ethnic performers new opportunities to preserve their cultural heritage. To cite as example the most popular prerevolutionary genre, gypsy romances, Ivan Rom-Lebedev's autobiographical history of gypsy performance shows both sides of the coin. Written in an era when he could not have published overt criticism of the Soviet state, much of what he describes nevertheless reflects a sincerely positive attitude toward the subsidies that removed economic insecurity and assured gypsy performers a stable base in Moscow's Romen Theater.[10] Rom-Lebedev exaggerates when he insists that Soviet power brought a respect for ethnic identities that had been lacking in the prerevolutionary era, but more important, his work underscores the dramatically new political role ethnic performers played after 1917. Now symbolic of triumphant multiculturalism in Soviet Russia, ethnic groups primarily performed their traditions, putting a politicized authenticity on display for a new kind of mass consumption. However, as Alaina Lemon has argued in her post-1991 study of the Romen Theater, "Its plays did display and produce social relations, but they emerged in ways not intended."[11] Therefore, although those categorized as "ethnic Soviets" continued to resist the state's ability to define their authenticity, these performers did not offer the same escapist flights of fancy that had established their predecessors' rapport with prerevolutionary audiences.

State subsidies of nightlife offered stability, but they depended on conventions that substituted a hokey nostalgia for politics.[12] The two capitals and other major cities maintained permanent operetta theaters, and the genre continued to be performed widely throughout the empire. Accusations of bourgeois influence were shrugged off with inflated claims that operetta was a fundamentally satirical genre, as though parody of the nine-

---

[9] As Clark argued, "The one thing that united most of the factions . . . was a scorn for the commercial theater. . . . The icon of commercialism for them was the *café-chantant*" (*Petersburg*, 84).

[10] I. I. Rom-Lebedev, *Ot tsyganskogo khora—k teatru "Romen"* (Moscow: Iskusstvo, 1990).

[11] Alaina Lemon, *Between Two Fires: Gypsy Performance and Romani Memory from Pushkin to Post-Socialism* (Durham, N.C.: Duke University Press, 2000), 234.

[12] As Peter Fritzsche has argued about this sort of "nostalgia without melancholy," when the past has become commodified, "its ability to indict the present and imagine the future is accordingly lessened." In "Specters of History: On Nostalgia, Exile, and Modernity," in *American Historical Review* 106, no. 5 (December 2001): 1618.

teenth-century bourgeoisie constituted a significant art form. Curiously, Valentinov's career had a Soviet epilogue in an operetta he wrote in 1928 about movie star Mary Pickford, who was almost as popular in the USSR as in the United States in the 1920s. As a sign of the Soviet times, Valentinov promised that *Meri Pikford* contained no romantic intrigues but rather exposed the hypocrisy of Prohibition in America. An operetta without intrigues was an oxymoron, and by concealing libidinous liaisons behind platitudes, Valentinov lost his audience.

The diminution of restaurant culture, combined with state-sponsored ethnic and operatic theaters, had a negative impact on the *estrada*. Variety shows did not disappear, but they played on a circumscribed venue until the expansion of television in the 1960s, when they began to dominate entertainment programming. The state's insistence on uncritical, traditional productions restricted the kinds of satire that had given performers their critical edge, but censorship itself was nothing new and the clever and talented could work with their audiences through a shared language of double entendres. Arkadii Raikin, for example, brilliant heir to the *kupletisty*, was especially revered for his multifaceted comic presentations.[13]

Live performances thus offered the possibility for spontaneity that went beyond official instructions. Motion pictures, in contrast, fixed actions. The epitome of cultural modernization, the cinema stood the best chance of transforming viewers into that idealized homo Sovieticus because of its unparalleled ability to show exactly the same performance to the broadest possible audience. Eager to exploit this potential, the new government established one of the world's leading film industries. In the 1920s official tolerance for fellow travelers among some of the prerevolutionary directors, such as Protozanov, together with the cinematic avant-garde headed by Sergei Eisenstein and Lev Kuleshov precipitated the growth not only of new themes but also of revolutionary cinematic techniques designed to help the spectator identify with the collective. The crowd as opposed to the single individual now played the protagonist in the pioneering works of Eisenstein, among others.

Artistic films, however, did not please the masses, who frequented imports, especially American movies.[14] In 1928, the government proclaimed that "a purely cultural approach to cinema would be incorrect."[15] The term "cultural" was invoked as a code for the *intelligentsia,* who the government rejected in its search for formulas that would sell tickets as well as ideology. In a reversal of cultural fortunes, the new milkmaid heroine

---

[13] *Arkadii Raikin v vospominaniiakh sovremennikov,* compiled by E. Raikina, ed. L. Mikhailova (Moscow: Izd-vo Act: Mezhdunarodnyi fond im. Arkadiia Faikina, 1997).

[14] See, for example, Denise Youngblood, *Movies for the Masses* (New York: Cambridge University Press, 1992).

[15] Ibid., 30. Politboro member Stanislav Kosior made this statement.

on the collective farm found a high level of contentment in the final reel, happiness that had been denied the prerevolutionary seamstress. The "unhappy" ending deemed so culturally significant before 1917 was now rescripted according to the mandates of the Hollywood formula. Soviet dream factories manufactured fantasies according to a bourgeois model, despite the differences in cinematic vocabulary. The triumph of the happy ending signaled the embourgeoisement of Soviet society.

The Soviet middle classes, though, have suffered much the same fate as their tsarist antecedents: contemptuous denunciation on the basis of their habits of consumption.[16] The Soviets, ironically, have been credited with significant political influence. Vera Dunham, one of the few to venture into the terrain of middlebrow Soviet culture, attributed the success of Stalinism to this social group, concluding that Stalin established his power when he "enter(ed) into a mutually rewarding alliance" with the social equivalents of "the young Russian bourgeoisie."[17] She identified the middle class as those who agreed to Stalin's "Big Deal": they "wanted careers backed by material incentives," and were not "interested in ideology or further revolutionary upheaval."[18] Writing in 1976, Dunham betrayed the characteristic *intelligentsia* intolerance for this social category because it "represents today, as it did before, a middle-class mentality that is vulgar, imitative, greedy, and ridden with prejudice."[19] Dunham recognized that the culture of consumption was fundamentally political, because it unified post-Stalinist society, where "the goals of the top and the bottom are the same: acquisitiveness reigns."[20]

In her study of the links between culture and power during the Stalinist 1930s, Sheila Fitzpatrick has supported Dunham's thesis. Connecting the rise of a "new elite," or those schooled more in engineering than in disciplines favored by the old *intelligentsia,* with the growth of cultural tastes that sounded distinctively bourgeois (despite the repudiation of the word itself), Fitzpatrick argued that homo Sovieticus wanted "art to make . . . life happier and more beautiful, not complex and depressing."[21]

This tendency to conflate the values espoused by Soviet and western middles classes can be seriously misleading, however. It implies that one need

[16] *Intelligent* V. P. Kranikhfel'd described Russia's middle classes at the turn of the century: "Complete material satisfaction intersects with self-satisfied, self-confident narrow-mindedness." Quoted in Ira Petrovskaia, *Teatr i zritel' Rossiiskikh stolits, 1985–1917* (Leningrad: Iskusstvo, 1990), 15.

[17] Vera S. Dunham, *In Stalin's Time: Middleclass Values in Soviet Fiction* (New York: Cambridge University Press, 1976), 15.

[18] Ibid., 17.

[19] Ibid., 19.

[20] Ibid., 241.

[21] Sheila Fitzpatrick, "The Lady MacBeth Affair: Shostakovich and the Soviet Puritans," in *The Cultural Front: Power and Culture in Revolutionary Russia* (Ithaca: Cornell University Press, 1992), 199.

draw no significant distinction between the role of the Soviet state and that of a liberal society's commercial marketplace when comparing the two as custodians of mass culture. If the subject is "taste" alone, then the Soviet state and the bourgeois market are comparable in that each will produce banality in its own self-interest. When the subject is more than simply "taste,"[22] however, we must draw a line between the state and the market. Commerce, as opposed to state subsidies, generates more opportunities for the individual to adjust to the wide spectrum of changes that accompany each technological development, every expansion of the notion of "mass," and every situation that requires the individual to find a new way of expression. Commercial leisure in prerevolutionary Russia was at times exploitative and reactionary, but it also created numerous occasions for the empire's citizens to learn about and adjust to the social reorganization precipitated by industrialization. For example, although the imperialist agenda of the prerevolutionary tourist may have been no more commendable than that of the later tourist-activist, the two are clearly distinguished by their mission: the tsarist-tourist set out to improve the self, whereas the Soviet counterpart was commissioned to enlighten society.

By striking out for purposes of self-fashioning, the tsarist-consumer-tourist looked to develop one more aspect of an identity that was fundamentally multiple and contingent. Mass-oriented commercial culture stimulates the pluralism that develops when consumers bring a variety of values and expectations into their uses of culture even when their choices are limited.[23] That said, in Russia the opportunities for pluralism were significantly greater before 1917 than after. In industrialized countries, pluralism has been a key component of modernization. The Soviet government's co-optation of leisure restricted this process by limiting the options available for citizens to experiment with their subjectivities. This is the point: that Russians in the late imperial era could play with far greater spontaneity than could their Soviet heirs. Such spontaneity did not foreordain a specific political or economic structure, but the limits imposed by the state foreclosed options for alternative cultural developments.

The extent to which this foreclosure contributed to the collapse of the Soviet Union has yet to be fully explored. The limitations that the state placed on opportunities for self-exploration, however, must be central to any analysis. Such a study must also address the extent to which consumers of a state-produced mass culture, like those in a commercialized market,

---

[22] Attitudes of the *intelligentsia* across countries and generations have complicated this problem of trying to separate taste from politics. As Andrew Ross has pointed out, "The problem of petit-bourgeois taste, culture, and expression remains to this day a largely neglected question for cultural studies and a formidable obstacle to a left cultural political." *No Respect: Intellectuals and Popular Culture* (New York: Routledge, 1989), 29.

[23] Fitzpatrick has argued that in the relationship between politics and culture "the rules of the game were not fixed; they were constantly evolving" ("Lady Macbeth Affair," 214).

found ways to make the official culture their own.[24] However much the Soviet state wanted to create an updated version of the Enlightened, modern individual, at the same time it had to satisfy the demands of mass consumption and ultimately could do no more than reduce the options for multiplicity in character development.

The flowering of commercialism in post-Soviet society has been connected to the rise of more democratic political values, but the normative western paradigm that makes democracy a function of commerce has not been realized. I would like to decouple the two and look instead at the possibilities for culture to evolve into an autonomous sphere that allows Russians to develop new ways of appreciating their place in their country and the world. One of the hallmarks of post-Soviet leisure among youth has been the explosion of nightclubs that, however modest in their entertainments in comparison with Tumpakov's enterprises, offer a place for open socializing more like the heterotopian clubs of old than the Soviet televised *estrada*.[25] Commercialism has also produced a vituperative anti-western culture, a greater outburst of antagonism than was expressed officially during the Cold War. The more pluralistic the options, the greater the opportunities for self-expression and self-fulfillment.

Leisure-time activities will always be a part of the larger social whole, intimately connected to the economic and political bases that ground those who participate in them. What they offer is a space above and beyond those bases, where *recreation* means just that, the possibility to re-create the self.

[24] Edelman, made plain that "spectator sports audiences did not share the seriousness of the state's intentions" (*Serious Fun,* 25). See also Richard Stites, *Russian Popular Culture: Entertainment and Society since 1900* (Cambridge: Cambridge University Press, 1992).

[25] Louise McReynolds, "Russia at Play: The Social Role of Commercial Culture in Post-Soviet Russia," *Report to the National Council for Eurasian and East European Research* (July 1998). I conducted numerous interviews among the youth of St. Petersburg in June 1998.

Bibliographic Essay

I found the original inspiration for this book in Andrew Ross's *No Respect: Intellectuals and Popular Culture* (New York: Routledge, 1989). Although Ross was writing about Americans during the Cold War, he was raising issues about the relationship between intellectuals and middlebrow consumers that were germane to questions that I thought needed to be raised in the historiography of late imperial Russia. Because of the obvious significance of the interaction between the lower classes and members of the *intelligentsia* in 1917, these two social categories have benefited most from the attentions of historians. However, this has led to an exclusion of the middle classes from the revolutionary equation, left out because they did not establish western-style political institutions. Ross's work made plain the political problems of dismissing middlebrow culture on the basis of a perceived banality, which led me to thinking about what kind of culture Russia's middle classes created for themselves. My first task was to find them, a project begun with my first book, *The News under Russia's Old Regime: The Development of a Mass-Circulation Press* (Princeton: Princeton University Press, 1991).

Historiographically, the search for Russia's "missing bourgeoisie," as Richard Pipes called them, had been organized around the perceived need to explain their political failure. The resultant scholarship was rich in detailing the lives of Russia's merchant estate, and I profited substantially from such secondary works as: Thomas Owen, *Capitalism and Politics in Russia: A Social History of the Moscow Merchants, 1855–1905* (New York: Cambridge University Press, 1981); Alfred Rieber, *Merchants and Entrepreneurs in Imperial Russia* (Chapel Hill: University of North Carolina Press, 1982); Jo Ann Ruckman, *The Moscow Business Elite: A Social and Cultural Portrait of Two Generations, 1840–1905* (De Kalb: Northern Illinois University Press, 1984); Edith Clowes, Samuel Kassow, and James West, eds., *Between Tsar and People: Educated Society and the Quest for Public Identity in Late Imperial Russia* (Princeton: Princeton University Press, 1991); Harley Balzar, ed., *The Professions in Russia* (Armonk, N.Y.: Sharpe, 1995); and James West and Iurii Petrov, eds., *Merchant Moscow:*

Images of Russia's Vanished Bourgeoisie (Princeton: Princeton University Press, 1998). None of these books, however, addressed the issue of a middlebrow culture, that is, one driven by commerce and reflective of the values of its consumers.

My search for a bourgeois culture began with Antonio Gramsci's "Prison Notebooks," reprinted in *An Antonio Gramsci Reader: Selected Writings, 1916–1935*, ed. David Forgacs (New York: Schocken, 1988). Gramsci's seminal ideas about the political workings of culture led me straight back to Ross and the cultural studies movement in which he has played such an important role. By crossing disciplines and looking for the nuanced ways in which culture functions as a political force, cultural studies allowed me to step outside the traditional historiographical narrative and search for Russia's middle classes as they identified themselves. Instead of looking for them at their workplaces, I set out to find where and how they played. I began with the first chapters of two books that concentrate on Soviet leisure: Richard Stites, *Russian Popular Culture: Entertainment and Society since 1900* (Cambridge: Cambridge University Press, 1992) and Robert Edelman, *Serious Fun: A History of Spectator Sports in the USSR* (New York: Oxford University Press, 1993). I gained much perspective from Neia Zorkaia's *Na rubezhe stoletii: U istokov massovogo iskusstva v Rossii 1900–1910 godov* (Moscow: Nauka, 1976) and D. A. Zasosov and B. I. Pyzin's *Iz zhizni Peterburga 1890–1910–kh godov* (Leningrad: Lenizdat, 1991).

Among the most valuable general histories that helped me to establish background I include: for the theater, V. N. Vsevolodskii-Gerngross's *Khrestomatiia po istorii russkogo teatra* (Moscow: Khudozhestvennaia literatura, 1936) and *Russkii teatr vtoroi poloviny XVIII veka* (Moscow: Izd. Akademii nauk, 1960); N. G. Zograf, *Malyi teatr vtoroi poloviny XIX veka* (Moscow: Akademiia nauk, 1960); I. F. Petrovskaia's *Istochnikovedenie istorii russkogo dorevoliutsionnogo dramaticheskogo teatra* (Leningrad: Iskusstvo, 1971); *Teatr i zritel' rossiiskikh stolits, 1895–1917* (Leningrad: Iskusstvo, 1990), *Teatr i zritel' provintsial'noi Rossii* (Leningrad: Iskusstvo, 1995); and M. G. Svetaeva, *Mariia Gavrilovna Savina* (Moscow: Iskusstvo, 1988). Beneficial histories of night life include: I. V. Lebedev, *Bortsy* (Petrograd: Gerkules, 1917); Evgenii Kuznetsov, *Iz proshlogo russkoi estrady. Istoricheskie ocherki* (Moscow: Iskusstvo, 1958); I. V. Nest'ev, *Zvezdy russkoi estrady* (Moscow: Sovetskii kompozitor, 1970); G. Terikov, *Kuplet na estrade* (Moscow: Iskusstvo, 1987); B. A. Savchenko, *Kumiry russkoi estrady* (Moscow: Znanie, 1992); and Liudmila Tikhvinskaia, *Kabare i teatry miniatiur v Rossii, 1908–1917* (Moscow: Kul'tura, 1995). Essential to researching the prerevolutionary cinema are: Veniamin Vishnevskii, *Khudozhestvennye fil'my dorevoliutsionnoi Rossii* (Moscow: Goskinoizdat, 1945); and Paolo Cherchi Usai, Lorenzo Codelli, Carlo Monanaro, and David Robinson, eds., with Yuri Tsivian, *Silent Witnesses: Russian Films, 1908–1919* (London: British Film Institute, 1989).

To build a theoretical framework, I turned to other authors who have been influenced by cultural studies or were founders of the movement themselves. Canonical texts include Pierre Bourdieu, *Distinction: A Social Critique of Judgment*, trans. Richard Nice (Cambridge, Mass.: Harvard University Press, 1984); Max Horkheimer and Theodor Adorno, *Dialectic of Enlightenment*, trans. John Cumming (New York: Continuum, 1997); Michel de Certeau, *The Practice of Everyday Life*, trans. Steven Rendall (Berkeley: University of California Press, 1984); Stuart Hall, ed., *Modernity: An Introduction to Modern Societies* (London: Blackwell, 1996); David Morley and Kuan-Hsing Chen, eds., *Stuart Hall: Critical Dialogues in Cultural Studies* (New York: Routledge, 1996); and Tony Bennett, ed., *Culture, Ideology and Social Process: A Reader* (London: Open University Press, 1981). Warren Susman's *Culture as His-*

tory: The Transformation of American Society in the Twentieth Century (New York: Pantheon, 1984) was also instrumental in the formulation of this project.

Books that helped me to frame chapters around specific issues include: Melvin Adelman, *A Sporting Time: New York City and the Rise of Modern Athletics, 1820–70* (Urbana: University of Illinois Press, 1986); David Bordwell, *Narration in the Fiction Film* (Madison: University of Wisconsin Press, 1985); Harry Brod, ed., *The Making of Masculinities* (Boston: Allen and Unwin, 1987); Michael Budd, *The Sculpture Machine: Physical Culture and Body Politics in the Age of Empire* (New York: New York University Press, 1997); James Buzard, *The Beaten Track: European Tourism, Literature and the Ways to Culture, 1800–1918* (New York: Oxford University Press, 1993); Katerina Clark, *Petersburg, Crucible of Cultural Revolution* (Cambridge, Mass.: Harvard University Press, 1995); Vera S. Dunham, *In Stalin's Time: Middleclass Values in Soviet Fiction* (New York: Cambridge University Press, 1976); Lewis Ehrenberg, *Steppin' Out: New York Nightlife and the Transformation of American Culture, 1890–1930* (Chicago: University of Chicago Press, 1981); Rita Felski, *The Gender of Modernity* (Cambridge, Mass.: Harvard University Press, 1995); Judith Butler, *Gender Trouble: Feminism and the Subversion of Identity* (New York: Routledge, 1990); Miriam Hansen, *Babel and Babylon: Spectatorship in American Silent Film* (Cambridge, Mass.: Harvard University Press, 1991); Susan Layton, *Russian Literature and Empire: Conquest of the Caucasus from Pushkin to Tolstoy* (Cambridge: Cambridge University Press, 1994); Lary May and Robert Strikwerda, eds., *Rethinking Masculinity: Philosophical Explorations in Light of Feminism* (Lanham, Md.: Rowman and Littlefield, 1992); Laura Mulvey, "Visual Pleasure and Narrative Cinema," *Screen* 16, 3 (1975): 6–18; Mary Louise Pratt, *Imperial Eyes: Travel Writing and Transculturation* (New York: Routledge, 1992); Rebecca Spang, *The Invention of the Restaurant: Paris and Modern Gastronomic Culture* (Cambridge, Mass.: Harvard University Press, 2000); Yuri Tsivian, *Early Cinema in Russia and Its Cultural Reception,* trans. Alan Bodger, ed. Richard Taylor (New York: Routledge, 1994); and John Urry, *The Tourist Gaze: Leisure and Travel in Contemporary Societies* (London: Sage, 1990).

Conducting the research was great fun. I put myself in the position of a nineteenth-century Russian looking to have a good time. I immersed myself in the journals, spending long hours in St. Petersburg's Saltykov-Shchedrin Library, now Russia's National Library, reading fan magazines, racing forms, synopses of films, restaurant guides, and nightclub reviews. The most critical journals to this project were: *Artist i tsena; Artisticheskii mir; Azart; Illiustrirovannyi zhurnal atletika i sport; Iskusstvo; K sportu!; Kino; Nasha okhota; Obozrenie kinematografov, sketing-ringov, i teatrov; Obozrenie teatrov; Pegas; Psovaia i ruzheinaia okhota; Rampa i zhizn'; Restorannoe delo; Russkii turist; Sine-fono; Sinii zhurnal; Sportivnyi listok; Teatr i iskusstvo; Tsirk i estrada; Tsiklist; Var'ete i tsirk;* and *Zritel'.* I also read numerous guidebooks, representative of which are: *Putevoditel' po Chernomu moriu* (Moscow: ROPT, 1897); *Predstavitel'stvo rossiiskogo obshchestva turistov. Spravochnik i programma ekskursii* (Rostov on Don: n.p., 1910); and Grigorii Moskvich, *Putevoditel' po Krymu,* 27th ed. (Petrograd: Putevoditelei, 1915).

Obliged to read a large number of plays, I felt the full force of Ostrovskii's insistence that plays were written to be performed. However, many of the manuscripts that I read in the Library of the Union of Theatrical Workers (Soiuz teatral'nykh deiatelei) were mimeographed copies with actors' and directors' notes to themselves, which helped to recreate some sense of performance. Happily, in addition to reading librettos of motion pictures, I was able to watch many of the films used in this study. The most significant collection of prerevolutionary films is the twenty-eight films put on ten cassettes by the British Film Institute and released by Milestone Film and Video (1992). This set covers the wide sweep of the cinema, from *Stenka Razin* to some of Evgenii Bauer's best works. In addition, the Library of Congress has more than thirty other Russian films available for viewing. Although most of these movies are incomplete, because not all reels survived the chemical deterioration that has destroyed most of the world's stock of silent films, what remained was indispensable to this project. The third location for these movies is the Mosfilm Archives in Belye Stol'by, not far outside Moscow, where I watched several classics, such as what reels remain of the serials *Light-Fingered Sonka* and *Sashka, the Seminary Student.*

Because my project was never considered politically sensitive, I did not suffer the problems of access to archives that many of my colleagues have. My problem was one of substance; although I worked extensively in numerous archives, the material was often of little or no use to my research. However, I did find several substantial collections that greatly enhanced my study. At the Bakhrushin Theater Museum in Moscow, I worked in well-maintained *fondy* for the Korsh Theater (f. 123) and Mikhail Lentovskii (f. 144). At the Russian State Archive for Literature and Art (RGALI) I read the personal files of Maria Savina (f. 853), Ivan Zaikin (f. 2347), and I. I. Miasnitskii (f. 45); the Collections of Small Music Publishers (f. 1980); and the business records kept by the Society of Russian Playwrights (ff. 675, 2097). I found materials for the imperial theaters at the State Historical Archives (RGIA; ff. 468, 497). In the Manuscript Division of the Russian State Library, I worked in the personal archive of P. P. Riabushinskii (f. 260) and collected information about movie theaters and public entertainments in Moscow's City Archive (f. 46, the *Gradonachal'nik*).

Memoir literature provided personal insights from several who lived through this era. The most useful to me included: Nikolai Karamzin, *Letters of a Russian Traveler, 1789–90: An Account of a Young Russian Gentleman's Tour through Germany, Switzerland, France, and England,* trans. and abr. Florence Jonas (New York: Columbia University Press, 1957); P. I. Orlova-Savina, *Avtobiografiia* (Moscow: Khudozhestvennaia literatura, 1994); M. G. Savina, *Goresti i skitaniia: Pis'ma, vospominaniia* (Moscow: Iskusstvo, 1983); G. M. Iaron, *O liubimom zhanre* (Moscow: Iskusstvo, 1960); Pavel Buryshkin, *Moskva kupecheskaia* (New York: Chekhov, 1954); Iu. A. Bakhrushin, *Vospominaniia* (Moscow: Khudozhestvennaia literatura, 1994); and the observations by American tourist Ruth Kedzie Wood in her *Honeymooning in Russia* (New York: Dodd, Mead, 1911) and *The Tourist's Russia* (New York: Dodd and Mead, 1912).

Index